The Spice of Popery

LAURA M. CHMIELEWSKI

The Spice of Popery

Converging Christianities on an Early American Frontier

University of Notre Dame Press

Notre Dame, Indiana

Copyright © 2012 by University of Notre Dame Press
Notre Dame, Indiana 46556
www.undpress.nd.edu
All Rights Reserved

Manufactured in the United States of America

Library of Congress Cataloging-in-Publication Data

Chmielewski, Laura M.
The spice of popery : converging Christianities on
an early American frontier / Laura M. Chmielewski.
p.   cm.
Includes bibliographical references and index.
ISBN-13: 978-0-268-02307-2 (pbk. : alk. paper)
ISBN-10: 0-268-02307-7 (pbk. : alk. paper)
1. Protestantism—Maine—History—17th century.   2. Protestantism—
Maine—History—18th century.   3. Maine—Church history.   I. Title.
BR555.M2C46   2011
277.41'07—dc23

2011046761

∞ *The paper in this book meets the guidelines for permanence
and durability of the Committee on Production Guidelines
for Book Longevity of the Council on Library Resources.*

In loving memory of

Mary T. Chmielewski

and to

Herman and Maria,

with all my love

Contents

Figures

Acknowledgments

When I began this study, I braced myself for a long, lonely scholarly endurance race. The process has proved to be anything but, becoming instead an opportunity for the joy of new discoveries and thoughtful, fruitful collaborations. Many people—friends, colleagues, professionals of various backgrounds, and family—have all put their stamp on this book. What follows is a long list of those to whom I owe my heartfelt thanks.

Topping it is Carol Berkin, who advised this work in its dissertation phase and continued to provide helpful comments and criticism throughout the revision process. She sets the bars of mentorship and collegiality very, very high. Angelo Angelis read many incarnations of this project and offered sage advice, as have David Jaffee, Barbara Welter, and Jonathan Sassi. The members of Carol's "writing salon"—Phil Papas, Cindy Lobel, and Iris Towers (in addition to Angelo)—were patient readers and encouraging critics. Emerson Baker, Edwin G. Burrows, and Julie Miller read portions of the manuscript and offered critical help for reshaping the narrative. I also owe a debt of gratitude to Ann M. Little and an anonymous reader who reviewed the manuscript for the University of Notre Dame Press and provided me with a compelling template for expansion and revision. The input of all these scholars and friends has made this an immeasurably better book.

Purchase College's supportive and collegial atmosphere has made it a second home. My colleagues there are quick to offer professional wisdom and cheerful encouragement whenever needed. They are too numerous to list here, but they know who they are. My sincere thanks to all.

The courteous and knowledgeable staffs of the Maine Historical Society, Maine State Museum, Library and Archives Canada, Massachusetts State Archives, Massachusetts Historical Society, and New York Public Library all patiently fielded my questions and pointed out potential avenues for exploration. I am indebted to them for helping me work through their collections in an efficient and timely manner.

My employer, Purchase College of the State University of New York, contributed in many generous ways to the completion of this project, most notably with a junior faculty sabbatical to finish this manuscript. Other funding from Purchase included the Provost's Faculty Support Awards Fund, the Greenwood-Labadorf Fund, and the Union of University Professionals JLM Fund. I also thank the Colonial Dames of America, the Colonial Dames of the State of New York, and the CUNY Writing Fellows Program for their financial support.

My family—father Stás Chmielewski, and sisters Christine Smith and Mary Kay Hauser and their families—is thanked, with lots of love, for providing years of moral support and cheerful hospitality. My daughter, Maria Theresa Eberhardt, who has never known life outside of the long shadow cast by *The Spice of Popery*, receives special thanks for understanding that I couldn't always "spend the time" as she would have liked. I hope she knows how much I look forward to making it up to her. My late mother, Mary Theresa Jas - kowiak Chmielewski, for whom my daughter is named, knew well the value of good books and lovingly fostered my childhood enthusiasm for all things early American. The seeds of interest she planted took deeper root than she likely ever imagined, but I think she would have been pleased with the result. For that reason, I dedicate this book both to her memory and to the beautiful little namesake she never met.

Finally, I thank my husband, Herman R. Eberhardt, for making all aspects of my professional life possible. I relied heavily on his brilliance as a historian and writer to guide me through the process of crafting this study. As if that weren't enough, his generous spirit, constant loving support, and skills as a parent and architect of family fun provided me with the greatest gift one can give an aspiring author— time. To say I never could have completed this work without him is an understatement. For all these reasons, I also dedicate this study to him, with all my love.

Brief Chronology

The Province of Maine, 1688–1727

1688   Onset of King William's War (War of the League of Augsburg).

1690   New England forces under the leadership of Mainer Sir William Phips attempts to take Quebec; repulsed.

1691/2   Candlemas Raid destroys York, Maine.

1695   Mathew Cary brings twenty-two captives back to New England, many of whom had converted while in captivity.

1698   Treaty of Ryswick ends King William's War.

1703   Onset of Queen Anne's War (War of Spanish Succession); Wells is attacked.

Compiled from Charles Clark, *The Eastern Frontier: The Settlement of Northern New England, 1610–1763* (New York: Knopf, 1970); Evan Haefeli and Kevin Sweeney, *Captors and Captives: The 1704 French and Indian Raid on Deerfield* (Amherst: University of Massachusetts Press, 2003); and Sybil Noyes, Charles Thornton Libby, and Walter Goodwin Davis, *Genealogical Dictionary of Maine and New Hampshire* (Baltimore: Genealogical Publishing Co., 1972).

1705   Forces under Winthrop Hilton attack Kennebec village of Norridgewock and its Jesuit mission and destroy its church.

1709   New England forces under Samuel Vetch seize French Acadia.

1711   Samuel Vetch attempts conquest of Canada; repulsed.

1713   Treaty of Utrecht ends Queen Anne's War, but boundary between Maine and French Acadia remains undefined; the Reverend John Williams returns to Canada with Captain John Stoddard to negotiate the release of New England captives.

1717   Arrowsic Conference; Joseph Baxter offered as minister to Kennebec Valley Wabanakis.

1722–27   Dummer's War rages throughout Maine.

1724   Norridgewock destroyed by New England militia; Sebas - tien Rale killed, flock scattered.

1727   St. George's River Conference marks the end of most of the scattered fighting of Dummer's War.

Introduction

In the history of early Maine's religious culture, few families stand out like the Wheelwrights. The first settlers to bear the name were dissenters, radical antinomian Puritans and associates of Anne Hutchinson who, unwelcome in Massachusetts Bay and having few other options, came to settle in the remote province in 1643.[1] In Maine the Wheelwrights prospered and multiplied, and the family's prestige grew in proportion to its size. For generations, they furthered the cause of godly society in northern New England as ministers, militia captains, and civic leaders. A few Wheelwrights, however, made their mark in less conventional ways. The intertwined stories of two of them begin in November 1753 when Nathaniel Wheelwright left Boston for French Canada on a mission to redeem captive Protestant children who had been seized in the most recent round of the violence that frequently wracked Maine's English settlements. Two months later, this heir to New England Puritanism could be found in seemingly unlikely circumstances: drinking wine and eating sweets in the company of Soeur Esther Marie-Joseph de l'Enfant Jésus, a nun of the Ursuline convent in Quebec.[2]

1

Figure 1. Nathaniel Wheelwright, by John Singleton Copley (ca. 1750).
Courtesy of the Massachusetts Historical Society.

In eighteenth-century North America, such an encounter—between a Protestant man and a Catholic woman, a layman and a cloistered nun, a New Englander charged with saving fellow Protestants from popish captivity and a Canadian who embodied Catholicism's extremes—was an unusual occurrence indeed. What brought these two together, however, was a consequence of the circumstances of religious life and culture in early American borderland communities. To Nathaniel Wheelwright, this cloistered nun was no random acquaintance. Named Esther at birth, she had been abducted from Maine as a child during Queen Anne's War. When the opportunity arose, she refused to come back; instead, she took the vows and veil of the Ursuline order. In doing so, Soeur (later Mère) Esther made a conspicuous religious commitment to Catholicism, a form of Christianity that in most ways was considered the antithesis to the professed beliefs of both her antinomian ancestors and her living New England Protestant relatives.[3] The latter included her nephew Nathaniel Wheelwright, whose father was Soeur Esther's brother.

Soeur Esther's transformation from Puritan girl to Catholic woman resulted from the Province of Maine's unique status as both an outpost of New England culture and a crossroads for the cultures of others. Much of this cross-cultural contact was a consequence of violent frontier warfare involving English and French and Native American forces which devastated Maine's frontier communities. The last years of the seventeenth century (termed *decennium luctuosum*, or "sorrowful decade," by Cotton Mather) brought violence, death, and loss of family and property to Maine's English settlements. These conditions persisted in varying degrees of intensity for three more decades, spanning 1688 to 1727. The destruction was more than physical: the conflicts with Catholic French and Indian forces also took a heavy toll on spiritual stability and orthodoxy.

This instability was exacerbated by Maine's preexisting conditions. As an intercolonial crossroads, Maine had long been regarded as a "pagan skirt" of New England.[4] The persistent violence of 1688 through 1727 reified this perception, as the forces of rival Christian visions curtailed efforts to create in Maine an extension of New England's godly society.

Contemporary witnesses to the *decennium luctuosum* and beyond feared the consequences of converging Christianities in times of war. Writing from a Massachusetts threatened by the loss of its charter—a consequence of the ill-fated Dominion of New England and Glorious Revolution, and the aforementioned frontier conflicts—Increase Mather fretted that the influence of Catholicism had already seeped into English Protestantism.[5] Mather called this spiritual contagion the "spice of popery," and he warned that, if left unchecked, it would infect New England's purer Protestant religious culture.[6]

Both Mathers' concerns were well placed. Decades of human movement and interaction, warfare, religious options, and discrete influences shaped a unique religious culture in Maine that reflected the province's diverse Christian population. How this happened and the consequences of Maine's position as a temporal and literal crossroads for converging Christianities are the subjects of this book.

Early Maine's religious culture defies conventional perceptions of religious life in colonial New England. Its diverse people, variety of religious experience, propensity to encounter the religious "other," geographical realities, and proximity to Wabanakia, French Canada, and Acadia render it an unconventional "artifact" of early American religion. Considering Maine on its own terms is a fairly recent phenomenon. For most of British North America's colonial period, the province was claimed by Massachusetts. This led generations of scholars to assume unquestioningly a rough equivalency between Massachusetts colonists and those found in Maine. The common, often-unexplored assumption was that Maine and Massachusetts colonists were indistinguishable in their social arrangements, religion, and culture. A major trend in early American scholarship of the last three decades, however, stresses the complexity of movement and encounter among various peoples of both European and Native American origin, as well as the intrinsic qualities of and inherent differences between colonial frontiers and contrasting metropoles.[7] *The Spice of Popery* contributes to this growing body of knowledge by arguing that, despite continued associations with conventional religious identities, Maine's Christian religious culture was far more complex than straightforward associations of "Protestant" and "Catholic" suggest.

Few of Maine's English settlers were the crypto-Catholics orthodox New England Puritans feared them to be. Nevertheless, significant differences in religious culture and experience separated them
from conventional New World, and specifically New England, Protestants. These deviating characteristics were fostered in large part
by the province's proximity to settlements populated by rival Christians. In the more religiously stable areas of New England, Protestants rarely observed or interacted with self-identified Catholics. In
contrast, Maine's English settlers were prone to encounters—some
fleeting, some sustained—with the religious "other." A thinly populated and loosely controlled borderland between Protestant New England and Catholic New France and Acadia, Maine was home to a
form of religious eclecticism that was found only where laws governing acceptable religious affiliations and behaviors, and the people
needed to enforce those laws for keeping undesirable Christians from
interacting with the local population, were ineffective. Maine's religious culture reflected the influences of nearby religious "others" and,
as a result, left a picture of early American Christian experience that
confounds rigid sectarian classifications.

In his groundbreaking 1990 study of early American religious
culture, *Awash in a Sea of Faith: Christianizing the American People,* Jon
Butler challenged his fellow scholars to "open up the discussion . . .
of the American religious experience by reconstructing a more complex religious past"—one specifically marked by religious eclecticism.[8]
He questioned the conventional idea that the seventeenth century
was a golden age of religious orthodoxy and fidelity among Euro-
American Christians and argued in its place that religious cultures
were shaped by multiple and sometimes contradictory or conflicting
traditions. In *The Spice of Popery* I apply a geographical perspective
to Butler's thesis to show how this eclecticism worked within an area
of colonial North America that placed a high priority on establishing
and enforcing an orthodox, Protestant religious culture. Conditions in
the Province of Maine during the seventeenth and early eighteenth
centuries provide rich examples of this complex religious past. For
much of its colonial history, Maine, though claimed by Protestant
New England, was contested ground for the various Euro-American

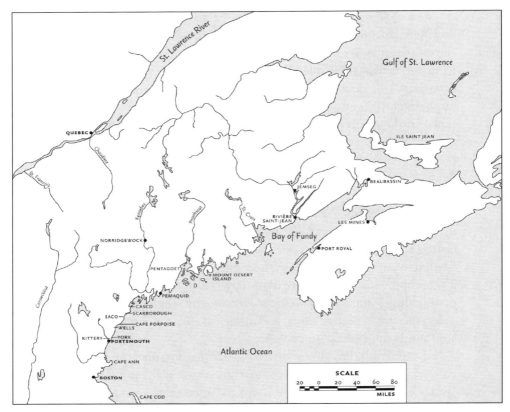

Figure 2. Maine and Its Environs, 1689. Courtesy of Jax de Leon.

Christians who lived in and around it, passed through it, and struggled to control it. As a result, the lived religion and religious culture of Maine's inhabitants was influenced by the competing forces Butler identifies. A complex culture resulted. The significance of this complexity lies in what it suggests about American frontiers and borderlands. Lacking in the traditional institutions and social tools that propagated and sustained orthodoxy, places like Maine actually harbored complex Atlantic World cultures. In describing the range of religious encounter and experience, *The Spice of Popery* defines one aspect of this culture, thus contributing to a deeper understanding of the interior lives and varied experiences of people long believed to be on colonial society's margins.

To comprehend this complexity, one needs to identify the origins and sources of Maine's Christian eclecticism. This is no easy task, as the volatile nature of the province's frontier during the years covered in this study took a heavy toll on source materials. For example, few sermons—traditional repositories of religious culture—managed to survive. If the consequences of frontier war did not destroy them, time, poor preservation, and acts of nature did the job. I was therefore forced to turn to less conventional sources partly as an act of necessity, but partly out of the need to identify the way religion was lived and expressed outside the predictable confines of meetinghouse and church. I found my evidence in letters that describe seemingly mundane matters; written descriptions of religious environments; records that use religiously laden language to describe gestures, objects, and people; colonial newspapers; and government records and correspondence, in which officials frequently complained about the precariousness of Maine's defenses, both military and spiritual, and plotted how to improve them.

I augmented these sources with the material culture of lived religion. Though subject to the same degradations of time and war that plague paper records, objects were often composed of more durable materials. Some were appropriated as war trophies or, as objects of transcendent value, put to new purposes. My research also uncovered a variety of forms of material culture that lacked explicitly religious design and function but nevertheless proved valuable when appropriated for religious purposes. *The Spice of Popery*'s historical actors reacted to religious objects in a variety of ways. Some scoffed at the real and symbolic power invested in them by Catholics. Others came to value what more orthodox Protestants might have derided as "popish trash." Both groups, however, recognized religious material culture when they saw it, suggesting that the size of the gap of understanding and experience commonly attributed to New World Protestants and Catholics varied according to time, place, and circumstance.

Eclecticism notwithstanding, Maine's English settlers usually brought to the frontier an aversion to Catholicism that was a consistent ideological feature of almost all English New World societies. Recent scholarship on anti-Catholicism in New England has established its prevalence and function in building a cohesive identify among eighteenth-century Protestants.[9] The New England colonies were places where Catholics were denied the rights of civil law and civic participation. At various times in colonial history, a Catholic priest faced possible execution for dwelling in a territory claimed by Protestant England.[10] Catholic areas had similar restrictions, with Protestants forbidden from settling in French Catholic New France unless they disavowed their religious beliefs and transformed themselves into Catholic French subjects.[11] In many parts of early North America, ideologies of anti-Catholicism and anti-Protestantism were commonplace. In the sense that Maine's English settlers consistently employed the rhetoric of anti-Catholicism, they fit an established pattern. I argue, however, that this particular early American frontier was subject to many confounding variables that inhibited the successful rooting of any single comprehensive ideology. For one, the institutions that supported Protestant orthodoxy and its attendant ideology of anti-Catholicism were often missing from frontier societies, or were kept from functioning effectively because of the near-chronic state of war between New England and New France. In addition, Maine tended to attract settlers who were dissatisfied with or consistently failed to meet the demands of life in more established New World Protestant communities. Though hardly crypto-Catholics, these early American Christians found that settling on the Maine frontier took them away from the watchful eyes of orthodox Puritan neighbors. Their removes challenged the rigid applications of anti-Catholicism by creating situations in which Christian people encountered one another and, on occasion, sublimated their religious differences in order to address the need for frontier cooperation among European Christians.

This is not to suggest, however, that straightforward, traditional religious identifications should be disregarded or reformulated. On the contrary, they serve a critical purpose. In his book of the same name, Thomas Kidd has identified the religious and ideological commonalities that formed "the Protestant interest," brought about by New Englanders' common hatred of Catholicism, their desire to play a role "in the eschatological destruction of Catholicism," and their eagerness to take up arms in its cause.[12] In *The Spice of Popery*, I write with the assumption that there were culturally dominant issues of theology, practice, politics, and very often ethnicity as well which bound Maine's Christians together under the collective titles "Protestant" or "Catholic." I use these titles of religious identification as freely as the colonists and Native Americans themselves would have. In this context, *Protestant* is used to describe anyone who adhered to any and all of the post-Reformation faiths that broke from communion with Rome. In early Maine, *Protestant* was used to describe peoples, settlements, and Christians who were not Catholic. For the most part, I apply the general title *Protestant* under the same circumstances. Nevertheless, adherents of multiple, often-competing Protestant denominations called the province home, and were sometimes in opposition to one another. I point out these denominational differences, and the societal fractures they reflected, when they apply directly to issues related to Maine's complex religious culture.[13]

Maine was located in a remote corner of the Atlantic World, but the roots of its religious eclecticism ran deep, reflecting the most pressing Christian theological debates of the seventeenth and early eighteenth centuries.[14] The theological adjustments and spiritual expressions of the Protestant and Catholic Reformations, whose religious representatives moved these innovations from the realms of the theological and intellectual into the world of lived religion, touched and influenced this distant region of North America.[15] Religious experimentation often accompanied reform which, in Maine's case, created often unwelcome or suspect Christian subcultures. Protestant experimenters such as Quakers and Baptists often escaped persecution by fleeing to frontier regions like Maine. There they were likely to encounter new expressions of Catholicism, which had been reshaped by European religious conflicts and its self-identified need to reform, and had fostered new religious orders, missionary tactics, devotional societies, and culture of personal piety. In contrast, the Catholicism that the settlers in Maine's English settlements encountered was indeed vastly different from the late medieval Catholicism that the Protestant reformers sought to escape.

Religious expression in early America extended far beyond the parish church or mission chapel, the meetinghouse, a protocol of personal practices, or a particular day of the week.[16] Like their European contemporaries, colonists viewed religion as a fully integrated daily reality, with applications reaching far beyond the circumscribed times and spaces for formal worship. It is in a broadly defined world of religious expression where one finds the most complex forms of New World Christian religious culture. This underscores religion's capacity to shed light on the distinct cultures of American borderlands and frontiers, which, in Alan Taylor's words, are most useful to scholars when regarded as "invitations rather than walls."[17]

I do not suggest that Maine's English settlers were eager to embrace a heterodox, tolerant world of religious experience. For most of them, zealous Catholics were almost always unwelcome, and at times of war, incredibly dangerous. But English Protestant settlers found themselves in an environment that underscored the limits of religious identity and the need for coexistence—if only for the benefits of wartime enterprise or peaceful initiatives—with the Christian "other" who shared the land.

✦ ✦ ✦

Maine's religious eclecticism was influenced by numerous factors that transcended belief or theology. When I began to research borderland religious culture, I worked on the assumption that religious identities were clearly defined among New England's frontier dwellers. That quickly changed as I applied new historiographical perspectives that challenge the metanarrative of English colonial conquest and expansion. Ultimately this led to a book that argues that early Maine's religious culture was informed and shaped by intertwined and dependent, versus parallel, communities.[18] *The Spice of Popery* thus became a contribution to "entangled history," a historiographical perspective described by Eliga Gould in his work on the English-speaking

Atlantic as a periphery of the larger Spanish New World empire. In "Entangled Histories, Entangled Worlds: The English-Speaking Atlantic as a Spanish Periphery," Gould describes how seemingly distinct colonial peoples can best be understood as part of the same "hemispheric system or community," a framework that encourages scholars to consider "mutual influencing . . . reciprocal and asymmetric perceptions . . . [and the] intertwined processes of constituting one another."[19] The shifting perspective of entangled history refocused my line of inquiry away from the narrative of English spread, settlement, and colonial consolidation. In its place emerged the complicated religious culture and equally complex religious people fostered by the borderland experience. Further support for this perspective comes from Claudio Saunt, who suggests that scholars of early America "might do well to plot a new course west" and move away from historiographical frameworks that reflect "the habit of conflating the vast territory stretching from the Bering Sea to the Gulf of Mexico with Britain's colonial toehold on the continent's easternmost edge."[20] While *The Spice of Popery* focuses on a landmass linked to colonies that were English and Protestant in origin, it supports the idea that peripheries like the Province of Maine, as Alan Taylor has argued, thrived on the "exchange of peoples, goods, and identities" natural to an early American "international crossroads" and were also spaces that "[drew] people together, rather than keeping them apart." In Taylor's analysis, Maine becomes "more representative of North American history than those artificially homogeneous towns of colonial Massachusetts."[21] My focus on religious culture supports this assertion. With major Indian and French Catholic players, Maine's early religious culture draws attention to the crossroads component, urging readers to focus on different contexts and cultural priorities. And while *The Spice of Popery* starts with an examination of the people living under the protection (such as it was) of the English colonial system, it rejects the foregone conclusion that the English (through population, weapons, and trade) would eventually bring the province under full cultural control. For one, the persistence of Catholicism among the region's Wabanakis long after the French had left the continent subverted efforts to make a holistically Protestant region out of Maine and prolonged the sense of a shared religious space, despite the conquest of the neighboring Euro-American Catholic colonies.

Maine's geographical entanglement was no doubt a curse for many of the inhabitants of the English settlements. What was challenging for settlers, however, is a blessing for historians of comparative early American social history. For one, the province produced a significant number of cross-cultural travelers compared with most areas of North America claimed by England or populated by Euro-American Protestant women and men. These travelers lived in, learned about, became part of, or relied on understanding another culture to interact productively with other borderland dwellers. While a good number of the people discussed in this book were captives, who moved among cultures involuntarily, others were in control of their religious destinies and made their living by negotiating multiple early American Christian cultures. Some were frontier diplomats whose encounters were by-products of their skills used in negotiating ransom for captives, trade relations and peace treaties with local Native Americans, and recognition of colonial boundaries. Some were even clergy, who at times sought to engage rival Christians in debate and shape their religious futures. These culture brokers often described their work in religious terms, using religious rhetoric to reinforce their positions, deride the beliefs of their enemies, or seek signs of God's blessing for their work. Their use of religious language, symbols, and behaviors further demonstrated the fact that they were acting in symbolic ways that their observers, who were otherwise considered cultural outsiders, could understand.

Such intermingling suggests that, though they believed that an actual religious conquest of the land was ideal, some of Maine's En - glish settlers resigned themselves to the possible persistence of religious others who, if peace were established and maintained, might prove to be useful neighbors despite their different faith. Certainly Maine's Protestant settlers observed, with some degree of regularity, behaviors that reinforced this idea. In Maine, syncretically Catholic Indians and, on occasion, their priests and *canadien* friends visited the English settlements for peaceful, even social reasons. Maine's English merchants traded willingly with the French Catholics of Acadia and Terre Neuve. Settlers born in heavily Catholic areas of Europe, such as Ireland and Portugal, lived among Protestants in English settlements like Pemaquid and Salmon Falls.[22] French-speaking Channel Islanders who settled on the northern frontiers were also a religiously diverse lot, a fact so universally known that, during the witchcraft crisis of 1692, Mainers and other New Englanders suspected them of being crypto-Catholics and secret allies of the French.[23] As early as 1645, a French Jesuit traveled from his mission on the Kennebec to make social calls at Cushnoc, a trading post on the Penobscot Bay affiliated with the Puritan Plymouth Colony, and as late as 1716, another Jesuit made regular visits for medical treatments to a Puritan minister and doctor who had set up shop at an English settlement on Arrowsic Island.[24] While such stories might appear anecdotal, they do serve to illustrate Maine's entangled nature as an early American crossroads. They also challenge us to reconsider the unyielding religious biases so often ascribed to early American people and supported by contemporary rhetoric.

The parameters of these encounters suggest that English Protes - tants in the northern New England borderlands succeeded less in reinforcing the differences between their own form of professed Christianity and one their ancestors and contemporaries rejected and reviled, and more in demonstrating the complex commonalities they shared with other New World Christians. Colonists who ventured forth from the protection of the established regions of Protestant New England were perceived by generations of scholars to be the vanguard of continental expansion by Euro-Americans, paving the way for the spread of Protestant Christianity and democracy throughout every corner of the future United States. I suggest that the migrants who moved north into Maine actually had more in common with their comrades back in Europe, where members of suspect religious minorities often lived side by side with the religiously orthodox. In doing so, they de - fied simplistic religious stereotypes. In this sense, the frontier dwellers of early Maine were just as likely to live amid a religious culture that reflected *backward* in time, toward the religiously polyglot communities of many parts of western Europe. In turn, the religious culture of this corner of America also manifested some aspects of late medieval Catholicism that the Reformation and transatlantic migration had supposedly swept away. Though converging Christianities rarely resulted in accommodation and tolerance, they introduced into religious life elements of religious culture that could easily be dismissed as either popish or heretical in the colonial metropoles, where consolidated religious ideologies were more pronounced, specific, and uniform.

This is not to suggest that Maine's English settlements did not experience the same centrality of religion that marked the lives of other New Englanders. Protestant borderland dwellers were indeed religiously minded people. Maine deviates from conventional New England patterns, however, because it tended to attract settlers who were prone to experiment with new religious beliefs and practices. Following the precedent of the great waves of religious experimentation that flooded England during the Commonwealth, many of these people were attracted to extremely radical interpretations of the Divine, human power, the soul, and society.[25] Thus, at least one historian has recently concluded that many Maine settlers were already "half way out the door" of Protestant orthodoxy, or at least averse to a heavy-handed implementation of Massachusetts Bay versions of Puritanism in the colony.[26] As suggestive case in point, many of the fami-lies who would later produce acculturated captives had during the province's early years participated in anti-Massachusetts agitation or dabbled in Protestantism other than Puritanism. Others came from families or regions in Europe where memories of late medieval Catholicism persisted. These influences lingered in memory, practice, and religious lore, even in the New World.

The entangled Christianities I describe in these pages were often produced by the Province of Maine's chimerical geographical definition and the near-chronic state of tension between the New World French and English.[27] Throughout the seventeenth century, French Catholics of Quebec and Acadia, their Native American allies, and even Anglicans, Quakers, and Baptists watched anxiously and sometimes angrily as New Englanders, inspired by new waves of Puritan fervor, pushed up into Maine and ever closer to Canada. This movement challenged a fragile religious status quo in the region. Like almost all New Englanders, the first generations of Puritan Mainers despised Catholicism in principle and, like their contemporaries in England, feared its influence. These fears were not without cause, as the influence of Catholicism and its defenders, especially among Maine's Wabanaki peoples, extended beyond the French-settled St. Lawrence Valley. Catholicism was manifest in countless borderland spaces that surrounded early Maine: in the missions that operated in contested New England territory, in the French-controlled trading posts that extended up the contested Maine coast toward the Bay of Fundy, in Canada and Acadia (French colonies almost as close to Maine as Massachusetts), and in the coastal waters. When war came to Maine, the proximity of these rival Christians lent itself to perceptions of conflict couched in religious terms.[28]

A critical issue affecting Maine's geographical definition was the fact that long before the arrival of Europeans, as well as long after, it continued to be Wabanakia, home to the People of the Dawnland, the North American people who were first every day to witness the rising of the sun. Many Wabanaki groups and allied native peoples of eastern Maine and Nova Scotia (collectively labeled "Eastern Indians" by English contemporaries) integrated some form of Catholic Christianity into their religious lives. The Wabanakis' interest in Catholicism was the result of religious realities on a hemispheric scale. Throughout seventeenth-century Europe, both Catholic and Protestant theologians and religious leaders grappled with the implications of introducing and sustaining Christianity among indigenous peoples. On the other side of the Atlantic in North America, the objects of these theological ponderings struggled to reimagine, rebuild, and maintain communities decimated by disease, warfare, and dislocation. For the survivors of this first wave of affliction, Catholicism as imparted by French missionaries provided a flexible spiritual framework for processing tragedy and, perhaps more importantly, fashioning a future with European allies around a common religious culture.[29] Christianity, and Catholicism in particular, also provided the Eastern

Indians with an opportunity to blend "old and new ways in a world transformed by the Columbian encounter."[30] In the Wabanakia of the late seventeenth century, the contours of this encounter were already well established. But Catholicism's importance to the Wabanakis was an independent reality. By 1727 France's waning political influence meant it could do little to sustain the religious culture of the Wabanakis who professed Catholicism. Yet the Wabanakis' syncretic Catholic culture and faith communities persisted as geographically based reminders of the convergence of Christianities on the Maine frontier long after those built by and for the French were reduced to ashes or dust.

Native Americans frequently used elements of Christian rhetoric or worship to improve or enhance conditions that predated their encounters with Europeans. In this way, Indians who accepted or adapted to their own beliefs parts of Christianity developed their own post-contact religious culture. Such uses of Christianity were often misinterpreted or misunderstood by contemporary European observers. One example is the common assumption that Indians allied themselves with Europeans for the simple reason that they had come to love Christianity. For centuries, historians accepted this interpretation at face value. The scholarship of the past several decades, however, suggests numerous alternative explanations for religious solidarity and its implications for active participation in borderland warfare.[31] These explanations take into account Native American ethnohistory, political structure and protocols, and longstanding relationships with other indigenous groups—factors that often eluded contemporary Euro-American observers. They also provide more evidence that pushes the concept of religious culture beyond the church, chapel, or meetinghouse.

✦   ✦   ✦

The "spice of popery" made its way into Maine through war between Protestant and Catholic people. I chose to focus on this violent time in the province's history mainly because it produced historical evidence describing, in unusual detail, the lives and habits of ordinary colonists who became pawns in imperial political struggles. Few borderland dwellers produced as many records as frontier captives—the women, children, and men who were seized by allied Indians and French during King William's, Queen Anne's, and Dummer's wars. Though many returned to New England to tell of their experiences, many others did not, and eventually took on all the cultural trappings, including religion, of their captors.

Because these convergences between Protestantism and Catholicism were born of exceptional—and, in Maine's case, frequently traumatic—circumstances, they impelled early modern Christians to appeal to traditional forms of comfort for consolation and guidance. These appeals appear most often in the records of captivity left by captives, their families, or others who found in them useful religious lessons.[32] The mostly Christian captors also had agendas for their captives that ranged from ritualized torture to ransom. For the most part, however, they wanted to keep their captives by binding them tightly to the captor culture, Indian or French.[33] Using the common (and commonly understood) appeals of Christianity, captors tried to entice or coerce captives into converting to Catholicism.[34] When purely religious arguments or threats failed to produce the desired result, captors attempted to promote overtly religious bonds (for Catholics, the sacrament of marriage or religious vows) to entice New Englanders to remain. Such techniques worked at converting a surprising percentage of New Englanders. For Maine families, a member who had converted to Catholicism while detained among enemy Indians or French blurred the line of God-ordained familial authority, placing children in the care of others who claimed the prerogatives of parental authority, and introducing to women (as seen with Esther Wheelwright) new paradigms for the role of religion in adulthood.[35] These religiously redefined family members were not merely reminders of the Catholicism that Protestantism inherently rejected; they also functioned as the Christian encounter of the future, grafting Catholic branches permanently to Protestant family trees. These ties remained intact long after French political power had been swept from Canada and Acadia.

By the middle of the eighteenth century, the frontier Province of Maine moved toward a mature colonial existence proportional with other English North American colonies. Protestant settlers who survived the early wars of empire and returned to the province quickly learned to turn frontier challenges into strengths. Some, like the Wheelwrights, continued to prosper. Their children left the frontier settlements and moved to established colonial merchant cities such as Boston and Portsmouth. This is precisely what happened when members of the Wheelwright family of Nathaniel and Esther left a life of uncertainty in Maine for the greater economic promise and physical security of Boston.

It was also during this time that the colonists in Maine's English communities developed a more unified identity as Protestants on territory claimed and defended in the name of Britain. This was the result of several trends that emerged from the sorrowful decades. For one, the Maine frontier continued to push northward, extending the geographical buffer for the older settlements to the Eastward and enhancing security through increased population for the badly battered southern coastal settlements. In addition, New Englanders in general grew more adept at protecting themselves, gaining the upper hand in frontier warfare and, on occasion, forming alliances with the indigenous population who for years had cast their lot with the French.[36] Though the lack of a formal definition for the American colonial border between New England and New France continued to cause severe friction, a better-defined New England Protestantism took a firmer hold, and worked toward ending the circumstances that contributed to interfaith encounter on the Maine frontier. A telling piece of evidence exists in the increased number of interdenominational squabbles among Protestants themselves, who now had the luxury of debating points of theology, as well as more worldly principles, that might have hitherto undermined the frontier unity they so desperately needed. Equally telling, however, was the persistence of Catholicism among the Wabanakis and within the families established by Catholic ex-captives, who were now subjects of the French Crown. Such factors suggest that, while borders could be defined and Protestant or Catho -

lic spheres of influence established and supported by law, the Province of Maine's religious culture was sufficiently rich and intricate to exist independently. Traditional and popular culture tell us that American frontiers and borderlands are places of innovation and Whiggish foresight, born of conflict, challenge, and ultimately, triumph. This study argues that this assessment is subject to place, time, circumstance, and perspective.

Monarchs, theologians, and philosophers all spoke of the potential of New World settlements to become New Jerusalems, blessedly free of the interfaith warfare that convulsed western Europe and spilled the blood of countless professed Christians. Though the religious differences of the colonial world appear to be simple and obvious, a far more complex story lies beyond the basic dichotomies of English and French, Protestant and Catholic, European and Native American. The peripheries of the colonial world presented opportunities to break down and reformulate these categories.[37] *The Spice of Popery* uses conflict and coexistence on an early American frontier to examine the complex dichotomies between Protestant and Catholic, godly and ungodly, civilized and savage, heretical and popish. But elements of this story also suggest that the Maine settlers who endured these trying times became more pragmatic—and less rigidly defensive of the righteousness of their own religious views—when faced with the basic humanity of rival Christians.

Nathaniel Wheelwright, a direct heir to the religious legacy of the *decennium luctuosum* and its aftermath, experienced this firsthand when one of his companions, a young New Yorker named Nicholas Lydius, lost his life to a high fever while the men were temporarily residing in Quebec. Already saddened by the loss of his friend, Wheelwright was further dismayed to learn that, in Catholic French Canada, the remains of deceased non-Catholics were "carried without the city & buried, as though the person had been a thief or a murderer." Such treatment of Protestant bodies was not inconsistent with colonial laws that clung to rigidly defined categories of religion and punished, even in death, those who deviated from explicit religious norms. However, Wheelwright found that the behavior of these fellow Christians contrasted sharply with the colony's official policies and legal realities. Before the ignominious burial could take place, a kindly French Catholic *habitant,* without regard for the traditional tensions between rival Christianities, offered to bury the young Protestant with dignity in his garden.[38] Though Nathaniel Wheelwright was no stranger to the anti-Catholic rhetoric of his Boston home, it took encounters with living Catholics, fostered by volatile frontiers, to introduce him to the basic humanity of the religious "other." In this sense, he was following a pattern established within his own Maine family that had already existed for decades.

CHAPTER ONE

"The Land That Was Desolate . . . Shall Flourish Like the Lily"

Christian Diversity in Early Maine

In 1646 Gabriel Druillettes, a Jesuit priest who had long worked among native peoples of New France, established the Catholic mission of Narantsuoak on the banks of the Kennebec River. Known as Norridgewock to the English, it grew and prospered as a center for Christian spirituality for the region's Wabanaki Indians, who took their regional name — the Kennebecs — from the local river. The mission managed to survive for almost eighty years despite its location at the center of a province that the English and French vied to control, while its Native American inhabitants were occasionally at odds with both local European powers. Norridgewock was an island of Catholicism in a terrain often hostile to Catholicism, serving the spiritual needs of the mission's Wabanaki adherents and walking a fine line between imperial spheres of influence and local interests.

In the early years of its existence, Druillettes claimed early successes in making new converts and developing a peaceful coexistence with his potentially resistant English neighbors. Indeed, the impulse to embrace Christianity appears to have predated him: the Jesuit reported coming to the region at the request of Noël Negabamat, a

Christian of long standing and a cross-cultural traveler who had lived among the Wabanakis and near the French at Sillery for years.[1] Negabamat spoke for a community of Kennebec Wabanakis that sought spiritual and political regeneration.[2] Since the Kennebecs had been decimated by disease and the alcohol that was sold to them illegally by English traders, their interests appeared to be best served by multivalent alliances with the Catholic French rather than the Protestant English.

Despite his status as a Catholic priest and Frenchman, Druillettes chose to chart a course for his new Maine mission that crossed national identities and transcended established Christian rivalries. The priest's plans were pragmatic as well as ecumenical. As a missionary, Druillettes likely saw one of his roles as seeking physical protection for would-be Christians, such as the Kennebecs, against their most dangerous non-Christian enemies, the Iroquois.[3] They threatened more than just the would-be Catholics on the Kennebec, which led the priest and the government of New France to conclude that all New World Christians shared an interest in seeing them subdued. In 1651, and with the encouragement of the colonial government, Druillettes undertook a diplomatic mission to New England to encourage its Protestant leaders in taking defensive action against the Iroquois.

Druillettes's first exposure to Protestant New England society came at Cushnoc, a Plymouth-owned trading post several miles downriver. There he developed an unlikely, though genuine, friendship with the post's manager, John Winslow. Both men's backgrounds underscore the uniqueness of this pairing. Druillettes was a Frenchman and a Jesuit priest who came to Cushnoc undisguised, Winslow, a member of a prominent Puritan Separatist family.[4] In building a friendship that transcended religious and national identities, the Jesuit and the Puritan demonstrated that borderlands were places where the common needs of Euro-American Christians could force older prejudices to give way to common interests.

Contributing to the friendship's novelty was Winslow's acceptance of the Jesuit as a diplomatic representative of another colonial power. At a time when a Jesuit on soil claimed by England could be accused of treason, Winslow seemed to accept out of hand that the priest was sincere in the peacetime goals of his mission and would not use his influence among the Kennebecs to harm English interests.[5] He stated as much when he welcomed Druillettes to Cushnoc and told the priest's Indian companions "I love and respect [him] . . . I will lodge him in my home and treat him as I do my own brother; for I know very well the good that he does among you, and the life he leads there."[6]

Cementing the spirit of cooperation between these rival Christians was their shared interest in proselytizing to Maine's Indians. In describing Winslow, Druillettes told his Jesuit superior that the Puritan had "special zeal for the Conversion of the Savages, as also has his brother, Edward . . . who is trying to institute a brotherhood to train and instruct the Savages, just as is practiced with the poor by the charity of London."[7] And though he might have objected in theory to the Jesuit's influence, and the vision for Christian belief and life it brought to the Kennebec Indians, Winslow found in Druillettes someone he believed could lay the groundwork for later Protestant missionary enterprises. Where Massachusetts's John Winthrop saw Puritan evangelization through example as "a bulwark against the kingdom of Antichrist, which the Jesuits labor to rear up in all places of the world," John Winslow, far from home and surrounded by potential enemies, saw accommodating the local Catholic as the best service to his—and Cushnoc's—interests.[8]

Despite his friendship with a prominent Puritan, and the mutual assistance they gave each other amid a challenging environment and potentially unreceptive Native American populations, Druillettes still appears to have been a peculiar choice to represent New France in New England, which was constantly on guard against the perceived threat of Jesuit-inspired, anti-Protestant designs.[9] Druillettes was a skilled Euro-American frontier dweller, however, possessing critical knowledge of multiple languages and an ability to move easily through diverse populations. He was furthermore a canny analyst of frontier interests that affected all Euro-Americans in and around New England, and knew enough about the English to pique their interest in alliances that helped them all. The priest drew on these shared fears when he wrote John Winthrop, Jr., that the Iroquois "not only have long harassed Christian Canadians near Kebec . . . but they intend by a general massacre to destroy my akenebek Catechumens dwelling on the banks of the Kennebec River, because they have been for many years allied to the Canadian Christians."[10] The implication was clear: an alliance would save the lives not only of fellow Christians, but of local ones who were potential customers for the English goods that came through Cushnoc.

Agreeing to travel to New England together, priest and Puritan set sail from Merry Meeting Bay on November 25, 1650. Anti-French, anti-Jesuit impulses, however, aroused fear in observers who witnessed the camaraderie between the two men, in particular local English fishermen, who complained of the arrangement within the priest's earshot. But the travelers persisted despite these objections, and ten days later the vessel they traveled on rounded Cape Ann.[11]

The interfaith cooperation forged on the Maine periphery was carried forward to the center of English New World Calvinist Protestantism, Boston. While among the Puritans, Gabriel Druillettes was consistently delighted with the courtesies he received from members of the local religious and civic elite. A noteworthy act of sufferance was extended by magistrate Edward Gibbons, who provided Druillettes with a key to a chamber with instructions to use it in whatever way he saw fit, implying, of course, that the priest was welcome to perform a mass there in private.[12] Catholic masses were outlawed in both old and New England.[13] However, what the Puritan could not see he could not report. Gibbons tolerated Catholic liturgical practices under his roof as a concession to his important guest. And Druillettes carefully locked himself away so that the Puritan did not have to observe or bear responsibility for the illegal rites taking place in his home.

This remarkable act of religious accommodation was later turned outward, with Puritans offering more public displays of tolerance and religious sensitivity. Arriving in Plymouth, Druillettes received further courtesies when he was served fish at a Friday conference of colonial leaders at Governor John Bradford's house. Though fish was a staple of the seventeenth-century Plymouth diet, Druillettes interpreted the meal as a deferential gesture to Catholic dietary practices.[14] The Jesuit also received an invitation by the Reverend John Eliot, Massachusetts Bay's "Apostle to the Indians," to winter at his Roxbury home.[15] Though learned men were not in short supply in Massachusetts, Eliot must have found the priest's successes in converting Indians particularly appealing. Three years earlier, Eliot had started his own mission to the local Algonquians. Perhaps the minister hoped to use the strengths of this colonial metropole — its sturdy structures, clearly defined Euro-American culture, availability of books, and populations of religiously minded people — to extend his missionary impulse to the Jesuit himself. Then again, it is impossible to dismiss mere kindness, or a desire for good company during a long Massachusetts winter, as the chief motive.

Still, the diplomatic component of Druillettes's visit was suspect in more than one New England corner, which contributed to its ultimate failure. Throughout his numerous meetings with New England authorities, Druillettes repeatedly represented himself as "an ambassador for my Catechumens of the Kennebec."[16] But the New Englanders likely perceived in the Jesuit secondary motives: to preserve French power in Canada, and assess New England's own. This made them justly wary. And their reservations, understandable under any circumstances, were well placed, as Druillettes was indeed using this opportunity to assess firsthand the Protestant colonies' perceived strengths and weaknesses. Armed with a functional knowledge of issues brought to the fore by England's midcentury internal strife and its consequences to the colonies, Druillettes speculated to superiors in New France that "the interest which Boston has therein is the hope of a good trade with Quebecq,—especially as that which it has with Virginia, and with the islands of barbade and Saint Christhopf, is on the point of being broken off by the war which the parliamentarians are agitating, in order to destroy the authority of the governors who still hold for the king of England."[17] The priest furthermore proved a shrewd analyst of New England's military might, reporting that the English were "so strong in point of numbers that, in the single colony of Boston, four thousand men can be put in the field. They number, in these four colonies, at least forty thousand souls; and besides, the route by which they can reach the Iroquois is very short and very easy."[18] The priest's population estimates were high in both accounts (modern scholars place the combined population of all New England colonies at about twenty-two thousand in 1650), but the message about New England he wished to impart was clear.[19] If allied with their fellow Christian colonists, the New Englanders could prove enormously helpful. If not, they were potentially very dangerous.

Though the Jesuit was confident that interfaith cooperation to protect Christian Indians would be forthcoming, a second mission ended with the New Englanders' refusal to cooperate.[20] The consensus among the New Englanders was that proactive war against the Iroquois was unjustifiable.[21] Additional reasons for the failure to give assistance, however, underscore the depth to which frontier necessities and interfaith politics were pulled into the far larger, more complicated venue of the Atlantic World. The 1650s would prove to be a turbulent time for Catholic-Protestant relations. It was during this decade that England, under the Protectorate of Oliver Cromwell, would strike at Spanish holdings in the Caribbean to remove the Catholic Spanish from the region. New Englanders had also begun their own efforts to Christianize Native Americans, and seemed to have little interest in protecting those the Catholics had gotten to first.[22] The laws against Jesuits on English soil, which reflected the Commonwealth's fear and loathing of the order, would be reinforced in 1651. And in that same year, Massachusetts would annex the settlements of southern Maine, rolling them into York County, with the sole intent of spreading Puritan settlement into the religiously nebulous northern frontier.

Despite his secondary motives and ultimate failure to achieve the desired results, Gabriel Druillettes's diplomatic mission to New England still stands as an apex of interfaith cooperation between Euro-American Catholics and Protestants. It was made possible largely by the relatively inchoate Christian landscape of Maine during the first half of the seventeenth century. Recognizing the fragility of this toehold on the Maine frontier, adherents of both faiths relied more on the common issues that united Christians than the differences that, in theory, should have kept them separate from and fearful of one another. The religious encounter of Jesuit Gabriel Druillettes and the Puritan John Winslow, fostered at its root by the request of the Christian Indian Negabamat, defied conventional expectations of hostility among Christians typically expressed in Old and New Worlds.

Protestant Maine in the Seventeenth Century: Shallow Roots, Deep Convictions

The early histories of Maine and the nearby colony of Massachusetts Bay are intimately intertwined. In conventional narratives of New England's founding and development, Maine has long been regarded as the natural extension of Massachusetts's influence spanning up the east coast of North America. The link with Massachusetts provided a convenient, predictable template for explaining the religious and cultural underpinnings of Maine's settlers. For much of the seventeenth century, however, the Province of Maine was in reality a welter of religious, geographical, and ethnic confusion. Though claimed by England and ostensibly reserved for development by settlers under English protection, Maine lacked a consistent, well-defined English Protestant presence for most of the seventeenth century.[23] For some Euro-American Christians, this void was the province's chief asset and attraction. Maine therefore became a haven for settlers who, though overwhelmingly Protestant, belonged to denominations that were unwelcome in other parts of New England.

This relative religious autonomy led to encounters between these Protestants and the Native and Euro-American Catholics who lived in and moved throughout the region. Though these encounters often reflected predictable elements of Christian rivalry, some, like Druillettes's friendship with Winslow, were chiefly notable for their disregard of these assumptions. Considered as a whole, the range of these encounters suggest that Maine's Euro-Americans could afford few of the stock, identity-building biases of their coreligionists who dwelled in more religiously homogeneous communities. Shaped by their frontier experiences, and common in times of peace between France and

England, their interactions with and perceptions of one another reflected a world of shared understandings of common cultural expressions of Christian belief. An added component—the lack of cohesion among Protestants—reflects the aforementioned frontier reality of Maine as a welcome possibility for Euro-American Christians who were religiously out of step with New England's overwhelmingly Puritan society. All of these factors influenced Maine's history from 1622 onward, when forces representing the interests of English Protestants attempted to reinforce their claims to the region, and others— Native Americans, Protestant religious outsiders, and the Catholic French—complicated their plans.

✦   ✦   ✦

Historically, most of Maine was Wabanakia, the traditional homeland of thousands of Native Americans. The Wabanakis of the seventeenth century were composed of scattered bands of eastern Algonquian peoples whose villages and hunting grounds stretched from Quebec to northern Massachusetts, and eastward from New Hampshire, through Maine, and into New Brunswick and Nova Scotia.[24] Anthropologists separate them into two branches, eastern and western. It was the eastern Wabanakis—Androscoggins, Kennebecs, Penobscots, Sacos, and Wawenocks—who inhabited much of the area the English called the Province of Maine. Close by were affiliated groups of Passamaquoddies, Mi'kmaqs, and Maliseets. English settlers and officials often did not identify the Wabanakis they encountered by their specific group, preferring instead to refer to them collectively as "Eastern Indians."[25]

From the beginning, Europeans had difficulty grasping the complexities of Wabanaki political culture and assumed after little observation that the eastern Wabanaki leaders were weakly organized, politically ineffectual, and inherently duplicitous. These assumptions obscured the fact that Wabanaki polity had traditionally rested on voluntary obedience, rather than the kind of explicit power used by area Europeans to compel or coerce.[26] This form of governance might also have been an innovative response to the first waves of European encounter, which left the Eastern Indians reeling from the effects of

European diseases, brought to shore by fisherman and other transient visitors.

Others came with designs of more permanent interaction. In 1604 Pierre Dugua, Sieur de Monts, a Protestant, and his Catholic associates, Samuel de Champlain and Jean de Biencourt de Poutrincourt, established a trading base at the Bay of Fundy in what is now Nova Scotia.[27] The trading post and settlement they christened Port Royal lasted less than a decade, hampered by internal problems and the withdrawal of royal support. Still, it managed to survive much longer than Maine's first English settlement, the Popham colony. Founded by Sir John Popham the same year as Jamestown, this settlement fell prey to the harsh climate and a lack of leadership, and ultimately lasted less than a year.

Yet the Popham colony's failure did little to discourage English interests in the area, which, due to its proximity to the North American cod fishery, had been promoted at that point for nearly a century.[28] By 1619, however, a thriving fishing settlement existed as far north as Monhegan Island.[29] And when John Smith explored the region in 1614, and wrote about its riches in *The Generall Historie of Virginia, New England, and the Summer Isles,* elite Englishmen continued to attempt to exploit the promising coastline Smith described. The two most successful were Sir Ferdinando Gorges and Captain John Mason, who received from the newly created Council for New England a grant of territory from the Merrimack to the Kennebec River.[30] The fact that Gorges was president of the council and Mason was its secretary no doubt helped the men establish and assert their claims.

Early attempts at settlement were tentative, oriented toward the sea, and underinstitutionalized in terms of religion and law. Small fishing settlements cropped up on the Isles of Shoals (now part of New Hampshire), and the very southern tip of modern Maine. The men who lived in them were for the most part "West Country men" from Cornwall, Dorset, and England's other southwestern coastal counties.[31] They were not Puritans—or even, for that matter, very convincing Anglicans. To at least one contemporary observer, they seemed to worship good fishing more than anything else.[32] Complicating the religious picture was the fishermen's desire to distance themselves from religious affairs that potentially interfered with business. Such was the case with John Winter, an agent for English merchant Robert Trelawney in the Casco Bay settlement of Spurwink. A budding and determined fishing entrepreneur, Winter knew that the best customers for his catch were Catholic France and Spain, and that Puritan contempt for Catholicism might retard the region's economic growth.

In 1629 Gorges and Mason separated their holdings. Mason took New Hampshire; Gorges took Maine, for which he envisioned a neofeudal society with himself as lord. To implement this vision, Gorges obtained from Charles I almost unlimited powers to build up his patent, including the ability to exclude Puritans and establish the Church of England.[33] The king likely granted such sweeping powers because he was beset by Puritan enemies at home; he no doubt valued the effort of loyal and grateful friends to check Puritan power in the New World as well. Maine had few settlements at this point, but Gorges had great plans for them. His grandiose vision for York, Maine (first called Agamenticus, then rechristened "Gorgeana" by Gorges, honoring himself), called for a large city to house the province's municipal offices and, more significantly, serve as an episcopal see for an Anglican bishop. The rest of Maine, with settlements so sparse they could barely lay claim to the title, were to be formed into a network of bailiwicks and parishes that recognized and supported the primacy of the Church of England.

Gorges's advanced age, troubles in the mother country, and the province's geography, however, combined to frustrate the proprietor's plans. Beginning in the 1630s, Maine experienced a string of events that, in historian Charles Clark's words, led to its "slow absorption" into Massachusetts. It began with the appointment of Thomas Gorges, nephew of Sir Ferdinando, to the position of deputy governor of the province. Unlike his uncle, the younger Gorges was sympathetic to the Parliamentary cause and Puritanism in general. He was also faced with the problem of declining New World migration in the wake of the English Civil War, which in turn hurt the colony's fledgling economy. In response, Thomas Gorges permitted important Puritan inroads into Maine. With the English Crown preoccupied with internal strife, Massachusetts continued to develop according to the vision of its own powerful men. When Thomas Gorges returned to England in 1643 to join the Parliamentarian fight against the king, he left behind a province in which some settlers were planning to import Massachusetts Bay–style Puritanism.[34]

The first Puritans to arrive, however, were unlikely partisans of Massachusetts. The Reverend John Wheelwright and his associates had been banished from the Bay Colony along with the minister's sister-in-law, Anne Hutchinson. On threat of yet another exile, this time from Exeter, New Hampshire, Wheelwright and his followers found safety in Maine.[35] Soon after, however, Wheelwright renounced his radical views and made his peace with Massachusetts, to which he would eventually return. Before that happened, he and his followers founded the town of Wells and established a congregation, making it the first "Puritan" town in Maine.

By the middle of the century, Maine had at least one community of committed Puritans. Thanks to Thomas Gorges's return to England, it also had a void in authority, which allowed the Church of England to maintain its presence. Events throughout the Atlantic World, however, were slowly turning in favor of Puritan control of Maine. In 1649 Parliamentary forces executed Charles I and ushered in the Commonwealth of Oliver Cromwell. Puritan sympathizers led by Sir Alexander Rigby secured the patent for the Province of Lygonia, the region between the Kennebunk and Kennebec rivers. Responding to confirmation of Sir Ferdinando's death, Edward Godfrey, a Gorges partisan, called an assembly in 1649 for representatives of Kittery, York, and Wells. The government they founded was sensitive to both the presence of Massachusetts Puritans in New Hampshire (they would effectively control that colony until 1680) and the new English government, as well as the diversity of Protestant affiliations already established in Maine. It included clear concessions to ensure that badly needed settlers, who were already accustomed to the province's relative freedoms, were not alienated.[36]

Godfrey's petition to Parliament requesting recognition of his new government was ultimately his undoing. Claiming jurisdiction over all territory south of the northernmost point of the Merrimack

River, Massachusetts authorities moved decisively to assert a counter-claim to the province. From 1652 through 1658, commissioners of the Massachusetts General Court steadily undercut Godfrey's power by securing the submission of all the major settlements from Kittery to Falmouth. Men friendly to Massachusetts were appointed as magistrates throughout Maine and the old Lygonia patent. This helped transform Maine, once noncommittal in terms of religion, into a "frontier outpost of Puritan society," at least for administrative purposes.[37]

With Massachusetts authority came the promise of greater settler numbers and more clearly defined civic organization, law and order, and protection. Even so, many Mainers of the mid-seventeenth century resisted the prospect of the Bay Colony's control. Resistance was so great that even Puritans doubted that their religious vision could compete with the loosely practiced Christianity of the original Maine settlers. In addition, orthodox Puritan ministers were in short supply and did not last very long in the province, and the close quarters of the small settlements created greater intimacy between minister and congregation than perhaps was ideal. One, the Reverend Richard Gibson, disappointed John Winter when he rejected Winter's daughter as a potential bride and chose to marry another. Later, Gibson sued fellow settler and Winter ally John Bonython for calling him "a base priest, a base knave, a base fellow" and labeling his wife, Mary Lewis Gibson, "a base whore, an impudent whore, a base strumpet," who "had or should have had a bastard three years since."[38] The court that heard the case awarded Gibson only a fraction of the damages he sued for, demonstrating to the minister that his status mattered little compared with the will of powerful local men like Winter and Bonython. During much of Maine's early history, no community minister was often preferable to one who did not yield to these secular leaders. Pure and orthodox churches, a fundamental element of civil organization in Massachusetts, were not easily organized in Maine.

In addition, there were still those in the colony who favored the Gorges family and remained faithful to the now-deposed English royal family. This faction greeted with pleasure the restoration of the

Stuart monarchy in 1660. Under the influence of the Gorges heirs, and determined to make the first round of Navigation Acts work, Charles II established royal control over the colony from 1665 to 1668. This new administration, however, proved ineffectual, and a new threat—the French, who persisted in strengthening their hold on the eastern and northwestern flanks of Maine—increasingly menaced the province's borders.

By 1668 many if not most Mainers were eager for a restoration of their own—of Massachusetts, and the protection it had initially promised. With control reasserted, the General Court of Massachusetts laid to rest any disputes of title by purchasing all rights to Maine from the Gorges heirs in 1677. With this transaction, and the creation of a royal province out of New Hampshire, Maine became, officially, Puritan Massachusetts's northernmost extension, as it remained until 1820.

The key colonies in France's plan for a New World empire, Canada and Acadia, composed New France and neighbored New England to the north. But in contrast to the English colonies, the French holdings were slow to attract settlement. For one, New France had brutally cold winters and a short growing season. According to Baron de Lahontan, an early eighteenth-century visitor to Canada, humans needed a brass body, glass eyes, and brandy for blood to survive a Canadian winter.[39] The simple realities of climate, along with other restrictions soon to be described, placed on pools of potential colonists kept settler numbers in New France chronically low. Still, the French persisted in their chilly clime, determined to subdue their piece of the New World, and to experiment with new forms of colonial organization.

Four years after he helped found Port Royal in 1604 and despite the obvious weaknesses that led to the settlement's downfall, Samuel de Champlain searched the banks of the St. Lawrence River for Stadacona, an Indian village visited by Jacques Cartier seventy years earlier. Champlain never found the village, but he did find an ideal spot for settlement: an uninhabited plain, perched high on a bluff for easy defense, which became the site for Quebec. In contrast to the English who were building settlements mostly in southern Maine, Champlain

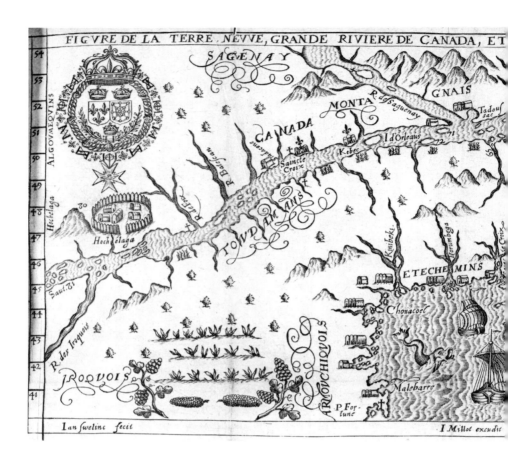

sent French representatives to local Indian villages to build trade relationships and map the country. But with few comforts and virtually
no institutions or social structures, Canada lost colonists who migrated back to France after a few years of work. Others, like the ad-
venturer Étienne Brulé, rejected the French colonial enterprise altogether and became completely transculturated Indians.[40]

   Those who stuck with Champlain's program, however, extracted
valuable resources of fur and fish to send back to the mother country.
In addition, Roman Catholic religious orders, most notably the Jesuits, claimed a harvest of their own—in Indian souls. Though not
the first French missionaries to come to the New World (the Récol-

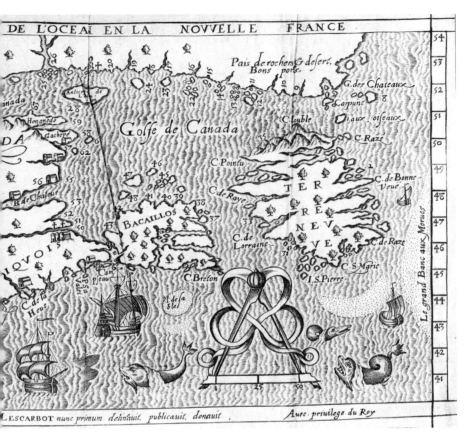

Figure 3. Marc Lescarbot's 1609 map emphasized French claims to Maine. Lescarbot, *Histoire de la Nouvelle France* (1609). Courtesy of the Osher Map Library, University of Southern Maine.

lets took that honor), the Jesuits seemed more likely than anyone else to stay. Their drive to build a Catholic spiritual empire in the New World hastened the development of badly needed institutions that served Frenchmen and Indians alike.

Still, colonial development was painfully slow. Seeking to stabilize the colony through migration, and encourage missionary work and self-sufficiency, France's powerful Cardinal Richelieu formed the Company of New France in 1627 and charged it with restructuring

New France. Financial support for the new enterprise came from pious and patriotic French men and women who wanted to play a role in spreading Catholicism's global reach. Richelieu also prohibited Protestants from participating in the enterprise, fearing they might create friction with Catholic settlers or worse, undermine French New World interests by joining the Protestant English.[41] The colonies thus took on an intrinsically Catholic patina, which undermined the original founders' humanistic goals of Christians and Indians living in tolerance.

What happened next, however, underscored Richelieu's assertions of Protestant perfidy. As the Company of New France prepared its ships to sail to Canada from Dieppe, Jarvis Kirke, a London merchant who knew the city well, received a letter of marque from the English government, granting him authorization to prey on French shipping. He and his brother, David, crossed the Atlantic, seized the company ships as they reached the mouth of the St. Lawrence, and then sailed downriver to take Quebec itself, which he succeeded in doing for a few brief months in 1629. At the same time, French Acadia was conquered by Scottish Protestant William Alexander. Proud of his conquest, Alexander rechristened Acadia "Nova Scotia" in honor of his birthplace.

European politics, however, thwarted the plans of Alexander and the Kirke brothers. By the end of 1629, France had reclaimed its two most important colonial outposts. The Jesuits quickly resumed their ministries to colonial Europeans and any Indians who showed an interest. Family groups, and later *filles du roi,* began to arrive in the colony with the goal of creating a New World version of French society. And in marked contrast to the New English who were spreading northward into Maine, the French cultivated political, religious, and even familial ties with Native Americans. These influences came into Maine from the surrounding northeast and northwest French territories.

Ironically, the strength of these ties, and the transformations they brought to Native American life also created serious problems that threatened New France's very survival. Beginning in the 1630s, the Iroquois, whose own allies were the Dutch and later the English, launched a series of attacks on French Indian allies and interests. Having depleted their local beaver populations and now largely dependent on European trade goods supplied by the Dutch of New Netherland, the Iroquois would continue these attacks, often with spectacularly terrible consequences, for more than six decades.[42] The Jesuits and their missions were frequent targets.

The violent deaths of various Jesuits, however, served only to inspire fresh waves of French Catholic missionaries. Inspired in part by the *Jesuit Relations,* a series of published letters and reports of mission activity made public by the Society of Jesus, pious French women and men migrated to New France in search of outlets for their zealous impulses. One of these was a devout nobleman named Paul de Chomedey, Sieur de Maisonneuve, who in 1649 led members of an ultra-pious Catholic lay society, the Companie du St. Sacrament, to what would become Montreal. Farther down the St. Lawrence than Quebec, Montreal soon became a more strategic entrepôt for the fur trade than Quebec, and grew quickly as an economic base for French interests.

Though their tiny populace was dwarfed by the population of Protestant New England, the French colonies continued to invent new and novel ways of increasing their trade networks and religious spheres of influence. Key to this effort were women. Chomedey's fellow *dévote* and partner in the Mont Royale enterprise was the laywoman Jeanne Mance, who, though not a professed religious, spurned marriage because of her belief that God had created her to convert Indians to Catholicism. Her example inspired other devout women to reject married life and devote their energies instead to founding schools, hospitals, and dispensaries.[43] These services were mission institutions for settler and Indian alike, and functioned as another tool for cementing bonds between the French and an increasingly far-flung population of diverse Native Americans—including those who lived in close proximity to the English in the Province of Maine.

Most of the connections between Indians and French Europeans, though, were facilitated by the Jesuits, who remained the most powerful religious group in New France throughout the seventeenth century. In the 1640s they continued to push out of New France in all directions. Such incursions worried other colonists and often aggravated the already tense situation with the Iroquois. From 1647 through 1649, the Iroquois struck out against their major foes, the largely Christian Hurons, with particular ferocity.

The Iroquois onslaught continued throughout the 1650s into the 1660s, when the colony came under royal rule and was reoriented by two particularly able administrators of Louis XIV, Jean-Baptiste Colbert, secretary of state for the colonies, and Jean Talon, the new intendant of New France. Both men were charged with improving the colony's economic viability and military defenses. Talon was one of a long line of professional military men who held the post of intendant, and his particular skills coincided with Colbert's agenda.[44] Colbert ordered Talon to continue to implement policies to "draw these [native] peoples, and especially those who have embraced Christianity, into the neighborhood of our settlements and, if possible, intermingle them there so that, with the passage of time, having but one law and the same master, they will form thereby but a single people of the same blood."[45] Like most seventeenth-century Euro-Americans, Colbert was not a cultural relativist, and he did not envision a syncretic society. His vision was for a transplanted French society, with dominant French language, customs, and religion that absorbed Indians. But with settler numbers still low and those of Indian neighbors still relatively high, this hypothetical society could not be created by fiat. Thus the French continued the process of cultivating Native Americans by identifying common goals and interests, and highlighting the deficiencies of the English, who, for the most part, neither welcomed Native Americans into their communities nor showed any signs of ceasing to pressure Indian lands with new settlements. Diplomatic and missionary endeavors that belabored this point continued throughout the latter half of the seventeenth century. As a result, the French influence was palpable, in varying degrees, throughout the upper frontier of North America, from Nova Scotia and Newfoundland to the Great Lakes. It also seeped into borderlands contested by the English.

In the meantime, Anglo-Wabanaki hostilities, created largely by English encroachment on the lands of Maine's Indians, boiled over in the wake of King Philip's War in 1675. This brutal conflict lasted for little more than a year in Massachusetts. A separate but related conflict between the New English in Maine and the Wabanakis, however, persisted until 1678.[46] The role of the French in this conflict was negligible, in part because tensions between the Wabanakis and English ran high enough on their own. By the end of the century, however, European events, and New France's implementation of Jean-Baptiste Colbert's policy of *le meme sang* (the same blood) began to bear fruit among Maine's discontented Indians.

Throughout the Atlantic World, the course of colonization never ran smoothly. Throughout much of the seventeenth century, attracting settlers remained a problem throughout the French regime. Thinly settled Euro-American communities remained easy targets for hostile Indians and Europeans alike. In northern New England, the threat and occasional outbreak of violence that pitted the English against the Wabanakis and other Indians also resulted in weak settlement patterns. Compounding the problem was that any sense of a border between the French and English colonies remained, as described by James Axtell, "dangerously undefined" throughout the seventeenth century and well into the eighteenth.[47]

The persistence of the French colonies despite their own internal problems ensured that English settlers who wanted peace and prosperity in seventeenth century Maine needed either to conflict with the French or, as the situation required, to accept them as fellow Christian Europeans in cooperation and coexistence. This is not to suggest that Protestant Mainers were religious relativists. They were not. They were, however, living in fragile communities located near formidable adversaries. During the seventeenth century, few Euro-American Christians, English or French, had the luxury of uncompromising zealotry.

Planting Christianity, Christian Plantations

Throughout the century, Maine's English settlements grew haphazardly—a by-product of the single-minded goal of its early settlers and proprietors to locate, harvest, and trade in the province's natural riches. For their part, Massachusetts ministers prayed that the Bay Colony's midcentury incursions would produce a rich harvest of the souls of (as Cotton Mather termed them) "men whose gods were fish and pine."[48] More worldly authorities hoped to harvest the fish and pine as well. By 1688 these settlements stretched from Kittery in the southwest to Pemaquid in the northeast. But a few miles east of Pemaquid, French territory began. The Penobscot Bay fort of Pentagoët, the westernmost settlement of Acadia, sat a mere thirty miles away.

The population of the English settlements grew throughout the century, but not in ways that supported the community cohesion found in nearby Massachusetts. According to Charles Clark, Maine's settlers "lacked the sense of community that came with close religious and social ties, and had felt no necessity for the consolidated arrangement by which the Puritans to the south had tried to foster moral and civic responsibility, church attendance, and public education."[49] The distance between settlements and the lack of a civic plan for their development contributed to the problem. It was thus impossible for Puritan officials to exert the same influence in Maine as they did in Massachusetts communities. This, combined with geographic proximity to Wabanakia and the French, made Maine a "dark corner" of piety in the eyes of New England's orthodox Puritans which attracted colonists out of step with the New England Way.[50]

Still, for some, the dark corners of the religious world were pockets of spiritual innovation, the origins of which could be traced to the experience of religious migration throughout the Atlantic World. All forms of Christianity on the Maine frontier were products of the powerful religious movements of the previous century which emphasized new modes of personal and collective religious expression. In seventeenth-century popular and print culture (not to mention actual religious practices), Protestantism and Catholicism appeared as Christian opposites, defining themselves against one another. To early modern Catholics, Protestants were heretics; emphasizing a perceived slavish devotion to the Roman papacy, Protestants countered by adopting the derisive term papists to describe Catholics.[51]

But both forms of Christianity that existed throughout the early modern Atlantic World were the results of their own reformations. Most forms of Protestantism revolutionized the Christian visions of their followers and introduced dramatic changes to theology, piety, liturgy, and daily life. The Catholic Reformation likewise reoriented, redefined, and occasionally jettisoned elements of late medieval Catholicism that the earliest Protestant reformers found insupportable. In some cases, Catholic reforms were strikingly similar to those advocated by early Protestants, some of whom influenced the Reformation yet did not themselves leave the Catholic Church.[52] Included among these were reforms in education and the greater use of vernacular translations for sacred and spiritual works. These changes coincided with increasing encounters between New World Indians and Europeans, which created a Catholic "sphere of influence" within the Atlantic World that allowed for the dissemination of reformed Catholicism. Initiating the drive to fashion the peoples of the Western Hemisphere into Catholic Christians were missionaries of new, post-Reformation religious orders. Some relied on techniques that were predicated on the most radical features of post-Reformation *Christianity*, let alone Catholicism, yet to be seen.

Key differences between Catholics and Protestants remained on every level. Even the very nature of a church, and the legitimacy it could claim as a Church of God, was contested. To most Protestants of early New England, a church in its ideal form was composed of members who lived godly lives, possessed an intimate understanding of Scripture, and deferred to the judgment of the church.[53] In contrast, anyone could easily become a committed Catholic through general knowledge of the church's creeds, participation in its liturgies, and access to its sacraments. This created the possibility for a much more extensive body of the faithful, not born to salvation but capable of attaining it.[54]

Differences persisted on every level. When the two faith systems collided in contested colonial regions, reformed Protestantism's exclusivity became a handicap. This happened in Maine, where mission Catholicism was by its very nature more flexible and adaptable than the mission Protestantism that would eventually rise to challenge it.[55]

Most of the elements of Catholic practice that proved adaptable in the missions were anathema to Protestant Puritans of the seventeenth and early eighteenth centuries, and reinforced the perception among orthodox New Englanders that the Church of Rome was not a true Christian church at all. Other northern New England Protestants, including Anglicans and, later, Presbyterians, also viewed Catholicism in terms of society and politics, seeing the Church of Rome's adherents as heirs to a post-Reformation history whose key purpose was to destroy God's visible churches and the states that protected Protestantism.[56] To New England Protestants, therefore, professed Catholics not only bore the historical stain of a corrupt set of theological and moral principles, they were also condemned for a historical past that included the primacy of foreign potentates, the perceived rapines of the Catholic Irish, and the campaigns in France and Spanish-controlled portions of Europe that had attempted to root out Protestantism.[57] Writing at a comfortable distance from the Maine frontier in 1702, Cotton Mather drew an explicit connection between Catholic practice and anti-Protestant warfare in his preface to a description of the borderland atrocities of King William's War in *Decennium Luctuosum.* Mather contended, "A Spaniard, that was a Soldier, would say, That if we have a good Cause, the smell of Gunpowder in the Field is as sweet as the Incense at the Altar."[58]

Nevertheless, early Puritan thinkers struggled to come to terms with the fact that the nature of election meant that the possession of true, saving faith could not be limited to the ranks of their adherents alone. Reluctantly, they admitted that Christians of non-Reformed churches, like Anglicans and Roman Catholics, could also be the recipients of saving grace if it was God's will.[59] Election is a theme that runs through many narratives left by returned captives from Maine, but it also emerges as a theme in the scattered evidence left by Maine captives who did remain with their captors and became Catholics. Even as Catholic converts, these Mainers found it difficult to escape the predestinarian impulse that was fundamental to so many early modern Protestant creeds. And for Protestants, and Puritans in particular, who would later lose family to captivity and apostasy to Catholicism, this modicum of hope in Providence's wonder-workings must have provided at least a modicum of spiritual comfort for their losses. In addition, some who encountered Catholics before or during the wars saw that their fellow Christians could bypass confessional differences to aid Protestants in mortal danger.

What is now modern Maine is the only area of New England that has experienced the persistent influence of both Catholicism and Protestantism throughout its entire colonial history. Euro-American Christian settlement within Maine was sporadic and mixed. The settlement patterns varied greatly. From 1620 onward, English settlements slowly but gradually nudged northward, expanding and contracting according to the state of relations with the local Wabanaki Indians and the Catholic French. The settlements of Catholic people — French or Native American — were more scattered, and their longevity varied greatly. Some were seen as threats to New England or Protestantism and quickly destroyed. Others withstood attack and reconstituted themselves or were absorbed into New England. Some persevered on their own for long periods, protected by the Wabanakis or the French or simply not challenged by the New English. Most, however, became stages for converging Christianities. Though often born of hostility, these encounters often demonstrated that Protestants and Catholics could find common ground with a common Christian language.

The events surrounding the creation and destruction of one of these religious settlements, the Jesuit mission of Saint Sauveur, show that clearly defined religious sensibilities and biases often gave way to other factors such as geopolitical alignments, a sense of solidarity in places where Europeans were far outnumbered by Native Americans, and empathy for fellow Christians. As the English eyed the lower littoral, Samuel de Champlain claimed the coast to the east of Penobscot Bay in the name of France and christened the landmass Isle des Monts Deserts.[60] Remote and unattractive to prospective farmers, it drew a small band of Jesuit priests and brothers who, armed with missionary zeal and a royal commission, attempted to found a mission there in 1611.[61] In addition to its proselytizing role, this mission was also meant to be part of a general French plan to occupy the littoral surrounding the Bay of Fundy. The coast, however, was also claimed by England, which despite an early failure at setting up a Maine colony, was disinclined to turn a blind eye to French occupation.[62]

The symbolic start of Saint Sauveur involved an enormous wooden cross that was "planted" on the landscape, according to the priests, "by way of consecrating the place."[63] For the missionaries, the literal planting of a religious symbol that all Christians understood tied Christianity to specific places and rendered the landscape a holy land of religious enterprise. It was through the use of objects of veneration and of sacramentals—everyday objects that were consecrated by a priest to perform certain religious functions—that the worldly and common became holy endeavors.[64] The ceremonies that symbolically planted Christianity were liturgical performances that also carried the secondary meaning of "consecrating" claims throughout the French New World. Thus the Saint Sauveur Jesuits, as in so many other places of the Atlantic World, became simultaneously evangelists and agents of a European Crown, claiming territory for God and King with one ceremony.[65]

In the use of crosses, however, Catholics were not alone. Protestants also employed them to identify their New World territory. English explorers Martin Frobisher and Christopher Newport planted them in Newfoundland and Virginia, respectively. So did George Weymouth as he explored Maine's coast in 1605. Weymouth's actions were described by crewman James Rosier, who attested, "In no place . . . we could discerne any token or signe, that ever any Christian had beene before; of which either cutting wood, diggine for water, or setting up Crosses . . . we should have perceived some mention left."[66] Planting a symbol so closely associated with Catholicism seems a strange choice for sixteenth- and seventeenth-century Englishmen, who have long been identified as enthusiastic iconoclasts toward anything that smacked of Catholicism. Yet the universal association of the cross with European Christianity had a pragmatic function, as warnings to other would-be colonizers that the land had already been claimed by other Christians. A cross left the actual faith of those colonizers ambiguous, thus reducing the risk of attack by rival Christian nations. Rejecting the cross as a legitimate Christian symbol was a potent element of post-Reformation English religious culture, but it remained a useful universal emblem that all Europeans understood.

No records describe whether the cross-plantings of Anglicans had a ceremonial component. In contrast, French ceremonies of possession, as Patricia Seed has called them, were carefully orchestrated, elaborate rituals that combined Catholic liturgy, French political ceremony, and the participation of indigenous people to create a symbolically unified faithful who, in turn, "christened" the land together. For the French, these were the actions of people who intended not only to develop a colonial presence in a region, but also to bring it into the Christian fold. The spreading of Christianity throughout its New World possessions was a longstanding French goal. Along with their king, the early colonization leaders Pierre Dugua, Sieur de Monts, and Samuel de Champlain agreed that this was one of the most important reasons for a New World colony to exist. De Monts brought both Protestant and Catholic clergy to his Acadian colony, though they argued constantly. Ruminating on this interfaith disaster, Champlain wrote, "Two contrary religions are never very fruitful to God's glory among the infidels."[67] Throughout the seventeenth century, various French authorities demonstrated their agreement with Champlain by preventing any meaningful Protestant presence to develop in New France. For this reason, the overt symbolism of Catholic conquest created a sacred bond between the nation and the land. Through ceremonial planting, French explorers and colonizers sought to demonstrate the grandeur of their spiritual vision wherever they went in the New World.[68] The cross itself served as a harbinger of spiritual and literal prosperity. The contemporary Jesuit historian Joseph Jouvency noted, "The land that was desolate and unpassable shall be glad, and the wilderness shall rejoice, and shall flourish like the lily."[69] In the case of Saint Sauveur (Holy Redeemer), even its name demonstrated that the land, and certainly its people, would flourish spiritually in the shadow of the French fleur-de-lys.[70]

The planting of crosses marked the establishment of a New World colony, but these could prove temporary, subject to weather, neglect, and vandalism. Far more resilient were the metaphoric "plantings" they harbingered: the subjects of various European powers, and the crops, livestock, possessions, and guns that accompanied them and became tools of conquest.[71] The horrors of King Philip's War showed the colonial world how much Native Americans resented these incursions into spaces that had long been their own. Often their attacks wiped the landscape clean of English habitations, livestock, and people, leaving, according to Nathaniel Saltonstall's account, "besides particular Farms and Plantations, a great Number not to be reckoned up, wholly laid waste, or much damnified."[72] Retaliatory measures also demonstrate the lengths to which the English would go to protect their regional interests. By 1688 attacks on the settlements of Christian people by other professed Christians, both Native American and French, became a standard form of warfare.[73] These attacks were so ghastly in their human toll to English contemporaries and subsequent historians that they often overshadowed all other elements of religious contact between peoples, and functioned instead as the whole story of religious culture on the Maine frontier.

For the French in and around Maine, the religious "plantings" that began with crosses proceeded differently. French attempts to compete with the English were impeded by low settler numbers, climate, and internal wrangling among the French proponents of colonization. French Catholic weaknesses, however, were also a source of strength: low French settler numbers in Acadia and along the upper Maine coast put little to no pressure on Native populations. In addition, the failure to develop consolidated settlements with large numbers of European Christians liberated French missionaries to concentrate on the explicit colonial priority of spreading Catholic Christianity to the Indians. Though marked by tensions, misunderstandings, resentments, and other problems, the Wabanaki/Jesuit alliance became one of the most enduring religious synergies between Indians and Europeans in seventeenth- and eighteenth-century North America.[74]

In Maine the French effort to consecrate and settle the land they called "Norumbega" began on Mount Desert Island with the Jesuit mission of Saint Sauveur. Had it succeeded, Saint Sauveur would have boldly proclaimed the French Catholic presence on the mid-Maine coast, and stood as a territorial bulwark against English expansion. Before that happened, however, it became the focal point

for European Christian claims that overlapped. The resulting territorial dispute played out on the Maine frontier, as competing Christians battled to have their marks on the landscape respected. For the
French missionaries who came to the Maine coast to proselytize, the
lengthy journey and its unexpected consequences led to multiple interfaith encounters. Some confirmed the priests' worst opinions of Protestants, others defied them. Taken together, these interfaith encounters constitute an early example of Maine as a staging ground for
converging Christianities.

For the Saint Sauveur Jesuits, these encounters began before they
left France in 1611. Their chosen vessel was owned by Protestants who,
upon learning of the priests' intentions, refused them passage. Though
Jesuits were free to dismiss them as "churlish Heretics" in their private
writings, they could not ignore the fact that their enterprise could not
proceed without the agreement of Protestant investors.[75] Desperate to
secure passage on the only ship that was fitted out for travel to New
France that year, the Jesuits turned to a wealthy and devout laywoman,
Madame de Guercherville, who purchased a partnership in the venture
and transferred it to the priests.[76] Thereafter, the Jesuits were not mere
passengers but owners on a vessel that included Protestants among
its crew and officers.[77] The initial tension gave way to the demands
of maintaining the camaraderie of the vessel, ultimately trumping the
scruples that kept Protestants and Catholics apart. This would not last;
divisions between the Jesuits and the colony's leadership forced the
priests to found a settlement of their own.

In 1613, the Jesuits settled on Mount Desert Island, whose stark
beauty included topographical features that served as natural conceal-
ments, and in welcoming Penobscot Indians the possibility for meeting all their goals as both French and religious men.[78] Other portents
were less promising, as infighting between the Jesuits and their settlers
left the tiny settlement dangerously fragmented. When English sailors
patrolling the coast and fishing for cod discovered the settlement and
determined to attack it, the missionaries and laypeople of Saint Sau -
veur were unable to muster an organized defense.

The English attackers came from Virginia. Their captain, Samuel
Argall, claimed authority to attack the mission from the Council for

New England, which had already laid claim to the territory and considered its defense a patriotic and moral duty that would pave the way for settlements populated by English fishermen.[79] With little warning, Argall fired on the ship that housed the Jesuits and companions, killing Jesuit brother Gilbert du Thet. The terrified survivors revealed their identities as Catholic priests and pleaded for clemency. As they reported,

> Our brethren approached [Argall]; frankly revealed themselves to him, as he was still ignorant of their identity; and begged him not, in elation over his easy victory, to adopt severe measures against their colony; they earnestly warned him to remember the conditions of human life, saying that just as he would wish his own interests mildly handled, if a similar calamity had fallen upon him, so he ought to act humanely in the case of others; moreover, that he should especially consider that he was dealing with innocent men, to whom no fault could be charged beyond the fact that, because of their blamelessness, they had been too careless in a peaceful spot. They were heard somewhat kindly by the Captain, and received with respectful address; the only thing of which he disapproved being that Fathers of the Society, who had commonly so good a reputation for piety and wisdom, should be among a band of runaways and pirates.[80]

The Jesuits were apprehended by the Protestants for the twin offenses of piracy and squatting on English land. But their explanations and plea for mercy ultimately received a sympathetic response from their captors. Though he kept the Jesuits as prisoners, Argall extended various courtesies to them, offering the services of an English Catholic and inviting the captive priests to dine at his table.[81] In a more unusual offer of interfaith cooperation, a pilot named Bailleur, a Protestant member of the fractious French mission, "came by night to Father Biard, and, taking him by the hand, with many protestations bade him and the other Fathers to expect from him, as far as faithfulness and devotion could go toward another, all the services of a Christian and a fellow-countryman, and to be persuaded that he would neglect nothing which might contribute to their safety; to employ his aid freely, and consider what they should decide upon, as to making their escape."[82]

By the time they arrived in Virginia, the Jesuits had succeeded in converting Samuel Argall—not to Catholicism, but to the belief that the English had detained innocent men.[83] Upon arrival in Virginia, the Protestant captain openly sided with the Jesuits against his colony's governor, Thomas Dale, who was prepared to deal harshly with the priests. In the end, the Anglican Argall's defense won the priests their freedom.[84]

The Jesuits' North American odyssey did not end there. After their ordeal among the Virginians, their attempt to return temporarily to France was thwarted by devastating storms, another accusation of piracy, an attack by a genuine pirate, and the near-destruction of their vessel by a Spanish treasure ship.[85] Their experience in Maine, however, had provided a rare opportunity, albeit under unusual circumstances, for Catholics and Protestants to encounter one another in ways that defied biases based on faith.

In the years following Saint Sauveur's demise, Jesuits like Pierre Biard were joined in their ministry by another order, the Capuchins, who occasionally worked the Maine coast from Acadian outposts.[86] The Sulpicians had a more limited presence, mostly in nearby Acadia, which, according to French reckoning, extended well into Maine territory claimed by England. Gabriel Druillettes's mission to the Kennebec began in this milieu, amidst both potentially hostile Protestants and fellow Catholics with whom they competed for souls. Massachusetts's understanding of Maine overlapped with New France's, creating a borderland where multiple Christianities could be found.

Perhaps emboldened by their ability to live and work unmolested so close to New England, at least one Maine Jesuit attempted to extend his ministry to the heart of New England itself. In 1674 Jesuit Jean Pierron took the bold step of visiting the heart of American Puritanism itself, Boston. Unlike Gabriel Druillettes, however, the priest traveled in disguise. En route to visiting fellow Jesuits in Maryland when his boat stopped in Boston, Pierron decided to stay in

Massachusetts to seek converts—or at least create some pro-Catholic mischief. Though disguised, he spoke openly about religious matters to Puritans who lived in communities outside of Boston. While he later complained that New England was filled with "naught but desolation and abomination among the heretics," the Jesuit still managed to secure a few abjurations of Protestantism.[87] Eventually his reputation for learned debate preceded him. When he went knocking on the doors of various Boston ministers, he found them open, and their occupants eager to engage in lively religious dialogue. Like his predecessor in New England, the undisguised Gabriel Druillettes, Pierron reported that the Bostonians treated him with "much civility."[88] As time passed, however, his methods and message cast suspicion on his true identity, and Pierron was summoned for questioning by the Massachusetts General Court. Wisely, he chose to flee, as his successes in Boston had been insufficient to encourage martyrdom.[89] And there were interesting challenges to be had in Maryland, where Catholics—even secret ones—were numerous. Pierron's adventures demonstrate that infiltration into New England by disguised Jesuits, by sea or land, was not merely the stuff of Protestant English paranoia.[90]

The Jesuit's impromptu mission to Boston perhaps carried greater significance than just the thrill of theological mischief. The audacious sojourn coincided with rumors from England that Charles II, who had strong Catholic sympathies, had engaged in secret diplomatic conferences with the French and was encouraging a "Popish Plot" to restore Catholicism to England.[91] From his perch on the edge of the Atlantic World, Pierron was likely aware that the future of Christianity in England was at a crossroads—and that his services might prove handy to those in New England who might secretly welcome such change. Of even greater interest is the fact that this rumor of events in far-off England managed to travel as far as the Maine frontier, where the Jesuit had spent the winter of 1674, leading to tempting speculation that the informants could have been Maine's English settlers themselves.

If Pierron interacted with Protestants in Maine's English settlements, he left no record of it in the *Jesuit Relations*. If they took place, such interactions might have suggested to the priest that New England Protestants were possibly open to experimenting with other forms of Christianity. From the beginning, Maine attracted settlers who were ethnically and religiously diverse. Settlers in Maine's English towns were likely to attend whatever church was at hand, if one existed at all. Their own religious preferences ran the Christian gamut from Eastern Orthodoxy to radical Protestantism. By the middle of the seventeenth century, Greeks, Scots, French, Portuguese, Channel Islanders, Dutch, Walloons, Irish, West Indians, West Africans, and Welsh had all come to Maine to work in its maritime and forestry enterprises.[92] While the Puritan Conquest of the latter part of the seventeenth century increasingly tipped the scales in favor of English Puritans, settlers of other religious and ethnic backgrounds continued to make their way to the province, with the fringe settlements and fisheries of New Hampshire and Maine attracting Christian Europeans who came for the maritime enterprises and timber, not religion. Though most of these groups (with the possible exception of the Channel Islanders) did not make a lasting cultural imprint on English Maine, they maintained a presence outside of the boundaries of Puritan orthodoxy that Massachusetts hoped to enforce. Though the European populations scattered throughout the Eastward's communities were small in number, their diversity suggests that the settlers of the post-Puritan Conquest were aware of, rather than isolated from, the wider events that shaped the religious culture of the Atlantic World.

Still, most of these settlers lived under the auspices of English settlement, which brought with it an intrinsic association with Protestantism. "Catholic" Maine was created through ceremonies of possession. Though Anglicans also used crosses, English Puritans tended to use different rituals to establish distinctly "Protestant" territory. Such rituals were nonetheless laden with symbolic understandings, born of an intrinsically Protestant sense of sacred space and religious landscape. Emphasizing "grace over place," as Jon Butler notes, communities of the Protestant faithful were driven by a desire to collect a church of visible saints.[93] It was the presence of people who had been converted through grace that made a place Protestant, not buildings, trappings of liturgy, or the presence of the sacramental technicians who formed the Catholic priesthood.

Which Protestant vision would prevail was often in question throughout the province's seventeenth-century history. The tradition of resistance to Puritan Protestants dates to Ferdinando Gorges's attempts to create a strictly Anglican province. He planned to make Gorgeana a seat of centralized church power and instill himself as the church's protector. Gorges saw in Maine, according to one historian, "a land of misty dreams rooted in England's feudal past."[94] To promote his plan, Gorges aimed to populate his province with committed Anglicans who would buffer Massachusetts Bay Puritanism and stand as needed as a bulwark of royalist support against the colony to the south's more radical elements. The very name of Gorges's manor—Point Christian—lent pious meaning to the proprietor's ambitions for the area. It also conjured a vision of England's pre-Reformation past, where places bore names that honored saints and other sacred affiliations, and likewise spoke boldly of the presence of Anglicanism, which preserved the tradition.[95]

Despite his ambition, Sir Ferdinando was thwarted from ever setting foot in his province. And his capable young cousin, Thomas Gorges, proved to be sympathetic to Puritans. While maintaining his primary commitment to family interests, the younger Gorges pushed his uncle to sacralize the land with Protestants by adopting a policy of Protestant religious tolerance which, in turn, would spur settlement.[96] In a letter to antinomian refugee John Wheelwright, Thomas Gorges gave assurances that he "[forced] no man to the common prayer book or to the ceremonies of the Church of England but allowed the liberties of conscience in this particular," suggesting that he hoped to people his family's province from the pool of those already used to life in the New World. [97] Their potentially devisive radical Puritanism notwithstanding, the Wheelwrights and their friends were experienced settlers—the very people the Gorges family required to establish an enduring settlement.

Attracting religiously appropriate settlers was never easy, and it became even more difficult after Thomas Gorges's return to England. Gorges's departure deprived Puritanism of its most powerful advocate and left Maine vulnerable to an Anglican resurgence.[98] The province already had an Anglican infrastructure, with Anglican churches at Gorgeana (later York) and Kittery. Later, Falmouth would be established as an "Anglican" town (its founders having come farther north from predominantly Anglican Portsmouth).[99] Devout Anglicans also continued to play key roles in Maine's development throughout the seventeenth century, and many of them disliked and resisted the incursions of Massachusetts Puritans. One of these was Richard Vines, who came to the province as a servant of Sir Ferdinando and rose to become the proprietor of Arundel (Kennebunkport). Vines shared his master's commitment to the Church of England and may have had sympathetic relations with recusant families in England.[100] Another was Captain Francis Champernowne, a cousin of Sir Ferdinando and an enthusiastic protector of the original proprietor's interests. For decades, he protested against Puritan control of Maine, though he later joined Puritan representatives at the province's peace conference after King Philip's War.[101]

Men of more modest backgrounds also kept Maine's Anglican vision alive, sometimes actively disrupting plans to create in Maine a Puritan commonwealth. Such men included an Anglican priest named Robert Jordan, "an Orthodox Deane for the Church of England," who settled on a large and particularly choice piece of land near Spurwink (later Scarborough).[102] An outspoken opponent of Puritan hegemony, Jordan often ran afoul of Massachusetts authorities after Maine was permanently annexed by the Bay Colony.[103] Even members of later generations of Puritans, like merchant and mariner John Alden, raised suspicion among Orthodox Puritans because they associated too intimately with the province's Anglicans, as well as Indians, French Catholics, and Quakers.[104]

By the middle of the seventeenth century, Puritans and Anglicans were actively vying to shape the Protestant religious culture of the Province of Maine. Still, Puritan migration grew throughout the century, and its members faced the challenge of exerting their vision over one that had become increasingly eclectic and fractured.

Like the increasingly marginalized Anglicans, Nonconformists were slow to relinquish their interests in the region. For one thing, Maine offered the promise of a spiritual haven for Christians who were deemed undesirable elsewhere. Quakers in particular had been attracted to Maine's remoteness and were tolerated in Maine communities, especially Kittery. Indeed, a substantial number of the townspeople were converted by Quaker missionaries.[105] Among these converts was Nicholas Shapleigh, a prominent merchant, magistrate, and appointee to numerous civil and military posts.[106] Quakers were a source of annoyance in any territory under Puritan control, but in Maine and neighboring New Hampshire, officials successfully excluded only the most outspoken Friends. Despite the doctrine of pacifism espoused in 1660, small groups of Quakers added to settler numbers and engaged actively in economic affairs, two positive attributes that led to toleration in Maine and New Hampshire even during the years of Massachusetts Bay's government.[107] Even the more outspoken Quakers had an unexpected allure: fines meted out to them for failing to attend services were a source of provincial revenue. Still, the most outspoken critics of Puritanism were not welcome, with the General Court of Massachusetts even considering execution as an appropriate punishment for the most egregiously outspoken.[108] Even the border wars with the French and Indians did not soften Puritan attitudes toward these radical Protestants, despite what they contributed to the English towns. As late as 1708/9, Governor Joseph Dudley complained to the Board of Trade of people inhabiting the eastern parts who were "Living Disorderly, and some of them being Quakers," as though "disorderly" and "Quaker" were synonymous.[109]

Even less desirable than Quakers were Baptists, who began to appear in the Eastward as early as 1681. In 1682 a bold Baptist minister named William Scriven, who was licensed to preach by the Baptist church in Boston, successfully built a congregation in Kittery.[110] Scriven's alternative Sabbath services offended a local magistrate, Francis Hooke, who levied fines against professed Baptists and attempted to run the minister out of town.[111] Contempt for this particular Christian sect is evident in the case of George Burroughs, the Wells minister who was executed as a witch in Salem in 1692. Among the many accusations made against him was the assertion that he was a secret Baptist.[112] To his Puritan accusers, this was a serious addition to Burroughs's long list of grievous sins.

With so many competing Protestant visions practicing openly in Maine, planting an orthodox, Puritan English colony would have challenged even the most persuasive gospel minister. Orthodoxy could not be taken for granted, or even expected, from those who self-identified as Puritans. Settlers often "became Puritan" in terms of law and custom only. The Anglican congregation in Kittery, for example, simply swapped its founding denominational structure for a Congregational one after the province's submission to Massachusetts. Ultimately, the Kittery settlers were much more interested in wresting control of the region away from the grip of Gorges's patentees than they were in debating points of religious principle.[113] Adopting Puritanism, even in name only, provided additional grist for that mill, and linked their commitment to Puritanism to explicitly worldly matters.

Denominational diversity was not the only stumbling block to forming a cohesive Protestant identity in the Province of Maine. Mainers who professed Puritanism were, in general, not as well educated as their fellow colonists in Massachusetts. Many possessed a less than intimate knowledge of Scripture and were thus bereft of a key theological underpinning of Puritanism. When Massachusetts first gained control of Maine in 1649, the General Court stipulated that "all gode people within the Jurisdiction of this province who are out of a Church way and be orthodox in Judgment and not scandalous in life" should "gather themselves into a Church estate, provided they do it in a Christian way" and select and ordain officers who were "able, pious, and orthodox."[114] Charles Clark observes that the terms *able* and *orthodox* come directly from the Bay Colony's statute books. The term *pious,* however, had been exchanged for what in Massachusetts was *learned.*[115] Seventeenth-century Maine lacked schools and a critical mass of well-educated settlers, which meant it also lacked a clear tradition of Puritan scriptural learning. Knowing the shortcomings of the population, the General Court was forced to take the first step toward orthodoxy with piety, an achievable form of religious expression for sincerely godly settlers.

Lower rates of literacy in Maine challenged more than just orthodoxy. Literacy had benefits that transcended reading Scripture: it was also the key means of cultural transmission that perpetuated the English anti-Catholic tradition. This tradition was a useful tool for galvanizing the faithful against the enemies of God and Protestant English settlers. The prevalence of John Foxe's *Actes and Monuments* (among the first texts printed in New England, and one critical to the argument that Catholicism and Protestant-defined Christianity were intrinsically incompatible) hints at the enduring popularity of anti-Catholic tropes for an educated Protestant New World readership. *Actes and Monuments,* commonly known as the *Book of Martyrs,* fired the passions of many Massachusetts ministers.[116] So too did John Cotton's sermons, which were printed and widely distributed in both London and Boston. Cotton's works affirmed the "anti-papal persuasion" as a key belief for all Protestants, and used current events in Catholic and Protestant Europe to predict that "Christian Princes, and State shall powre out the wrath of God, upon Popish Superstition and Idolatry."[117]

Print culture in Maine, however, was limited by points of dissemination and the abilities and enthusiasm of potential readers. Print material, regular ministry, and schools were all instruments that spread and reinforced antipopery throughout the more established regions of New England. But the communities to the Eastward experienced few means to transmit these messages. Though the rhetoric of anti-Catholicism was not uncommon in seventeenth-century Maine, this important identity and community-building sentiment was far more successful where print culture thrived. If not passed on and perpetuated in print or by word of mouth to many listeners, anti-Catholicism's potency as a tool for militant Protestantism became diluted.

Given the relative scarcity of reading material in the province and the lack of any practical means to disseminate it, Maine's English settlers actually had more in common with the colonists of Canada and Acadia than they did with New Englanders who lived closer to the colonial metropoles. Despite the development of the cities and institutions, New France lacked a printing press until well into the eighteenth century.[118] As late as 1750, Peter Kalm was claiming that during his extensive travels in New France, he never once saw a Bible in a private home. This seems unlikely, as Catholic vernacular Bibles had been in print and available in France and for export to French-claimed territories for more than a century.[119] Roger Magnuson believes that the Protestant Kalm's sweeping statement smacks of both exaggeration and persistent stereotypes that Catholics were forbidden by their clergymen to read Scripture on their own. Nevertheless, a kernel of truth can be found in the tie between class and book ownership in New France—which in turn connects most colonial Catholic Canadians with the English settlers Maine was likely to attract. Assessments of ownership show that books of any kind were indeed rarely found in the homes of New France's frequently illiterate lower classes.[120] Thirty-two percent of the members of the ruling and professional classes, however, did possess books, with one personal collection surpassing three thousand volumes.[121] In comparison, a survey of Maine estate inventories between 1678 and 1685 reveals that books, including Bibles, were found in less than one-third of the province's households. Of these, approximately only one in three texts was identified explicitly as a Bible or a "practice of piety."[122] In addition, those fortunate enough to own books treated them as precious objects, and were reluctant to submit these precious and expensive objects to the dangers of frontier life. This was the case with John Wheelwright, who inherited a collection of books but was loath to keep them in his Maine home. He sent them to Boston for safekeeping, an act that preserved them from some types of frontier harm but also took them out of possible circulation to the reading public of his own community.[123]

Unlike French and English communities to the south and the west, Maine's were also severely underinstitutionalized in terms of education. If literacy rates were reasonably consistent with other areas of mid-seventeenth-century New England, most of Maine's settlers were able to read.[124] Many, however, lacked the means or inclination to take their education to the next level, which entailed going to a school to learn to write and cipher.[125] Maine communities were frequently penalized for failing to comply with a Massachusetts law that stipulated that towns with fifty or more families engage a teacher (part of the strategy to keep the "old deluder Satan" at bay).[126] To a critic of frontier dwellers like Cotton Mather, the inability or lack of interest in forming schools was another indication that these particular Protestants were haphazard, at best, in their regard for religion.

In the towns to the Eastward, which were constantly vulnerable to attack by religious antagonists, piety and zeal were more important tools for forging a cohesive Protestant identity than texts that explicated Catholicism's intrinsic deficiencies. Maine's settlers knew the basic conventions of anti-Catholic rhetoric, but it took the very real interfaith violence of the last decades of the seventeenth century—experienced intimately by many Maine families—to give these sentiments a stronger, more unified form. The arrival of Protestants with well-defined Puritan leanings during the second half of the seventeenth century accelerated this movement toward unifying Protestantism against Catholicism. Even those who fumbled for their religious bearings in the province's scattered, inchoate frontier communities retained at least a vague ideological conviction that the Catholic Church and its adherents were enemies.

How, then, did these New Englanders experience Catholicism? The answer lies in Maine's heritage of frequent comingling between native peoples and settlers. In the seventeenth century, settlers who knew of Catholicism through firsthand experience had most likely witnessed the syncretic practices of the Eastern Wabanakis, who were frequent visitors to the Eastward communities. As syncretic Catholics, Maine's indigenous people valued their missions, priests, feast days, and devotions. But Indian pragmatism outweighed unquestioned allegiance to the Catholic French, and they traded and worked with the English as community needs dictated, which meant that alliances between English and Wabanaki groups were not uncommon. Still, Christianity and Indian-ness struck many provincial Protestants as fundamentally incompatible. Some simply dismissed all Catholic Indians as professed yet defective Christians. To others, the very idea of a "Christian Indian" seemed beyond contemplation. As late as 1712, Massachusetts governor Joseph Dudley wrote to the Board of Trade in London that French officials allowed English captives "to be made Heathen, and Wives" by the Wabanakis, many of whom professed Catholicism.[127] In contrast, other Mainers would later argue that any exposure to any form of Christianity was a potential starting point for building bridges with Native communities. For them, the challenge was to mold defective Christian knowledge into their own vision. Finally, reflecting the diversity of early Maine Protestantism itself, there were some who simply did not care, as long as the Wabanakis left the English to pursue their own interests in peace or traded for worldly goods from English warehouses.

✦ ✦ ✦

By the onset of King William's War, Protestant Mainers were tackling both internal and external religious enemies that threatened their Christian plantations. Maine's position on New England's northern border heightened settlers' fears that enemies of Protestantism lurked everywhere — even in the most homogenously Puritan pockets of New England itself. Like their coreligionists in Massachusetts, they feared that the colonial administrators and merchants of the colonial metropoles were trading with (and were therefore secretly allied with) borderland Catholics. This heightened the fear that the "spice of popery" was being dished out liberally at the expense of poor settlers and their meager frontier enterprises. For example, during the early years of King William's War, colonists in both Massachusetts and Maine perceived that the witchcraft crisis in Salem was the culmination of a supernatural conspiracy that united greedy Boston merchants, the anti-Protestant factions of both North America and Europe, practitioners of unorthodox religions on the northern frontier, Catholics from various corners of Europe (including England), and Satan himself.[128]

Events in the life of Sylvanus Davis illustrate how frontier violence transformed Maine's eclectic religious culture. Davis came to live in the province as early as 1659, the same decade that the Jesuit Druillettes dined at various Protestant tables. The first document that records his presence is a deed for land in Damariscotta purchased from the local Wabanakis, among whom he lived uneventfully for sixteen years.[129] His life in the province proved both long and profitable, ultimately lasting until 1700. He filled civic posts for colonial governors from Thomas Danforth to Joseph Dudley and acted as a local agent

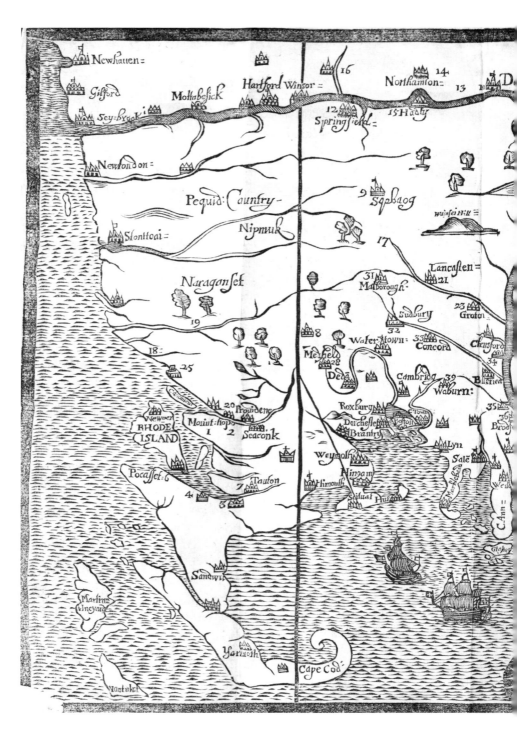

A MAP OF
NEW-ENGLAND,

*Being the first that ever was here cut, and done
by the best Pattern that could be had which being
in some places defective, it made the other less
exact: yet doth it sufficiently shew the Scitua-
tion of the Countrey, and conveniently well
the distance of Places.*

The figures that are joyned with the Names of
Places are to distinguish such as have been assaulted by the *Indians* from others.

A Scale of forty Miles.

The Wine Hills

Dover
P. scatequa R.
Winter Harbor
Cap.o Bay
Kenebe
Pemaquid

Figure 4.
The first to be
printed in America,
this 1677 map shows
Maine's English
settlements from
Cape Cod (lower
left) to Pemaquid
(lower right).
William Hubbard
(after a woodcut
by John Foster),
*The Present State of
New-England . . .*
(1677). Courtesy
of the Osher Map
Library, University
of Southern Maine.

for wealthy Boston merchants. He ran a trading post and a sawmill, farmed, traded in livestock, and purchased more property.[130] And, tellingly, he traded with English, French, and Indian partners.

All of Davis's activities were possible thanks to the relative peace of the frontier, reflecting a time when productive economic enterprise could, for some, take precedence over religious or political rivalries. For a man like Sylvanus Davis, who had not come to the region for any discernible reason other than economic gain, the challenges of life were grounded in corporal, not spiritual, concerns. His diverse trading partners and ability to navigate among the many groups in early Maine suggest that Davis wore neither his ethnic nor his religious identities on his sleeve in his dealings with others.

But Davis faced significant challenges as well. As was the case for many settlers in English communities, his successes alternated with downturns in fortune that often accompanied the outbreak of hostilities among the English settlers, the French to the north and east, and the Native Americans. These trials started during King Philip's War, when Davis narrowly escaped capture, or worse, when local Wabanakis attacked the Arrowsic Island trading compound of his employers, the Clarke and Lake Company.[131]

Maine's economic promise justified Davis's perseverance. For a good portion of the seventeenth century, and in spite of periods of violence, the gamble he and others took to realize the province's economic promise often paid off. But this good fortune was destroyed at last. At the end of the 1680s, tensions in Europe between England and France erupted into open conflict on imperial frontiers. Sensing danger, Davis cast his lot with his fellow English settlers and took command of Fort Loyal at Casco Bay. It was then that Maine's inability to develop and maintain a cohesive Protestant identity (which in times of peace was a blessing to outsiders of the New England Way) became fully apparent. Troubled by his inability to convince the Casco settlers to unite against the threat and appalled by their lack of corporate commitment, Davis informed the General Council in Boston of the situation, and complained that the region's "Inhaebitance Are Gon ought of our Towne & Are dayly Going of soe that wee Grow weaker & weker every day as all soe such a speritt of disorder amongst soom of our peopell that there can hardly bee Any order kept all though it been for the presarvation of thaire owne & thaire naibours Lifes."[132] His complaint underscored the fact that Casco's settlements, like others clustered throughout the parts of Maine claimed by the English, lacked the cultural and religious conformity that contributed to discipline in times of stress and provided the cohesion necessary to support the militia and communal life. The Casco settlements did not have a meetinghouse or a settled minister until well into the eighteenth century.[133] Given the multiple services that such spaces performed within New England towns, the absence of a meetinghouse meant missed opportunities to spread news, reinforce community solidarity, and concentrate group defensive measures.[134]

Colonial leaders were also suspected of withholding valuable intelligence from the Casco settlers. News of the impending attack on Fort Loyal came not from New England but through the providential intervention of a Dutch privateer, Abraham Fisher, who reported to the Casco group that the Wabanakis and French "Resolved to use theire uttermost Indevor to Destroy Casco: perteculerly & all the Engles in Jenerall."[135] Without this vital piece of information, the coming attack on Fort Loyal might have been a complete surprise.

Despite this warning, the frontier dwellers could not stop the French and Indians from heaping destruction upon Casco. When the attack finally came on May 16, 1690, it was devastating. Combined forces numbering about five hundred under the leadership of an experienced French frontier fighter, Réne Robinau de Portneuf, began their assault just a day after a Massachusetts unit left the fort to join William Phips's expedition against Acadia.[136] This left only seventy-five local militiamen to defend the fort. Poorly prepared and desperately outnumbered, they somehow managed to resist for four days. The exhausted defenders surrendered on May 20. As commander of the fort, Sylvanus Davis negotiated with Portneuf for safe passage to the next English town for the fort's noncombatants.[137]

Or so Davis thought. As the English combatants and civilians exited the fort, Portneuf reneged on the terms of quarter, declaring instead that the fort's inhabitants were in a state of rebellion against their rightful Catholic monarch.[138] With this action, the assault on

Fort Loyal became a microcosmic religious war, echoing in particular the problems that plagued European Christians of the post-Reformation age who lived with or near one another. The second half of the sixteenth century witnessed frequent bloody conflicts between the religious rivals that, by some estimates, took the lives of upwards of two million French soldiers and civilians.[139] The Edict of Nantes quelled the violence but not the tension, which took on new forms. The seventeenth century saw the rise of royalism, which associated Catholicism with loyalty to the French Crown, and sanctioned proactive acts of bias against religious rivals.[140] The situation was exacerbated further by the revocation of the Edict of Nantes in 1685, which reset the French stage for religious warfare and ended a century of mild toleration. These trends were reflected in Portneuf's declaration that the Fort Loyal Protestants were rebels, an act that combined the militancy of the sixteenth century with the royalism of the seventeenth. This declaration also changed the defenders' status. Defined as rebels (in lieu of prisoners of war), in French eyes they deserved no protection or even honest treatment. As a result, Davis noted, "as soon as [the French and Indians] had us in theire Coustady thay Broker theire Articuels surfed out wiming & Children & our men to be mad Captiffs in the Hands of the Heathen to bee Cruelly murdred & Destroyed many of them wonded men, only the French kept my self & 3 or 4 more & Carried us over Land for Canada."[141] Davis was one of the lucky few who survived, albeit as a captive. Scores of these perceived rebels lost their lives. Their remains were left without burial, devolving into bleached bones that lay scattered on Casco's beaches for years to come.

For Davis, Maine still had treasures that made resettlement worth the risk. Four years after he returned from Canada, the entrepreneurial Englishman purchased substantial tracts of land in the St. George's River valley, far north of the English line of settlement, thus implying that he looked at the conflict as a temporary impediment to trade.[142] But such assurances were not to be had in the Maine of the late seventeenth and early eighteenth centuries. Sylvanus Davis, who knew firsthand that Maine needed peace and prosperity to flourish economically, left after almost fifty years of effort to live out the remainder of his life on Nantasket, in Boston Harbor.[143]

While the young Sylvanus Davis had prospered with the help of French and Indian trading partners, the older one emerged from captivity convinced of their pernicious presence in the region. Fresh from captivity in 1690, he wrote a letter to the Massachusetts General Court warning that, left unchecked, the enemies of New England would come "throw the Country farther & farther upon the Backs of the English." If this unfolded, only God himself could "prevent [the] Jesuiticall Bloody Designes" of the New World French.[144] Barring divine intervention, Davis argued, the English should take proactive measures to check the French themselves. "The only way to prevent [the French] from their Bloody Desing," he insisted, was "to subdue theire Country."[145]

At the end of his letter, Davis told the General Court he prayed that "the Lord will finde ought a way for the subdoing those Blood thursty rechess that have joynd with the Cruell heathen to bucher soo many poore Innocent lambes."[146] If the English failed to recognize their divine responsibility to the appointed task, Davis implied, the Massachusetts leaders' sole remaining recourse would be prayer.

Before the wars of empire engulfed the Maine frontier, Sylvanus Davis had profited from alliances that transcended differences of faith. Yet he emerged from his ordeals during King William's War as a different type of colonist, with his Protestant identity playing a very different role. Influenced by the explicit religious implications of an imperial conflict, he had become a fully realized militant Protestant, who now felt that Maine could not and, on religious principles, should not be shared.

At the beginning of King William's War, Maine's Protestants still faced many challenges to promoting a unified, holistic Christian vision. For one, they faced seemingly unified Catholics, who exploited Wabanaki knowledge of Maine's topography to launch a devastating attack on Protestants. In addition, many of Maine's English settlers had fled, instead of banding together, at the mere threat of a Catholic juggernaut, leaving fellow Protestants who had nowhere else to go to fend for themselves. The power of the pulpit, both to encourage a proper response to the French and Indian menace and to disburse information, was also severely challenged. Laxity in enforcing the established church and the relatively peaceful coexistence among disparate interfaith groups—the very things that made Maine's English settlements attractive to so many who either left or bypassed Massachusetts altogether—ultimately proved to be the downfall of those unfortunate enough to live there during King William's War.

For many settlers, religious odysseys began before the wars of empire and the arrival of zealous agents of religious homogeneity in New England and New France. The ethnic and religious diversity of settlement under the Gorges proprietorship; the irregularities of congregational development; the failure to attract and settle committed ministers; and the close proximity of substantial numbers of Catholic Wabanakis and French collectively worked against establishing a robust Protestant identity in Maine. Despite the best efforts of Massachusetts to bring Maine into the fold of Puritan orthodoxy, many of its settlers had already undergone a partial religious transculturation of their own choosing before captivity forced the issue. For some, the actual conversion to Catholicism that is discussed in this book's subsequent chapters was more a step than a leap. For others, however, exposure to Catholicism's people, objects, and built environments reinvigorated religious sensibilities that may have been atrophying. This was certainly the case with Sylvanus Davis, who brought back from French Canada a hardened sense of Protestant conviction.

Throughout the next several decades of tension and all-out war, many of Maine's English settlers used their encounter with Catholicism to help develop a vigorously Protestant religious culture. But others did the opposite. Though the colonial wars between Catholic France and Protestant England ultimately aided in the formation of a solid Protestant identity in Maine, they also left a complicated legacy of religious encounter which increased religious unity and orthodoxy could not undo.

In the seventeenth century, Catholic people were familiar to many Maine settlers. Catholicized Indians were numerous. Some of Maine's Europeans came from parts of Catholic Europe and were likely at one time Catholics themselves. The unsettled state of the boundary between New England and New France frequently forced these contacts to continue over lengthy periods of time. Paradoxically, as divisions between Maine and its Catholic neighbors grew more distinct and were increasingly viewed in terms of religious identification, the two regions grew more similar as early modern religious societies. And some Mainers experienced firsthand both types of religious societies, and even both Christian faith traditions, as they flourished in the upper reaches of early North America.

CHAPTER TWO

"Satan's Prey" or
"L'esclavage de l'hérésie calviniste"

The Imperial Battles for Maine's Frontier Souls

Maine's lack of religious cohesion haunted orthodox New England ministers, who feared for the souls of the province's settlers. The most vocal warnings came from Cotton Mather, who asserted that the province's religious instability jeopardized New England's entire holy experiment. Mather cautioned Maine's frontier settlers, known as "outlivers," that dwelling in the "more Pagan [out]skirts of New England" would lead to death—or worse. "Satan terribly makes a prey of you," Mather warned, "and Leads you Captive to do his Will."[1] These prophesies seemed to come to pass when King William's, Queen Anne's, and Dummer's wars brought death, permanent separation and, most important to this study, spiritual reorientation and confusion to many Maine families.

Mather took aim at Puritans like Hannah Swarton. Swarton and her family were typical of the outlivers whose choices Cotton Mather so strenuously condemned. The basic contours of Hannah's life provide little indication of the religious odyssey into which she would be drawn. The daughter of committed Puritans, Hannah spent her early life in the Essex County, Massachusetts, town of Beverly. Wealthy by neither birth nor marriage, she and her husband, John, found land in Essex County beyond their means and were forced to seek opportunities elsewhere.[2] Maine was the kind of place that appealed to people of limited means like the Swartons, for in the 1670s, it was still possible to procure decent parcels of land for relatively low prices or in exchange for service. If Maine's remoteness, climate, and deficiencies in organized civic or religious life worried the Swartons, they left no record of their concerns predating King William's War. Later writings would be filled with such concerns, at least on the spiritual level.

Moving far beyond the safety of the established Puritan communities of northern Massachusetts, the Swartons settled in North Yarmouth, a new community on the northern edge of Casco Bay. Like Casco Bay's other settlements—Falmouth (now Portland), Spurwink (Cape Elizabeth), and Falmouth Neck—North Yarmouth seemed poised for prosperity, thanks to its location on the bay and the interest this inspired among land speculators from Massachusetts. The town's economic promise was ostensibly protected by Fort Loyal, built in Falmouth to protect the Casco settlements from local enemies.

While the region was economically promising, life there also demanded significant personal sacrifices, including the civic and religious stability the Swartons had known in Beverly and its attendant protection of thick settlement. At the time of their arrival, North Yarmouth also lacked a meetinghouse, a minister, and any semblance of organized religious life. To Hannah Swarton, the baptized child of parents who were church members, the move to Casco "where there was no church or minister of the Gospel" would lead to punishment.[3] This came on May 16, 1690, when René Robinau de Portneuf's combined force of French and Wabanakis attacked Casco. Hannah's husband and most likely one of her sons were killed in the attack. The rest of the fort's inmates, including Sylvanus Davis, were carried into captivity in Wabanakia and Canada. Separated from her three surviving children, Hannah bravely navigated through the multiple worlds of her captors. Stripped of the material symbols of her identity as a New England wife and mother, she clung instead to Reformed religion—the sole element of her precaptivity life that remained.

Like other Maine captives of the frontier wars, Hannah likely encountered Catholics of various strata—Indians, priests, nuns, laypeople—who sought to claim her soul for the Church of Rome. Still, she returned to New England a Protestant.

Upon her return to New England, Hannah's story attracted the interest of Cotton Mather, who tailored her resistance to Catholicism into an eloquent defense of her Puritan convictions. "A Narrative of Hannah Swarton Containing Wonderful Passages Relating to Her Captivity and Deliverance" first appeared in 1697 as part of *Humili-ations Followed with Deliverances,* and later appeared in an expanded version as part of Mather's monumental work *Magnalia Christi Americana* in 1702. The extent to which Mather actually consulted Hannah on the details of her religious life in captivity is unknown, but he clearly found the basic outlines of her experiences (which were consistent with those of other Maine captives) of high instructional value. In his retelling of her life in captivity, Mather links Hannah's story and the terrible consequences of Maine's religious fragility, to the greater story of New England Christianity.[4] Hannah's story remained in print long after the French Catholic threat was removed. As late as 1837, it was being reprinted as "The Narrative of Mrs. Hannah Swarton," and used in New England Protestant Sunday schools to illustrate the workings of Providence, resignation to God's will, and the value of spiritual fortitude.[5]

What is known for certain about the real Hannah's life is that she was redeemed from captivity in 1695. She returned to little or nothing: a widow since the fall of Fort Loyal, she had but one of her four children with her.[6] At least one of her other two sons was dead (and likely the other as well). And significantly, her only daughter, Mary, married in New France and never returned to Protestant New England.

After 1695 Hannah virtually disappears from historical records. At least one source claims she married Edward Belcher of Beverly by 1708.[7] If she married a Beverly man, Hannah's days most likely ended in that community, which had seen its share of strife from the Essex County witchcraft crisis of 1692.[8] Ironically, it is Mary Swarton's life that continued to be documented in historical records long after her mother's trail went cold. A teen at the time of her captivity, she converted to Catholicism, became a fully acculturated subject of the French king, married another acculturated captive, and bore many children whose births and religious rites of passage are found through-out Canadian sacramental records.[9]

✦   ✦   ✦

The Hannah of Mather's "Narrative" continued to be a recognizable figure long after the Hannah Swarton of history was lost to memory. The narrative's descriptions of a pilgrim who lost loved ones, en-dured the cruelty of Indians, and resisted the machinations of zeal-ous and threatening priests is a standard trope for captivity narratives related to King William's, Queen Anne's, and Dummer's wars. That so many of the captives immortalized in these narratives were from Maine by birth or settlement was a consequence of the province's unique geographical position between rival frontier empires.

Hannah's odyssey, in history and literature, concluded with her redemption to her proper spiritual home, New England. For other Maine Protestants, however, redemption — at least the kind that re-turned them to a Protestant religious culture — never came. Others did come back, but only after contemplating, or even taking steps to-ward, committing themselves to the religious culture of a rival form of Christianity. For Hannah, captivity was a spiritually galvanizing event that renewed her flagging Puritan spirit. But other Maine set-tlers had little spirit to prop, or found the lure of the other religion's arguments too great to resist.[10] Maine's religious diversity bred diverse responses to religious challenge.

The likelihood of any Protestant, frontier or otherwise, willingly converting to Roman Catholicism subverts traditional assumptions about the identities of early modern Christians. Many early modern Protestants, and Puritans in particular, defined their theology, their sense of national identity, and many aspects of their religious culture in express opposition to the teachings of the contemporary Catholic Church.[11] How could such people even contemplate participating in Catholic liturgies and devotions in Catholic households? How could others take these interactions a step further to conversion, along with the additional steps of sacramental marriage, baptism for children, and even, in several cases, professions to a religious life? And if such critical steps were the result of pressure applied by Catholic captors, how did others successfully resist?

Plausible answers to these questions are rooted in an examination of the nature of Maine as a mere outpost of New England Puritanism—a borderland between Protestant and Catholic territories—and as a place where Dissenters and diverse religious eccentrics of the early modern Atlantic World could live in North America in some degree of disengagement from the predominant religious culture. The Province of Maine was intrinsically fragile, making it fairly easy for religious aggressors to challenge prevailing religious identities and build new ones that drew on foundational elements common to all professed Euro-American Christians. With the Province of Maine itself functioning as one enormous frontier, these demonstrations of its inherent fragility no doubt led some to conclude that life there was futile—particularly if their families, in addition to their property, had been destroyed. As Emerson Baker notes, many of Maine's settlers were "people on the edge" with few personal options when frontier violence destroyed their fortunes.[12] For some, these fortunes were tied to their religious beliefs only from necessity and shared culture.

The acculturation process from English Protestant colonist to French Catholic *canadienne* seen in Hannah Swarton's daughter, Mary, as well as many others, is rendered more understandable against such a backdrop. The French went to great lengths to demonstrate that these new immigrants, involuntary as they were, were welcome and invested in New French society. That metaphorical welcome was extended, at almost every stage of captivity, by the still recognizably Christian Roman Catholic Church. A stable colonial institution with uniformity of liturgy, prayers, and professed beliefs, Catholicism offered a potent spiritual counterpoint to the uncertainty of life in the borderlands as a captive Protestant.[13]

Catholic clergy, religious, and laypeople used multiple strategies to demonstrate the stability and unity of Catholicism and deploy it to convert Protestant captives. As the experiences of Hannah Swarton and another well-documented captive, Mary Plaisted of York, will show, these encounters fell along a broad spectrum of encounter that ranged from simple introduction and catechesis to coercion and threat. These spiritual contests took many forms and had diverse results: some New England Protestants successfully resisted Catholicism, some temporarily converted, and some changed their religions and, as a result, recast their Euro-American cultural identities as well.

The paths to these possible outcomes were far from prescribed. Captive English men, women, and children were pulled into entangled networks of relationships that transcended imperial boundaries, as well as familial and religious categories. Even those who managed to return to New England only did so after they had navigated several sets of challenges to their religious identities. Furthermore, they frequently left pieces of themselves behind—children, siblings, and, in at least one case, a parent—which meant that returning Maine captives often continued to have ties to their captivity experience among New World Catholics.

Neither the "pagan skirt" of Cotton Mather's nightmares nor a firmly secured bastion of Puritan orthodoxy, Maine remained throughout the seventeenth and the early eighteenth centuries a religiously challenged New England outpost. The province had yet to find illumination through the civic, theological, and moral order that religious conformity could produce. Uniformity of this kind was ironically much more apparent in the Euro-American settlements of New France than it was in the Maine of Mather's day, and thus hewed more closely to the idea of the religiously homogeneous society so cherished by American Puritans.

✦   ✦   ✦

It was the first colonial war of empire that set Hannah Swarton, York settler Mary Plaisted, and their families on their involuntary journeys among New World Catholics. King William's War was heavily influenced by its Continental counterpart, the War of the League of Augsburg. In 1688 England deposed its despised Catholic king, James II, in favor of his Protestant daughter Mary and her husband, William of Orange. Catholic France perceived this as an insult to the man they considered the rightful, albeit Catholic, English king. Hostilities in Europe began in earnest when the newly proclaimed king, William III, joined the League of Augsburg in alliance against the French, an event that sanctioned acts of war wherever French and English people came in contact with one another. European political entanglements created real crises for the borderland dwellers of northern New England, where military protection could not be taken for granted.

The Glorious Revolution restored a Protestant monarch to the English throne and sent shock waves throughout the Atlantic World that penetrated even remote outposts of English influence like Maine. New Englanders initially lauded events on the other side of the Atlantic and used them as a pretext to break up James I's despised Dominion of New England. In Massachusetts, colonists forcibly removed royal administrators from office. In some cases they even jailed them, a potentially treasonous act. In New York a group of ambitious Protestant merchants led by Jacob Leisler seized power, and maintained it through their claim that they were protecting the colony from pro-French crypto-Catholics and acting in the best interests of English Protestantism.[14]

Even before news of war between England and France reached North America, long-festering resentments in the borderlands surrounding Maine boiled over into open raids. In 1688 an expedition led by Massachusetts governor Edmund Andros attacked and looted the trading post of Jean-Vincent d'Abbadie de Saint-Castin, a minor French nobleman who had set up a trading post on central Maine's Penobscot River and married the daughter of a powerful sachem, Madockawando.[15] Saint-Castin and his Indian kin and allies retaliated by sacking nearby Pemaquid. Andros, who was already hated throughout New England, was soon jailed, not only because he represented the deposed king, but because he aroused suspicion that he had conspired to give Maine into the control of the French.

Maine's inhabitants, Europeans and Indians alike, suffered terrible personal and property losses during King William's War. The attack on Fort Loyal that made Sylvanus Davis a prisoner and killed most of his comrades, including Hannah Swarton's husband, John, took place in May 1690. Shortly after, New Englander Benjamin Church led an expedition against Indian villages on the Androscoggin River and at Purpooduck, on Cape Elizabeth. With each raid, Church allowed his own Indian mercenaries to take some prisoners and left the remaining captured Wabanakis to face execution.[16]

At the same time, patriotic New Englanders, led by Pemaquid native Sir William Phips, undertook a campaign to rid Maine and the rest of New England of the French Catholics who had developed colonies on the province's rim. For the third time in its brief history, Acadia's Port Royal fell to English invaders. This victory emboldened Phips and his men to aim for a bigger catch. Confident and well armed, Phips's force of over 2,300 men, packed into thirty-four vessels, left Boston to take Quebec in the summer of 1690.[17] This time, however, French military power and fortifications combined to repulse the attack. In addition, the New England forces were buffeted by every form of bad fortune—from shipwrecks to pathogens—that could befall them. While only thirty men died in combat with the French, an additional three to four hundred succumbed to drowning, disease, and other misfortunes. The expedition limped back to Boston, where Phips faced harsh criticism for its handling.[18] Additional forays against New France's seats of power during King William's War also ended in failure for the invading New English.

The French and Indians were more successful in their bid to roll back the line of English settlement in Maine. In February 1691/2,[19] French and Indian forces swooped down on York, killing forty-eight settlers and taking another seventy-three prisoner. They burned the town, killed settlers and livestock, and assassinated the minister, Shubael Dummer. Among the prisoners were the aforementioned Mary Plaisted and at least two of her children. Four months later, French and Indian forces attempted a similar blow on nearby Wells, which repulsed the attack but lost critical structures and livestock.[20] Many Mainers fled. Some went to Essex County, Massachusetts; others found safety as far south as New Jersey. The flight of these colo-nists drained the province of its English population. Determined to hold the province, the English built new forts at Biddeford and Pemaquid, which inspired some Eastern Indians to talk peace with the English. In 1693 Wabanaki groups from all over Maine agreed to renounce the French, restore captives, and normalize relations with the English.[21] French authorities and Jesuits, however, countered these actions and encouraged the resumption of hostilities.

By 1695 the French were fighting vigorously against the English and allied Iroquois, who later sued the French for peace. Additional maneuvers against the English came under the leadership of Pierre Le Moyne d'Iberville, the son of a well-established Canadian military family and the future founder of permanent colonial settlements in Louisiana. D'Iberville led attacks on English targets throughout 1696, destroying the new fort at Pemaquid as well as English fishing settlements throughout Newfoundland, and securing the Hudson Bay region for France.

King William's War began with New France on the defensive. In the early years, the English and Iroquois allies held their own against their enemies. But as the war proceeded, the tide turned in France's favor. The French forced the Iroquois to sue for peace, demonstrated their ability to seize valuable English possessions, reinforced their relationships with Indian allies, and forced New Englanders to all but abandon Maine. In the end, however, the Peace of Ryswick stipulated that all territories be returned to their original claimants.[22] This meant the borderland between French and English claims would in fact remain undefined, a state of affairs that contributed significantly to the next conflict, Queen Anne's War. The stage was set for more suffering among the Mainers who returned.

By 1699 many Maine settlers remained in captivity among either the Indians or the French. The knowledge that captives lived far beyond New England's ability to redeem them scarred the province's war-torn families. Most of Maine's English settlers likely knew or were related to a captive. Thus they did not need Cotton Mather's perspective on Hannah Swarton's ordeal to understand the consequences and potential pitfalls that the "pagan skirts" of New England posed to the Protestant soul. They knew all too well from personal experience.

Maine Captives in Print and Record:
Hannah Swarton and Mary Plaisted

Hannah Swarton and Mary Plaisted were common women whose lives are uncommonly well documented. The specific details of their lives and the ways their lives were used by others for didactic purposes suggest much about the nature of early American frontier women's lives. The experiences that lifted them out of these conventional existences have attracted the interest of scholars of women's history and gender studies, who use them as models for describing the ranges of possible experience and the limits of a world where the importance of gender was omnipresent.[23]

In my effort to map out the range of reactions to alien Christian cultures, I take a different approach, using Hannah and Mary as representative witnesses of and reactors to converging Christianities in and around the Province of Maine. Like other captives, Hannah and Mary experienced a range of Christian experiences not open to many New World Protestants. They attended masses, knew convents, met Catholic priests, viewed environments suffused with Catholic visual culture, witnessed miracles that Catholics claimed were wrought by the relics of saints, and refused or accepted communion with the Roman Catholic Church through sacramental participation. Neither woman desired to live among the papist Indians or their allies to the north — indeed, their lives among Catholics were the product of terrible personal experiences. Yet their experiences reveal attitudes and reactions to Catholicism that add nuance to our understanding of the religious lives of those on the entangled edge of Indian and Euro-American settlement.

Hannah Swarton was one of several captive Maine settlers who left behind a record purporting to describe her entire captivity experience, including an array of Protestant interactions with Catholics. Though the basic facts of Hannah's life — war and loss, captivity and return — included issues that transcended religious ones, the story of a Protestant retaining her faith despite severe tests was ready-made for Cotton Mather's didacticism. As his father, Increase, had done before with the narrative of Mary Rowlandson, Cotton Mather saw in captivity a test from God meant both to strengthen the faith of the orthodox and to warn would-be emigrants from the orthodox fold of the potential terrors that awaited them.[24]

Scholars of history and literature have pointed out that Cotton Mather highlighted those elements of this encounter to serve a greater instructional purpose. However, it cannot be concluded that the essence and goals of the interrogations reported by Mather were fabricated for didactic purposes.[25] Instead, it is critical to acknowledge that the *range* of Hannah's own religious encounters described in the "Narrative" (Mather's invented dialogue notwithstanding) matches that of other captives, who in turn left records of their own varied responses to the religious challenges they encountered in captivity among Catholics.

On the surface of Mather's "Narrative," Hannah Swarton appears to be a rather unremarkable Puritan woman who finds herself in remarkable circumstances. Few details in the "Narrative"—except her remove to the infamous "pagan skirt" of New England—place her beyond the pale of conventional Puritanism. But Hannah's life in the historical record—before, during, and after captivity—reveals an intercultural complexity that Mather either did not perceive or chose not to discuss. Like many Mainers, Hannah left Massachusetts for Maine because of a complex set of circumstances. Her captivity led to additional complications. Hannah, the seemingly archetypal Pilgrim wandering in the wilderness, arrived in Maine with wide ties to the Atlantic World that transcended her local Protestant community. If New England frontiers were worth defending (and even Cotton Mather acknowledged that this was a worthy goal), then the Hannah of both historical record and literature would have been the right kind of settler to contribute to the cause of creating a holistic Protestant culture in northern New England. She was a church member. Likewise, she was literate and knew her Scripture. She had also fulfilled her godly destiny as a Puritan woman through motherhood.

There was, however, one core contradiction at the heart of Hannah's life as an orthodox Puritan woman: her marriage. As a married woman, Hannah would have accepted subordination to her husband as a matter of course, accepting such an arrangement as preordained by God and mirroring his own relationship to creation.[26] Unlike his wife, though, Hannah's spouse was not a New Englander. It is possible he was not an adherent of Reformed Protestantism either. This made the Puritan Hannah subject to the control of an outsider to Massachusetts religion and order.

The spouse in question was John Swarton, a native of the culturally French, francophone Channel Island of Jersey and an iconic Atlantic World traveler whose own background reflected numerous influences. Ambitious Channel Islanders who migrated throughout the Atlantic World found plenty of outlets for their energies in New England. The unique cultural mix of the Islands made these often well-educated and well-connected New World settlers particularly valuable to the New English. The savviest among them employed linguistic skills perfected in the Old World to bridge gaps of language and custom between English- and French-speaking trading partners. They also brought important contacts to potential markets in continental Europe.

Channel Islanders gravitated toward New England's coastal industries, and could be found in Boston and the seafaring communities of Essex County. Some exploited their European trade connections and enhanced their status in New England by perfecting their knowledge of the local language and customs and, perhaps most importantly, adopting New England religion. Among these was the notable Philip English. Born Philippe L'Anglois on the island of Jersey, English developed a sophisticated and lucrative intercolonial trading network that linked Boston to the Caribbean, western Europe, and French Catholic Acadia. Church membership, marriage to a New English woman, a fine home, and an anglicized name all suggest that English transformed himself to conform to the standards of New England Puritan society.[27]

But as the contours of John Swarton's life demonstrate, Channel Islanders of modest means were not equally valued by more mainstream New Englanders.[28] Those who were less invested than Philip English and others like him often clung to French language and customs. This led some English Puritans to fear them as potential religious deviants, and reinforced the foreign-born Channel Islanders' outsider status. And technically they were outsiders: despite centuries of political ties to England, the Channel Islands of the seventeenth century were still culturally and linguistically French. Unconventional in language and habit, their outward differences were thought to betray the same intrinsic religious and cultural defects that Catholics from mainland France were presumed to harbor. These marginal Channel Islanders were further confined within the economic and social boundaries that affected even American- or English-born Puritans of humble birth or modest talents. With the added handicap of cultural difference impeding their advancement, poor and middling Channel Islanders were truly at a disadvantage in New England society.

The surviving evidence of John Swarton's life suggest that he was of the poor or middling sort. When Swarton took an oath of fidelity at Beverly on December 3, 1677, he identified himself as a tailor, a respectable profession, though also humble.[29] In addition, he barely spoke English. As militia captain Benjamin Church would later attest, Swarton's old Norman French *patois* was nearly impossible to understand.[30] He also appears to have been landless. Armed only with a humble trade and scant ability to speak the local language, Swarton, unlike his wealthy compatriot Philip English, was not likely to have been a valued member of New England society.

Deficient in two key ways, Swarton was likely a religious outsider as well. His wife's Puritanism was a religion of words, and in Essex County those words were almost always English. A linguistic inadequacy did not by definition impede piety, but it may have imposed a barrier to full participation in a Puritan congregation. This might have reinforced a sense of alienation.

John Swarton thus followed the same trail to Maine blazed by other cultural misfits from New England: he went to the province to improve his fortunes, and possibly to enjoy some respite from communities he might have found stifling. In 1686 he applied to the Massachusetts government for a grant of land in "North Yarmouth in Cascoe." In his petition, he stated proudly that he had "formerly served his Late Majestie King Charles ye second of Blessed Memorie in ye wars in flanders under ye Comand of Colonell Marloe and elsewhere."[31] For a man like Swarton, who had defended the Stuart cause in Europe, the new royalist government with its High Church inclinations gave the impression that men like him, who could never join the Puritan elite, would find favor with the colony's new leadership. His identification with the restoration of the Stuarts and the timing of his petition—1687—are suggestive. Swarton likely saw an opportunity to press his case to a government that would look on his military service with a friendly eye, especially since that most faithful of Stuart supporters, Edmund Andros, a Channel Islander who flaunted his Anglicanism, had become the royal governor.[32]

Whether because of his service to the Stuarts, or because he provided warm bodies to populate Casco Bay and its environs, Swarton received fifty acres in North Yarmouth. His new start, however, would be in a settlement devoid of churches, ministers, or the predictable religious identities that his wife had known so well. The Hannah Swarton of Cotton Mather's "Narrative" grieved for "the Public worship and ordinances of God where I formerly lived."[33] In contrast, religious coexistence was likely not a new experience for John Swarton. The Channel Islands of his birth were home to a diverse mix of French-speaking Anglicans, Calvinist Protestants, Catholics, and, later in the century, an increasingly large Huguenot population, especially after France revoked the Edict of Nantes in 1684.[34] The Jersey of Swarton's younger days was fraught with interfaith tension. Despite the strong Calvinist influence on its churches, the island gave refuge to Prince Charles, Anglican son of a French Catholic mother and future king in his own right, after the execution of his father. After the prince left the island, Puritan-leaning ministers like Increase Mather flocked to Jersey to purge it of any vestiges of Anglicanism, and expected their efforts to be welcomed. Many Channel Islanders, however, considered the religious incursions presumptuous, and "persecuted out" the Puritan minister, Cotton Mather's grandfather, Richard.[35] After this failed Puritan experiment, Jersey and the other islands for the most part returned to the Anglican fold.[36] Though Swarton's birth religion remains unknown, he could have come to New England as a Calvinist, an Anglican, or even possibly a Catholic.[37] Rich in lumber and fish, and with good farming poten-

tial, Maine offered men like John Swarton not only economic promise, but relief from a well-defined religious culture that was no doubt
often oppressive to those who did not hew closely to its beliefs.

The Swartons were still relative newcomers when war came to
Casco in 1690.[38] Unlike many other Mainers who fled at the prospect
of war, John was a good neighbor and stayed to defend Fort Loyal
alongside Sylvanus Davis and a few others. Perhaps too this choice
was made because the Swartons had nowhere else to go.[39] The head
of his family with the ability to compel their movements, this culturally and religiously ambiguous man fell with his colleagues in arms.
Hannah and their children, who ranged in age from five to sixteen,
were taken captive as soon as they left the fort, and were soon separated by their captors.[40]

John Swarton likely had many religious encounters throughout
his life. For his widow, such encounters were new. The first stop on
many routes that brought captive New Englanders to the centers of
French Canada was Norridgewock, the mission that had long before
been administered by the English-friendly Jesuit, Gabriel Druillettes.
Isolated by design from other Maine captives, Hannah was, according to Mather, subjected to repeated taunts by an Indian woman who,
raised and catechized among English Puritans, was now "married to a
Canada Indian and turned papist."[41] Such ridicule likely underscored
the degradation of Hannah's captivity.

After nine months among the Wabanakis, Hannah was ransomed
in the winter of 1690/1 by one of the most powerful people in New
France, Jean Bouchart de Champigny. This was a welcome turn of
events, for Wabanakia had been for Hannah a place of spiritual and
physical deprivation. The hardships she endured included little food,
repeated threats of death, the heartbreaking news that her son Samuel
had been killed, and no "Bible, or good book to look into, or Christian friend to be counselor in these distresses."[42] The French, however,
mitigated the worst of these abuses. In the home of the intendant,
Hannah was "kindly entertained . . . and had French clothes given me
with good diet and lodging and was carried thence to the hospital
where I was physicked and blooded and very well provided for. And
I must speak it to the honor of the French, they were exceedingly

kind to me at first."[43] As Ann Little notes, "European Catholics were perhaps even more disturbing than Indian enemies because they were not all that different from English Protestants. They dressed the same, they did the same work, they ate the same food, they worshipped the same God—and thus they could be plotting and scheming just about anywhere and at any time."[44] The French used these common elements of European heritage, as well as physical comfort and the gratitude it engendered, as tools for proselytization. Detained in the Champigny house, Hannah was a literal captive audience for Catholics who wished to convert her. These interactions ranged from theological interrogations by "nuns, priests, and friars" and the intendant's own pious wife, to the excitement of the household over a supposed miraculous healing of the intendant's hearing. The "Narrative" asserts that Hannah's interrogators found her resolve frustrating, and even threatened to take her to France and publicly burn her. Such dramatic turns from kindness to cruelty are rare in accounts of captivity left by Maine Protestants. They may reflect the expectations of Mather's contemporary readers, who would have expected the kinds of Catholic cruelty to Protestants described in popular texts like Foxe's *Book of Martyrs*.[45] During this time, Hannah was also reported to have been forced to attend a Catholic mass. After failing to change her, however, the spiritual aggressors gave up, and left Hannah alone to contemplate Scripture and work for them in peace.

Relegated to the world of solitary work—which was again consistent with accounts of other Maine captives who could not be lured to apostasy—Hannah reportedly enjoyed relative freedom on the Quebec streets as she went about her daily business. The world outside the Champignys' walls exposed Hannah to a proselytizing onslaught of a different sort. Catholic culture suffused Quebec visually and aurally, providing yet another test to Protestant resolve. The cityscape was thick with steeples that marked parish churches and other Catholic religious institutions. Building names and places reflected the French Catholic association with dozens of canonized saints. Sounds of liturgies and the chanting of Divine Office bled out of sacred buildings and onto the streets. Public feast days brought processions and other religiously oriented public celebrations.

Figure 5. Allain Manesson Mallet, *Description de l'Univers . . .* (1683). Mallet's otherwise highly stylized view of Quebec emphasizes religious institutions. This was the urban environment that Hannah Swarton, Mary Plaisted, and other Maine captives would have experienced. Courtesy of the Emmet Collection, Miriam and Ira D. Wallach Division of Art, Prints and Photographs, The New York Public Library, Astor, Lenox and Tilden Foundations.

Whenever possible, captive Protestants attempted to build their resolve by seeking out each other for comfort, solace, and support. In Quebec Hannah lived near Maine native Edward Tyng and Massachusetts captive John Alden. Margaret Gould Stilson of Pemaquid was her housemate. All of these captives resisted conversion attempts too, and all eventually returned to New England.

There was one Protestant in Hannah's circle, however, who ultimately lost whatever resolve she had. Like her mother, Mary Swarton was a captive used as a servant, and lived nearby in the town of Trois-Rivières. Hannah saw Mary twice during her four-year captivity.[46] Whether mother and daughter discussed the religious component of their captivities has gone unrecorded, but what is certain is that the teenage girl had assented to Catholic baptism even before her mother was redeemed. The act of converting by individual family members complicated the legacy of Maine's Protestant families for decades to come—and longer—adding Catholic children, in-laws, and descendants. In a number of cases, these new relations were Native American as well. Hannah might have known of Mary's transformation, but it went unrecorded in the "Narrative." Both the 1697 and 1702 editions simply describe Mary as "captive at Montreal." By the time the later edition was published, however, Mary was fully transformed into a French Catholic. She had received the sacraments of baptism and marriage (she wed John Lahey, an Irish Protestant captive in the home of the wealthy Montreal merchant Jacques Le Ber), and had already had at least two of her eventual thirteen children baptized in a Catholic church.[47] In short, Mary was no longer a captive at all, but a particularly fecund, appropriately Catholic subject of the king of France. New France was grateful for every conversion and showed that gratitude with earthly rewards: on the occasion of their formal naturalization in 1710, the king awarded Mary and John Lahey the handsome sum of seventy livres apiece.[48]

Little is known of Hannah's own post-captivity life or her involvement, if any, in the publication of the "Narrative." As a widow from a decimated community, she had nothing to return to in Maine. The Casco settlements would remain in disarray for years, and rebuilding without a husband or grown sons was all but impossible.

Returning to Beverly would have made the most practical sense for Hannah, for numerous Hibbard relatives continued to live there. It also would have brought the possibility of remarriage, which would have saved the impoverished outliver from becoming a dependent of the community.[49] And last, it had a church. If she indeed returned to Beverly, the "pagan skirts" of Maine, which had proved so disastrous for her family, became a thing of the past. Having left with four children, she now returned with, at best, one son, who, like his mother, disappears from the historical record. Ironically, the Catholic branch of the family continued to thrive.

+ + +

On board the ship *Province Galley* with Hannah Swarton and Margaret Stilson were two other Maine women, Elizabeth Tozier and Mary Plaisted. Unlike Hannah and Margaret, both women had endured multiple captivities and had ultimately assented to baptism. To Elizabeth and Mary, and many other Maine captives, the open-ended nature of captivity, the stresses and challenges of post-captivity life, and the uncertainties of the frontier life they had left behind (and were perhaps obliged to go back to) were likely contributors to their taking a different road, which turned temporarily toward Rome.

For New Englanders living in uncertain circumstances in the French colonies of New France and Acadia, an explicit commitment to Catholicism through baptism opened up new channels for active religious experience in New France. It offered captive converts an immediate community of coreligionists. In this sense, it would have represented an improvement to Mary Plaisted's life, which throughout had consisted of a series of deprivations—of loved ones, homes, and personal freedom. By 1691/2, her life was already a trail of personal loss, including at least two and possibly three husbands, two children, and family prestige and fortune. At thirty-two, Mary Plaisted had endured more hardships than most settlers could have expected in a lifetime—even on the pagan skirts of New England.

Unlike many Maine women, Mary was born into an elite Puritan family. She was the daughter of a Wheelwright, related through her maternal line to the province's most notable family. Her male kinsmen were provincial representatives to the General Court and had closer connections to the Massachusetts leadership than most others in Maine. The most prominent among them were also instrumental in attempting to bring Puritan orthodoxy to Wells.[50]

Orthodoxy, however, had not historically been her family's strength. There were prominent Dissenters on both sides of her family, including her maternal grandfather, the aforementioned Reverend John Wheelwright, who was an outspoken antinomian and associate of Anne Hutchinson. He was banished from Massachusetts with some of his followers, including Edward Rishworth, Mary's father and Anne Hutchinson's nephew. Rishworth married Susannah Wheelwright, Mary's mother and one of John's daughters, around the time that the dissenting group was forced to leave Exeter, New Hampshire, in 1643.[51] It was around this time that the Reverend John Wheelwright would renounce his controversial religious views. Not long after his group of followers fled to Maine, Wheelwright penned an apology for his views to the Massachusetts General Court and Governor John Winthrop.[52] His banishment was then revoked, and he was free to move back to orthodox New England.

His older children, however, remained in Maine to make their own way. In a gesture antithetical to Wheelwright's original religious designs, his sons worked hard to make Maine "a frontier outpost of a Puritan society."[53] Mary Plaisted's Wheelwright uncles were subsequently rewarded with judicial appointments, salaried administrative posts, and military protection for Wells. Sharing in their good fortune was their brother-in-law Rishworth, whose protean political attitudes preserved his personal interests and position, though they managed to alienate many less powerful associates.

As an only child, Mary Plaisted served as executor of her father's will and was his sole heir. By the time of Rishworth's death, however, there was little to administer. Like so many other New English Mainers who tied their fortunes to Massachusetts speculators and investors, Rishworth suffered a devastating financial reversal. Bad investments, debts, and failed land speculation reduced his personal fortune to a mere thirty-nine pounds at the time of his death.[54]

Still, despite various economic downturns and spiritual crises, Mary's maternal relatives were the closest thing Maine had to a ruling elite. And, thanks to her multiple marriages, Mary also formed relations with other ambitious frontier entrepreneurs who hoped to build the colony's strength through trade and association with Massachusetts. She counted among her in-laws Henry Sayward, father of her second husband, John. Sayward was among the earliest settlers in York and Kennebunk and built one of the region's first lumber mills. He also helped raise funds for the construction of York's first church, for which his mills supplied the building materials. When the burning of the York mills in 1669 deprived him of his livelihood, Sayward and his family were invited to resettle at Wells, where he built a larger gristmill and sawmill complex near the Mousam River, the first set of permanent structures in Kennebunk. The fact that the mills were built with the help of Wabanaki labor indicates that relations between Native Americans and Europeans had not yet reached a point of alienation, and that Sayward himself, whose granddaughters and daughter-in-law would one day be Indian captives, had amicable relationships with them.

But as happened with the Rishworths, the Sayward family's fortunes fell victim to the all-too-common tangle of loans from Boston merchants, mortgages, and failed business partnerships.[55] When Henry died, his widow attempted to eke out a living selling unlicensed liquor. Her sons, including Mary's husband, John, were forced to sell their inherited interest in the mills to reduce an inherited debt.[56] Then John also died, leaving Mary a widow again, this time with four small daughters and, as tradition dictates, an infant son.

The reversals of fortune of the Rishworths and Saywards were passed from one generation to another, a common trajectory for frontier families. It was Henry Sayward who built a church and several mills — two types of structures critical to the definition and function of a permanent settlement — yet these efforts to ensure community permanence held no guarantees for his own family. Effort did not guarantee upward mobility in Maine. Too many variables linked to the vagaries of frontier life were part of the Maine experience during times of peace as well as war. Eventually, some Rishworth and Henry Sayward grandchildren managed to break out of the family cycle of economic stagnation and ruin. For two of them, Mary's daughters, that meant attaining rewards of both wealth and spirit in French Canada.

This most ironic reversal of fortune began tragically on January 26, 1691/2, while Mary was married to her fourth husband, James Plaisted, and living with him and five children in an outlying area of York called Cider Hill.[57] On that day, a band of French-supported Eastern Wabanakis surprised and overran the town at dawn and left forty-eight settlers dead. Eighty York residents were taken as hostages. The fallout from the horrors of the attack on York, known commonly as the Candlemas massacre, was so severe that some scholars consider it the watershed event that touched off Salem's witchcraft hysteria.[58] York, one of the oldest and best established of the English settlements in Maine, was almost completely obliterated. Seemingly sturdy garrisons were breached, houses and dependencies reduced to ashes, and dozens of animals slaughtered. From his home in Wells, almost fifteen miles away, the Reverend George Burroughs, who was soon to suffer his own deadly ordeal as an accused witch, wrote a vivid description of the terrible plume of smoke he saw spewing forth from the burning town.[59]

In the sense that they suffered no immediate casualties, the Plaisteds were luckier than most other families, some of whom lost all their members to the attack and its aftermath. But Mary and two of her daughters, eleven-year-old Mary and seven-year-old Esther, were among eighty captive Protestants.[60] They were forced to march quickly to the wooded areas near Cape Neddick Pond where their captors camped for the night. Before dawn, the captives were hustled toward Wells, where the Wabanakis stopped at Storer's garrison "under a flag of truce," and presented an opportunity for the English to redeem some of their fellow countrymen. Ten days later, Captain James Converse and John Alden arrived at Sagadahoc, almost one hundred miles up the coast from York, with enough donated money from settlements throughout New England to redeem thirty-six of the eighty captives.[61]

Mary and her daughters were not among the redeemed. Instead, they were hastened deeper into the northwestern wilderness of Wabanakia. James Plaisted's failure to redeem his family remains a mystery. Though Mary and James had but modest means themselves, both were connected to Maine's important governing families.[62] The Plaisteds were also among the largest landowners in Salmon Falls and were civil and militia leaders. Mary's personal kinship networks, courtesy of birth and marriage, extended to almost every community in Maine. Her continued captivity, therefore, suggests two possibilities: either the funds raised in Boston for the relief of the York captives were earmarked for specific persons, or the process was subject to the judgment of the captors, who kept those individuals best suited to their needs and allowed others to be ransomed. The first scenario seems particularly plausible in light of the fact that four wealthy Portsmouth residents who were well connected in Boston and had the misfortune of being in York when the raid took place were among the first to be ransomed at Sagadahoc.[63] The second scenario, however, was common among groups of New England captives throughout the empire. Women and children were perceived to be more likely candidates for cultural and religious conversion, and thus more likely to bolster the population of French and Indian communities. They were highly valued spiritual conquests who could be used to demoralize the Protestants to the south.

Where Mary's encounter with Catholicism began continues to inspire scholarly speculation. She lived among the Wabanakis for as long as two years, and it likely started there. But Catholicism's appeal was not universal among the Eastern Indians, and by no means accessible to English captives due to, among other things, differences in culture and language. The encounter more likely took place while she served in the household of Catherine Gauchet, widow of a recently deceased royal judge and seigneur, Jean-Baptiste Migeon de Branssat.[64] When she returned to New England two years after her arrival in the Gauchet household, Mary had agreed to receive the sacraments that, to the French, made her a proper Catholic. Her French captor, Catherine Gauchet, also had the means, connections, and piety to coerce her servant into religious submission. Other incentives,

like access to her daughters at the nearby school of the Congrégation Notre-Dame, no doubt encouraged apostasy from Protestantism as well.

Through conversion, Mary's life likely became much easier. Conversion would have offered her a means to become once again a more
fully vested member of a colonial Euro-American society. And in
contrast to Hannah Swarton, she also gained steady access to her
daughters. So it appears surprising that she left both her children and
her new religion, and returned to New England with Mathew Cary
in 1695, reappropriating her life as a New England Protestant as the
wife of James Plaisted and mother to additional children.[65]

The reunited couple led fairly uneventful lives. After Mary's return, James requested a license from the Court of Quarter Sessions
"to retayle bear syder and victuals at his now dwelling house."[66] After
James's death, Mary was continually granted renewals for a license to
retail liquor.[67]

It is not known whether Mary ever saw her *canadienne* daughters
again. She was alive as late as 1723, two years before her daughter
Esther visited the Eastward in the company of several other acculturated French captives. Daughter Mary and Esther continued to experience seemingly content lives as rebaptized Catholics in the captor
colony. The younger Mary Plaisted became Soeur Marie-des-Anges
of the Congrégation of Notre-Dame, and her sister Esther became
Madame Lestage, the wife of a wealthy Montreal merchant. Despite
Mary's life commitment to the convent and Esther's marriage into
wealth and privilege, their mother persisted in the hope that they
would return. As late as 1715, she pressed a suit against her own son
to prevent him from claiming his sisters' modest inheritances of less
than twenty pounds apiece.[68]

Like Hannah Swarton's narrative, Mary Plaisted's story was disseminated throughout New England, again through the pen of Cotton
Mather. It appeared as an anecdote in his *Magnalia Christi Americana*. Like Hannah's story, it served a didactic function, one that il-
lustrated the perversity of the tormentors of New England Protestants. In Mather's account, Mary was taken captive not only with her
daughters but with a newborn son whose cries impeded the progress

of his mother and called unwanted attention to the fleeing Wabanakis and their hostages. As a result, the baby was killed by his Wabanaki captors. Though the actual existence of this baby is in doubt
(family, church, and civil records confirm the existence of his siblings,
but not of him), Mather's emphasis on this story added to the already grievous losses of the mother and demonstrated the barbarity
of her captors. But with or without the putative baby, the real Mary
had lived a life of diverse losses which had begun long before she was
seized by Wabanaki and French forces and carried against her will to
Canada. In Canada, however, complying with expected deference
toward Catholicism guaranteed rewards. And, if necessary, such religious defections could be undone.

Captives from Maine: Common Experiences, Diverse Responses

A comparison of the life circumstances and reactions to captivity of
Hannah Swarton and Mary Plaisted reveals similar patterns. For one,
the promise of fresh starts and material prosperity that Maine seemed
to offer both families had not come to fruition. In addition, both
women experienced periods in their adult lives in which they were
bereft of critical sources of identity: husbands, fathers, extended family,
and offspring. Furthermore, both were subjected to the same challenges to religious identity once they were imprisoned in New France.
Last, both were ransomed back to New England but had children
who remained behind as Catholic subjects of a French king.

   Though the circumstances of their lives also diverge in significant ways, the experiences of Hannah and Mary suggest a range of
common experience, action, and response for Maine captives who
crossed frontiers of culture and faith. Maine's English settlers are the
focus of this examination because many, like Mary and Hannah, had
already breached frontier boundaries. By virtue of their placement
on New England's pagan skirts, Maine's outlivers were more likely
than most New England settlers to share intimate contacts, voluntary or otherwise, with the religiously and ethnically diverse populations of the northern frontier.[69] To an observer like Cotton Mather,

an established theologian and authoritative social critic writing from the secure perch of Boston, the tragedy for both women (and for other captives as well) began long before they ever faced foreign foes.[70]

How do the experiences of Maine's Protestant captives compare with those of New England captives overall? Of the 201 Maine captives taken between 1688 and 1727, Emma Lewis Coleman and Charlotte Alice Baker identified 109 who returned and 51 who lived out their lives in Canada. Of the remaining 41, some were killed or died shortly after they were taken captive, and a few lucky ones experienced captivities of only a few days. Maine captives were a diverse group in terms of age, occupation, and station in life. Among them one finds soldiers, small children, infants, and the elderly. Several of the women taken from Maine were pregnant. When the infants they bore did not impede the progress of the raiding party, they were valued as a source of increased ransom or (if their mothers could be persuaded to remain in New France) additional settlers.[71]

Whether women or men, adults or adolescents, the Protestant colonists who took the first critical step toward acculturation into the captor culture—Catholic baptism—were far more likely to do so while among the French than the Wabanakis. Despite the proselytizing, haranguing, and taunting by Wabanaki Christians and the nearly constant presence of aggressive Jesuits, few captives were baptized in the missions. This is striking, especially since missions functioned as sacramental stations, places where a sacramental technician of some sort was usually present.[72] Indeed, Catholic priests were more predictably present at the missions than in the smaller parishes of New France. As the most learned and zealous of proselytizers, they would have set to work on captives quickly.[73] With the religious potency of the missions in mind, how can one account for the failure of captives to convert while detained in the missions of Wabanakia and Canada? Many factors suggest themselves, but all coalesce around the same theme: the clash of cultures was far too great to encourage and support substantial numbers of conversions, especially among adult captives.

It is unlikely that captives, especially those taken in later wars (Queen Anne's and Dummer's), resigned themselves to long or permanent stays among their captors. They had seen enough friends and neighbors return to have at least a rough idea of how redemption unfolded—and the redeemed more than likely came home through New France. In addition, many English Mainers would have rejected most if not all elements of Native American culture out of hand—even those elements that were clearly Christian and European in origin.[74] To captive observers, even the syncretically European elements of postcontact Wabanaki culture were relentlessly alien. Almost always suspect to English settlers to begin with, they were associated with the terror of the raids and a form of Catholicism imparted by French missionaries which made this alternative Christian vision seem doubly strange and perverse. All Wabanakis, even those who professed Christianity, were still regarded by Protestant observers as "heathens" and "barbarians," "diabolical" in all their religious practices, regardless of the origins of those practices.[75] One settler, Francis Tooke, saw in the murder of York minister Shubael Dummer "Gods dreadfull displeasure agaynst us, the first minister kild in all our warrs."[76] The possibility that God had chosen the Wabanakis as emissaries to punish the New Englanders did not render them less sinister or anti-Christian in their own right. The latter sentiment was confirmed to all captives when their captors, some of whom paraded in the dead minister's clothes, led their prisoners into the wilderness while delivering mock sermons, singing *Te Deums,* matins, and vespers, and raising a common component of Catholic liturgy to a cry of victory in war.[77] Though clothes of the dead were a common form of booty, the sight of a Wabanaki warrior dressed in Dummer's clothes of his office would have been viewed as not merely abominable but literally satanic. To Cotton Mather, the Wabanaki who donned Dummer's clothes was "a Devil as an Angel of Light."[78]

Worse still, according to Protestant writers, were mission Indians who engaged in far greater anti-Christian acts: the targeted killing of Protestant babies and young children. Accounts like Mather's of Mary Plaisted, as well as records on captives from other sources, attest to the fact that frontier warfare posed particular dangers to the young and, through them, the long-term survival of frontier settlements and families. Mather related that Mary's captors "forced her to Travel in this Weakness . . . without any Respect of Pity."[79] Her baby's particularly savage death came at the hands of a "Diabolical master," who "took her Child from [his mother], and carried it unto a River, where stripping it of the few filthy Rags it had, he took it by the heels, and against a Tree dash'd out its Brains, and then flung it into the River." The death of this child offered proof to Protestant readers that the "heathen," even those who professed to be Christians, were inherent savages and beyond the reach of redemption. To Mather and his readers, a chilling demonstration of this savagery came from killing Christian babies who might not have had access to baptism because of their outliver parents' choices, and were therefore now excluded from the Puritan covenant forever.[80] Many Maine babies were not baptized in their infancy. This sacrament, one of the few that Puritanism retained from the pre-Reformation Church, brought children into covenant with God and their families. Death before baptism foreclosed that possibility.

The murdered Plaisted baby might have had his origins in someone else's story and did not exist in his own right. But the anecdote reflects the reality that death was an all-too-common fate for infants and the very young in captivity, as their Native captors sought to relieve adult captives of their physical burdens on the wilderness trails. The practice of killing young captives was not applied in any consistent manner. Death or survival depended on the time of year, the condition of the mother and the child, and the perceived level of jeopardy that these human impediments caused to the greater effort of keeping captives and captors out of the hands of the pursuing English.[81] The practice was also not restricted to the very young. Older children who became problems for their captors and were too large to be dashed against a tree were killed in other ways if they became troublesome. To the English, even Indian mercy appeared cruel to child and parent alike, and devalued the lives of young Puritans. For example, Mather wrote that one small child, on the verge of being roasted for food, was saved only by the timely appearance of a dog, who took the baby's place as the evening meal.[82]

These horrifying images would not have been completely new to Mather's New England readers. Accounts in his writings of burned churches and homes, slaughtered ministers, and brutalized children all demonstrated that French and Indian enemies were aggressively and mercilessly targeting the symbols of permanent settlement in a particularly vicious way. Such accounts would have been familiar to a Massachusetts population that had endured the horrors of King Philip's War and were urgent reminders that their enemies strove for nothing less than complete annihilation.[83] As residents of a frontier region with few spiritual protections, many potential Puritans were similarly lost, including the youngest, most vulnerable, and most promising. It is little wonder that conversions were unlikely to happen among these Native American captors and their mission priests, who were despised and fearful tropes of a maturing New England literary genre.[84]

Death was only one form of permanent separation for the members of captive families. Among their captors, Mainers were subjected to an informal process of sorting. This took into account each captive's age, sex, and potential receptivity to religious and cultural transformation. If sorting achieved its goals, it resulted in permanent religious and cultural alienation, depriving the surviving young captive of the familial support structures that guided him or her into a mature spiritual existence.

Those who were determined to resist any form of acculturation refused to acknowledge basic human elements that Wabanaki culture shared with their own, which allowed them to cling to their English Protestant identities. This type of resistance, however, took a toll on their bodies and spirits. When Hannah Swarton cataloged the losses she endured while among the Wabanakis, her list included "friends, neighbors, house estate, bread, clothes, or lodging suitable."[85] Such an environment was unlikely to produce enthusiastic converts.[86]

Heathenism was considered by all Euro-American Christians to be a terrible human state, but for particularly zealous Protestants, the concept of a "papist" Indian was at once both a confirmation of Catholicism's intrinsic flaws and a perversion of Christian belief. While living among the Eastern Indians, Hannah Swarton was forced into servitude by an Indian woman who had lived among the English at

Black Point but had married a "Canada Indian and turned papist."
This Wabanaki convert delighted in chiding her captive for her religious beliefs, tauntingly telling the captive that "had the English
been as careful to instruct her in our religion as the French were to
instruct her in theirs, she might have been of our religion."[87] In this
world turned upside down, Hannah Swarton and her Protestant companions paid a heavy price for local ministers' inabilities, or lack of
inclination, to make religious inroads among the Eastern Indians.

Things were little better at the Jesuit missions, where numerous
captives spent months, even years, still living among Indians and
waiting for redemption to New England or relief at the hands of the
French. Though most of the violence that marked the raids and subsequent treks through the wilderness was quelled at the missions,
conditions there reinforced for most Protestant adults the alien nature of Native American expressions of Christianity. The Jesuits alone
were present in at least six Maine communities at various times in
the province's pre-Revolutionary history. Panawamske, Cowass, Pig-
wacket, Ameseconti, Norridgewock, and Naurakamig all operated
within territory that was claimed by the English but not yet settled.
As will be seen, Norridgewock's existence was a particularly thorny
issue that eventually unleashed a three-year cycle of violence. Other
Wabanaki groups outwardly avoided conflict by migrating to missions closer to the French metropoles. Récollet Franciscan and Sulpician missions also operated in the province, mostly in areas east of
those staffed by Jesuits. Their establishments spanned from Pentagoët
on the Penobscot Bay all the way to Plaisance, in modern-day Newfoundland.[88] Though records are scant for most Wabanaki missions,
two—Norridgewock and St. Francis, in Canada—are particularly
well-documented thanks to their size, stability, and voluble missionaries. Other missions are documented by English informants, including ex-captives, who with good reason associated these communities
with fear and pain. Bias notwithstanding, their accounts tell scholars
much about the religious culture of Maine's missions and about the
missions that attracted Maine Indians. Taken together, they paint a
picture of religious life that was often beautiful and full of promise
for those Euro-American Christians who embraced it, and repellent

or even comically blasphemous for those who did not. Unsurprisingly, the vast majority of conversions took place in Canadian and Acadian towns and settlements, where more recognizable forms of Euro-American Christianity were preponderant and fellow Euro-Americans were the worshippers and proselytizers.

The intrinsic "Indian-ness" of Wabanaki Catholicism was key to these reactions. For the Indians, Catholicism was a means of accommodation rather than transformation.[89] The fact that Catholic conversion did not require the Wabanakis to denounce all preexisting aspects of their culture, as Puritan missionaries thought fitting, no doubt contributed to the revulsion toward Indian religion reported by so many returning Maine captives. When the primary encounter with Catholicism happened at Wabanaki communities, English men, women, and children met an expression of Christianity yet another step removed from the various Protestant forms with which they were familiar. In Wabanaki Christian communities, religious identity and activities were manifest in the built environment, in methods of religious expression, and even on the physical person. When combined with Native American habits and customs, Catholicism must have appeared to Maine captives to be even stranger and more alien than before. Its unfamiliar qualities were enhanced by the fact that most of the elements Protestants witnessed were extreme in physical and sensual ways. Though all the major forms of frontier Protestantism had their own connections either to Catholicism or forms of Christian expression that went beyond the written word, Indian Christianity must have shocked the spiritual system of any novice Protestant observer.[90]

For English settlers, the religious "other" in the shape of an Indian stood out in terms of physical appearance. Catholic bodies could be covered in overt symbols, such as crosses, beads, and medals that bespoke the owner's religious identity. Encouraged by mission priests, Catholic Indians who had access to rosaries often wore them around their necks, not only to proclaim their faith but also to act as "a defense from temptation."[91] Their fingers and necks might also boast "Jesuit rings," inexpensive trade goods made of a copper alloy that were commonly given to Indians by French priests. Though small, their escutcheons could be decorated with crucifixion groupings, crosses, or short Latin phrases, all things that would have identified them as vaguely Euro-Christian in origin.[92] Other Indians had similar Christian symbols permanently incised into their bodies through tattooing. Called *piquage* by the French, tattooing was common among most Native American groups, including the Wabanakis and their indigenous neighbors. The tattoos themselves, however, were less unusual than the fact that some Native groups incorporated Christian symbols in their iconographic repertoire. Europeans found this phenomenon notable. In 1708 a French surgeon named Dièreville wrote that Acadian Indians were lavishly tattooed with "all kinds of Devices" including "Crosses, Names of Jesus, Flowers; anything in fact that may be desired."[93] While their tattoos might have been covered by warm clothing during a significant part of the year, Catholic Wabanakis encountered Englishmen, in peace as well as war, throughout the year. Proclaiming these indelible marks of Christian alliance relayed the Wabanakis' association with familiar Euro-American Catholics. Yet their unorthodox methods of displaying these symbols (coupled with the Puritans' visceral aversion to them) added to Protestant concerns that Indians had yet to learn true Christianity, or whether they were even capable of grasping it. English religious culture held that altering one's body was a sinful act because it turned the human body, considered an image of God, into an object.[94]

Once detained in an Indian village with a strong missionary presence, captives and noncaptive Protestant emissaries encountered Catholic worship spaces, as well as the worship that went on in them. Though frontier (and most certainly captive) Protestants witnessed individual or small bands of Catholic Indians performing their devotions outside of the missions, it was here that they saw Catholic bodies in action *en masse.* Catholic ritual demanded physical activities that accompanied acts of personal piety and liturgy. Genuflecting, kneeling, making the sign of the cross, keeping track of prayers by fingering beads, processing, receiving sacraments, chanting, singing—all were common physical components used in Catholicism to express spirituality. The Jesuit missionary Sebastien Rale found proof of his success as a missionary in the level to which Wabanakis were willing to commit themselves or (from the Jesuit's perspective) discipline their bodies to conform to Catholic ritual and moral codes. In 1723 he wrote to his nephew, "I can say to you that generally you would have difficulty in restraining your tears were you in my Church, with our Savages gathered there; and were you to witness of the piety with which they repeat their prayers, chant the divine Office, and participate in the Sacraments of Penance and of the Eucharist."[95]

Protestant English captives and other religious outsiders also witnessed Catholic Indians using their bodies in ways that undermined the Wabanakis' claims as pious Christians. Extreme liquor dependence and sexual activity that deviated from Christian ideals of conjugal love were sources of chronic tension between the Indians and the missionaries. They subverted the latters' sense of moral order and undermined the sacrament of marriage. Mission converts were expected to marry in the Catholic Church and adhere to its demands of monogamy, indissoluble union, and male authority in marriage.[96] Persuading the new faithful to accept these mandates, however, proved difficult. Jesuit Joseph Aubery's complaint to his superior, Joseph Jovency, that he "profited naught or little by admonishing, chiding, and beseeching" his flock to avoid drunkenness and fornication was a common lament among spiritual workers who lived among Native Americans.[97] Though their behavior was considered religiously deviant by mission priests, the Wabanakis were engaged in long-standing normative patterns of marriage and sexual behavior.[98] Such behaviors demonstrated that, despite their commonly expressed enthusiasm for Catholic cosmology and French military alliance, a gulf in understanding still existed between the priests and the mission's neophytes.[99] It is likely that any Protestant adult who spent any amount of time within a mission would have some knowledge of these tensions, and from observing them come away with the lesson that Native Americans were incapable of truly embracing Christianity.

Indian bodies engaged in Catholic prayer, especially on holy and saint's days, often determined the rest of the day's rhythms, which for most Protestants would have represented an unnecessary disruption of daily, worldly patterns. Though days spent in worship paralleled the Puritan Sabbath, the sheer number of these special days, and the ways in which Indians went about expressing these devotions, were far removed from Protestant, and especially Puritan, sensibilities regarding proper use of time and space. Jesuit Jacques Bigot described the spiritual bustle of a mission on a sacred day. It involved movement throughout the mission's geography, especially the overtly holy spaces of the churches and chapels, and, according to the importance of the day, brought a sense of sacred space outward into homes, fields, and hunting grounds. Bigot gave a hint of this integration when he wrote to his superior describing how baptized Wabanakis celebrated the feasts of their patron saints who, the priest reported, felt "the utmost Joy when I notify them of the Day of their Patron's feast: and some of the principal persons have, after their Devotions, chosen to manifest their Rejoicing through feasts,—sometimes in their Cabins, sometimes public ones for all the people." Adding to a sense that some days were more holy than others was the way the Wabanakis enhanced the spiritual environment. Bigot asserted, "I can make no one a more Esteemed present than to give him some fair-sized Image of his patron Saint. They put away these Images as best they can, in order to Preserve them, and display them in their cabins on the Days of the great feasts."[100] During their time in the missions, some New Englanders might also have witnessed a ceremony of public penance called *hotouongannandi* by Claude Chauchetière, a Jesuit at the mission of Kahnawake, near Montreal. According to the priest's description,

> The men, gathered together according to the savage custom,— that is, at a feast,—expressed their detestation of drunkenness, which mastered them. This was done as follows: after agreeing together as to what they could do to give satisfaction to God, they came to the conclusion that each should speak for himself in full meeting; and that they who on account of illness, or for any other reason, were unable to do so, should have someone speak in their names. This was done to prepare for the festival of Christmas. Each spoke as the spirit of penance moved him; and some did so more eloquently by the tears that flowed in abundance from their eyes, than by their voices broken by sobs.[101]

English Protestants who belonged to Reformed sects that rejected Catholic concepts of holy time and holy space would have found it nearly impossible to reconcile such a ceremony, which had as many indigenous religious elements as Christian ones, with their own.

In describing special prayers for feast days, Bigot noted, "The more fervent showed an admirable ardor to know this prayer as quickly as possible, and some Days later they Inserted It in their usual prayers; It is now said four times a Day—twice in the Cabins, and twice in The Church. Although I did not have them receive Communion on the Day of The death of St. Francis de sales, because they had received communion three Days before, they Nevertheless spent almost the whole Day in prayers."[102] Later, at a mission at Nauraka-mig, on the Androscoggin River, Bigot described how "others on returning from the forest, after depositing their loads of fuel in their cabins, go at once to adore Our Lord." [103] Breaking the day in such a fashion puzzled Protestants, who seemed to regard these pious pauses as a waste of daylight. John Gyles, a young captive servant from Pemaquid who lived among the Maliseet Indians and the French for nine years, offered a simple alternative to such pieties. When his master's fields were plagued by blackbirds, the captor family invited "a Jesuit" to banish them. Thirty French farmers processed through the field with the priest, who rang little bells and sprinkled holy water in an attempt to banish the birds. When this failed, Gyles remarked to a nearby French youth, "The friar hath done no service; he had better take a gun and shoot the birds."[104] Gyles's conclusion was a logical one, but it missed the larger point. Religious ceremonies helped integrate the community and develop a sense of solidarity. In Acadia, where settlers were few, French control was tenuous, and tension was high regarding the better-armed and more numerous English on the horizon, public displays of religious culture reinforced identity and strengthened community ties, a role the local Catholic clergy enthusiastically embraced after the Treaty of Utrecht.[105]

Protestants held captive in the missions who refused to conform to a Catholic liturgy's gestures and movements were sometimes forced to do so: John Williams, the Deerfield minister, reported that while he was a captive at St. François, a mission near Montreal, his

Indian master "took hold of my hand to force me to cross myself, but I struggled with him and would not suffer him to guide my hand; upon this he pulled off a crucifix from his own neck and bade me kiss it, but I refused again. He told me he would dash out my brains with his hatchet if I refused. I told him I should sooner choose death than to sin against God . . ." Faced with his captive's committed opposition to being forced into pieties he neither respected nor understood, the Indian captor dismissed Williams as "No good minister, no love God, as bad as the devil."[106] In this fight for the right to control the ways that bodies were allocated to worship, Indian and Puritan held each other in mutual contempt, regarding each other's pious practices as impious or defective.

Williams's reactions to Catholicism represent an extreme example of Puritan revulsion. Nevertheless, it is telling that so few mature Protestants, including some who would later accept or even embrace a Catholic identity in New France, were lured to accept the faith while living among the Wabanakis. The Deerfield minister had suffered horrifically at the hands of Catholic people, which no doubt contributed to his disdain for their expressed methods of belief. Most alienating, however, was their liturgy, which he was forced by his Indian master to attend at least once. Williams describes the Catholic mass at a mission as a babel of confusion, filled with strange prayers, languages, movements and objects. He reacted to it with amusement: "One of the Jesuits was at the altar saying Mass in a tongue unknown to the savages, and the other between the altar and the door saying and singing prayers among the Indians at the same time saying over their Pater Nosters and Ave Mary by tale from their chaplets, or beads on a string. At our going out, we smiled at their devotion so managed, which was offensive to them, for they said we made a derision of their worship."[107] That a gospel minister, especially one who had just gone through Williams's ordeal, should have such an unfavorable view of Catholic liturgy is unremarkable. What is surprising, however, is that Williams revealed through his ability to identify a chaplet and the specifics of Catholic prayers that he had actually acquired some knowledge of Catholic material culture and pious practices. As with Williams, converging Christianities might lead to derision, but also led to exposure and experience with the religious "other," which few in New England had.

The minister's reaction to the worship space itself is missing from his account, leaving one to wonder whether the chapel matched the alien nature of the Christian bodies and practices of the Indian adherents. These worship spaces, though, exposed Protestant English men and women to the objects and practices that Indians valued. Catholic observers recorded for others what the Indians used and the English saw. Jacques Bigot provided his Jesuit superior with detailed descriptions of the worship spaces the Indians built, adorned, and prepared for special church holidays. He reported, "[The Wabanakis and their missionaries] chose the Day of The death of Saint francis de sales; and, on The day before, an altar was set up in The Church of our Mission, where was exposed The Image of the Saint, which the savages adorned with everything most beautiful in their possession. The whole Altar was covered with a great number of Collars, made in all sorts of designs; Bugle beads and strings of porcelain; and articles worked with glass Beads and, porcupine quills."[108] Turning such profane, overtly Indian ornaments as beads and quills into expressions of the Christian God must have been anathema to New Englanders. Indeed, even some of the most progressive Euro-American Christians seemed a little uncomfortable with worship spaces that reflected Native American understandings of Christianity. Jesuits, for example, preferred church ornaments that were created by Euro-American craftsmen. Bigot thrilled to the gift from his superior of "the most beautiful ornament on this Altar, which was a very large Image of St. Francis de Sales on satin. I had It enriched with a wide border of gold and silver. I may say that I have not seen in france a more beautiful Image of St. Francis de Sales, or one more handsomely adorned than that one is."[109] Almost forty years later, Sebastien Rale took delight in reporting to his nephew that his mission church was decorated with forms and objects that made it more compatible with European notions of worship spaces. He told his young relative, "I have built here a Church which is commodious and well adorned. I thought it my duty to spare nothing, either for its decoration or for the beauty of the vestments that are used in our holy Ceremonies; altar-cloths, chasubles, copes, sacred vessels, everything is suitable, and would be esteemed in the Churches of Europe."[110] Though the priest reveled in his life as an Indian in other ways, he equated worship that reflected Euro-American origins with a mature Catholic colonial church.

For most Maine captives, the various villages and missions of Wabanakia were just intermediate stops on the way to the final destination, French Canada or (for a few others) Acadia. For many captives, this transition marked the end of their ordeal in the wilderness among those the English termed "salvages" who shared collective responsibility for attacking their settlements and killing their family members, neighbors, and livestock. Arriving in Quebec, Montreal or Trois-Rivières — all settlements that Mainers would have recognized as inhabited by fellow European Christians — they found familiar physical comforts. Even the most defiant captives, such as Hannah Swarton, reported an ease of life in New France and a quantifiable improvement in their material circumstances once they were placed in French hands.[111] For most adult Mainers, conversion, if it happened at all, happened here.

There was, however, one captive population that was as likely to embrace Catholicism in Wabanaki as in New France. These were children, who for logistical reasons had been separated from their parents (if they had managed to survive) and placed in the care of particularly pious mission families. Maine's young children were far more likely to enter Euro-American captor communities already baptized as Catholics.[112] The process was fostered (New Englanders claimed forced) by the French missionaries of Wabanakia, who used more advanced neophytes to encourage newcomers. Though incorrect in his assessment, the Jesuit Jacques Bigot observed Protestant children and noted with concern that they did not know how to pray. Bigot credited the Wabanakis with providing a positive example of Catholic devotional practices for captive children. Bigot wrote to a fellow Jesuit, "At first I find [captive children] greatly prejudiced against us, but they gradually allow themselves to be persuaded by the devotion of our Abnaquis and their zeal for prayer — which they do not find, they say, in their colony."[113]

Bigot's misconceptions of Protestant, and particularly Puritan, prayer illustrate a critical difference in the ways each faith viewed and partook in it. Early modern Catholics said prayers that were the same for all adherents. What is more, they recited them in Latin, a language that was alien to all but the most learned of English frontier dwellers. The exception to this rule were Native Americans, for whom priests, and Jesuits in particular, adapted prayers to Native tongues.[114] The results, however, were the same: though they might express similar relationships to God through prayer, Protestants and Catholics, even the most erudite ones, were unlikely to understand each other's methods of accessing the Divine. Christian commonalities were therefore not likely to be inspired by the act of prayer.

Opportunities to encourage the learning of Catholic prayers increased when captives, adult and child alike, left the Wabanaki villages and came to live among colonial Catholics. By emphasizing Protestantism and Catholicism's common roots, clever proselytizers attempted to break down the perception that their religion was as radically different as Wabanaki Christianity had suggested. This technique was used by Père Meriel when he closely quizzed Joseph Bartlett, a teenage captive from Haverhill, Massachusetts, on the youth's knowledge of Scripture. In the ensuing debate, the priest employed a Scripture-based defense to demonstrate that the critical common text for all Christians affirmed Catholicism's intrinsic truths. Though ultimately unsuccessful at winning a convert, the priest's technique did succeed in at least cultivating in Bartlett a respectful interest in Catholicism and an affection for individual Catholics, even the clergy, who treated him well.[115] Even Hannah Swarton expressed gratitude when her French captors, who had abandoned hope of conversion, provided her with a scrap of Scripture in English and left her to her own devices to use it.[116]

Arrival in French Canada changed the religious lives of adult captives. In some instances, they were granted greater personal freedoms. But in other instances, the pressure to convert and the clear benefits that religious conversion could bring to daily life were a source of unease. Narratives assert that, once they were in New France, adult captives banded together in support of one another and to reinforce their collective resistance to conversion. One way was through participation in prayer groups with coreligionists. Jacques Bigot's assumption that Protestants did not engage in communal prayer is contradicted by numerous sources, French and English alike, which describe prayer meetings among New England captives. French authorities even took the step of attempting to forbid them.[117] These attempts were recorded by John Williams, who wrote in his own narrative that when he and other New Englanders arrived at New France, they "were forbidden praying one with another, or joining together in the service of God."[118] The problem surfaced again during his 1713 mission to New France to redeem captives, when the French intendant warned Williams and his companion, John Stoddard, that they would face house arrest if they preached to or held Sunday meetings for any English prisoners.[119]

Hannah Swarton's account and the lives of others show that a Protestant could live among aggressive "papists" for years without becoming a Catholic. The antipathy of Protestant English men and woman toward Catholicism was for the most part well established, and Protestant captives could evade conversion or refuse it outright. Why, then, did so many of Maine's English Protestants convert? Scholars speculate that the reasons range from general religious apathy to gratitude toward kindly Catholic captors. The possibility exists, however, that New France Christians were less alien to these often religiously lax settlers than they would have been to more orthodox Puritans. Put simply, acculturation was an integral and often irresistible force in early America.[120] Distance from the religious establishment of New England suggests a greater tendency toward acculturation during times of upheaval and war. In New England, few places were father from the seats of orthodoxy than Maine.

There were other, more pragmatic considerations as well, stemming from New France's relative stability. Many captives must have found the chance to establish some semblance of stability and peace an increasingly tempting reason to convert. Mary Plaisted, Elizabeth Tozier, and another Maine woman, Mehitable Goodwin all avoided conversion for three years. But the Catholic Church offered married women, who through captivity were separated from the living husbands who gave them their identities, an element of protection and prestige that they had not enjoyed since before they came to New France.[121]

Other captives of both sexes might have made conscious decisions to stay in New France, but prisoner exchanges, paid ransoms, and other incentives eventually brought them back to Maine. Hannah Parsons, Martha Grant, and Anne Batson, all widows with children living in captivity with them, assented to baptism, and either brought their young children or allowed them to be taken into the church with them. York captive Charles Trafton, one of the few men to convert, was an adolescent when he was taken. But he became a baptized Catholic, took up a French identity, and learned a trade before he too returned to Maine, well into his adulthood.[122] Children with or without parents in captivity also converted and returned, though their captors often went to extraordinary lengths to entice them to stay.[123]

Others were won, or almost won, with kindness. Deposing against the Norridgewock sachem, Bomazeen, Grace Higiman of Pemaquid conceded that the French at Quebec had treated her well and provided her with comfortable quarters, in contrast to the Indians, whom she claimed had beaten her.[124] Abraham Johnson, an English sailor who was taken captive off Maine's coast during Dummer's War, preferred a more restricted life among French Catholics to offers of freedom for remaining among the Wabanakis and marrying an Indian woman.[125]

New France offered special incentives to males who would consider making the French colony and religion their real and spiritual homes. Most male New England captives resisted their captors and ultimately returned to the English Protestant colonies. Proportionally speaking, however, most of those who remained were from Maine. Although they represented only a small percentage of Maine's unredeemed captives, this reinforces the idea of religious permeability among the province's settlers. As will be seen, it also underscores their marginality. Like captives from other parts of New England, most of these Maine men were taken in childhood or adolescence. At least two adult males, John Edmunds of Pemaquid and William Lucas, remade their lives within the captor culture.[126] Joseph Fry, Aaron Littlefield, Richard Nason, and George Gray were well into adolescence at the time of their captivity, and were nearing adulthood when they were finally redeemed to Canada. By that time they had converted to Catholicism and become fully acculturated to the French colony. Other males followed the same pattern until stipulations on inherited wealth brought them back to New England to claim their share.[127] The common theme among these male captives was their modest origins, suggesting that the Canadian *concession* (a grant of farmland) most were given, as well as the opportunity to build a more productive life than they might otherwise have been able to obtain in Maine, was well worth the price of reforming themselves as Christians. Men like Fry and Nason were already familiar with borderland religious experimentation, as both men came from frontier Quaker families who were sufficiently outspoken to run afoul of local authorities.[128] Gray and Littlefield seem to have formed sincere attachments to Catholicism, with Gray refusing redemption "for love of his new religion."[129] Littlefield, whose story forms the core of chapter 6, was initially tricked into remaining in New France, but after marrying, fathering numerous children, and creating a productive adult life in Catholic French Canada, he clung to his new identity, even when it put his valuable inheritance at risk.

Counterproductive as it might have seemed, persistent resistance to conversion frequently ended with the captives' desired result—exchange or ransom back to New England with their Protestant integrity intact. But other adolescent or adult captives concluded that Catholic baptism opened more than just the gates of heaven. Conversion could add considerable ease to their lives—both in and beyond captivity. Captives who took this step were admitted into the wider world of public participation in Canadian society, which in many ways revolved around the feast days and sacraments of the Catholic Church. The sacrament of baptism provided entry into the well-established colonial world of New France, and the reintegration of English captives into the company of one another.

But before any of this could happen, the captive was subject to sacramental entry into the church. Preparation for the sacrament of baptism varied. Some captives, particularly the very young and very frail, received the sacrament immediately. When time was less of an issue (a rare occurrence in an age when news of peace negotiations that might affect captives was slow to reach frontier communities), captives who consented to baptism were prepared with care. For adult women, preparation took place in the households of elites. Younger women and girls prepared and learned their catechism in Canada's convents and convent schools, places of peace, tranquility, and female learning that contrasted starkly with both Maine and the Wabanaki missions.[130] Passing time in a convent school did not guarantee that a young New England captive would live out her life in Canada, but it did increase significantly her chances of remaining. Over half of the girls who stayed in Quebec had at one time been schooled by the Ursulines in their *pensionnat* (boarding school).[131]

Captive networks among detained Mainers and other New Englanders in Canada were often facilitated by sacramental association, a form of fictive kinship within some forms of Christianity intended to create a special spiritual and worldly bond between the recipient of the sacrament and his or her godparent. The actual conversion of the captive, made explicit in baptism, also possessed an overarching meaning for the whole captor community. For this reason, captives were frequently baptized on major feast days. These were holy days of obligation when the churches of New France were busy, active spaces, teeming with the faithful, who created an instant audience for one of French Catholicism's triumphal moments.[132] The captive minister John Norton observed the "women from the Eastward" tended to seek one another out and make common cause.[133] Historian Barbara Austen has shown that Norton's comment had many facets, with the camaraderie of female ex-Protestants extending to many of life's transitions, sacramental and secular alike. Captives served as godparents and sacramental witnesses for one another's families. Notably, godparents pledged to raise and educate children as Catholics—which means they had to possess sufficient knowledge to do so themselves.[134]

Choosing to celebrate the baptism of a former Protestant on an important feast day reinforced the role that the veneration of the saints played in Catholic religious life. December 8th, the Feast of the Nativity of the Virgin Mary, was a particularly popular choice for the celebration of baptism for female captives. The feast to honor the conception of the Virgin Mary, which is predicated on the dogma that she had been conceived without original sin, was loaded with obvious ritual symbolism for bringing female captives into the church. Bringing female captives forth in a symbolic "rebirth" after the corruption of heresy was a fitting way to celebrate the feast in New France. This connection is evident in the timing of the baptisms of Mary Plaisted and her two daughters, which all took place on the Feast of the Nativity of the Virgin Mary in 1693, but in two different churches. This coincidence suggests it was the date, not the family connection, that drove the decision to baptize these women on the same day.[135] The fact that Deborah and Mary Cole, two young girls from Saco, were baptized together on December 8th, 1703, supports the idea that the day was singled out for sacramentally welcoming female Protestants into the captive church.[136]

In baptism, all five of these captives now bore the name "Marie," presumably in honor of the Virgin Mary and her feast. Mary Plaisted and one of her daughters already possessed the English version of the name, but the fact that they kept them was unusual, as most captives either took or received names unconnected to their Protestant natal identities. Certainly "Marie" was an extremely popular name in New France. First-born daughters frequently bore it in honor of the Virgin Mary and her perceived power to protect the young.[137] But frequently their subsequent sisters did as well, and it was left to a distinctive middle name to differentiate female children from one another. The conventional names for women in French Catholic culture were frequently paired with Marie, yet Charlotte, Louise, Madeleine, Thérèse, Marguerite, Jeanne, and Françoise were also popular, with French women born in Canada and New England alike bearing them. The fact that all three Plaisteds emerged from Catholic baptism with some variant of Mary suggests that the day of their baptisms gave them a special connection with the Virgin. This connection, however, crossed the boundaries of baptism date, and even gender. Renaming a captive New Englander through Catholic baptism was a form of religious power. For those overseeing the baptism of Maine females, the use of the name "Marie" created an obvious bond with the Virgin Mary, as if the Virgin herself bore responsibility for redeeming these new coreligionists from "*esclavage de l'hérésie calviniste*" (the slavery of Calvinist heresy). The name was used for rebaptized males as well. Coupling it with the name of a male saint who had a particular connection to the French was a double honor. In taking the name "Louis-Marie," Charles Trafton of York was thus renamed after two great Franco-Catholic protectors, the Virgin Mary and King Louis IX, the thirteenth-century French crusading monarch and canonized saint. For those who were born English, had spent their early years speaking English, and had, in many cases, strong memories of their birth culture, it could also serve as a constant reminder *to them* that Providence had brought them to New France.

When onetime captive Protestants emerged into French colonial society as acculturated French Catholics, they lived lives that ran the gamut of colonial experience. They could be found on farms, in workshops and convents, and in the grand stone homes of the New French elites. These onetime New Englanders, however, were prone to seeking each other out. Recognizing this tendency, *canadien* captors created a system of alliance among converted captives who had passed through the process of religious acculturation. By encouraging rebaptized New Englanders to act as godparents and to witness marriages and other important religious rites of passage that involved Catholic sacraments, captors mimicked the idealized form, minus the theology, of New England community religious life. This privilege afforded to the rebaptized allowed them to sustain a fragment of New England life: relationships with family, friends, and neighbors who shared their cultural roots and memories.

Focusing on captive women from all areas of New England, Barbara Austen has demonstrated the range of female kinship networks that these captives relied upon during their captivities.[138] Maine Protestants also formed links across gender lines. These connections preserved some remnant of family and neighbor ties left behind. They also created new families and, through the use of Catholic sacramental life, new forms of fictive kinship. The networks that linked these ex-Protestants are most evident in the extensive and thorough sacramental records of Canada's Catholic churches. These records tell the stories of the rebaptized who became active in the spiritual lives of others. Baptism was the key to this form of community participation. Captives who embraced the Church of Rome earned the privilege that most Catholics in French Canada enjoyed: full participation in a critical form of community life. In contrast, those who resisted baptism were restricted not only from their families and friends, but from the ceremonies and related activities that added shape and substance to the lives of colonial people. Baptism therefore served simultaneously as a unifying force for captives who had assented to it and a wedge between captives who converted and those who did not. It created fictive kinships, based on sacrament, with other New Englanders while simultaneously blurring the lines between blood kin and spiritual kin, encouraging Catholics to bond with converts to whom they were not related by blood or marriage and reorienting them away from family who remained steadfast in their Protestantism.

The sacramental connections of Mary Storer St. Germaine of Wells open a window on a wider circle of New England connections. When Mary wrote to family in Wells and Boston, she sent the regards of Aaron Littlefield, also originally of Wells, who now lived a short distance away in Chambly.[139] Several members of Mary's extended French family, the Gaulthiers, served as godparents to several of Aaron's children.[140] The husband of Mary's cousin, Priscilla, witnessed two of the three French marriages of New Hampshire captive Paul Otis, including his union with Elizabeth Weber of Purpooduck.[141] Converted New England Protestants like Mary St. Germaine were channels through which the alien nature of Catholicism, hitherto the religion of enemies, was rendered more palatable and familiar to others. This was also the case with Cape Porpoise's Anne Odiorne Batson. Anne and her distant cousin Abigail Cass Turbet were members of one of Cape Porpoise's original families when they were taken captive in 1703 during Queen Anne's War. When Abigail neared death several years later, Anne, who had converted shortly after her captivity, kept vigil over her deathbed and served as witness for the three sacraments that Abigail received—baptism, penance, and unction—before expiring. Stephen Williams, a captive from Deer -

field and the adolescent son of minister John, witnessed Anne and Abigail's prolonged bedside conversation about the step the dying woman was about to take. According to Williams, Père Meriel, who served as a de facto "chaplain to captives," found the conversation so moving that he recorded it in his diary.[142] Anne Batson performed the same deathbed service for Esther Jones, a captive of Northampton, Massachusetts. Those who gathered for Esther's death included Charles Trafton, the acculturated York captive, who witnessed her passing along with several French nuns.[143]

Anne Batson witnessed many sacramental ministrations to others and later partook in them herself. In 1705 she was married in the Catholic Church to another Maine captive, James Stilson, of Pemaquid. When a daughter was born to them, she like her mother was christened Anne. But here Anne Batson's perceived commitment to Catholicism becomes somewhat hazy, with her actions reflecting not just the religious culture of her newly professed faith, but also that of her old religious culture. Naming the baby Anne suggests many possible influences that bridged Protestant and Catholic practices. In Catholic late medieval England (as in other parts of Europe) it was common to name a baby girl Anne when the child was the result of a difficult (or surprising) pregnancy. The name honored Saint Anne, the mother of the Virgin Mary and the patron saint of the childless and of childbirth, whose cult in Europe was at its peak at the time of the English Reformation.[144] From the Protestant perspective, naming an oldest daughter after her mother was an established practice common to New England Protestants.[145] Though an appropriate name for a child from the perspective of both faiths, its use underscores the fact that rebaptized New Englanders moved through multiple religious cultures—a distinction few claimed in early America.

Baby Anne's older half-brother, born a few months into his mother's captivity and while she still professed Protestantism, bore the marks of captor culture much more strongly than did his Catholic sister, who was born after the parents became Catholics. This child received the highly suggestive name of Clement. This name was given to two other baby boys born to captives in the same captor household. As William Foster has noted, this suggests the name was forced on him by his mother's captors, as the name also happened to be that of the current pope.[146]

Rebaptism of adult New Englanders and Catholic baptism of their infants often proved temporary. For the Maine captives who returned and reestablished themselves as Protestants, Catholic baptism in captivity presented no obstacles to full social and religious reintegration. Marriage, in contrast, did introduce new complications, and bound onetime captives far more strongly to the captor colony. The subject of the next chapter, the sacrament of marriage in French Canada created religiously tangled family trees throughout the Eastward. One of the most complicated of these captive family trees involved Mary Austin, a captive from York, the Edmunds family from Pemaquid, and the Gibau family of Montreal. Mary, an older cousin of Aaron Littlefield, was eight years old when she was taken from York in the Candlemas raid of 1691/2.[147] In 1695 Mathew Cary reported to Massachusetts authorities that Mary was among "thos Remaining Still in hands of the French at Canada."[148] Her cousin Josiah Littlefield met with her during his own brief captivity in 1708. In a letter back to Maine, Littlefield noted that his four captive cousins, including Mary, Rachel and Priscilla Storer, as well as Mary Austin, were all in good health. Through their cousin, the captive women wished to "remember their duty to thear father and mother and their kind love to all thear friends and relations, hoping in god you are all well."[149] As described by Littlefield, the long-absent Mary Austin seemed impassive about her fate, accepting without further pleas that her life was now in French Canada. It is possible too Mary's attitude toward her captivity made her a model for her Storer cousins, who saw in their cousin's reorientation to French religion and colonial life a pattern for possible future happiness that did not require the challenges of redemption.

Unlike those who stayed in New France because there was no one to lobby for their return, Mary Austin came from a prominent and well-connected family. Her father, Matthew, was a militia captain and active in York County affairs. So was Mary's maternal grandfather, Captain John Littlefield. Furthermore, at the time she met Josiah she was not yet naturalized, which meant no legal impediments existed to block her return to New England. By the time she met with her cousin Josiah, she was twenty-six, not a French subject, and still unmarried. Nothing, except possibly religion and personal preference, bonded Mary Austin to Canada.

Why, then, did she persist in her life in New France? The most obvious answer is that she wanted to. Mary was only eight when taken, just one year older than Eunice Williams, the daughter of Deerfield, Massachusetts, minister John Williams and another permanently "un-redeemed captive." Like Eunice, the young Mary Austin had witnessed the failure of her father, a powerful man within the community, to protect his besieged family.[150] And also like Eunice, she remained with her captors during her formative years. Mary, however, spent only three years among the Wabanakis before being ransomed by François Hazeur, "marchand-bourgeois" of Quebec.[151] By the late 1690s Hazeur was one of the wealthiest and best-connected merchants in the colony. The contrast between the fragile settlement of York, completely destroyed in a short period of time, and Hazeur's house in the well-developed and fortified upper town of Quebec must have been striking.[152] For Mary, as for other captives from the towns to the East - ward, the points of contrast must have been profound, especially for the young and vulnerable. In addition, these religiously suffused environments demonstrated to New England women that females played important roles in New French religious culture. Statues, paintings, and female-led religious institutions filled with and staffed by women reinforced this perception.

As Mary Austin matured, so must have her awareness of other captives around her. Her 1710 marriage to Étienne Gibau (a joiner, who, though illiterate, was well connected) brought her into a close circle of French families interlaced with Maine captive connections.[153] The sacramental life of the Gibau family provided opportunities for additional interactions with the English Canadians. Madame Lestage, the former Esther Sayward and another York captive, was godmother to Mary's first child, Marie-Elisabeth. The marriage of another of Mary's daughters, Marie-Thérèse, was witnessed by Joseph-Daniel Maddox, a joiner and immigrant from England to New France who had also witnessed the marriages of Wells-born Aaron Littlefield and Matthew Farnsworth, a captive from Groton.[154] Maddox might have been an associate in trade with her husband, Gibau. Expanding the captivity circle was Mary's nephew in marriage, another Étienne Gibau, who married Marguerite Edmunds, the daughter of acculturated Pemaquid captives John and Mary Edmunds. Mary Austin Gibau's Montreal house was right next door to the Edmunds family home.[155]

These networks were fostered in the homes of the Catholic elites of New France: wealthy merchants like Hazeur, administrators like the devout Champigny and his wife, and officers of rank, with their wives and daughters. Many of these elite families shared a connection to a key priest, the Père Henri-Antoine Meriel, whose influence in the colony gave him the power to assist elites in furthering worldly, as well as spiritual, goals.[156] Would-be godparents, despite their titles in French colonial society, could always use the help maintaining their positions and influence within the government, military, and trade hierarchies. Captive sponsorship raised the prestige of elites in the eyes of their peers, but money and other economic favors one might assume they could give to their new spiritual charges were most likely reserved for the promotion of their own, often-numerous children. These godparents tended to belong to a deeply ambitious, unstable class in New France, one in which working to promote family honor and prestige was a full-time occupation.[157] But though they eventually left their spiritual children to their own worldly devices, *marraines* and *parrains* nevertheless played a key role in transitioning them into lives as French Catholics while improving their own standing in church and community.

Elites had other pragmatic connections to captives. Unlike devout *canadiens* of limited means, elites had the ability to court captives aggressively to a new religion, put them to productive labor, or both. When their captives proved spiritually resistant, these would-be *marraines* and *parrains* had to employ diverse means to convince them otherwise. Hannah's Swarton's captors, Jean Bouchart de Champigny, the Jesuit-educated intendant of New France, and his wife, Marie-Madeleine de Chaspoux, stand out as examples. Known for their religious fervor, and one of the most powerful couples in New France,

Champigny and Marie-Madeleine had the clout to ask priests and nuns to aid them in their efforts to convert Protestant captives. Each had a confessor priest, a clergyman who would be a consistent presence in their home, dispensing spiritual guidance, worldly advice, and absolution for sins. Champigny's connection to the Bureaux des Pauvres, his personal piety, and his willingness to house and, essentially, entertain captives as a first step toward conversion all reflected the realities of a man of means. When conversion failed, the Champignys had sufficient property to find work for recalcitrant heretical New Englanders.[158]

Religious affiliation clearly mattered less than labor potential to other captors. One was Agathe Saint-Père, who kept not only the Adams family of Wells, but Hannah and John Sheldon, Judah Wright and Warham Williams (all of Deerfield, Massachusetts), and another Mainer, Pendleton Fletcher of Saco. She used her captives for her own business enterprises, and contented herself with baptizing their infant children rather than engaging in heavy, possibly distracting proselytizing with adults who had valuable skills to contribute to Saint-Père's business enterprises.[159]

After redemption to New England, captives who had not been subjected to aggressive proselytizing (or had managed to resist it) had little invested in the French colony, and no doubt a good deal of anger and resentment toward it. They left when opportunity arose. Others, like Mary Plaisted, might have been more hesitant. Unlike Hannah Swarton, Mary Plaisted left no account of her perceptions of her experiences in French Canada. But evidence suggests that her temporary conversion to the Church of Rome was neither wholly genuine nor wholly practical, but something in between. Mary assented to baptism much more quickly than most adult captives from Maine, and this act gave her easy access to her children, thanks to the intervention of the Gauchet family, with whom she lived. And though she was baptized by another priest, Mary had managed to meet and make an impression on Père Meriel, the famed proselytizer. Meriel even asked after Mary a full sixteen years after she returned to Maine, sending his "commendations" to her when he exchanged letters with another ex-captive, Johnson Harmon.[160] Perhaps the memory resulted from her active engagement in religious affairs. If that was the case, Mary would have been in good company with other New Englanders. Other converted Protestants, like Grizel Otis Robitaille of New Hampshire, played an active role in lay affairs almost from the time of conversion, as had New England converts Anne Batson and Charles Trafton. Like Hannah Swarton, Mary also lived under the roof of a forceful model for Catholic female piety: her mistress, Catherine Gauchet, the widow of a French official. It was most likely Gauchet, a woman of means, who ransomed the Sayward/Plaisted trio and arranged for the girls to attend school at the Congrégation de Notre-Dame.[161] Her devotion to the Congrégation was so steadfast that she later took up residence in the convent.

The impetus to participate actively in New France's spiritual life also likely came from within the captives themselves. As William H. Foster notes, playing an active role in the church may also have been Mary's means of maintaining family ties with her older daughter, who was brought into the Catholic fold almost immediately.[162]

Despite similar circumstances, Hannah Swarton and Mary Plaisted responded in different ways to the reality of Catholicism's overarching presence in the captor culture. The circumstances that brought them to live among French Catholics, their varied responses to the beckoning of new religion, and the new life it offered reflect the diverse religious backgrounds, motives, and experiences of the Maine frontier's settlers.

✦   ✦   ✦

Whether baptized in captivity or not, redeemed captives were quickly reintegrated into New England religious and family life. Understood on both sides of the Christian coin to be *sous condition,* Catholic baptism that proved temporary was no more a permanent stain on a Protestant soul than it was for a committed Catholic convert to have been born in New England to heretical parents.

Upon her return, Mary Plaisted soon reestablished her role within her marriage, resuming married life with her husband and bearing him a child within a year of her redemption.[163] Why Mary resumed her proper New England Protestant domestic role after doing so much to integrate herself into the fabric of her Catholic captor society remains open to speculation. But her choice is less mysterious when viewed in the light of her status as a married woman whose husband continued to live on the Maine frontier. While James might have pursued a divorce from Mary on the grounds of abandonment if she had remained, by choice, in New France, Mary had no such option in Canada.[164] She was also blocked from remarrying in Canada unless she could prove that James had either successfully divorced her or died in her absence. And despite her ingratiation into the wealthy, comfortable Gauchet household and her proximity to her daughters, she had once known greater freedoms and enjoyed higher status as the wife of a freeman in Maine than she did as a servant in an elite French household.

Furthermore, the fundamental challenges of the early Maine frontier bred pragmatism in the face of adversity. For many captives, conversion was a way to render a terrible ordeal more manageable. A year after her redemption, Mary Plaisted was fined four shillings "for not attending ye public worship of God on ye Lords Day."[165] Her husband told the court that she had been ill on the day in question and paid the fine. Historians of frontier religion and captivity have suggested that this was an act of defiance against the established church, of homage to vestigial Catholicism, or disgust with religion in general.[166] Or perhaps the issue was with the Protestant minister, Samuel Moody, York's "spiritual dictator." His sermons about hell and the "howling, roaring, yelling [and] shrieking" of the damned might have awakened painful memories that were all too real for any of Maine's redeemed captives.[167]

With the onset of King William's War, it no doubt appeared to many Protestant New Englanders that Satan and his minions were no longer disembodied spiritual threats, but had taken physical form in the Eastern Wabanakis of Maine, their Catholic missionary priests, and their French allies. Though Hannah Swarton's "Narrative" credited the return of captives to the wonder-working and mercy of God, the number of captives who stayed among the French, or let down the guard of true religion while in captivity, challenged the narrative's lessons. Such cases were not publicized in New England, as they suggested disturbing weaknesses in Protestant fortitude at a time when religious foes seemed to have numbers, distance, crafty conversion strategies, and perhaps, most disturbingly, God's approval on their side.

Maine's underdeveloped communities were vulnerable to both physical attack and spiritual conquest. Their proximity to New France, the hostility of the Wabanakis, and their weak defenses made them ideal frontier targets. The sporadic presence of French trading partners, decades of interaction with local Wabanakis during times of peace, and the presence of Jesuits and other missionaries on Maine's northwestern and eastern frontiers provided the enemies of New England with ample opportunities to observe the spiritual poverty of many down east settlers. And, as Mather predicted, a surprising number of Mainers who were taken captive in the frontier violence that ensued did become "Satan's prey" when they adopted the alternative Christian vision that labeled all Protestants heretics. An ideal Puritan was, in all things, the antithesis of a Catholic—at least in the world of religious rhetoric. But the porous nature of early American borderlands gave Maine's settlers many opportunities to test the assumption.

When the Reverend John Norton and his Protestant cohort were taken captive at Fort Massachusetts during King George's War, they demonstrated how much they had learned from the experiences of decades of captives. They negotiated the following terms with their captors:

1. That we should be all Prisoners to the French, the [French] General promising the Savages should have nothing to do with us.
2. That the Children should live with their parents during the Time of their Captivity.
3. That we should all have the Privilege of being exchanged the first Opportunity that presented.[168]

These terms demonstrate that, between King William's War and the end of Dummer's War, Norton and his companions had clearly learned a few of the reasons why the French were such successful spiritual colonizers. What proved far less predictable over those decades was the lengths to which Maine settlers would go to retain their Protestant identity.

CHAPTER THREE

"Pits of Hell" and *"Ménages des anges"*

The Protestant Dilemma of Sacramental Marriage

The Treaty of Utrecht ended Queen Anne's War in 1713. Among its provisions, the treaty addressed the return of all prisoners seized in the war, including frontier captives. English settlers who had lost family to captivity and were aware of the stipulation no doubt looked forward to the imminent—and permanent—redemption of their loved ones.

Still, return was rarely immediate, especially for captives who had made life-changing decisions involving religion or family while in French Canada or Wabanakia. The processes to return the lucky and willing were often long and convoluted, with many requiring arduous case-by-case handling by colonial diplomats. Even when diplomatic efforts to redeem captives unfolded with ease, such transfers were subject to other impediments once the captives themselves were involved. Though many were eager to resume their lives as New England Protestants, others were ultimately indecisive about, reluctant about, or even hostile to leaving New France or, in a few cases, Wabanakia.

Some of the reluctant had established productive lives and identities as French colonists. Others even found themselves New Englanders again not by design but from the unpredictable circumstances and geopolitical realities of the constantly shifting borderlands between New England and New France. A significant number, however, did not return at all, or came only to visit without resettling in New England. When these unredeemed captives resurfaced under these circumstances, they had different names, family circumstances, cultural affinities, and religious affiliations.[1] And it was to these new identities, and with corresponding new family and religious connections in Catholic New France, that these Protestant-born New Englanders returned once their business among their kin had been concluded. To the Maine families whom they now willingly left behind, these events must have been a source of confusion and emotional pain.

When seized from their frontier families in childhood or adolescence, captives reached maturity under the guidance of their Catholic captors instead of their own Protestant parents. Their new names, new dress and habits, and new religion were sources of strength and communal affinity in Canada, yet made them aliens to their birth families. Still, many elements of New French and Catholic acculturation such as language, clothing, personal habits, and even rebaptism as Catholics could be undone. But when New Englanders further engaged with Catholic New France by entering into a sacramental marriage, they were forming relationships to the Catholic colony that could not be undone as easily. Though Protestants and Catholics had different views of the marriage ceremony (for Puritans, marriage was a civil contract; for Catholics, a sacrament), both faiths considered the unions to be indissoluble except in the most extreme cases. Thus even Protestants who married Catholics in captivity were considered, by both faiths, to be bound to their spouses until death.

It was through sacrament that Catholicism extended out beyond the borders of French Canada, binding diverse peoples from the peripheral areas of New England, and drawing them into a wider network of colonial Catholic people. These Catholics revered the sacraments and believed in their importance as connections to the sacred. But sacraments also had more worldly applications. In New France, every Protestant who abjured his or her birth religion and accepted Catholic sacraments represented an addition to the French colonies' settler numbers, a tiny population that was dwarfed by that of New England. For the Protestant families of these apostates, the marriage sacrament proved to be the most durable of these bonds, as well as the most problematic. The very existence of these marriages, and the expectations for procreation that went along with them, meant that many New England families had Catholic branches that would persist long after the death of the original convert captive. These realities complicated negotiations to bring a captive home, the patterns of inheritance within families, and the status of offspring within families. Sacramental marriages between Protestant-born New Englanders and Catholics highlight both the boundaries of Protestant parenthood and the long-term legacies of war that burdened Maine's English settlers for generations. The complications they introduced to frontier religious culture were among the most enduring.

Sacramental marriages presented frontier Protestants with a range of problems. For one, captive kin who married without securing the support of their parents were engaging in "self-marriages," a term applied to all marriages transacted without the permission, or in express opposition to the will, of one's parents.[2] Under Massachusetts law, marrying without parental consent was a prosecutable offense. Fueling the fire was that fact that, in the New England colonies, marriages that dispensed with the publication of banns and, by extension, parental knowledge and agreement, were unlawful, and could be punished by fine, public whipping, or, when the bride was younger than local laws allowed, imprisonment.[3] Parental approval of marriage choices made also good civic sense for Puritans, who saw basic compatibilities as the key to a functioning union. Ministers echoed popular public opinion, such as this anonymous homilist who asserted "the happiness of marige life consists much in that Persons being equally yoked draw together in a holy yoke . . . there must be sutable fitness for this Condition equality in birth, education, and religion."[4] Self-marriages further endangered New England civil order by stripping Protestant parents of some of their most cherished, God-ordained prerogatives: guiding children to a calling, encouraging and approving spouses for them (and by extension, the connections their future grandchildren would have), and conveying material wealth to them when they reached adulthood.[5] Throughout the English colonies, families who could not reconcile themselves to the unions created by self-marriage used the power of local courts to dissolve them.[6] In New England in particular, however, the power of parental authority was derived from a source higher than the courts. As Cotton Mather described it, family hierarchy was "the First Society, that by the Direction and Providence of God is produced among the Children of Men."[7] Similar in situation to Quakers and other Dissenters, but for different reasons, New England–born Puritans who married Catholics appeared to allow the dictates of conscience, or their own individual preferences, to trump obedience, which in turn subverted the natural godliness of parental authority. Puritans alleged that the new religious trends unleashed by unapproved, interfaith marriages would undermine the critical established hierarchies that demanded a wife's subordination to her husband and a child's subordination to its parents.[8]

Puritans marrying Catholics unhinged Puritan structures in more ways than one. But they came about due to complications on the side of the Catholicized Puritans that parental and civic authorities were unlikely to anticipate. Like their errant peers in New England, young women and men who married in captivity did indeed create their unions without the approval of their parents. But in part this resulted from the logistics of the situation, in which parents lacked access to the captive, and the captives themselves were far beyond the reach of New England's laws governing unauthorized marriages.[9] The sacrament of marriage in New France could occur only between two baptized Catholics.[10] Whereas baptism had a host of immediate physical rewards attached to it, a proper Catholic marriage was a considerably more involved spiritual process, usually involving a captive who had reached adulthood by the standards of both New England and New France.[11] Sacramental marriages took time and planning, and often came about with the guidance of Catholic *canadien* adults who assumed the parental role. Under these circumstances, marriage between a converted New Englander and a native French Catholic could be perceived as a religious act that reflected a conscious choice, as well as an act of sexual or social self-determination. Marriages that brought forth children also created new French subjects who, like their parents, were bound to the French colony by regulations regarding movement in and out of Canada. Ultimately, the sacrament of marriage added new Catholics to French Canada while fracturing the familial, civil, and religious relationships between Maine-born captives and their natal families. In some ways it created new freedoms; in others, new limitations.

Before the Treaty of Utrecht and other initiatives that returned captives to their points of origin, the marriage of a captive child in Canada could have been explained away by distressed Maine parents as a coerced perversion of marriage as defined by New England Protestant societies. But as years and then decades rolled on, and peace was established between the two colonies, the strength and constancy of these unions (and others created *after* the treaty's stipulations regarding New England captives became widely known) pointed to other realities that suggested an act of will on the captive's part. To marry in Canada meant that one must become a Catholic—*truly* a Catholic, who had been confirmed, was receiving the Eucharist according to Catholic rites, had married in the church according to proper sacramental protocols, and was prepared to present one's offspring for Catholic baptism. Family members who remained in Canada crossed the line that separated the unfortunate and debauched from the intrinsically corrupt and disobedient. New Englanders at various stages of captivity and redemption warned that this could happen, as John Williams's *Redeemed Captive Returning to Zion* attests.

Years became decades, and some Maine captives who through diplomacy were granted the right to return to Protestant New England failed to do so. To New Englanders, these unredeemed captives must have seemed irreparably lost to new Catholic families. Records left by or that mention these captives, however, register few hints of dissatisfaction with their new relationships and religious affinities. More in evidence is the sense that Providence had brought them to New France and shaped their futures in the Catholic colony. For Maine's English settlers to agree, however, would necessitate recognizing the validity of Catholic sacramental life, and accepting that God meant for their children, and their children's children, to be Catholics. Such recognition would challenge the English sense of godly purpose among Maine's settlers.

In this colonial existence, Philip Greven notes, "no individual was utterly alone and private; instead, each was always obligated by a series of relationships and connections that bound him to an ever-widening circle of people, from the most intimate and domestic ties to the ties of public life and religious duty"; in this context it is difficult to imagine a less desirable connection for a New England family than to "frenchified" Catholics.[12] Conversion to a form of Christianity that was feared and reviled in New England rhetoric, coupled with the attendant subversion of parental authority, could have, by right and principle, resulted in a clean break of bonds between these parents and their captive children. But this did not happen. Instead, most borderland families attempted to cope with the reality of captive Catholic kin without adopting a stance of religious relativism. In what became an early American twist in the convention "hate the sin, love the sinner," some Maine families who established contact with family members who had deviated from New England marriage and settlement patterns offered incentives for a return to rectitude and threatened punishments for continued defiance. These included material enticements and pleas for the one-time captive to remember his or her duty to family.

In spite of the implicit disobedience of those who had made critical life decisions on their new religion's terms, and the alien guises of these visiting kin, Protestant Mainers struggled to engage the complex and enigmatic figures who briefly entered their lives with requests for familial recognition and affection. The interactions between unredeemed captives and their New England kin demonstrate that the process of religious encounter initiated in the borderlands lasted long after the religious enemies themselves were subdued or vanquished. The eighteenth century saw a hardening of the ideological and geographical borders of faith. But Maine families with unredeemed captives among them experienced a sustained encounter that kept these emotional lines persistently vague and undefined for decades.

A Tale of Two Siblings: The Storers of Wells and Montreal

In his classic study of generational changes in American slavery, Ira Berlin observed that history is the study of changing relationships.[13] In the case of Maine's rebaptized New Englanders, these changes unfolded slowly, brought about by the rare opportunities for contact that borderland entanglements permitted. The relationships within one of these families, the Storers of Wells, who had three captive family members, provide several points of departure for examining the changing relationships created by religious conversion, the acceptance of further sacraments culminating in marriage, unredeemed captivity, and the vagaries of imperial politics.

Wells had been the target of French and Indian raids several times before the turn of the eighteenth century, and it organized its defenses to face frontier threats effectively. As a result, it was one of the few settlements to the Eastward to remain populated after King William's War.[14] Along with other large and important local families like the Wheelwrights and the Littlefields, the Storers had called Wells home for decades and were reluctant to evacuate. The garrisons of these three families alone could house half of Wells's population in times of crisis.[15]

But on August 10, 1703, Wells fell to an intense assault by a combined force of Wabanakis and French.[16] Thirty-nine New Englanders were killed or taken captive. Among them were three members of the Storer family: Mary, the eighteen-year-old daughter of Joseph and Hannah Storer; and Rachel and Priscilla, seventeen and nine respectively, the daughters of Joseph's brother Jeremiah and Ruth Storer.

The attack on Wells came early in the conflict known as Queen Anne's War, the second conflict with France to leave an indelible mark of sorrow on frontier families. At the end of King William's War, New France had established its position as a formidable military and political force in North America. New Englanders, and Maine's settlers in particular, were charged with defending themselves. Though this new conflict between the New World's European Christians would ultimately end with the French North American empire in an ambiguous position, and the English claiming significant territorial gains in Acadia that stretched all the way to the central Maine coast, it still resulted in ambiguous understandings of colonial boundaries and alliances. Most importantly, the Treaty of Utrecht, which ended the conflict, left the border between New England and New France again subject to local interpretation. This uncertainty would wreak havoc on Maine on at least one occasion and set the stage for Dummer's War.

Like King William's, Queen Anne's War began with an imperial crisis of European origin. The death of the mentally and physically feeble Spanish king, Carlos II, passed the crown to his French cousin, Philip, duke of Anjou, grandchild of Louis XIV and potential heir to the French throne as well. The prospect of these two colossal powers unified terrified most of the rest of western Europe, Protestant and Catholic alike. The conflict on the European side of the Atlantic, known there as the War of Spanish Succession, was an attempt to prevent or contain the power of a united Franco-Spanish crown and, in the colonial world, prevent expansion of French and Spanish territorial claims to North America that also blocked English expansion. Between 1699 and 1702, the French moved to cement their claims to Louisiana, which by their calculation spanned the land from the Gulf of Mexico to the Great Lakes. The French reified these claims by establishing forts at Biloxi, Mobile, and Detroit.[17] The ever-growing population of Maine provided a potential threat to these ambitions. Friction between England and France provided an opportunity to reassert alliances with the Wabanakis, test the peace established with the Iroquois, and demonstrate their intolerance of English incursions into conflicting northern land claims.[18] Within the region resettled after six years of relative peace, Maine's coastal settlements remained prime targets for those who wanted to counter English expansion.

Maine's English knew this, and attempted to broker peace with the Wabanakis at Canso. When the effort faltered, however, it opened the door for the French and Eastern Indians to reestablish common cause and launch additional attacks on the Eastward communities. This happened during six bloody days in August 1703, when a force of five hundred French and Indians sacked Wells, Cape Porpoise, Winter Harbor, Scarborough, Purpooduck, and Falmouth. Over one hundred settlers were killed, and many others were taken captive.[19] Less than six months later, Deerfield, a frontier town in western Massachusetts, was caught off guard and virtually obliterated. Other raids targeted communities throughout northern New England, including Amesbury, Dover, Exeter, Groton, Haverhill, Northampton, Oyster River, and Westfield.[20] These frontier depredations led to another draining of the frontier communities, with refugees again fleeing for safety.

Aware of Maine's strategic importance and wealth of economic resources, New Englanders actively defended their regional claims. This determination reached beyond simple strategic targets to ones that challenged a religious culture of Protestantism as well. Favorite among these were Maine's Jesuit missions, places believed to encourage and reinforce Wabanaki anger toward the English and their settlements. Determined to end the problem, a force of primarily Maine Englishmen under Winthrop Hilton attacked the mission at Norridgewock in 1705. The Englishmen rendered the entire complex uninhabitable and made particular targets of its religious identity enshrined in its church and chapel.[21] At the same time, the French settlers who lived in relatively isolated pockets on the Maine/Acadia coast were the targets of Benjamin Church, the "old Indian fighter," and his militia. Alone and unprotected, these settlers surrendered quickly and likely surrendered their claims to the area.[22]

Such successes emboldened New Englanders to revisit the 1690 plan to conquer all nearby French Canada, a strategy that pursued the enemy at the seat of empire instead of at far-flung frontier outposts. Captain Samuel Vetch, a merchant and relative newcomer to New England, became the strategy's outspoken advocate. Vetch used his knowledge of the French colony (acquired not only through two other planned invasions, but from engaging in illegal trade with French as well) to formulate a new invasion plan, which he presented to the Board of Trade in London. Enthusiasm for the plan grew. In 1710 Vetch captured Port Royal and permanently secured Acadia for the British. Emboldened by this conquest, the British committed more resources toward taking the even bigger prize of Quebec. A larger force combining imperial troops under Sir Hovenden Walker and colonials under Vetch was assembled for this operation. But it failed when bad weather and inexperience with the treacherous St. Lawrence claimed eight hundred lives. Another initiative, to seize Montreal using allied Iroquois groups, ended with fewer English casualties but much frustration.[23]

Stalemate, exhaustion, and limited resources brought the French and English to the bargaining table in 1713. Though French losses were steep (Acadia, Hudson Bay, Newfoundland, and half of St. Kitts were all surrendered), the Acadia that the French turned over remained poorly defined.[24] After Utrecht's ratification, complications quickly arose. The French continued to place the southern boundary of Acadia, now Nova Scotia, at the Kennebec River. New Englanders insisted the true boundary lay at the St. Croix River, considerably farther east. The people who knew the complicated geography of the upper Maine coast best—the Wabanakis and their French Jesuit missionaries—reinforced Indian and French claims by returning to the Kennebec and rebuilding their mission. And in the English settlements that remained after Queen Anne's War, families awaited the return of their surviving captives, many of whom had lived among Catholics for almost a decade.

While most of these anticipated returns eventually happened, some never did, and others came about under unanticipated circumstances. It took Mary Storer almost a dozen years after the Peace of Utrecht—and a full twenty-two since her capture—to return to her Protestant New England family. In 1725 she and another of the 1703 captives, Aaron Littlefield, received permission from the New French government to "*voir ses parents et régler ses affaires domestiques*" (see their parents and put their personal affairs in order).[25] They traveled to Maine in the company of Madame Lestage (Esther Sayward, the comfortably married daughter of Mary Plaisted) and Jean-Baptiste Dagueil, a sergeant in the French army and an experienced emissary for New France to neighboring English colonies who was also the husband of Mary's cousin Priscilla.[26] All of these cultural and religious apostates planned to visit only; none intended to stay.

Mary, who in Catholic baptism and marriage had become Marie St. Germaine, used her time in New England to visit her parents and siblings, in particular her younger brothers, Ebenezer and Seth. Her reflections on this visit, recorded in later correspondence, betray a particular affection for Ebenezer and Seth, the younger brothers she undoubtedly had cared for as little boys.[27] Also retained (in contrast to many New England captives) was Mary's knowledge of and ability to write and speak in English.[28] Mary's ease with English and ability to express her emotions is one contributing factor to the value of the family's correspondence, as it gives scholars a rare glimpse into the interior lives, emotional complexities, and range of interactions of a New England family separated by distance, fate, and religion.[29] Mary's letters, however, suggest as many questions as they answer. Chief among these are Mary's motives for reestablishing contact with her Protestant family. Though her letters are filled with heartfelt claims of love for the New England Storers, the fact remains that she waited more than a decade after the Peace of Utrecht to reestablish her ties with them. More importantly, why did she not come home after the treaty seemingly granted her freedom of movement between New France and New England?

Part of the answer might lie in the specific details of Mary Storer's borderland experience. The 1703 attack on Wells through which the young Mary lived demonstrated the very real vulnerability of Maine's English settlements. Late seventeenth- and early eighteenth-century Wells was a challenging, often frightening place for children. When Mary was six, she undoubtedly saw the survivors of the Candlemas massacre as they stumbled, stunned and wounded, into Wells to beg for help and shelter. Many took refuge in the Storer family's garrison. Given the general lack of privacy in most frontier homes this meant that the little girl was likely exposed to the survivors' descriptions of their terrifying ordeals. Mary likely experienced some of this terror herself when Wells successfully repulsed its own attack four days later.[30] And she, along with everyone else, must have been severely disquieted when George Burroughs, the town's minister, was accused of witchcraft and associated crimes (including the murder of two of his wives through supernatural means) and was taken into custody at her family's garrison.[31]

Wells's families took whatever steps they could to guard themselves. The town became a military zone, its population swelled by soldiers and experienced frontier fighters, whose ranks included Mary's father and uncle, Joseph and Jeremiah Storer.[32] Still, it remained isolated from regular contact with other frontier communities, most of which had been destroyed or severely depopulated during the previous round of hostilities with the Wabanakis and French.[33] But despite all its efforts, the town was unable to withstand the force of a coordinated French and Indian attack in the summer of 1703. Samuel Penhallow, a contemporary chronicler of the New England frontier wars, described its end: Wells "suffered great spoil, nor could it escape the loss of 39 that were killed or taken."[34]

To Mary, the infiltration of the family garrison and fortified town leading to her captivity must have impressed upon her that preparation, fighting skill, and zeal guaranteed nothing in the face of determined enemies. The towns of French Canada in which she soon found herself, however, lacked those fragilities intrinsic to frontier communities. In stark contrast to Wells, the Montreal to which Mary was quickly ransomed must have appeared stable, safe, prosperous, and protected.[35] Such an environment may have held an immediate attraction for a frontier girl who had already experienced so much fear and witnessed so much destruction.

Mary's stay among the Indians was brief, as were those of her two young cousins, Priscilla and Rachel Storer, so the girls' formative years were spent chiefly among the French, who were practiced in coaxing young Protestant females toward acculturation.[36] Mary had the particular good fortune to be ransomed by Pierre Boucher, master of one of the most prosperous *seigneuries* in all of Canada.[37] The wealthy, well-connected Bouchers offered assurances of physical stability that the Maine Storers of the early eighteenth century could scarcely match. Like other elite *canadiens,* Pierre Boucher and his family took a particular interest in New England Protestants. It was Boucher's son, Jean-Baptiste Boucher de Niverville, who became Mary's godfather when she was baptized by the ubiquitous Père Meriel in February 1704.[38] Members of the Boucher family, including the seigneur Pierre, attended Mary's wedding four years later. The man Mary would eventually marry, Jean Gaulthier *dit* St. Germaine, was a prosperous young Boucherville farmer connected to the seigniorial family.[39] Children quickly followed, and the family prospered. By 1725 a Storer family acquaintance and ex-captive, Theodore Atkinson, attested that Mary was "very well marryed . . . & Lives very Grandly."[40]

Shortly after Atkinson made this observation, Mary returned to her Protestant family. She spent a month among them, visiting parents and siblings. The record of her visit describes a warm and happy reunion. Yet it also describes tension, born of Mary's new religion, and her refusal to return permanently to Protestant New England.

In goods and comforts, however, Mary's lifestyle was compatible with her prosperous New England relatives. As a woman in an early modern colonial society, Mary had an economic and social standing within her own community that bore strong similarities to that of her New England family, particularly those relatives of her own generation, who had learned to turn frontier vulnerabilities into worldly successes. Ebenezer had become a prominent Boston merchant; Seth had entered the ministry and been ordained to a pulpit in Massachusetts. As a woman who had married into a well-connected elite family, Mary was at least their equal, and, arguably, their superior.

Though Mary's journey toward comparative prosperity began involuntarily, it followed an established pattern of migration, also blazed by Ebenezer and Seth, that took their generation off the Maine frontier and into colonial metropoles.[41] Like many of his peers, Ebenezer pursued his fortune not in the Eastward but in Boston. He left Maine to attend Harvard College. Remaining in Boston, he seized opportunities to move his home province's indigenous goods into the wider Atlantic World and, in the process, made a fortune for himself.[42] Like his sister, he lived very grandly, turning a handsome profit from his home province's bountiful resources. Ebenezer also married well and with his wife, Mary Edwards, and eight children, lived in a large home in the center of Boston, complete with extensive gardens. Family portraits by John Singleton Copley proclaim that this generation of Storers had risen above their relatively humble Maine origins.[43] In addition to acquiring worldly wealth, Ebenezer pursued civic and, like his sister and other brother, spiritual riches. He served as a justice

Figure 6. Ebenezer Storer, by John Singleton Copley (ca. 1767–69). Courtesy of the Metropolitan Museum of Art/Art Resource, NY.

of the peace, an overseer of the poor, and a church warden. When he died a wealthy man in 1761, Ebenezer was remembered publicly for his "kindness, charity, and devotion to good works."[44]

Seth Storer also left Maine for Massachusetts, where he studied at Harvard, was ordained, and remained. At twenty-five he received the comfortable pulpit of Watertown, Massachusetts, where he served as minister for fifty years.[45] In 1734 he married Mary Coney, with whom he led the stable life of a Congregational minister whose abilities had secured him a pulpit for life. The sole controversial moment of his career involved his refusal to invite George Whitefield to speak at his church. In doing so, Seth showed he preferred the stern stability of Old Light religion to New Light's emotionalism.[46] It is tempting to speculate that his preferences were influenced by the spiritual relativism his sister introduced into the Storer family.

Mary Storer's passage into adulthood paralleled her brothers' conventional, consistent, and comfortable lives. Life in eighteenth-century Montreal was comfortable for its elites, who built themselves large, sturdy, warm stone houses in locations that gave them easy access to the city's places of business, and for social purposes, other elites.[47] Mary's house also would have been surrounded by churches and religious establishments in which Mary regularly participated in the sacraments and dutifully presented each new baby for baptism.[48] As her husband would later attest, Mary was ideally suited to all the demands of elite women in New France, a perfect helpmeet who made their home a *"ménage des anges"* (household of the angels).[49]

In terms of economic and personal success, Providence seemed to have blessed this generation of Storers. But seasoned by religious differences and prejudices, Mary's successes were a function of perspective. To her family, Mary's successes in marriage and material wealth must have appeared to come at a great price—her acceptance of Catholicism, and participation in its rites and liturgies. As postvisit correspondence between Mary and her family demonstrates, this difference created a nearly insurmountable barrier despite other fundamental compatibilities—of parentage, social status, marriage, and parenthood—which defined their lives. And though it did not result in outright rejection, it did leave Mary's family with the task of assigning a role to her, suitable to the unusual nature of her religious trajectory and appropriate for their own level of comfort. Family entreaties to her to return to New England and Protestantism, however, demonstrate a lack of knowledge of the level to which participation in sacraments bound Catholics, as well as their children, to French colonial culture.

It fell to Seth Storer to take a leading role in attempting to bring his sister back to true religion.[50] Though he ultimately failed, he did succeed in leaving her with a good deal of spiritual discomfort. From Rhode Island, Mary wrote of these effects to Seth:

> I had but litel time with you who I thought woulde show and teach me more then eney bodey sir but what you have saide to me I will not for gett it and I hope god will in able me in all my afflictions and that it may be for the best and good of my soule deare brother doe not for get me in youre prayers which I hope will be a counfort to me and what eure paines and trouble I have and shall have in all my jorney . . . I hope god will have merce on me and help me.[51]

Perhaps Mary was truly disturbed. Or she might have been telling the family what she thought they wanted to hear: that her life as a captive had been one long affliction, and that persisting in the path assigned her was an act of resignation, not will. Or, as Seth's biographer has argued, her decision may have been little more than a hedged bet: "[Seth] was at a hopeless disadvantage in this matter, for, as a Puritan, he had to admit that sect alone was no bar to salvation, but Mary had learned in Canada that heresy was automatic damnation. Naturally she played it safe."[52]

What such an assessment overlooks, however, is that Mary's sacramental marriage in the Catholic Church and status as a subject of the French monarchy bound her to French law and custom. In a colony where Protestantism was still outlawed, a married woman like Mary would have had little choice but to remain a Catholic, or to conform outwardly to Catholicism. Negotiating to repatriate captives after the Treaty of Utrecht, the French agreed to the English demand that "English women should not be compelled to tarry with their French husbands."[53] Children and movable goods from these marriages, however, were to remain in the colony. Returning to New England, therefore, would have required Mary to leave her home, spouse, and children, as well as the security of a comfortable existence in New France in order to lead a dependent life as a single woman among people who were beloved, yet still strangers.[54] The union wrought by the sacrament of marriage had given Mary much of her identity, just as it would have for many other colonial women, regardless of their faith. She was better situated as a wife and mother, albeit a Catholic one in New France, than she would have been as just a sister or daughter in a Protestant New England family.

Such realities of women's roles in colonial society were fairly uniform among colonial Euro-Americans. Mary's interactions with her family suggest, however, that when a woman converted to an unpopular religion, and was dependent on her new identity to maintain her status, she was regarded as corrupt, and perhaps more importantly, corrupt of her own accord. In addressing her "deare brother," Ebenezer, Mary hints at a conversation between the siblings that raised these uncomfortable issues. Sister told brother, "I remember what you have saide to me I thanke you and all that has spoek for my goode."[55] Others had joined in the effort, with Seth lending his ministerial experience to the discussions and Ebenezer providing his sister with a pious book as a reminder of their conversations. Thanking him for this tactile reminder of her Protestant roots, Mary reassured Ebenezer that she would put the book to use "for my good."[56]

"For my good." The phrase appears several times in Mary's letters to her Protestant brothers. It seemingly offered assurances that she was sympathetic to their arguments for her well-being. Yet despite these rhetorical acknowledgments that her best interest lay elsewhere, she remained faithful to her own post-captivity life course. Placed squarely between her Catholic present and Protestant past, the best Mary could do was reiterate her gratitude for their concern for her soul and welcome their prayers for the good of her soul—even if these prayers came from those who professed Calvinist heresies.

Failing to turn his sister back to New England, Ebenezer applied his efforts to the next generation. During Mary's visit to Boston, Ebenezer discussed with her the possibility of taking one of the St. Germaine sons to live with him and learn his business. A Boston business connection of this caliber would have been a good one for the Quebec family, and the arrangement was a common one among colonial families. Had this happened among the Storers and St. Germaines, however, it would have placed the Protestant brother in charge of the nephew's soul as well as his body, guaranteeing that the boy would at least have some exposure to the Protestantism that his mother had sadly lost.[57]

Other methods were also deployed to pull the errant Mary more closely to her family. Ebenezer's third child, a daughter, was born during Mary's visit and named in honor of her aunt. Mary was clearly flattered: her subsequent letters refer lovingly to "little cosine mary who is my name sake." Her hope for the parents, to "have the comfort to see her a woman grone," is poignantly reminiscent of her own years of maturing among strangers.[58]

Theological and intergenerational ties aside, Mary went against family assertions that were "for her good." She returned to Canada—to her marriage to a stranger to her family, to Catholicism, to her persona as Marie St. Germaine—and once again became a stranger. And though Mary had proved to be a good French subject by obeying the terms of her *pérmis,* she does not appear to have applied for additional visiting privileges. Storer family hopes for redeeming part of Mary's line suffered another setback in 1727, when Mary wrote to Ebenezer that her son, who possessed so much promise for restoring a Protestant line of Storers derived from Mary, was "not willing to goe from us."[59]

The final challenge to acknowledge the apostate Storer sister came after the death of Joseph Storer, the family patriarch, in the winter of 1729–30. When Joseph made a will in 1721, he virtually disinherited Mary, leaving her ten shillings—a paltry 1 percent—of the patrimony that was promised to her other sisters, if she refused to come home.[60] If she returned, however, she would be rewarded with a full

Figure 7. This daughter of Ebenezer Storer was likely named after her aunt, Mary Storer St. Germaine. *Mrs. Edward Green (Mary Storer),* by John Singleton Copley (1765). Courtesy of the Metropolitan Museum of Art/Art Resource, NY.

share of fifty pounds, an amount identical to that promised to her New England sisters.

In the intervening years between the creation of his will and his death, Joseph had seen his daughter again, spoken to her, and undoubtedly learned about the life that kept her bound to Canada. Whether unmoved or simply forgetful, Joseph Storer did not change his will after becoming reacquainted with his daughter. After Joseph died, however, Mary persisted in the belief that he had and pressed her siblings for the fifty pounds she considered to be her rightful share.[61] It was over this issue that the hope of restored family bonds created by the 1725 visit ended, to be replaced by a dispute over the terms of the will, and Mary's conflation of recognition with a full share of her patrimony.

The ensuing family altercation illustrates the limits of tolerance for profound religious differences among family members. Mary Storer St. Germaine and her French family were worthy of recognition through correspondence, but not in the more tangible form New En - gland Protestants provided for their good children—patrimony. The gatekeeper to this higher form of recognition was Ebenezer Storer, who opted for a strict interpretation of his father's will. He therefore refused to let the fifty pounds pass into Catholic hands. This surprised and angered Mary, who defended her claim to her brother, asserting, "We are al the same blode you can not denie it."[62] She then took her case to their mother, Hannah, asserting, "My brother Ebenezer wright to me that my deare father maide his will that I may be equall to my sisters you may belive my deare mother why I am far frome you and my deare familie I belive that is for me who is youre one childe."[63] Perhaps Hannah tried to intervene, but Ebenezer never - theless persisted in refusing the recognition of full family communion that inheritance validated. Months later he reiterated his determination to honor his father's religious bias by insisting to his sister, "I . . . will do any thing yt is proper if it be not against ye will of our Father."[64]

As with any dutiful Puritan son, it was natural for Ebenezer to uphold his father's judgment, even when the father in question no longer lived. In addition, the terms of New England wills were not easily—or legally—ignored. But Mary's physical separation from her family meant that she never had to know the terms of the will. Clearly someone had apprised her of its basic terms, which left fifty pounds for each of Joseph's daughters. Certainly Ebenezer had the means to give the money to his sister himself, an act that would have respected his father's will and made his sister feel invested as a Storer family equal. But he did not. Instead, he used the terms of the will as an opportunity to demonstrate his own feelings about his religiously wayward sibling. Mary's value as a Storer was materially diminished by her unredeemed status, her commitment to Catholicism, and the many entanglements of religious identity and participation that came with it. This outweighed her status as a well-married, and pious, wife and mother: achievements of virtue for Protestant women, liabilities for Catholics born of Protestant families.[65]

Mary's push to receive her portion of Joseph's will seems rooted in a need for recognition rather than a concern over money. She sought recognition of her status within the Storer family, of the misfortunes she had turned to her advantage, of her marriage and children, of the affection and charity implicitly confirmed by inheritance, and of the God common to Protestants and Catholics alike, which such a bequest would have implied. But given the persistence of Mary Storer as Marie St. Germaine, even in the face of personal contact, arguments, and letters, it was perhaps asking for more religious tolerance than the New England Storers were capable of giving. She was eventually forced to settle for polite discourse and tepid expressions of filial affection.[66]

When Mary died in 1747, her *canadien* husband, Jean Gaulthier, related the sad news to her New England kin. Jean wrote to Ebenezer that Mary had died "*en parfaite chretienne*" (in a perfect Christian manner).[67] This observation must have been galling to Ebenezer, who likely scoffed at the idea that his sister's husband knew what Christian perfection entailed. Though Jean would write to him several more times, Ebenezer was a less than enthusiastic correspondent, having little enthusiasm for the Frenchman's assertions that it was God himself who had handed Mary, his "*une des meilleur femmes du Monde,*" over to French Catholicism.[68]

In life, Mary Storer St. Germaine failed to conform to Protestant expectations of embracing true religion and obedience to her parents. The transgressions of religion and marriage which, through French law and religious structure, could not be easily undone, placed her in a category of family relations that constituted neither acceptance nor rejection. Catholics and Protestants continued to encounter each other throughout Maine's colonial period because of captive conversion and durable sacramental marriages, but the modes and byproducts of contact demonstrate that these interactions did not lead to comprehensive accommodation or understanding.

Catholic sacraments, and, as the case of Mary Storer demonstrates, the sacrament of marriage that Catholicism demanded, were technically and spiritually problematic for Maine families. Unions created by the sacrament of marriage fractured religiously diverse families. But deeply rooted ideas about the prerogatives of Protestant parenthood made their children and their new connections offensive in the sight of God. Part of the problem lay in the nature of the New England family, a primary vessel of religious culture and the paramount social unit of the community.[69] Family was the single most important bridge between religion and society, and the structure of its relationships was considered analogous to God's omnipotence over all living things. Parents claimed from their children the same love and fear that all Puritans were expected to give to God.[70] Even though many Mainers were not orthodox Puritans, elements of the classically Puritan conflation of family as a dispenser of religious experience and as intolerant of family religious deviations—in both private devotions and public worship—could be seen in families of other colonial Protestant denominations, including Quakerism and Anglicanism.[71]

But when Protestant family bonds transcended borders and cultures, the ability to use fear to compel obedience was lost. Parents' efforts to bend these children to their will and ensure that they lived lives in accordance with Protestant principles were thwarted by distance, inaccessibility, and new kinships (voluntary and involuntary) that captives formed within captor society. For Maine's English Protestants, a relative who became a papist through baptism and then took steps that virtually guaranteed that he or she would stay a papist had abdicated the familial rights that dutiful Protestant children enjoyed.

Redemption from the Pit of Hell: The Sacramental Ordeal of Rachel Storer

Few New England families had first-hand knowledge of the extremely complicated world in which Canadian captives found themselves — a world that facilitated the captive's acceptance of a new religion and the creation of new kinship ties. Little is known of the processes, decisions, or interactions that created Marie St. Germaine from the former Mary Storer, but much more evidence exists documenting the process for Rachel Storer, who, like her cousin, engaged in Catholic sacramental life beyond baptism and into marriage. The details of Rachel's connections made through sacrament led to a very different sequence of choices, hazards, and, in some cases, manipulations young New Englanders encountered as they attempted to navigate the spiritual terrain of a new religious culture. A Protestant convert's compliance in partaking in the sacrament of marriage with a French subject had potential civil, political, or diplomatic implications. As the events of Rachel's life show, sacramental marriage in New France could be complicated by additional, though ultimately less than sacred, factors that took advantage of the indissolubility of the sacramental marriage bond in French Catholic society. Allowing marriage to be trumped by colonial diplomacy was all but unthinkable, as it would not only subvert French assertions that ex-Protestants were happier as Catho - lics, but would also challenge the immutability of sacraments conferred by the church. Nevertheless, a welter of issues of European political origin had the potential to reach across the Atlantic and, in ways unforeseen by Euro-Americans throughout the colonies, shape and even upend prevailing religious norms. In Rachel Storer's case, the sacrament of marriage ultimately became the catalyst (as opposed to a deterrent, as it was for Mary) of her return to the Protestant fold.

Before that happened, however, Rachel found herself navigating an alien, often unforgiving world of sexually aggressive French soldiers, ambitious colonial elites, zealous Canadian officials, and clergy. Like other youths in similar circumstances, crossing the divides of culture and faith presented Rachel with a specific set of challenges. Because many of Maine's captives were young children when taken, they were the easiest targets for cultural and religious conversion. Unlike older captives, they remembered little or nothing of New England and their birth families. In terms of French colonial law and the church, *canadien* families were structured no differently than their New England counterparts. But French custom and tradition, along with the added layer of New World encounter, led to the development of more permissive forms of parenting in New France.[72] Diverse European observers, from the Jesuit Charlevoix to the eighteenth-century Protestant travel writer Peter Kalm, observed that the New World French raised their children "in the manner of the savages," giving them wide latitude and personal freedom.[73] For captive children this translated to a wider range of personal freedoms than they likely would have enjoyed among their New England natal families. By harnessing these parenting styles, captor-surrogates did their duty to their colony by working to supplant the captive's love for his or her biological parents with an attachment to his or her new surroundings.[74]

Catholic clergy joined lay adults in working to bond young captives to their new communities. To do so, they used techniques they had learned as missionaries and founders of colonial schools. This practice appalled Deerfield's Reverend John Williams, who believed that clergy had lost the God-given prerogatives of adult parenthood because of their vows of celibacy. Williams echoed New Englanders' aversion to celibacy when he condemned French Catholic clergy who claimed for themselves the same rights as birth parents to shape lives and determine vocations for children of all ages and cultural origins.[75] He was even more scandalized at the thought that the "callings" fostered by Catholic clergy could push Protestant children into Catholic holy orders. And there were precedents for this happening: Protestant-born Esther Wheelwright and her cousin Mary Sayward pursued callings that led them to celibate religious lives. So did at least six other young women from various corners of northern New England.[76]

With every day lost to New France, the critical elements of the life courses of captive children and youths were developing far beyond the reach of their natal families. This often unfolded at the very time of life when those parents would be encouraging their children toward a calling and providing a role model for them.[77]

The development of callings among captive youths coincided with spiritual formation, which revolved around Catholic sacramental life. If New England captives simply modeled French Catholicism while in captivity, or accepted baptism, there was no stigma or other impediment to their reintegration into Protestant communities. As Mary Storer's case illustrates, complications arose if the captive married while in the captor culture, which erected real barriers to redemption. Unlike baptism, the sacrament of marriage was more than a spiritual gift conferred upon an individual: it was an arrangement between people who had reached a certain level of maturity. It involved conjugal love, reproduction, property, legal identity, and status. Though Protestants could scoff at the sacraments they rejected as mere idolatrous rituals, the consequences were real and tangible, and the connections of spouse and parenthood they created could not easily be undone.[78] Why then were captives tempted to take this critical determinative step? Certainly attraction, love, and the desire to marry cannot be discounted. Yet captives likely contemplated such a move with additional factors in mind. While historical records are silent on their inner deliberations, evidence suggests that some Maine captives might have eventually concluded that home had given up on *them,* and thus felt liberated to seek opportunities for fulfilling relationships elsewhere. Older captives like Mary and Rachel Storer had witnessed those who returned, and more importantly, those who did not, among the Mainers taken captive from King William's War. Even so, resistance to marriage suggests that some captives deliberately postponed marriage to keep hope for redemption alive and resist a higher level of commitment to the captor colony. This might explain why Maine captives who relented and married—out of love, pressure, or preference—tended to be older than their *canadien* counterparts. Allan Greer has shown that the average age for first marriages among *canadiens* by 1740 hovered around twenty-two.[79] In contrast, Mary Storer was twenty-four and had lived in Boucherville for five years before she married Jean St. Germaine. Mary Austin had lived in New France for more than a decade and Esther Sayward for almost two before they committed to sacramental marriage. They were twenty-six and twenty-seven, respectively, at the time of these marriages.[80] Mary Scammon, a Dummer's War captive, married for the first time shortly before her thirtieth birthday after more than ten years of life in the Ursuline convent at Trois-Rivières.[81]

Most captives seem to have been content with their marriages. They lived in comfort; their children were numerous. In contrast, Maine was not well situated to compete in material comforts. The end of Queen Anne's War brought a measure of economic stability to the province, with peacetime settlers free to focus on agriculture instead of the region's extractive industries, fishing and lumber.[82] But the women and men of Maine's postwar generation were still likely to live in structures that had changed little from the seventeenth century. As late as 1748, almost every house in Wells was assessed at less than the paltry sum of twenty pounds. These houses were mostly one-story affairs, and not one had glass windowpanes.[83] Prosperity was hampered by the relatively poor condition of the soil. Flax, hay, and corn grew relatively well, and most farmsteads could support at least one cow. But surplus was rare, and there was little to spend on ornamental non-necessities like glass windows and house paint. Serious food shortages were common to the Eastward, and persisted throughout the first half of the eighteenth century.[84]

In contrast, Maine's adolescent Protestant women who converted and partook in the sacrament of marriage were sometimes propelled to the highest strata of a cosmopolitan colonial society and enjoyed its material privileges. Mary Storer, Mary Scammon of Saco, and Esther Sayward of York all married elite men. Like other wealthy Canadians who shared their rank, these women spent their married lives in sturdy stone houses well furnished and provisioned. As described by Louise Dechêne, these homes were likely to contain abundant linens, finely wrought furniture of native cherrywood, multiple beds, pewter and silver tableware and cutlery; iron stoves, tapestries, and books were common household items for New France's wealthier residents.[85] Even the Maine captives who joined the ranks of the *habitants* seemed to be materially better off. Though their relative wealth and household goods were comparable to those of Maine farmers and fishermen, common Canadians took a special delight in displaying the few goods they had. Charlevoix compared the wealthiest English colonists to the poorest French in terms of enjoying rewards, and found the former wanting. Based on his own observations, as well as the stories of others, the Jesuit concluded, "In New England, and the other provinces of the continent of America, subject to the British empire, there prevails an opulence which they are utterly at a loss how to use; and in New France, a poverty hid by an air of easy circumstances, which seems not at all studied. . . . The English planter marries wealth, and never makes any superfluous expense; the French inhabitant again enjoys what he has acquired, and often makes a parade of what he is not possessed of."[86]

The priest Charlevoix admired neither the French nor the English responses to material wealth, but he believed his colonial coreligionists were more capable at extracting pleasure from their toil. To captive Protestants steeped in a work ethic that discouraged ostentation and mired in a frontier poverty that reinforced the philosophy, the new example of Catholics taking pleasure in even limited prosperity offered a different, and likely appealing, model for Christian living.

Even captives from less respectable backgrounds could flourish in New France thanks to conversion and sacramental marriage. Among these was York captive Barsheba Webber, who came from a poor and troubled family. Her mother was punished for public drunkenness, her brother for profaning the Sabbath, and her sister for fornication, bastardy, and falsely accusing a man of fathering her child—all in the course of one year.[87] Yet Barsheba's captivity wiped clean the taint of her disreputable family. In Canada she married Joseph Saleur, a *bourgeois,* in 1714 and bore four sons. Materially and socially, the marriage to Saleur was a good one for a young woman from an unpromising family who might have been shunned by more respectable suitors back in Maine.[88]

James Axtell notes that successful marriages between converted captives and French colonial elites were powerful instruments of pro-French propaganda.[89] Still, the fact that these marriages happened at all was the source of deep suspicion for New England Protestants. In some cases, these suspicions had merit. Such was the case with Rachel Storer, Mary's cousin. Marriage in New France was subject to a captive's protectors, who controlled captives' access to others. Mary Storer had powerful protectors in New France who saw that she married well. Rachel Storer did not at first, and it took the potentially embarrassing crisis of a misguided relationship to procure them for her. The sacrament of marriage became a key action in controlling the damage. Though it created bonds that were sacred, marriage in this case was put to less than holy uses.

The man from whom Rachel Storer—and through her, the dignity of the Catholic convert—needed saving was a soldier named Jean Berger. Like his wife, Berger was an immigrant to New France. Born in Lyons in 1681, he enlisted in a French regiment as a teen and was sent to New France around 1700.[90] His Atlantic World trajectory was a common one for males who left France for its colonies. Soldiers like him constituted over 30 percent of the entire immigrant pool in Canada and Acadia.[91] Arriving in the colony some time before 1706 (the year he married Rachel, known in Catholic baptism as Marie-Françoise), he was by 1707 out of the army and working as a painter in Montreal. This was an uncommon career for an ex-soldier, whose comrades were far more likely to turn to farming or return to France when their enlistments ended.[92] Berger, however, possessed some talent for his craft and was awarded several prestigious commissions. His work still decorates the altar frontal of the church of La Sainte-Famille in on Île d'Orléans. And in contrast to Mary's husband, Jean Gaulthier, who tried to engage with and please his Protestant New England in-laws, Jean Berger celebrated victories over the colonial English by painting portraits of the Hertel brothers, two members of the famed military family whose leadership of the Salmon Falls and Deerfield, Massachusetts, frontier raids made them notorious among the English.[93]

By 1707 these two immigrants to New France appear to have found conventional roles within New French society: Rachel in marriage, Jean in marriage and a valued trade. But they had arrived at this state in unconventional ways. Rachel herself disclosed as much to John Williams, whom she chanced to meet in the spring of 1706. Weeping, she described to him how she had been "debauched, and then in twenty-four hours of time published, taken into their communion, and married." Williams noted that "the poor soul has had time since to lament her sin and folly, with a bitter cry; and asks your prayers." The minister told his readers "that God of his sovereign grace would yet bring her out of the horrible pit into which she has thrown herself."[94]

Already bemoaning the seduction of popery and its effects on young captives (including his own son and daughter), Williams was primed to hear Rachel's message of a young Protestant woman manipulated into a religious state that bound her, seemingly irrevocably, to Canada. He reported grimly that "such [captives] were sent away who were ungainable, the most of the younger sort still kept. Some still flattered with promises of reward, and essays were made to get others married to them."[95] Rachel's story was consistent with what he and others had long suspected about captives who converted and married.

What had led Rachel, "debauched," as the minister called her, to the pit of hell Williams described? Undoubtedly to the New England minister, the captive's conversion to Catholicism contributed to her damnable state. But he might have been describing the circumstances that led to her marriage as well. These circumstances suggest that Rachel's "debauch" was not just to Catholicism but into illicit sexual exploration as well.

Indeed, the minister's chosen word is a complicated one that in period usage conflated the loss of true religion to lost innocence of both soul and body. But other evidence favors a literal understanding of a sexual encounter that eventually bound Rachel and Jean together in wedlock. This connotation of *debauch*, as Sharon Block has suggested, was commonly understood throughout New England, where the term appeared in legal proceedings, sermons and personal correspondence throughout the colonial period, and beyond.[96] The term *debauch* was distinct from *rape* in the sense that it involved two parties coming together in common understanding and agreement. Debauchery could begin with men attempting to coerce women into sexual activity. But unlike rape, the onus was ultimately on the woman to participate willingly.[97] Applying this context of the word offers a compelling alternative explanation for Rachel's fall into the French Catholic "pit of hell" described by John Williams. Whether or not women completely understood the implications of consensual relations is a different matter. For Rachel, who was still an adolescent in a world of new cultural understandings, languages, and behaviors between the sexes at the time of her marriage, the broader implications of enjoying the romantic attentions of a French soldier were likely unclear. They would have been very clear, however, to Rachel's captors. Catholic sacraments were the only tools they had to hide the potentially embarrassing end products of debauchery. Children born to unmarried captive women would have undermined arguments by French Catholics that captives had been brought to the colony by acts of Providence, and were the recipients of loving and attentive care from their captors. The undermining of such claims could cast doubt on the legitimacy of any marriage between a captive and Catholic colonist, as well as any claims that New Englanders came to Catholicism for love of the new religion and of Catholic New World people.[98]

Although her captors failed to act before Rachel's debauch by Jean Berger, they were swift to act once it happened and proactively forced a marriage. This interpretation explains several puzzling elements surrounding this captive's participation in the sacrament of marriage. One such puzzle involves Rachel's age at the time of her marriage. She was only nineteen, below the average age for French brides and considerably younger than most Maine captive brides (whose ages at the time of their marriages suggest they delayed as long as possible).[99]

In addition, the church itself expedited the marriage. Preparation for the sacrament of marriage in New France normally required the public reading of marriage banns, a measure that was taken to ensure that both parties were free to marry. This was of particular importance in all Christian New World colonies, where bigamy was difficult to trace and could lead to a host of unwelcome social problems if not detected and deterred. In French Canada, it fell to the Catholic Church to aid in preventing bigamy.[100] The tool of choice, for both Catholics and many New World Protestants alike, was the publication of banns, a public announcement over the course of several days, weeks, or even months, which called the public's attention to a couple who intended to marry. Normally, banns were presented at High Mass on three successive Sundays, with at least two or three days between publications. Yet for Rachel and Jean there were none at all, and the sacrament was conferred a mere two days after Rachel's baptism in the Catholic Church. The speed of these developments suggests the need to effect the marriage quickly.[101]

Even more compelling is the timing of the marriage, which took place on April 17, 1706, while negotiations by Ensign John Sheldon for Deerfield captives and others were under way.[102] The conferring of these two critical sacraments, which completed Rachel's transformation from a New England Protestant captive into a French Catholic colonial subject, were performed at the very moment that her liberation might have been at hand. Thus were the negotiators robbed of at least one potential redeemed soul.

A final piece of evidence involves Rachel's godfather at her rebaptism, the signatory to her marriage contract, and a witness at her wedding, Jacques Levasseur de Néré, who was a captain in the army, a military engineer, and a knight of the order of Saint-Louis.[103] He was also Jean Berger's commanding officer before the latter left military service (in disgrace, as will soon be described).[104]

With friendship with a subordinate like Berger highly unlikely, why did someone of Levasseur de Néré's stature play multiple, active roles in the marriage of a common soldier to a New England captive? The answer likely lies in the nature of the relationship between military elites and common soldiers in Canadian society. The presence of so many soldiers in the highly militarized colony presented a special challenge to the colony's ideal moral order, with soldiers posing the chief danger to the virtue of the colony's women, captive or free. Keeping young, rootless, armed men out of trouble was serious business. Military officers, colonial administrators, and even bishops made special efforts to keep these by nature sexually unruly colonists in order. Their efforts included adopting a hard line against fornication and illegitimacy, two problems with severe consequences for the young unmarried women (and no doubt married ones as well) who lived in areas with large concentrations of soldiers. Jean de la Croix de Saint-Vallier, François de Laval's successor as bishop of New France, made a special point of denouncing soldiers who promised young women marriage in exchange for sex.[105] Believing these promises sincere, the bishop claimed, young women were enticed to fornicate, resulting all too frequently in illegitimate children and abandoned, unmarried mothers. Savvier families covered up the threat of bastardy and preserved family honor by arranging for hasty marriages — to the often unwilling seducer or to someone else — to preserve family honor.[106] Jean Berger had already proved himself capable of playing the role of the seducer: a year before his marriage to Rachel, he had fathered an *enfant naturel* with Louise Boucher, the daughter of a local *habitant*.[107] Without the oversight and clout of parents or elite captors who could protect her, a seduced captive ran the risk of becoming a shameful statistic that undermined French claims that they cared for captives holistically, body and soul.[108]

The daughter of a poor colonial family, Louise Boucher and her child did not merit special consideration. A captive like Rachel Storer fell into a special category, with her overall well-being a matter of both political and religious honor. The reality of an unmarried captive who had been seduced and abandoned by a soldier would have seriously challenged the colony's claims to moral authority. Jacques Levasseur de Néré's active engagement in Rachel Storer's Catholic rites suggests that arranging for the captive's baptism and marriage was tied to a broader concept of family honor, in which the French colonial state assumed the role of a father asserting patriarchal control over female sexual activities.[109] If Jean Berger had usurped that privilege by debauching a captive, Levasseur de Néré had the power to reclaim it by using his weight as a representative of the state to convince the church to legitimize the relationship hastily. Perhaps he went to such lengths because of his own social ambitions. Levasseur de Néré was a newly created knight of the highly prestigious order of Saint-Louis. The shameful treatment of a powerful political tool like a captive by one of his soldiers would have cast dishonor on a leader who was supposed to enforce moral order among his subordinates.[110]

Narratives like John Williams's *Redeemed Captive Returning to Zion,* which described beatings and other abusive treatment toward captives who did not come to heel, reinforced the belief that Protestants who embraced popery could only have done so in ignorance or under threat.[111] In the case of Rachel Storer's marriage, the flurry of sacramental activity challenged French assertions to the English that captives came to Catholicism and all the sacraments of their own free will. Worldly factors sometimes took precedence, making Catholic sacraments, and those who received them, tools of temporal concerns.

Once she was married, however, separation from sympathetic and powerful New Englanders left Rachel little choice but to persevere in married life. The sexual debauch of 1706 might not have resulted in the feared pregnancy, for Rachel and Jean did not present a baby for baptism until more than a year after their marriage.[112] By this time, the couple had moved to Montreal, where Rachel lived near her sister Priscilla and cousin Mary. Priscilla, who was happily married to the aforementioned Jean-Baptiste Dagueil, served as godmother to Rachel's first baby, Marie-Françoise.[113] Through her immediate family, Rachel now had access to the greater network of Maine captives, who could offer her support in the transition into adulthood and marriage and add a touch of familiarity to her spiritual life.[114]

In the thriving metropole of Montreal, Jean also had opportunities to develop his chosen career as a painter. The growth of the Catholic city expanded the number of religious institutions that required sculptures, depictions of religious themes, and other decorations. The recent death of Pierre Le Ber, Montreal's most prominent painter of religious themes, left openings for others to enter the trade.[115]

The newlyweds thus stepped into a conventional world of family and work. But Rachel's prospects for crafting her own *ménage des anges* were undone by her husband's behavior. Jean Berger was, at very best, temperamental, and at worst, violent, and possibly mentally unstable. He also possessed a documented talent for mischief, and repeatedly attracted the attention of New France's civil authorities. Berger's troubles with civil order began the year before he married. In 1705, while still a soldier in Levasseur de Néré's company, he was arrested for lending his artistic talents to Pendleton Fletcher and James Adams, Maine captives and onetime neighbors of the Storers who stood accused of counterfeiting card money.[116] The fortunate Fletcher and Adams were returned to New England while Jean was left to stew in jail and face discharge from the army, his sole means of support.[117] Though eventually cleared of the charges, Jean tangled with the law again in 1710. This time, he stood accused of beating almost to death an apothecary, Claude Saint-Olive, during a street brawl. Though he was again cleared of the charges, continued suspicion of his character suggests Jean had earned a reputation for unsavory behavior. He might have disappeared from the eyes of the law had he not chosen to ridicule his prosecutors publicly. Instead of going quietly away, Jean Berger composed a bitterly satirical song that lampooned both the injured apothecary and the judge who presided over the case.[118] He even managed to distribute multiple copies of his work, a determined feat of mischief that, considering New France had no printing press until after 1749, required some effort on his part.[119] He was arrested yet again and ordered to pay stiff fines to both the king and the offended apothecary. Far more importantly, however, Jean was also ordered to leave Montreal. Faced with this extreme punishment, Berger was still incapable of self-restraint and indulged in yet another public display of contemptuous doggerel.[120] A chronically underpopulated New France needed all the men it could retain, but when a man resorted to bold public acts of ridicule of established civil authority, he threatened the civil authority that held the colony together. These authorities had had enough, which they demonstrated by banishing Jean from New France altogether.[121]

   If Rachel Storer had told John Williams that she "bitterly regretted her folly" after a mere few weeks of marriage, her distress over this development must have been profound. As a married woman, Rachel was bound to the fate of her husband, sharing the shame of his scandals and ultimately his exile. But had these events happened after the Treaty of Utrecht, which contained language allowing for the return of captives, would the outcome have differed? Would Ra -chel have been able simply to leave her troublesome French husband and return to her New England family? The answer is no — in the sense that such a fluid transition from the French colony into New England would not have been simple. In sacramental marriage, captives became French subjects, and the ability of these onetime New Englanders to move between colonies now, ironically, subjected them to the same regulations governing the movements of all other French subjects within and without the colonies. New Englanders had expected Utrecht's stipulations to alter these circumstances: when John Stoddard traveled with John Williams to New France in 1714, he voiced the expectation that decisions to return would be left to ex-captives and their spouses. But Stoddard soon learned he was mistaken. Like other French colonists, acculturated captives now required official *lettres de naturalité* from the French king to move from colony to colony. It was as French subjects, therefore — and not as onetime New Englanders — that the movements of English-born naturalized colonists were restricted by the French colonial government.

New Englanders refused to concede this right. When Williams and Stoddard argued that the treaty overruled the status of native New Englanders as French subjects, Governor Vaudreuil compromised by allowing that "French women might be at liberty to go with their English husbands, and that English women should not be compelled to stay with their French husbands."[122] A critical distinction, however, was made for the children of these unions, who would have to remain in New France among Catholic relations. In the simple calculus of bringing bodies and souls that had once been Protestant back to New England, the concession seemed logical, at least in religious terms. An apostate Protestant was at liberty to return to the faith of his or her birth, but children who had known only Catholicism were not to be separated from the church. And as shown in the case of Mary Storer, New Englanders who left French spouses would also have forfeited many of the defining aspects of their lives as Euro-American colonial women. If they returned to New England, they would have had to leave their French subject children behind. They would carry the taint of a previous marriage to a man who still lived. Without benefit of acceptable grounds for divorce (available, though still rare in New England), such women had little hope of marrying New England men unless they could verify that their French spouses had either died or deserted them. The choice for Maine's female captives, and indeed all New England–born women, was unambiguous: they could remain in Canada with spouses and children who gave their lives definition, or they could return to New England to a life devoid of marital, maternal, and social fulfillment. Understandably, they chose the former.

Perhaps this outcome would have differed had colonial laws that kept former captives in the French colony sat quietly on the books. But such laws were instead enforced with rigor. The Storer women would likely all have been aware of the sad details of the life of their fellow captive and neighbor, Christine Otis Le Beau Baker, who had been taken from Dover, New Hampshire, during King William's War. The mostly intact Otis family was ransomed to French Canada, where Christine's mother, Grizel, was quick to adopt the religion of her own Irish mother and become an active Catholic laywoman and enthusiastic proselytizer to New England captives. Grizel's children, including Christine, followed their mother into the Catholic Church. Christine matured in New France and married *habitant* Louis Le Beau in 1710. When Louis died three years later, he left Christine a widow with two small daughters. But the young widow had the good fortune to fall in love again, this time with Captain Thomas Baker, a New England Protestant and member of the Stoddard/Williams mission. Eager to return to New England with Baker, she was forbidden by the French colonial government to take her daughters with her. In what must have been a wrenching decision, she chose to leave the children in the care of her zealously Catholic mother and marry Baker.[123] Christine's experience demonstrated that the decision to return would entail sacrificing one form of flesh and blood for another. In the tight-knit world of New England–born *canadiennes*, this must have been seemed unconscionable, especially since so many Mainers had been violently separated from their own parents when they themselves were children.

✦ ✦ ✦

English families who endured life on the Maine frontier during the early wars of empire rarely moved in a world uncomplicated by geographical realities. To those they left behind, the Maine captives who stood by their French marriages after they were guaranteed the right to return to New England were souls lost to these borderland travails. For the captives, new connections and the wills and needs of others often played a role in limiting or foreclosing choices altogether. Larger events that influenced the boundaries of the Atlantic World powers also played a role in eclipsing personal relationships and choices and influencing the lives and relationships of colonists from even the most humble backgrounds. These larger events had unintended, yet likely welcome, consequences for Rachel Storer Berger and her "pit of hell" marriage wrought by sacrament.

Rachel's redemption came thanks to a combination of factors ranging from Jean Berger's chronic bad behavior in Canada to the cessation of Queen Anne's War. Banished from Canada in 1710 in the aftermath of Saint-Olive affair, the Bergers still had choices for settlement, including France itself. For reasons that might have ranged from economic advancement to a desire for isolation, they went to Plaisance, a cold, weakly developed settlement on the edge of the French colonial world of Terre Neuve (Newfoundland), which owed its existence solely to the North Atlantic fisheries.[124] Once settled, Jean Berger pursued both trade and painting, though he probably got very little call for the latter: Plaisance was among the poorest of the French New World settlements and lacked even a parish church, let alone a local aristocracy that hungered to preserve family glory in portraiture.[125] For Rachel, the adjustment must have been difficult. In contrast to Quebec, Plaisance was underdeveloped, isolated, and colder still. Alone except for her husband, and having lost both her children in infancy, Rachel was once again deprived of her family through the will of others.[126]

But within three years of the Bergers' arrival in Terre Neuve, the capriciously shifting boundaries of the eighteenth-century Atlantic World brought Rachel Storer back to an English colony without ever leaving Plaisance. Under the terms of the Treaty of Utrecht, all the French settlements of Nova Scotia and Terre Neuve were ceded to Britain.[127] No longer subject to the *congés* and *permis* that restricted the movements of French subjects in New France, Rachel was now free to move throughout the territories claimed by England—New England included. Jean Berger's flights of temper and imprudent judgment, his volatility and propensity for mischief which affected more than just himself, had the ironic consequence of procuring for his wife the freedoms that French naturalization could not. And Rachel, once a pawn of the imperial politics that tied her to France's New World territories, now benefited from their ability to shift New World geopolitical landscapes. Though little is known of her post-captivity life in New England, it is certain that she returned and re-established relationships with the extended Storer family. Proof of the reconstructed relationship is that Jeremiah Storer left "Rachel Bargee" a share of his estate equal to those of her remaining New England–based sisters.[128] This contrasts with the lot of his still-living French subject daughter and Rachel's sister, Priscilla, who, like Mary Storer St. Germaine, was a faithful *canadienne* wife and Catholic communicant, yet received no recognition in her father's will. If Rachel indeed regretted her folly as the Reverend John Williams suggested, her fidelity to the path paved by debauchery and the sacrament that mitigated its consequences eventually accomplished the very goal it seemed to undermine. Such were the wonder-workings of Providence on a complicated early American frontier.

✦   ✦   ✦

In July 1727 Mary Storer wrote to her Boston brother, Ebenezer, requesting that he "inquier after an ingliesh man which is maried in bostowne his name is greenhill his wife is yet living and his two sons in Morial I pray you to send me some nues of him whear he is a dead or a live ask my cousin barger knows him well."[129] The object of Mary's query was Joseph Greenhill, a once-captive New Englander who became a naturalized French citizen in 1713.[130] During his captivity, Greenhill entered into the sacrament of marriage with a French woman and had several children. A Catholic convert like many others of his origins, he was sacramentally active and served as a godparent to at least one other New England captive.[131] Yet Greenhill abruptly left his *canadienne* wife and their children when an opportunity to return to New England arose.

Mary wrote Ebenezer to enlist Rachel Storer in helping to repair the broken union. To Mary, whose bonds of sacramental marriage proved tighter than those of than her natal family and religion, the sanctity of the union itself transcended the violent circumstances that made such unions possible. Rachel likely saw things differently. Though she may have helped to locate Greenhill (the records are silent on this), it is easy to imagine how her own feelings toward the captor culture and the bonds of marriage within it might have been clouded by the memories of her decidedly less happy journey. Her own imperial odyssey was marked by symbols of her fundamental powerlessness as a young, unprotected female in an unknown land. The raid on poor, struggling Wells in 1703 lacked the ironic effect of raising Rachel's material fortunes, unlike the situation of her sister and cousin.

To Protestant Maine families, onetime captives like Rachel Storer Berger and Joseph Greenhill were more obedient children than Mary, living grandly in her *ménage des anges* as a devoted helpmeet and mother. Despite her "follies"—dalliance with a French soldier, Catholic baptism, sacramental marriage, and falling prey to the manipulations of others—Rachel escaped from the horrible pit of French religion and marriage to which John Williams had consigned her. The larger factors that brought her to Canada in the first place eventually worked to favor her, despite thwarting on every level her ability to shape her own fate. Redemption was not always an issue of personal agency. Like the Protestant definition of salvation itself, the factors that led to redemption seemed to be as incomprehensible as saving grace itself.

Regardless of their worldly success, an apostate son, daughter, brother, or sister had taken an enormous step backward on the path to salvation, to Protestants. If Protestants were heretics to Catholics, Catholics were idolaters and slaves of despots to Protestants.[132] If a captive accepted only baptism, the possibility for redemption was still strong. When captives went a step further and received the sacrament of marriage in New France, the possibility for both physical and spiritual redemption was severely curtailed. Maine's captives often had reasons for remaining in the captor culture which eluded the New England families they left behind. Those who changed religion now faced a series of life choices that necessitated deeper ties to the captor colony. But their Protestant families back in Maine would not completely relinquish them. To do so would be to allow the poor captive to wallow in his or her vices in Catholic New France and would be a gross abnegation of familial duty.[133]

John Demos's *The Unredeemed Captive: A Family Story from Early America* describes the captivity of the oft-quoted Reverend John Wil - liams and his family, and offers a psychological reading of that of the minister's daughter, Eunice. Unlike most of the Maine captives in this study, Eunice Williams remained among the Christian Mohawks at Kahnawake, outside of Montreal, and became a fully transculturated Native American. Her father and brother, Stephen, on the other hand, both returned from captivity and brought none of its trappings with them except the will to fight popery.[134] Captives like Mary, Rachel, and Priscilla Storer—married and acculturated *canadiennes*—fell somewhere in between the extremes represented within the Williams family. The contact captives shared with their blood kin shows that these families attempted some form of rapprochement with acculturated kin. Acceptance, however, was another matter. To Maine families, children and siblings who sought sacraments with binding consequences complicated the borderland of faith that the province's location and circumstances engendered. It added both theoretical (the rights and duties of families) and emotional ("love the sinner, hate the sin") elements that all members of mixed-faith families were challenged to transcend. Some captives lived among Catholic colonists and returned to New England to tell tales of either spiritual victory over popery or gratitude to their wrongheaded, yet sympathetic French hosts. But captives who took the Catholic

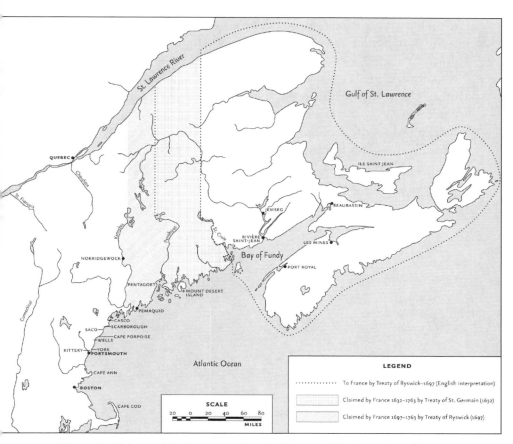

Figure 8. Maine and Its Environs. French Claims, 1632 through the Treaty of Utrecht, 1713. Map by Jax de Leon.

sacrament of marriage with a French subject and raised families in New France persisted in dual relationships to Protestant New England and Catholic Canada. Unlike their counterparts who returned, these captives became the objects of encounter themselves. Though their parents and siblings might have been spared the experience of a captive life in the French colony, they would now remain tied to it for generations. Consequently, married captives were responsible for incorporating a larger circle of Maine settlers into the greater story of the religious encounter of competing Christian visions on the Maine frontier. In borderlands like Maine, a world frequently turned upside down by religious encounters, the saints and sinners who ventured back from Canada were sometimes hard to distinguish from one another. Certainly, their life choices, and the limitations placed on those choices, were more complex than their New England loved ones knew or acknowledged. And though colonial Maine made steady, though episodic, progress toward stabilization after the Treaty of Utrecht, many of its captive daughters and sons remained hostages to the fortunes of intersecting geographies and competing religious cultures.

CHAPTER FOUR

The Ways of Christian Industry

Missions and Ministries on the Maine Frontier

Sebastien Rale, a Jesuit missionary at the established Catholic mission at Norridgewock, had problems with his neighbors. In 1722 he wrote a long letter to his nephew in France that described his troubles:

> Some years ago, the Governor-general of new England sent to the foot of our river the most able man among the Ministers of Boston, that he might open a School there, instruct the children of the Savages, and maintain them at the expense of the Government. As the salary of the Minister was to increase in proportion to the number of his pupils, he neglected nothing to attract them; he went to seek the children, he flattered them, he made them little presents, he urged them to come to see him; in short, he worked for two months with much useless activity, without being able to win a single child. The disdain with which his attentions and his invitations were treated did not discourage him. He spoke to the Savages themselves; he put to them various questions touching their faith; and then, from the answers that were made to him, he turned into derision the Sacraments, Purgatory, the invocation of the Saints, the beads, the crosses, the images, the lights of

165

our Churches, and all the pious customs that are so sacredly observed in the catholic Religion.[1]

The Jesuit understandably viewed these aggressive Protestant incursions with derision. The neighboring English were avowed enemies of Catholicism, and they had sheer numbers on their side to enlist others in a quest to rid the area of their religious rivals. Proof of this antipathy was evident in the highest ranks. Joseph Dudley, royal governor of Massachusetts from 1702 to 1715, expressed the Protestant aversion toward the Catholic presence near New England in explicit, unambiguous terms when he insisted to the General Court that "it is plain to every Considering man that while there is a French Nation in Europe so bigoted to the Romish Religion & so set upon perfidy and Destruction of all protestants that have dependent Colony's in our Neighbourhood, we shall have no rest or Ease, as plain that if they are removed ye Indians must inevitably become Vassals & Servants to us, having no possible means to be supplied wth Arms or Ammunition but from our selves."[2]

Between Dudley's public insistence on the dangers nearby in 1709 and Rale's 1722 description of his interactions with the offending neighboring minister, however, came an insightful missive sent to the Jesuit by a New Englander who professed deep concern for Maine's Christian fate. Its author was Samuel Shute, the royal governor of Massachusetts who replaced Dudley in 1716; its recipient, Sebastien Rale. In the letter, the governor assailed the Jesuit for, among other things, the latter's putative shortcomings—*as a fellow Christian.* At the heart of Shute's argument was Rale's behavior toward Joseph Baxter, the gospel minister about whom the Jesuit had complained with such bitterness. It was true that Baxter had set up his spiritual shop near the Jesuit's mission with the intent of bringing some of Norridgewock's self-identified Catholic Indians to Protestantism. By Shute's reckoning, however, the real root of the problem between the two men came chiefly from the Jesuit, who had, by the governor's reckoning, fallen short in Christian brotherhood. The governor argued that all Christian men of God should be bound together in some form of frontier common cause. Shute therefore freely rebuked

Rale in the name of all Christians, and maintained that the Jesuit should have been more inclined to band together with Baxter to address spiritual challenges. He wrote to the Jesuit:

> [It] seems strange to me, That one who professes himself a Christian Missionary, as you do, among the same People, should not only Oppose, But even Ridicule a Mission in the same Glorious Name, and for the same Blessed end; Altho the Method taken may be very differeing; Your Conduct in this Affair does not seem to be Agreeable to the spirit and Practice of the Great Apostle. . . . Notwithstanding every way whether in pretence or in truth Christ is preached, and I therein doe Rejoice year & I will rejoice. Upon which Catholick Principle I had reason to Expect that instead of hindring and Abusing Mr Baxter you should have Embraced & bid him Wellcome; If not as a Brother on all Accounts, yet at least as a Fellow Labourer in the Work of the Lord, & rather when the harvest was so plenteous, and the Labourers so few; And instead of Ecomunicating and Unchristian Treatment of the Poor Indians for only Attending on Mr Baxters Instructions, you had Recommended him and his Labours, to those poor People; This had been not only for the Glory of God, the promoting the Common Cause of Religion, but your own honour & Comfort.[3]

Shute's scolding was clearly disingenuous. Catholic Indians and French priests on the northern frontier were unenthusiastic about the spread of Protestant New England, and it was unlikely that any New Englanders rejoiced when the successful deliverer of the Christian message was a Jesuit. In noting Rale's faults as a "Fellow Labourer" in frontier Christian missions, the governor described a level of ecumenical cooperation, toleration, and fellowship that would have been exceedingly rare in any corner of early eighteenth-century America. After all, Rale was committed to implementing the dogma and practices of his own form of Christianity. And, of course, so was Baxter. In a world where coexistence rarely equaled tolerance, Shute's suggestion that the goals of both faiths were compatible was more likely an attempt to shame a Jesuit who was well aware that English Protestants were eager to supplant him and his Catholicism.

Yet despite the likely insincerity of its sentiments, the language of the letter suggests a great deal about issues of frontier Christian convergence affecting its most clearly identified religious actors: ministers and priests. These men of God attempted to define orthodox religious culture and oversee its spread throughout their spheres of influence. Though the goal of Shute's letter was to issue a written warning to the Jesuit of the consequences of failing to respect geopolitical boundaries, its author employed commonly understood issues affecting all frontier men of God. These included the difficulty and multiplicity of mission tasks; the unevenness of clerical preparation to perform these tasks; Christian encounter in "unchurched" environments; and the interfaith encounter (hostile or otherwise), which was a common feature of borderland life. The last issue was one that particularly affected Sebastien Rale and Joseph Baxter as each struggled to expand his religious sphere of influence in overlapping regions.

Analyses of frontier Protestants and Catholics frequently focus on their intrinsic differences. While these differences should not be downplayed, it bears noting that certain fundamentals of frontier Christianity underscore the presence of a borderland of shared religious understandings, motives, backgrounds, and experiences. In short, the men of God who found themselves on the Maine frontier knew more of each other than less. While "papists" and "heretics" were subject to derision in the popular culture of the more settled regions of the colonial world, frontier men of God were encountering Christian linkages that served to reinforce common roots, experiences, goals, problems, and shortcomings. Furthermore, frontier men of God looked to their rivals for examples of success and failure in their mission work, and capitalized on these as they could.

Frontier religious culture was rarely denominationally pure. The interactions between the minister Baxter and the Jesuit Rale, with the additional input of the Protestant Shute, show just how eclectic the seemingly clear-cut boundaries between Christian faiths could be.

Like its settlers, Maine's competing Christian men of God were a diverse lot in terms of background, creed, preparation for the ministry, and the goals they set for themselves. In the battle for Christian souls, no others served so consistently on the fractious frontier of spiritual conquest, especially in the years between 1688 and 1727. Maine's men of God faced numerous challenges to effective spiritual leadership. This sprang not only from conditions of time and place, but from the unique circumstances that brought these men to a corner of the Atlantic World that was as resistant to religious conformity.

If religious life in the early years of the province had achieved some level of homogeneity, the borderlands would likely have attracted only Protestantism's and Catholicism's most militant and orthodox defenders. In most cases, however, the special needs and challenges of the borderlands delivered the opposite. For some men of God, borderland catechesis and ministry provided an opportunity for real encounter with successful rivals. In these circumstances, ministers and priests who expressed revulsion for the Christian vision of these rivals nonetheless borrowed, added, or adapted the others' conversion and ministerial techniques. In other cases, the unsettled nature of Maine provided cover for religiously trained men whose personal lives undermined their ministries. Others were men of God in name only, who abandoned or reshaped their vocations to suit the environment and their own interests. Still others tried to pattern their actions on the example of self-sacrificing predecessors, yet preferred to preserve their own lives by taking up arms. For all these men of God, life in Maine reinforced the idea that behind the simple dichotomies of Protestant and Catholic and minister and priest lay a far more complex story of frontier encounter, where men who deviated from expected norms of orthodoxy, piety, and missionary self-sacrifice were common, and the demands of frontier life conditioned their responses to the challenges of superimposing structured Christianities onto the jumbled religious culture of the Maine frontier.

As with other cases of unconventional religious behavior in the borderlands, change came with time, and narrowed the possibilities, desirable and otherwise, for multiple, complex forms of interfaith encounter among these men of God. Before that happened, however, Maine witnessed a variety of unorthodox interfaith interactions.

In 1713 the Treaty of Utrecht was supposed to define a permanent boundary between Maine and French Acadia. But the treaty failed to do so, and the border remained dangerously fluid, causing even more tension in the decade after Utrecht. Within a decade, these disputes led to Dummer's War, a conflict that unlike its predecessors had no real European counterpart. It did, however, pit the usual Maine players—French, English, and Wabanakis—against each other for three years. At stake for French colonials was the right of the Catholic missions on the Kennebec and Penobscot rivers to exist. For the English, it was the right to extricate them, and purge their influence from the frontier. Local Wabanakis sought to keep the English colonies from encroaching even further on their already diminished homelands and construct political relationships with Euro-Americans that suited their interests.

Maine's settlements had been all but decimated by Queen Anne's War. Virtually all colonists who were spared or managed to flee the early attacks did not attempt resettlement until the war ended. By 1714, however, resettlement was under way in earnest.[4] Towns that survived the conflict attracted new settlers and brought back old ones, thus establishing what Charles Clark has termed "a mature colonial system."[5] Additional settlements that grew without New England's specific blessing lurched ever northward up the Maine coast, marking a renewed confidence that the English had the ability to hold their enemies at bay.

What force or critical mass could not accomplish in subduing local Indians was to be achieved through new rounds of diplomacy. One of these was the 1717 Arrowsic Conference, in which Massachusetts governor Samuel Shute attempted to negotiate with Wiwurna, a Kennebec Wabanaki sachem, for trade and land rights. The conference ultimately failed to resolve the land issue, but it did introduce another key element of New England's plan to deal with the Wabanakis.[6] Shute encouraged the Kennebecs to welcome a mission that would spread Protestantism among Indians who had been catechized by the Jesuits.

The leader of this effort was Massachusetts minister Joseph Baxter, a competent man of God who, up to 1717, had dutifully fulfilled the numerous spiritual and civic roles his position demanded in his Medfield, Massachusetts, congregation. Some of his congregants, though, were not satisfied with his leadership. They demonstrated their displeasure by withholding worldly things, making Baxter's tenure in Medfield an often unhappy one, fraught with internal congregational tension and concerns for his own compensation. Presented with an offer to engage in active ministry to a new community on the Kennebec and some patriotic missionary work, Baxter was likely influenced by his assessment that Maine's promise outweighed its drawbacks.

But he was under no illusion that life there would be easy. Ministers like Baxter who committed themselves to the province faced a long roster of environmental, linguistic, cultural, and denominational challenges that increased their burdens. These ministers fretted about converting the "heathen," and feared and loathed their competitors in faith—Catholic missionaries from the French territories—who had arrived before them and managed to entrench themselves among the local indigenous population. In the battle to win souls to a Christian vision, the Jesuits had assets the Protestant ministers lacked. These often gave the order critical advantages. Key among these was that the Jesuits did not bring settlers with them who competed for Wabanaki lands. In contrast, Maine's Protestants wanted and needed ample room for their settlements and economic enterprises. Any manifest attraction to Protestantism among the Wabanakis, therefore, was tempered by the fact that it brought in its wake the thing that the Eastern Indians found most objectionable about English colonization.

This perspective appears to have been lost on Joseph Baxter. When he committed himself to ministry in Maine, he did so willingly and was driven at least in part by piety: Baxter's own journal provides ample evidence that he approached his spiritual tasks with sincerity.[7] But he also knew the settlement's ability to attract and retain a robust Euro-American population was key to his own interests. Joseph Baxter was an investor in local industries, a move necessitated by his years with the parsimonious Medfield congregation.[8] Since he did not come from a wealthy family and had not married into one, he had little choice but to engage in extraministerial activities to support his six children. As a minister of the gospel, Baxter was doing God's work by contributing to stabilizing Maine in the greater service of New England. This in turn could guarantee profits for investors in its lands.[9] Along with schoolmasters and managers of trading posts, New England ministers like Baxter helped form a triumvirate of key figures that fostered security, prosperity, and Protestant stability. High settler numbers were therefore a benefit on multiple levels.

A year later, Baxter emerged from Maine as both a loser and a winner. He failed in his struggle to counter the influence of the rival Christian faction. But he left the Maine frontier with prime parcels of land and the goodwill of the Massachusetts authorities—a lucrative reward for a minister who had actually done very little to advance a spiritual frontier.

Samuel Shute blamed Baxter's failure to make inroads among the Wabanakis on the entrenched Jesuit, Sebastien Rale. Widely perceived as the "great Incendiary" of Anglo-Wabanaki hostilities in the Kennebec region, Rale had worked among the indigenous people for decades.[10] Still, he too had motives that transcended pure religion. Similar to Protestant ministers, the Jesuits and other missionaries from Catholic religious orders had characteristics that distinguished them from more conventional specimens of the French colonial clergy. Jesuits in particular married zeal for their enterprise with a working knowledge of Reformed religion and local political alliances. Zealous and adaptable, the Jesuits had long-established ties to many of the Wabanaki groups and vowed to help protect their interests against invading New Englanders, even if they had to take up arms themselves. The centers for Indian-Jesuit communications were the missions—religious villages that in Maine came to focus on common purposes that often blended religion with diplomacy. With well-established ties to New France, and well trafficked and fortified as well, these missions loomed large on the Maine frontier and constituted established settlements in their own right, complete with the elements of the built environment that any New Englander would recognize. They threatened Protestant expansion, not just in spiritual terms but in geopolitical ones as well. Indeed, many of their inhabitants and their French allies wished to roll it back.

Opposing men of God prepared for spiritual competition in 1717. Baxter had motivation, a greater degree of freedom to accomplish his goals, military power, and the potential for personal gain. Rale likewise had motivation and freedom, as well as a long history of successful missionary efforts by members of his order and the goodwill of the Wabanakis. As Christian missionaries, the two men shared key strengths in philosophy and ability, despite the differences of faith that stood between them.

These connections between faiths would have shocked a mainstream New England minister like Cotton Mather, who like most other New Englanders had probably never met a genuine "popish priest" in person. Mather's ideas about Catholic missionaries were formed largely by his knowledge of their role in the European wars of religion, popular literature, and accounts of the borderland hostilities that rocked New England between 1688 and 1727.[11] The reputation of the Jesuits as highly effective missionaries preceded them, and the minister spoke with authority about Jesuit conversion strategies and alliance-building techniques that, in his opinion, could put Protestant ministers to shame. "God forbid, That a Popish Priest should outdo a Protestant Minister in his Industry," he lamented.[12]

Thanks to his tenure in Maine, however, Joseph Baxter had managed to meet at least one Jesuit in the flesh. So did other Puritan ministers who had business in the province.[13] For these ministers and the Jesuits they encountered, Maine became a staging ground for flesh and blood post-Reformation encounters which in most parts of the colonial world existed only in history, political rhetoric, and the conventions of popular literature and culture.

Ungospelized Plantations, Unusual Ministries

For Maine's Protestants, attracting and retaining ministers for already established Protestant communities was a priority throughout the seventeenth and early eighteenth century. Most desirable were of course good ministers: hard working, zealous, doctrinally sound, and committed to spending their lives and building the godly communities the Maine frontier so desperately needed. However, the ministers who landed in Maine often failed to meet the standard. With its near-chronic tensions with French and Indian neighbors, often impoverished and spiritually apathetic settlers, and challenging climate, Maine was an unattractive option for most Protestant ministers, who sought more stable and fulfilling pulpits elsewhere.

The few Protestant ministers who committed to Maine, therefore, often did so because they failed to conform to the conventions of a stable New England minister. As a group, they displayed characteristics that distinguished them from their peers who succeeded to pulpits in the more settled parts of New England. Many were young and inexperienced, and eager to move back from the frontier before they married and had children. Others possessed talents for mischief, making Maine's remoteness a good place to conceal at least temporarily their unorthodox views or less-than-holy pursuits.

Once they arrived in the province, these ministers learned quickly that they needed to counteract other forms of Christianity that had taken hold among both Native Americans and, in a significant number of cases, their fellow Euro-Americans. Some responded by adapting their ministries to conform to their unorthodox communities. Others merged spiritual with literal warfare, taking up arms and defending frontiers with piety. Still others took advantage of the proximity of rival Christians, studied them, and attempted to appropriate their techniques to use against their rivals instead of battling them directly with words or weapons.

To do so effectively, however, New England Protestants needed more than a passing practical knowledge of contemporary Catholicism. Ministers in the more orthodox and settled regions of New England persisted in equating the post–Counter-Reformation Catholic clergy with the late medieval variety, which relied heavily on incorporating Christian piety into congregants through the senses instead of the intellect. Often they mistakenly assumed Catholic priests were steeped in superstition and collectively determined to "keepe the Scriptures shut up in an unknowne tongue."[14] Even John Eliot, who would later welcome the French Jesuit Gabriel Druillettes into his home, voiced his disapproval of Catholic missionaries with stinging sarcasm.

He wrote, "If wee could force them to baptisme (as the Spaniards do about Cuzco, Peru, and Mexico, having learned them a short answer or two to some Popish questions) . . . we could have gathered many hundreds, yea thousands it may be by this time."[15] Eliot penned this observation some time before he met Gabriel Druillettes in 1648, and applied his vitriol to the Spanish model of religious colonization. But it is unlikely that he would have felt any differently about the work of French Jesuits who came to the mission field from Canada. Frontier ministers, however, knew from experience that there was more to Catholic missionary success than incense, statues, medals, and rosary beads. Though Catholics continued to rely on objects of piety to attract the faithful, the missionaries of the Maine frontier took their cues from the Puritan tradition of "heart religion," which drew on devotional forms that it shared with Catholicism.[16] This transformation to a more emotional form of Catholicism was a direct by-product of the Catholic Reformation, which supported basic literacy for the faithful and championed reforms in education. The late medieval church was just as alien to post-Reformation priests as it would have been to their Protestant counterparts.

Geographically separated from the reformist movements in the Church of Rome that unfolded throughout Europe during the late sixteenth and early seventeenth centuries, many New World Protestants were less likely to comprehend the ramifications of these reforms for Catholic educational and missionary practices. Had they known (as they later would), they would have recognized profound similarities between their own Reformed faith and post-Reformation and Counter-Reformation Catholicism. The Society of Jesus produced proselytizers who valued elements of post-Reformation Christianity. The society's schools were among the most innovative educational environments, in curricular terms, in all of Europe.[17] Moreover, the society required the highest levels of education available to European Catholics for those scholastics who wished to become foreign missionaries. Leading Jesuit colleges like Le Flèche became incubators for priests hoping to carry the gospel into the American wilderness. As James Axtell notes, the vast majority of these Jesuits had spent most of their lives in colleges and universities and did not come into the mission field until they were in their midthirties.[18] Expert in Latin, they were also skilled in preaching and writing in the vernacular, encouraging the reading of Scripture among the literate faithful, adapting pious readings to serve new populations, and applying lessons in linguistics learned at home to indigenous languages. Such skills were vital to success in the North American mission field. Both the Reformation and the Catholic Reformation stressed the need for a well-educated clergy. Jesuits and New England missionary ministers alike were proud of their education and of the schools that produced them. The verbal feuds that played out between clergymen like Rale and Baxter were not exclusively bound to creeds: the honor of Harvard, Cambridge, La Flèche, or the University of Paris was also at stake.

Once established as missionaries, however, most Jesuits did not have much time to devote to intensive contemplation of classical texts. Neither did their Protestant counterparts. Protestant missionary ministers were expected to perform multiple duties while ministering to Maine's Euro-American Christians and attracting Native Americans to the faith. The challenge was even greater when one considers that, even under the best circumstances, ministers in Maine encountered Euro-American communities that lacked denominational homogeneity and cohesion. They were frequently caught in the middle of interdenominational tensions, which, in turn, diverted Protestants away from serious missionary work among the Wabanakis.

Jesuits too were often similarly torn. Virtually none of the priests who labored in New France and the surrounding areas from 1688 to 1727 had the luxury of giving undivided attention to Maine Indians. Instead, priests like Vincent Bigot, Rale's predecessor at Norridgewock, divided their time between provincial missions and the established parishes and schools of the French colonial metropoles. A consistent, sustained presence of an ordained priest in a Maine mission was rare.

Despite their elite education, however, ministers and priests came to recognize that Christian conversion depended on more than the simple word of God or the teaching and perfecting of pious practices. Adapting Christianity to the tactile world was a critical first step.

Early in his Kennebec ministry, Joseph Baxter asked the Massachu-setts Assembly to supply him with funds and "curiosities" to attract Indian children to the school he established.[19] Reliance on such items to grab the attention of potential converts most likely would have scandalized the average Massachusetts minister. But a borderland missionary might have viewed such tactics as tested methods that Catholic missionaries had used with great success.[20] Borderland evan-gelization during the wars of empire demanded innovative tactics, even if they were rooted in Catholic sacramentalism.[21]

Catholic clergy were likewise not uniform in their mission prac-tices. The Society of Jesus was but one Catholic order operating in New France, and its members had no choice but to depend on the regular French clergy to reinforce their teachings among the Indian neophytes; these clergy also traveled and lived among the French Catholic settlers who were attached to established parishes. But the regular clergy were not always successful at keeping the Euro-American population sufficiently devout and supportive of mission-ary work. Indeed, the *canadiens* were considered so remiss in every-day piety that missionaries tried to limit Indian convert exposure to their corrupting influence.[22] With a French population not known for its piety and few other incentives, the church in Canada faced simi-lar issues with the quality of its priests and missionaries. Some hun-gered for the spiritual glories of missionary work and had little inter-est in the French colonists themselves, whose pious habits left much to be desired. This was a particular problem in places where regular curés were few and far between.[23] Bemoaning the scarcity of colonial priests to minister to the colonial population, Bishop Saint-Vallier complained, "La perte d'un seul Prêtre est considerable dans un temps où n'a pas encore assez d'ouvriers évangéliques" (The loss of one priest is considerable at a time when there still are not enough to do the work).[24]

Yet missionary work came with its own drawbacks, influenced by the rise of new concerns for missionary priests, and different forms of response. For those whom the Catholic *canadiens* counted as their greatest spiritual assets—zealous missionaries—warfare, death, and, worse yet, the possibility of cultural apostasy lurked everywhere.

Sebastien Rale felt the tug of transcultural conversion: his years among the Native peoples of North America led him to attest that he saw, heard, and spoke "only as an Indian."[25] Priests in the missions also ran the risk of straying from their initial purposes by becoming entangled in borderland politics. In Rale's case, his critics perceived his actions as smacking of pride — and to have contributed significantly to the destruction of his mission and even his death. Perhaps most significantly, however, Rale and his fellow frontier Jesuits neither courted nor welcomed the martyr's death that had been so glorious for their members of an earlier generation. He wanted to preserve his own life along with those of the mission Indians. Furthermore, he was not alone in favoring action over martyrdom: his fellow priest on the Penobscot River, the Franciscan Louis-Pierre Thury, adapted fighting techniques of the mission Indians and deployed them with enthusiasm during raids against English settlements.

The Christian ministries that collided in Maine suffered from labor shortages and other shortcomings that hindered their service to Euro-American Christian populations. Work with Native Americans was at times even spottier. Both Protestant and Catholic frontier colonies struggled to secure capable men and supplies to meet their population's spiritual needs. Once in Maine, Christian men of God of both faiths needed to be adaptable to thrive.

Despite the fact that frontier men of God from all Christian traditions met with similar obstacles and limitations, Protestants faced a key disadvantage compared with the materially unencumbered Jesuits. For Protestantism to gain a firm foothold in all corners of Maine, it needed a regular ministry. This required a critical mass of ordained, married Protestant ministers with established congregations and adequate life provisions in terms of homestead, land, and livestock, which in turn required levels of demanding daily work to preserve home and family. Missionary work became, at best, an extracurricular activity for Maine ministers who needed to protect and provide for their wives and children. Even unmarried ministers, who had less to lose in personal terms, committed themselves only briefly to frontier work, and then moved on in search of a more suitable situation for a spouse and children.[26] Reformed clergy regarded marriage and offspring as the fulfillment of their duty to God. This mandate seriously undermined their ability to make the sacrifices required of a missionary to Wabanakia.

In contrast, Catholic missionaries entered the mission field without spouses and children. Still, lack of family was not tantamount to comprehensive physical deprivation. Priests often did their best to live as comfortably as they could within the limitations of the missions. Sebastien Rale, for one, displayed a delight in corporal concerns: when his neophytes stole from English ships, the priest enjoyed his full share in their booty of good wine.[27] Others, like Vincent Bigot, dabbled enthusiastically in regional politics and made sport of tweaking English officials. Tradition and religious affinity cemented the bond between the Kennebecs and Catholicism, but in the contest of Christianities, clerical celibacy ultimately played a key role. As celibates, Jesuits were not weighted down with the literal legacy that most Protestant ministers brought to Maine. To the Kennebec Wabanakis who repeatedly threatened to "plunder and burn ye Englishman's Houses if they did not move off their lands," minister Joseph Baxter, with his family needs and business interests, did not appear to be a suitable person to address the problems that plagued Indian-Anglo relations on the Maine frontier.[28] Baxter's joint duties to his ministry and his family rendered him part of that problem. Protestant men of God brought to the frontier a mandate to be fruitful and multiply. This, by its very definition, would eventually mean containment or displacement for the Wabanakis.

As eager students of Indian languages, Jesuits had another critical advantage over Protestant missionaries. Through trial and error, effective communication on the Indians' terms endeared the priests to their would-be converts. Jesuits like Sebastien Rale recorded local Indian dialects so that future missionaries could learn from their expertise. The Wabanaki lexicon Rale assembled was one of these enduring keys to French-Wabanaki religious compatibility.

With few exceptions, their Harvard-trained rivals lacked this key element of pre-missionary training that the Society of Jesus insisted on for all its members. Efficient and effective communication with Native American groups remained a persistent problem for Massachusetts ministers.[29] It was not that New England missionaries rejected the learning of Indian languages out of hand: John Eliot, Thomas Mayhew, and Richard Bourne all devoted considerable time to learning them.[30] Later ministers relied on translators or lexicons prepared for various Native populations by others. Joseph Baxter attempted to compose his own lexicon of Wabanaki words but, pressed for time, abandoned the project after recording only a few words. Lacking the most basic ability to communicate, he had no way of knowing that the "Indian Bible" he brought with him was John Eliot's Natick translation, written in an Algonquian dialect unfamiliar to the Kennebec Indians.[31]

The enduring image of the dreaded Jesuit missionary, a potent relic of the Gunpowder Plot and ideally suited to the frontier wars of empire, persisted in New England memory and popular culture long after the order was universally suppressed in 1773. The Jesuits' legendary successes with Indians were attributed to a dark supernatural ability to mislead potential Christians. In reality, however, the Jesuits also had some practical shortcomings as missionaries that were far more significant than their contemporary detractors suggested.

Jesuit missionaries attracted a significant number of Wabanaki converts, but they did not control them. While the Wabanakis accepted and even embraced Catholicism, they did not view Christian interests and French interests as one. Frequently, Jesuit initiatives to bind the Indians exclusively to French interests were blocked by assertive Wabanaki leaders, who jealously guarded the prerogatives of leadership. This complicated their relationship with Jesuits. And when cooperation with the English suited them — and occasionally it did — the Wabanakis cooperated.[32] This angered the Jesuits, who feared that a Wabanaki embrace of *l'hérésie calviniste* would surely follow. Even the seasoned Sebastien Rale occasionally mistook religious identification for political allegiance. Indeed, when it came to the Kennebec Wabanaki, Jesuits like Sebastien Rale lacked the authority to compel them to deviate from their own goals.[33]

To distant English observers, the Jesuits who lived in the Wabanaki missions were pernicious enemies of the New England Way.[34] Fabled Jesuit cunning alone, however, could not account for Catholic successes and Protestant limitations. Though ministers would eventually try to supplant Catholic priests, they first had to devise methods of meeting their neophytes' needs. Given the many drawbacks of English Maine as a place to settle and secure one's future, it took many men, and many decades, before a mission such as Baxter's could be assured of the logistical support that a qualified minister needed to survive and thrive.

For years, Massachusetts regarded the state of religion in Maine with great concern. Porous boundaries, unregulated migration and settlement, upheaval from war, and lax application of laws and community standards that supported religious conformity fostered an unstable religious environment. Good ministers could have helped address the problem, and Massachusetts officials were always anxious to find men of God who were content to go to the Eastward. But instead of effectively spreading the word of God and community stability, ministers sometimes did the opposite.

Throughout the seventeenth and early eighteenth century, the Province of Maine continued to attract religiously problematic settlers. The ministers who came to lead their congregations exhibited many of the same traits. Included among their ranks were suspected or accused Quakers, Baptists, apostates, witches, drunkards, wife-killers, and adulterers. Others were pious and took their ministerial role seriously but became outspoken opponents of the extension of the Puritan sphere of influence from Massachusetts. These ministers were often indistinguishable from their most unruly lay neighbors. Some were even accused of partaking in the very subversive activities that their ministerial influence was meant to counteract.

One of the most troublesome was George Burdett, who came to York while it was still controlled by the Gorges family. He soon ran afoul of his neighbors and congregants amid accusations of seducing at least four married women. Put on trial, Burdett was found guilty of disturbing the peace, incontinency, and "dangerous speeches the better to seduce that weake sex of women to his incontinent practices."[35] While Burdett might have been an ill-tempered rake, he was also a radical antinomian partisan who might have been seen as a challenger to the Anglican see that Ferdinando Gorges desired to erect in York. This might have contributed to his downfall as much as the putative "incontinent practices."[36]

The lack of religious conformity or even predictability among men who identified themselves as clergy created frequent headaches for the Massachusetts authorities. In 1659 Henry Josselyn and Robert Jordan accused the minister of Black Point, John Thorpe, of "preaching unsound doctrines."[37] Two years later, Thorpe's congregants issued their own denunciation, accusing Thorpe of "notorious Crimes in his Convarsation as may appere by severall testimonies upon oath and sevarall prsentments in Court of Drunkenes & Revilings & slaundring of neightbours & others and divars Inordinat Cariges verie unsemly for any Christian much more uncomly for a minister of the gospel of Jesus Christ." They found Thorpe unsuitable "to Instruct us in the wais of salvation," and relieved him of his spiritual duties.[38]

An ironic twist to Thorpe's case is that one of his most vocal opponents, Robert Jordan, was himself a controversy-courting man of God. Jordan's problem was his outspoken commitment to the Church of England and his profound dislike of Puritanism. A devoted "Orthodox Deane of the Church of England," an admirer of the policies of William Laud, and outspoken enemy of Massachusetts Puritanism, the English-born and Oxford-educated Jordan hoped to restore the province to the Anglicanism of Ferdinando Gorges.[39] In addition to his ministerial duties, Jordan was an active civic leader and lawyer, one of the new, aggressively self-confident frontier settlers who knew that leadership in the province could lead to glory and stability for himself. In 1660, at the height of his provincial career, he ran afoul of the province's new Puritan administration and was jailed for "baptizing his children in the episcopal mode."[40] Angered at the criminalization of a practice that had hitherto enjoyed protection, and unable to hold his tongue about it, Jordan was fined for "saiing the Gov. of Boston was a Roge."[41] After that, the minister saved his vitriol for the Massachusetts ministerial elite and was subsequently brought before the court in 1667 for calling the late Puritan minister John Cotton "a liar, [who] died with a lie in his mouth, and . . . has gone to

Hell with a pack of lies."[42] In yet another court case, the minister was accused of breaking up a marriage not through adultery but by fostering a married woman's interest in Anglicanism.[43]

Robert Jordan's difficulties demonstrate the peculiar religious situation of late seventeenth- and early eighteenth-century Maine. On the one hand, Puritan officials wanted conformity to Puritan orthodoxy in the Eastward settlements. On the other, they needed living English bodies to populate the region. But few orthodox ministers who could procure pulpits in less challenging locations were interested in settling the frontier. Consequently, Puritan Massachusetts walked a fine line and practiced at least a modicum of toleration. This explains Jordan's persistent presence in Maine and his relative freedom of movement. Despite the growth of Puritan control in the region, Jordan continued to hold Anglican services in Spurwink, interrupted only by the onset of King Philip's War, which drove him and his family to New Hampshire. There he enjoyed the protection of Major Nicholas Shapleigh, a less vulnerable friend and fellow opponent of Massachusetts. A Quaker, Shapleigh was himself a religious outsider who had sought safety in New Hampshire after he also ran afoul of Massachusetts authorities.[44] Through canny maneuvers and with the aid of powerful friends, Robert Jordan managed to retain his sizeable Maine plantation, preserving it for his children. Returning to Maine to claim their patrimony, however, Jordan's children suffered the same acute personal and financial losses during the wars of empire as their Reformed neighbors did. Several members of subsequent generations were killed in raids on English settlements. Others were taken to Canada and never returned.[45] Perhaps the Jordan family's devout Puritan neighbors might have been tempted to attribute the family's misfortunes to Providence had they not suffered from the same depredations themselves.

As the seventeenth century wore on, the situation regarding quality ministers changed little. Unlike Burdett, Thorpe, or Jordan, who stayed in the Eastward settlements long enough to spread vice, sow discord, or both, rogue ministers passed in and out of the region with ease, claiming the benefits of ministerial status while working their mischief until they were unmasked. This was not uncommon throughout New England. As late as 1690, Increase Mather complained about the activities of "a Debauched Priest" who was making the rounds throughout New England and who, "besides the good work of Baptizing a noted whore or two of his acquaintance, made private marriages without the Publication of Banns." This rogue minister later quit New England entirely for the freedom of southern New Jersey's nearly barren coast.[46]

Other ministers came to the frontier with sincere intentions and appropriate credentials, but cast them off in favor of other work once the challenges of the frontier became apparent. Minister to merchant was a common frontier transformation. In the case of Benjamin Blackman, this included military leadership as well. Blackman, a Connecticut minister's son, was a new Harvard graduate when he arrived at Black Point shortly after graduation to take up the post at the town's church (the first to commit to the region in the wake of the disastrous tenure of John Thorpe). By 1680 Blackman left the ministry for all intents and purposes. Declining to settle at the church at Black Point, he moved to Saco and pursued multiple business interests, including milling, timber, and land speculation.[47] Blackman later became a justice of the peace and militia captain. In contrast to the ministers who left Maine to pursue their calling elsewhere in New England, Blackman persevered in the province, forging civic and business connections and standing fast on the frontier when war threatened the English settlements. He protected these assets with force: too much for some of his neighbors, who accused him of excessively tough dealing with the Wabanakis. Blackman was generally thought to have triggered the sequence of events that released the full fury of Indian and French hostilities on Maine, leading directly to the local outbreak of King William's War. It began in 1688, when Blackman apprehended twenty Wabanakis near North Yarmouth for killing cattle, and sent them to Boston to be jailed.[48] In response, the Wabanakis took sixteen Mainers captive and killed four others in the process, leading to an escalation in hostilities.[49] Perhaps the narrative might have been different if the ministry had taken Benjamin Blackman in another direction.

For the Harvard men who drifted toward the frontier, Maine could be a place of both spiritual and physical destruction. Some early ministers drank, swore, insulted Puritan saints, seduced married women, cultivated dissent against the Puritans, Anglicans, or their neighbors, or abandoned the ministry altogether. But few outdid George Burroughs in terms of depravity. Burroughs, a minister at Wells who already had a roster of complaints against him, was accused of witchcraft in the Essex County hysteria of 1692 and executed. His story, as Mary Beth Norton has noted, reflected the general unease that Massachusetts residents harbored about the northern frontier. The case against Burroughs conjured the image of evil, subversive men disguised as gospel ministers who murdered their wives, swore fealty to the devil in exchange for superhuman strength, and bewitched soldiers to keep them from triumphing over God's enemies.[50]

Some of Burroughs's misfortunes might be attributed to the fact that he had inherited a troubled pulpit in which no gospel minister lasted long. Wells had chronic difficulties attracting and maintaining a minister, a problem that persisted throughout most of the second half of the seventeenth century. The long succession of ministers began with Hugh Gunnison, who came to Wells at the start of his ministerial career in 1654. He quickly left that pulpit to assume one in Kittery. The congregants there soon refused to ordain him because of his "low character."[51] Shortly thereafter, Seth Fletcher was called to Wells to preach, and ordained to the church three years later. But he too courted controversy and departed in 1660 for Saco, leaving behind descendants who later allied themselves with the highly unpopular, anti-Puritan and pro-Anglican Andros faction.[52] Next came Joseph Emerson, who served two brief stints in Wells before moving back to Massachusetts.[53] After Emerson came John Buss, who stayed in Wells for at least a decade and struggled through King Philip's War with his congregants. But postwar accusations that he was "indifferent to religion" proved too much for this seemingly sincere man of God. Buss moved on to Durham, New Hampshire, where he was later ordained. He then spent the remaining thirty-three years of his career in relative peace and ministerial fulfillment—suggesting that it was

Wells, not Buss's orthodoxy or conviction, that was the problem.[54] Next came Percival Green, who died young after only a year in Wells. Green's loss was doubly grievous since he had been close to establishing a badly needed school for the town's children. His death deprived Wells not only of a minister but of a much hoped-for symbol of the community's persistence in trying times.[55] Afterward came Richard Martyn, a classmate of Green, who came to Wells in 1688. In 1690 he too died young from another omnipresent frontier danger, infectious disease.[56]

In total, Wells had six ministers in thirty-six years—a high turn-over by any standard, given the long tenure that other ministers enjoyed in the more established parts of New England. No one managed to stay more than a decade, and there were large gaps between pastorates. Perhaps the Wells pulpit had come to be regarded as tainted, making the accusations against the ill-fated George Burroughs (who was already unpopular and suspected of unorthodoxy) all the more credible.[57]

If Wells's failure to keep its pulpit puzzled ministerial candidates, the killing of York's minister, Shubael Dummer, hammered home the very real and constant danger posed by the Indians and their French allies.[58] As the town's Protestant leader, Dummer was deliberately targeted by the French and Indian raiders, who shot the minister during the Candlemas massacre in full view of his terrified congregants. Cotton Mather's memorial of this ministerial death describes Dummer's killing with religious metaphors that his readers were sure to comprehend. Mather described Dummer as struck down "[as he] was just going to take his Horse at his own Door, upon a Journey in the Service of God, when the Tygres that were making their Depredations upon the Sheep of York seiz'd upon their Shepherd; and they shot him so, that they left him Dead among the Tribe of Abel on the Ground." Mather believed that the minister's death had been plotted by "some Romish Missionaries [who] had long been wishing, that they might Embrue their Hands in the Blood of some New-English MINISTER."[59] Adding to the terror, the assassins then mocked their victim by stealing and donning the garb of his office.

To New Englanders, the murder was a particularly ungodly act on multiple levels: murder and mockery aside, Dummer had been one of the few settled ministers who seemed content to stay on the troubled Eastward.

Ironically, Shubael Dummer's murder was invested with symbolism for both the French and the frontier English. Having heard a different account of the killing, the intendant of New France, Jean Bouchart de Champigny, told his own version of the story, reporting matter-of-factly to Governor Frontenac that the minister was shot "while escaping on his horse."[60] Champigny's version suggests that New England ministers, unlike the martyrdom-seeking Jesuits, were cowards whose first impulses were to abandon, rather than protect, their congregants. Where Cotton Mather saw a saint, Champigny saw a coward. Regardless of the perspective, the English, French, and Wabanakis appear to have agreed that a gospel minister like Shubael Dummer was a key symbol of settlement, stability, and cohesion. Killing him in front of his congregation sent a potent psychological message to friend and foe alike about the persistent vulnerability of Maine's settlements.

The death of Shubael Dummer provided ample proof that Maine's dangers were numerous. This grim reality slowed efforts to fit Maine with a regular ministry. And furthermore, enemies also came from within. Chief among these were Edmund Andros and his supporters. Long suspected of playing the French and Wabanakis against the English, the hated royal governor was suspected by his detractors of plotting to hand New England over to the French, cavorting with Native American women, supplying Native American men with English weapons, and overtly practicing popery.[61] Facing removal from office and jail, Andros struck back against his colonial enemies, accusing the Puritans of failing to evangelize the Indians and, through arrogance, bringing the full wrath of these Indians upon their own heads. One pro-Andros author damningly charged that "French Priests and Jesuits have dwelt and inhabited [among the Wabanakis], and endeavored to propagate their Religion amongst them, which is more than any of our English Priests or Teachers have done, for although by the Piety of our Forefathers Considerable Sums of Mony have been given, and a corporation erected for the Evangelization of the Indians in N-E, very small progress hath bee hitherto made therein."[62] If the colonists played the popery card, so did the besieged royalists, and they tossed in accusations of hypocrisy and theft of missionary funds for good measure.

To some Puritans, the royalist accusations pointed to a sad reality. Even Cotton Mather chronically bemoaned the failure of the New England ministry to provide spiritual reinforcements for the frontiers and to divert the spiritual interests of the Indians toward the metaphoric Puritan city on the hill. Through Hannah Swarton's narrative, Mather stated as much when he told of the taunts Hannah endured from her Catholic Indian mistress, who chided the Puritan captive for her faith's reluctance to proselytize to the Wabanakis.[63] Mather was careful not to cast blame on the ministers who were already tending provincial flocks. Instead, he argued that the government had failed to support further efforts for Native American proselytization.[64] New England collectively bore responsibility for the spice of popery's persistence on the Maine frontier, and it was best countered through ministers charged with challenging the Jesuits who operated so openly on Puritan New England's doorstep.

Ministerial Challenge to the Eastward: Black Robes and Harvard Men

By the end of the seventeenth century, Maine's Protestant religious culture was a spiritual shambles. In 1700 Lord Bellomont, who was serving a brief term as the governor of Massachusetts, suggested diverting a French-speaking minister from New Oxford to counteract the effects of "French Jesuits debauching . . . Indians."[65] Bellomont knew well the effectiveness of the Jesuits in supporting Indian war against English interests. For fifty years the frontiers of New York, over which he had also been governor, had been pierced multiple times by Indian raids in which Jesuits were complicit. Bellomont hoped to counter these effects by bringing badly needed spiritual workers to the area. By 1700 there were only nine ministers serving all the English settlements to the Eastward. Of these, only John Newmarch (Kittery), John Wade (South Berwick), Samuel Emery (Wells), and Samuel Moody (York) were ordained and serving regularly constituted churches.[66] The ministers Bellomont hoped to secure would serve two functions: communicating religion in French, which mirrored the Jesuits' own mother tongue, and challenging the Jesuits in their language of greatest fluency.

Massachusetts governor Dudley was likewise concerned over the province's deficit of Protestant ministers and appealed to the Board of Trade for help, reporting, "There was nothing done towards the Maintenance of a Minister in several places."[67] New England had a strong tradition of local support for the ministry, with each community caring for its meetinghouse, minister's house, and salary. Other forms of compensation in the form of food, drink, and firewood were donated by congregants as well. But in settlements that had been decimated by King William's War, the remaining settlers had little or nothing to give in support of the ministry. Intervention from London was needed to sustain orthodox ministers and their families. With its broad mandate to address numerous problems pertaining to the management of Britain's American colonies, the board seemed well suited to provide the money, goods, and other resources needed to attract quality ministers to Maine.

But even government assurances could not guarantee that ministers would be protected from the ebb and flow of hostilities between the Maine settlements and their neighbors. Maine ministers who managed to stay on the frontier during the wars of empire shared every disadvantage with their neighbors. They too lost their homes, livestock, and personal belongings. Compounding their losses was a lack of funding for ministerial salaries, usually a community responsibility. Settlers who had to reconstruct their own lives often lacked the means to contribute to a minister's upkeep, and ministers, with no help and since they had lost as many resources as their congregants, took advantage of the fact that their trade was movable and left.

At least one minister who wanted to stay in Maine devised a workable solution. Samuel Moody of York successfully merged spiritual and military duties, becoming a living model for frontiers well defended in the process.[68] Like many of his peers, the Massachusetts-born, Harvard-educated Moody was not native to the frontier. When he came to York after the death of Shubael Dummer, he found a congregation eager to avoid the devastation of another Candlemas massacre. Together they built a stockade, complete with flankers for added defense, to enclose the meeting- and minister's houses. This new spiritual architecture evoked the design of Maine's Catholic missions, where physical protection and worship spaces had long been intertwined.

Samuel Moody had a personality to match his godly fort, where he claimed a spiritual authority that mirrored his military experience.[69] Moody's public assertiveness with his Protestant congregation resembled the absolute spiritual authority that the Catholic mission priests aimed to establish over their neophytes. Assertive and voluble, Moody became, in Charles Clark's words, York's "spiritual dictator."[70] The spiritual militarization of York and "Father Moody's" militant ministry thrived there for decades until the minister's death in 1747.[71]

Moody's firm hand and his dual role as spiritual leader and fighter further resembled Jesuit missions by blending both to develop a holistic frontier community bound together in a common cause of identity, origins, and most importantly, religion. Like Jesuit priests, who served political functions as well as religious ones, Moody increasingly played multiple roles that straddled both the spiritual and material worlds. A case in point was the minister's attempt to woo Christian Indians away from the influence of local Jesuits.[72] Massachusetts supported Moody in this effort, and Joseph Dudley advised him. "The next visit the Indians make you at the fort," the governor wrote, "receive them friendly and acquaint them that in order to a firm and lasting peace between the Queen of Great Britayn & the french king there is a cessation of arms Concluded for four months to give the Necessary time to make it perfect & that the governments of the french and English are commanded not to Hurt each other till they shall hear the

Issue and be further Directed."[73] "Further directed" suggests proselytization, a strategy for winning the English friends and allies which had seemingly worked for the French. Certainly the Jesuits saw the resulting interactions that way: the same year Dudley wrote to Moody, Sebastien Rale countered with the threat that any attempt to woo his neophytes to Protestantism would be considered an *acte d'hostilité*, regardless of the state of relations between the French king and British queen.[74]

The Jesuits resented Moody's attempts, as well as those of other Protestants, to supplant them among the Wabanakis. To mission priest Jacques Bigot, the English represented a potentially serious challenge to the Jesuits' work among the Maine Indians—so threatening, in fact, that he complained to his superior that they had damaged his health: "My return caused great joy among my beloved savages, who thought me dead. I at once set about visiting the three villages to confess the savages, to make them perform their Easter duties, and to strengthen them against the solicitations of the English—who do everything in their power to induce them to receive ministers. All these fatigues have brought on a second attack of fever. Nevertheless, I perform all my duties; and not a day has passed without my having the consolation of saying mass."[75]

Additional threats to the Jesuits came from Protestant people who were not ministers but had come to believe that the Christianities that converged in Maine could not share the land. Bigot himself witnessed an attempt by an English sea captain to convince the Wabanakis to accept an English minister, which rattled the priest so much that he refused invitations to dine on board the captain's ship for fear of being kidnapped.[76]

Even as France and England were at peace, their New World missionaries were discreetly prosecuting the war for souls on their own. By the time Rale threatened Moody, the Massachusetts government had for years been looking for ways to contain or evict the Jesuits who inhabited what they considered to be English territory. It had begun with a war of words. In 1700 Jacques Bigot's fellow Jesuit and brother, Vincent, sent a letter to George Turfrey, commander of the English garrison at Saco. The tone of the letter hints of at least one earlier confrontation between the two men, which produced lingering hostility. Mocking, derisive, and, by eighteenth-century standards, insultingly informal, Bigot informed Turfrey that he had no intention of backing down in the battle for souls. Bigot wrote to Turfrey, "My George, believe me, this one thing I aim at in writing, warning . . . that you may be sensible in the vanity of your Religion . . . take care of your Salvation; which if it were possible I would willingly secure to you with my blood."[77] Massachusetts authorities did not take such threats to their province's commanders lightly. In 1701, with the support of a strengthened English law that forbade Jesuits from English territories on pain of death, William Stoughton wrote a stinging rebuke to Bigot. Addressed "to Vincent—a *Bigot,*" the letter accused the priest of "a Licentiousness of tyrañising over our Consciences and destroying our Souls." Stoughton warned Bigot to "speedily [betake] your self to Quebeck, or Paris, or Rome or where you please out of this Jurisdiction. Except you can find it in your heart to forego your superstitions for Christ and embrace the true reformed Religion which most firmly retains everything that is Christian in yours." Stoughton's letter reinforced the governor's conviction that the priest was squatting on territory that was Protestant, even if Protestants had yet to secure the claim through settlement.[78]

The English had good reason to suspect that Bigot's threat was not an idle one, for they knew that frontier priests like the Pentagoët Sulpician, Louis-Pierre Thury, had joined mission Indians in the attack on Pemaquid during King William's War. A decade and another war later, Rale was making similar threats of violence toward the English. In contrast to the Jesuit martyrs of an early age, the members of the generation that matured in their work during the wars of empire used their position within their missions to work as active agents of both Indian and French interests, even if that meant taking up weapons themselves.[79] In general, these extraspiritual activities by priests enjoyed the support and protection of Canada's governor. But that governor could—and sometimes did—disavow priest-inspired anti-English agitation when it blatantly jeopardized French interests. Ultimately, the only protection the Jesuits could truly count on came from their faith in their righteousness, their neophytes, and each other.

Still, the Society of Jesus had a powerful model for the warrior priest in the example of its founder, Ignatius Loyola, the militant yet erudite soldier-saint of post-Reformation Catholicism. Implementing Ignatian teachings that encouraged the order's members literally to combat heresy molded the Jesuits, as one modern historian notes, into the "shock troops" of Catholic Reformation reforms.[80] The military metaphor for the spiritual fighters who followed Ignatius's example found numerous outlets on the Maine frontier—and some Protestants knew it. One of these was Joshua Scottow, a Black Point settler, an Englishman who knew well the Jesuit reputation for the literal spiritual combat meant to dispel Protestant heresies. Writing "Igne-nate, Hell-born Loyola" whose "Jesu-ite" priests should "Depart from Jesus," Scottow punned with Jesuit-specific words to illustrate his contempt for the order.[81] Scottow denounced Jesuit activities that, to him, diverged from spiritual work and were therefore unchristian.

From the perspective of Jesuit missionaries, however, activities that blended proselytization and the vigorous fighting of Protestantism allowed them to apply their talents to a diverse set of useful purposes. Jesuit Joseph Aubery, a onetime missionary at Norridgewock, lent his cartographic talents to arguing that implementation of the Treaty of Utrecht would cheat the French out of what was left of mainland Acadia.[82] Sebastien Rale was both a missionary and a reliable intelligence agent of the French state during Dummer's War.[83] As he matured in the mission field, another Jesuit, Étienne Lauverjat, became increasingly active in his attempts to maintain political control over the Penobscot Indians and subdue an unruly French settlement in modern-day New Brunswick. Pierre Joseph de La Chasse publicized the activities of Maine missionaries in both Canada and abroad, and kept money and other forms of support flowing into his order's missions.[84]

And these were just the Jesuits. For Protestants, the most notorious missionaries were the seminary priests, like Louis-Pierre Thury, the Pentagoët Sulpician who actively engaged in combat against English; and Henri-Antoine Meulan de Meriel, who, based in Montreal and with close ties to local colonial elites, had formidable resources at his disposal, the full effect of which he turned toward converting captive English women, men, and children.

The Catholic priests of New France possessed a diverse array of talents, and found diverse outlets for them. And with no literal families to protect, they had the time and inclination to develop them. It is little wonder that English settlers like Joshua Scottow, who clearly knew something of their reputation as dangerous spiritual enemies, found their presence nearby alarming.

During the early eighteenth century, Massachusetts demonstrated its concern over the spiritual health of Maine's Protestant people, as well as Protestantism's explicit connections to other types of colonial stability, such as local governance and economic activity. It spearheaded new efforts to shore up the Protestant identity of the province's settlers. Stabilization led to a new militarism among the ministers themselves. The most successful (and resilient) were both ministering to civilians and offering spiritual protection and military leadership to the militia. Rival Catholic priests were engaged in similar enterprises, ministering to the Wabanakis and, when appropriate, providing intelligence to the government of New France in exchange for protection of mission territory. It was into this world that the Protestant missionary Joseph Baxter stepped in 1717.

Despite powerful Catholic establishments, Joseph Baxter would be a well-supported competitor in the mission field. In contrast to many of his predecessors, Baxter was orthodox, zealous, and learned.[85] He could also count on aid of various kinds from the Massachusetts Assembly, which not only supported his efforts in principle but had provided for his physical comfort. Most importantly, he was willing to go, and his home congregation seemed willing to part with him. As late as 1743 Baxter was still receiving only fifty-five pounds annually for his ministrations to the community. With a list of disputes among congregants and a large family to support, the minister likely looked to Maine not as a frontier of last resort but as a land of opportunity.[86]

Baxter's reaction to Maine as an opportunity represents a transition among ministers. Increased efforts to stabilize the territory and economic incentives made Maine a viable alternative to unsatisfactory pulpits elsewhere. Economic incentives were indeed readily available: the minister's compensation offered by the Pejepscot Proprietors included assurances that Baxter's "known zeal to do good & serve the interest of religioun" and "the great good not of a particular congregation only but the whole land" would be rewarded generously with tracts of land, appropriate for both harvesting resources and for future development.[87]

In the eighteenth century, offers that paired the drive to extend Protestant religious culture with the promise of worldly goods were common and desirable. Baxter was, after all, a father of six, who dispatched one of his religious duties by creating and providing for a large family. Though his promised salary was small (£15 less than Medfield was paying him), the land grants held significant promise, bringing the minister's total compensation to £150 and offering him additional ways, through land transactions and trade contacts, to contribute to the well-being of the region's Protestant people.[88]

Even Samuel Shute himself wrote to the minister to assure him that his interests would be safe. The governor promised Baxter that Massachusetts was "carrying forward settlement [in Maine] & having entered into engagements with the Province to build a Fort, there, have lately finished it beyond all expectation, which is owing not so much to our industrious application, tho that was not wanting—as the remarkable smiles of Providence on the undertaking too long here to relate, & which gives us hopes of our future success: It is a fine strong stone fort well built with lime, mounted with ten pieces of canon & garrisoned with a captain and fifteen men."[89] In referencing the role Providence played in the early completion of the fort at Arrowsic, Shute reminded Baxter that extending English settlement was a blessed endeavor. This assurance also followed the model devised by Samuel Moody at York, where physical safety went hand-in-hand with proselytization.

With a significant increase in income came a vast increase in work—of maintaining a congregation, preaching to the Wabanakis, undermining the Jesuits, and developing his own business interests—which helped not only the minister and his family but the settlement overall, and expectations for Baxter's success would be high. To ensure he understood all that was expected of him, the Pejepscot Proprietors wrote to Baxter, "We desire religion, not only among the garrisons and the inhabitants which we expect will be a good number went thither in the spring, but also the Indians, who are almost daily there. It is necessary that the person engaging in this work should be full of self-denial, zeal for religion & compassion to ignorant & perishing Idolaters & one who will be constant to forego many . . . enjoyments & endure some hardships & hazards for the satisfaction of doing good here & the prospect of a future reward."[90] To bring the Kennebec Wabanakis to "the same Religion" as the English required Baxter to bring a forceful Protestant vision into a region suffused with "foolish superstitious and plain Idolatries."[91] This was an exercise in spiritual multitasking expected of relatively few New England Protestant ministers. Yet it bore a strong resemblance to the efforts of the nearby Jesuits, who were likewise expected to serve the already-Christian faithful, manage the mission's physical environs, attract new converts, and prevent the spread of false religion.

Certainly these were all tasks that Sebastien Rale, the man who would be Baxter's nearest ministerial colleague, performed very well. Now he would face a concerted, organized, and well-funded effort, launched by rival Christians, to undermine his religious enterprises. The priest likely knew such an effort was coming: in the years following the Peace of Utrecht, a sizeable number of speculators from other parts of New England were convinced that the terms of the treaty ensured the safety of their investments. These proprietors included the well-connected Pejepscot group, who pushed for the quick establishment of fortified settlements. What actually constituted the post-Utrecht boundary, however, was still mired in vagueness and confusion long after 1713. The Kennebec River region remained contested, and Rale's Norridgewock, the largest Jesuit mission in the Province of Maine, was situated right in its heart. By hiring their own missionary to work among the Indians, the Pejepscot Proprietors were firing an unambiguous shot across the bow of mission Catholicism, and by extension, French claims to the region.

The unsettled nature of the competing claims to the Kennebec led to frequent cultural encounters that were personal, ideological,

Figure 9. Sacramental vessels likely used by Sebastion Rale found at the remains of the Norridgewock mission. Courtesy of the Maine State Museum.

and religious. Rale himself was like any other borderland dweller who coexisted with the English as time, place, and circumstance suited. During Queen Anne's War, French authorities accused the priest of discouraging the Wabanakis from supporting the French by taking up arms against the English.[92] Word of Rale's fondness for lively and even humorous theological debate with Protestants reached as far as Boston's ministerial community, where Cotton Mather fantasized about converting the Jesuit with pro-Protestant arguments laid out artfully in Latin.[93] Perhaps taking Mather's fantasy one step further, Samuel Sewall, who never met the priest but was well aware of his reputation as an effective minister and linguist, sent him a gift in 1717. Sewall chose for Rale a collection of personal meditations in English, and inscribed in the cover, "*Samuel Sewall Sebastien Rale salutem mittit*" (Samuel Sewall sends greetings to Sebastien Rale).[94] While it is tempting to speculate that the gift was meant as both a compliment and a barb that highlighted the contrast between the "secret tongue" of Latin and the importance of the vernacular in Reformed religion, the inscription also hints at a theological and cultural rapprochement by connecting a common thread that united educated Christian Euro-American men of God, even those in the wilderness. Rale also recognized that the English, as fellow Euro-Americans, brought with them settlers with a range of talents, and he was not averse to seeking them out when he found himself in need.

When he suffered a serious leg injury in 1716 falling off a church steeple he was repairing, he turned to Hugh Adams, a onetime Puritan minister who had settled at Arrowsic and set himself up as a physician. Adams willingly treated the priest and admitted to enjoying his company.[95] According to contemporary historian Jeremy Belknap, Adams also cherished the hope that Rale, whom he found accommodating and reasonable, "would thenceforth exert his influence for peace" in the region.[96] To Adams, there was nothing intrinsically defective about the Jesuit that would keep him from living in harmony with his neighbors. Real encounters could also humanize the image of the shadowy papist agent on the frontier.

Joseph Baxter's first encounters with a Jesuit other than Rale, the man he was charged with supplanting, were similarly nuanced. His first meeting was with either Pierre de La Chasse or Étienne Lauverjat, the Jesuit who replaced the Sulpician Thury at Pentagoët and was in close council with Joseph d'Abbadie and Bernard Anselm d'Abbadie de Saint-Castin, the half-Wabanaki sons of the settlement's French proprietor.[97] Like Druillettes and Eliot almost seventy years before (and more recently, Adams and Rale), Baxter and the anonymous Jesuit greeted each other with civility. The Jesuit visited Baxter at least once and corresponded with him several times.[98] The encounters included, by Baxter's reckoning, "a great deal of Discourse," which perhaps focused on English assurances that their designs on the area were peaceful. Other events added to this hope. At one point, John Gyles, an ex-captive cum culture broker for the English, reported to Baxter that Lauverjat had told his mission Indians that "there is a strong Peace between ye French and English and I believe it will be a lasting one," and he thus seemed to be encouraging the Wabanakis to maintain the peace on their end.[99]

But as Baxter would soon discover for himself, the Society of Jesus attracted dynamic individuals and their approaches to comprehensive mission management varied. Factors influencing their responses to the Protestant challenge included geographical isolation, their physical separation from established Catholic hierarchies, and the length of their tenure among the Eastern Indians.[100] A relatively new or untested missionary like Lauverjat might err on the side of religious accommodation. But an experienced veteran like Rale, who had long been exposed to the intricacies of borderland politics and their implications for frontier Christian culture, would likely act with greater assertiveness in his dealings with local Protestants. The older Jesuit drew the line at English ministers who sought to change the prevailing religious culture. And in this he was not alone, as demonstrated when New France's Governor Vaudreuil wrote Rale, "I am of the opinion that, if the [Wabanaki] have taken a Sincere resolution not to allow The English On Their Land, they must not hesitate to Drive them Therefrom as Soon as Possible."[101]

Supported by New France and valued by the Wabanakis, Rale was ultimately far better equipped than Lauverjat to reject Protestant overtures. Seasoned by years of field work, Rale was well grounded in Kennebec culture and more acutely aware of their motives. This Jesuit who claimed to see, hear and speak "only as an Indian" juggled not one but three masters: mission community, state, and faith.[102] The Norridgewock he helped create reflected these loyalties, and Rale's activities displayed these multiple allegiances.

The skirmish between Baxter and Rale for the souls of the Kennebecs was relatively brief. The minister attempted to reorient existing patterns of religious devotion by substituting Protestant meetings with Scripture readings and hymns for Catholic liturgies, Protestant works of piety for Catholic ones, alluring objects for the tactile elements of Catholic worship. The "curiosities" that Baxter elicited from the Massachusetts Assembly were a particularly cunning tool, used to attract children, who in turn, it was hoped, would be educated in the school Baxter planned to found. These children were then expected to bring Protestant Christianity into the mission via a younger generation, subverting the prevailing Christian culture from within and elevating the place of Protestantism among the Kennebec Wabanakis.

Faced with an effort to undermine his work through the use of tools that Jesuits had themselves employed, Rale acted swiftly to counter the threat, sending the minister a one-hundred-page letter in Latin that systematically refuted the tenets of Reformed religion. The Kennebec courier who delivered the letter was instructed to leave the following day with the minister's reply, an impertinent gesture

meant to put the minister on the spot and reveal his lack of learning.[103] Other initiatives to keep the Kennebecs Catholic were directed
toward the Indians themselves. Baxter heard told of

> an Apparition yt the Jesuit at Nerridgewock saw who Lying alone
> in his wigwam, awaked in ye night and saw a great Light as if his
> wigwam had been in fire, whereupon he got up, and went abroad,
> and after some time he returned to his wigwam, and went to sleep
> again; and after awhile he waked, and felt as it were a hand upon
> his Throat yt almost choaked him, saw a great light again, and
> heard a voice saying it is in vain for you to take any pains with
> these Indians, your children, for I have got possession of them,
> and will keep possession of them.[104]

In relaying this vision to the mission's Indians, Rale deployed the
apocalyptic horrors described in the last book of the New Testament
and cannily applied them in ways that complemented Native American beliefs in the power and truth of dreams. These purported dreams
by a religious leader of long standing were sure to strike a chord with
older Wabanaki leaders who, despite their connection to Catholicism, demonstrated some willingness to make peace with the English
and accept, at least in theory, the presence of a potential Protestant
proselytizer in their midst. Rale warned these advocates, "You will
do ye Devils work, &c., the Devil will take you."[105] To Rale and the
Indian coreligionists he castigated, the figure of the Devil himself, a
living frontier presence, loomed sufficiently large to menace Indian
appeasers of English interests. Describing these fiery prophetic terrors
of the torments of hell was a powerful mnemonic device for evoking
the horrors of frontier warfare, from which Maine's Indians suffered
as much as local Euro-Americans.

In the end, these visions, along with the bonds of genuine spiritual kinship between the Kennebecs and their Catholic missionary
and persistent diplomatic ties to the French in Canada, were likely
responsible for severely hampering Joseph Baxter's success as a Prot -
estant missionary. By 1718 Baxter was back in Medfield serving the
same difficult congregation. His personal financial situation, how-

ever, had improved considerably. Despite his failure to supplant Rale, Baxter still claimed a secondary, more worldly prize of Maine land, including an island that to this day bears his name.[106]

Sebastien Rale did not fare as well. His victory over the Protestant missionary was small compared with the battles with the English yet to come. In the years after 1718, Rale continued to be regarded by Massachusetts governor Samuel Shute as the instigator of anti-English sentiments among the Eastern Indians, who persistently thwarted peace and trade negotiations.[107] The claim was not without merit. Assuming a role he had rejected earlier in his ministerial career, Rale now actively assisted the French government in Canada against the English. As a result, and despite a state of peace between Britain and France, tensions between the Wabanakis and provincial Euro-Americans ran high.

Back in Boston, Samuel Shute was eager to avert another war to the Eastward. But he was also wrestling with problems created in part by his own unorthodox religious background and the lack of trust among Puritan elites that it engendered. Shute was the grandson of Joseph Caryl, a noted English Nonconforming minister, in whose faith he was raised. As an adult, however, Shute turned his back on his grandfather's Puritanism and joined the Church of England. Sent to Massachusetts as a royal appointee, he attempted to appease Puritans while remaining true to his own religious preferences by attending the church services of both.[108] This politically expedient strategy was one of several Shute adopted to please the difficult Massachusetts Assembly, on whose cooperation he relied for the smooth governance of the colony. But as neither fully Puritan nor fully Anglican, Shute continued to be regarded as religiously suspect. This contributed to his poor relationship with the assembly, which deteriorated more with each passing year. By 1718—the year of his letter to Sebastien Rale scolding the Jesuit for unchristian behavior—the governor was likely aware that the assembly was eager to point to his missteps as grounds to remove him from office—the fate of the despised Edmund Andros of the not-so-distant past. Certainly tolerating a Jesuit in such close proximity to Puritans stirred up memories of the pro-Catholic conspiracy to the Eastward of which Andros had been suspected. With an agitated frontier Jesuit threatening to undermine imperial peace by inflaming anti-English sentiment among the Wabanakis, and powerful enemies in the assembly, the governor needed to find opportunities to protect his interests.

Shute's 1718 letter to the Maine Jesuit for his uncharitable treatment of a Puritan missionary demonstrated both his awareness of the Eastward's key problems and his allegiance to colonial Protestants. The letter elevated universally held Christian principles above all other concerns. In this way, it provided Shute with an appropriate venue for setting his own record straight while underplaying the tensions between two Euro-American powers that were trying to cling to a fragile peace.

Years passed, but tensions between Protestant settlements and Catholic missions persisted. In the winter of 1721–22, a New England unit militia under Thomas Westbrook descended on the Norridgewock mission. Warned by scouts, Rale hid in the forest, but left behind letters implicating him and the government in New France in encouraging anti-English violence among the Wabanakis by promising arms and ammunition.[109] This would later give the English the justification they needed to press for the mission's destruction. In the meantime, local Wabanakis avenged Westbrook's attack by burning Brunswick and taking hostage nine English families. Samuel Shute was eager to declare war, but political sparring between the governor and the Massachusetts Assembly prevented it. The frustrated Shute then sailed to England to plead his case to the king, leaving his difficult office in the hands of his lieutenant-governor, William Dummer.[110] Attacks on English towns and settlers persisted throughout 1723 and into 1724. The Massachusetts Assembly eventually authorized two incursions into Wabanaki territory meant to wipe out the anti-English mission centers, and, with them, their Jesuits. In February 1723/4, Thomas Westbrook destroyed Étienne Lauverjat's deserted Penobscot mission. Westbrook's troops targeted the church for symbolic destruction.[111]

Norridgewock was the next. On August 12, 1723, over two hundred New Englanders under Maine-born leaders Johnson Harmon and Jeremiah Moulton (his cousin through marriage) launched their assault.[112] Norridgewock's residents were not forewarned, as they had been in 1722. Surprise was complete and destruction comprehensive, with the English, who suffered no casualties, taking twenty-seven scalps. Included among these was that of Sebastien Rale, which was taken as a prize back to the Boston of Cotton Mather and Samuel Sewall.[113]

Like that of Shubael Dummer, the story of how Sebastien Rale died varies according to the religious perspective of the storyteller. As told by the fellow Jesuits La Chasse and Charlevoix in ways that echo Cotton Mather's description of Dummer's downfall, the priest was shot down without mercy at the foot of the giant cross in the middle of the mission. The Jesuit chroniclers thereby placed Rale in the same continuum of Jesuit sacrifice that included the North American martyrs of an earlier age. Johnson Harmon, who had his own perspective on the Franco-Wabanaki alliance and was himself a zealous Protestant, attested that Rale died while huddling in his house trying to load his gun. The Englishmen ordered him to come out, to which the Jesuit declared he would neither give quarter nor take it. Rale got his wish and was shot dead in an instant by New England lieutenant Benjamin Jaques.[114] Like Champigny's description of Dummer's cowardly flight, Harmon's description speaks of a hypocritical man desperate to preserve his own life. Thus, in death, the Jesuit and his work fell far short of the Christian ideal of martyrdom.

But neither Rale nor his temporary nemesis, Joseph Baxter, appeared to crave frontier martyrdom in the name of spreading Christianity. They both knew they occupied borderland spaces that were in the process of change. Each man tried to develop his own niche and prepare for his own, living future among a growing number of Christian coreligionists. Each was also willing to exercise other options, including military support, diplomatic negotiations, direct communication, and the ability enabled by geographical closeness to spread potent threats directly without making good on them, in order to preserve the Christian culture of the settlements and missions they valued.

The similarities between the men long predate their exposure to one another on the Maine frontier. Both embodied their respective European religious reformations, which privileged ordained men who could bridge the worlds of theological erudition with the more emotional counterparts of heart religion and liturgy. Both were committed to using their knowledge to bring souls to the Christian God. And though they disagreed over the definition and uses of erudition in the mission field, both were members of a cadre of religious men known as much for their learning as their piety. Baxter and Rale were also sufficiently clever to learn what they could about the other's techniques, selectively applying and adapting them to suit their purposes. Lacking the security, resources, and time that allowed contemporaries in Quebec and Boston to turn to contemplation and pious texts, they borrowed or improvised, even if such practices meant teetering on the edge of orthodoxy in the company of papists or heretics.

Finally, both men ultimately failed to realize their overarching goals for their frontier ministries. Baxter could neither instill orthodoxy nor convert Native Americans away from their Jesuit-inspired syncretic Catholicism. Rale could not protect his cherished Norridgewock Indians from English guns and became in death what he actively sought to avoid: a martyr in the tradition of the first wave of frontier Jesuits like Jean de Brébeuf, Isaac Jogues, and René Goupil, instead of a warrior saint like Loyola, who combated heresy at every turn yet died in peace.

The Limits of Influence:
Indian Religion and the Politics of Coexistence

Contemporary accounts by New Englanders of the wars of empire on the northern frontier confirm that French Jesuit missionaries were important political players in Maine's Native American communities. Throughout the nineteenth century, historians of Maine's communities assumed that Native groups were inextricably tied to French interests, needing the Euro-Americans' protection and absorbing their religious and political views.[115] As described previously, modern scholars have found much to debate in this claim, and have demonstrated convincingly that whatever influence the missionaries could claim over the Eastern Indians was limited by numerous factors, including trade, political identity, and preexisting intertribal relationships. Jesuits played circumscribed roles in networks of political, social, and trade alliances that were largely of Indian devising and designed to serve village or group interests. That they also acted as cultural mediators between the Wabanakis and the French government in Quebec is indisputable. Nevertheless, their power and ability to effect change varied from village to village and depended largely on a given Indian group's attraction to Catholicism, the spiritual charisma of the particular missionary, the nature of preexisting relationships, and, perhaps most importantly, the priorities of the Wabanakis themselves. Some missionaries played no political role at all, and were valued only for their skills as leaders of the Catholic component to Wabanaki spirituality.

One can find evidence of this in a letter sent by the Norridgewock Indians to Governor Shute in 1721. Addressed to the "Grand Capitaine des Anglais," the letter set down facts that the Norridgewocks wished to make incontrovertibly clear. An anonymous leader asserted, "My land is not thine by right of conquest, gift, or purchase . . . the King of France could not give it. I am not his subject."[116] Though dictated to and presented by a Jesuit, Pierre Joseph de La Chasse, the letter implies that both Protestants and Catholics who lived among the Wabanakis were there on sufferance. While military force could bring about changes in custom, certain prerogatives remained those of the Wabanakis alone.

When priests and ministers encountered each other in Maine, familiarity increased. In the aftermath of Dummer's War, Jesuits continued to be regarded with distrust even after peace was declared, despite the fact that the loss of Norridgewock and Rale's leadership marked an end to priests serving as frontier political agents of French interests. Nevertheless, a Maine-born interpreter and ex-captive, John Gyles, risked ruining a conference with the Penobscots in 1727 because the Wabanaki delegation included a Jesuit. Gyles refused to allow the offending priest (most likely Étienne Lauverjat or Joseph Aubery) to partake in the conference. The Jesuit resented the implication that he would somehow deal dishonestly. But Gyles was unmoved, asserting, "I think it altogether Improper for any Jesuitt to

Pen Down my Enterpretation."[117] Gyles further insulted the priest by contesting the Jesuit's right even to be present at the proceedings. Addressing the Jesuit and his Franco-Indian companion, Bernard Anselm d'Abbadie de Saint-Castin (son of the aforementioned Jean-Vincent d'Abbadie and his Penobscot wife), Gyles stated firmly, "I must aquaint you Mr. Jesuitt & you Mr Casteen if you are Com as Privat Gen'men to Give me a Vicett you ar Welcom, & shall be treated Sinely, but if as Spies & to take advantig of my Interpretation & Insult me, I shall Resent it, &c. And I must further a quaint you chief Indians, and you Mr. Jesuit it not Custemay wth Us for Ministers to set in Council, only as Sent for before & after Council to pray & move off."[118] The Jesuit replied that he attended "not . . . to Insult but to hear." Nevertheless, he agreed to give up his role as scribe. But for John Gyles, who as a boy of the frontier had once thrown away the food his Jesuit captor gave him because he believed it was bewitched, this gesture was insufficient. He ordered his own man, a militia captain, to draw up his own account. Hoping to convince the Penobscots to solidify their peace with the English (and perhaps learning a lesson from the mistakes of Joseph Baxter), Gyles sought to recast the once-politicized role of the French Jesuit as apolitical.[119] The message to the Penobscots was clear: Jesuits in Maine had been overstepping the proper boundaries of conduct for men of God for decades and had ruined previous negotiations that might have stemmed the tide of war. Bargaining took place between the two explicitly political parties alone. The Jesuit, however, remained at the conference, though with a severely curtailed role. Now a voiceless observer, the priest had to content himself with berating his Wabanaki companions for drinking too much English rum.[120]

Incidents like the St. George's River conference were a serious cause for concern among Jesuit missionaries. Alarmed at the prospect of English incursions, Joseph Aubery wrote to Jean-Baptiste DuParc, the new Superior of the Canadian missions, that "religion has up till now been the only motive that has made the Abenakis French, and as soon as there are no more missionaries they will become English and will be capable by themselves of putting the English in possession of the whole country at the first war."[121] Despite the Jesuits' concerns, many northern indigenous groups remained tied to their priests and elements of Christian practice. In 1728 the Penobscot sachem Loron and two other Indians wrote to Massachusetts governor Burnet (in a letter delivered by John Gyles, no less) to protest that their "Priest has been us'd very Ill by the Gouvernour of Annapolis in being stript of his Cloathes and alsoe has been prevented performing his Priestly Office due." The Wabanakis reminded the governor that they had promised to communicate freely any problems with their terms of peace with the English, provided that "as to our Religion, Wee were not to Interrupt one the other in the Injoyment of itt."[122] They also continued to make annual journeys to the shrines of Quebec and Montreal in accordance with the Catholic liturgical calendar. Their Christian vision was now under their control, and the Wabanakis directed and protected it to the extent they wished, using Euro-American intervention selectively.

The English eventually won the battle to set their own limits on the meeting, but they could not completely dislodge the influence of French priests among the Wabanakis. Though some Indians expressed dissatisfaction with the Jesuit interpretation of Christianity, New England Protestantism never succeeded in gaining a strong hold among the Wabanakis during the colonial period. Nor, however, did the pure, reformed version of Catholicism advocated by the Jesuits. In the scramble to gain and keep souls for a particular Christian vision and, by extension, related geopolitical alignments, the actions of neither Protestant nor Catholic missionaries displayed the purest forms of reformed Christianity.

✦ ✦ ✦

In the early modern English-speaking world, the myth of the Jesuit was cloaked in simplistic stereotypes of good and evil. New England writers of the seventeenth and eighteenth centuries described these priests as skulking, plotting, covert villains whose identities as Christians were destroyed by their zealous defense of a worldly, papal Catholicism. Nineteenth-century historians of the colonial period like Francis Parkman, Samuel Adams Drake, and even Reuben Gold Thwaites, the translator of the *Jesuit Relations,* were more subtle in their denunciations. But they too projected their own cultural values onto their interpretations of the historical record. More recently, some historians have regarded Jesuits as the destroyers of Native American culture and implementers of Europe's hegemonic, inflexible religious systems.[123]

Literate colonial New Englanders were among the most vociferous of the historical denouncers of the Society of Jesus. Nevertheless, their writings demonstrate a subtle understanding of the use of *friar* to describe Catholic missionaries. The word itself derives from *frère,* the French word for brother. Male religious orders were self-described brotherhoods, creating fictive kinships of *frères,* or friars, in the English form. But the image of the friar was a dubious one in English history. English literary traditions, even before the Reformation, supported Chaucer, Shakespeare, and many other English popular writers who poked fun at the supposed debauchery and skullduggery of local and Continental mendicants. The tradition gained greater currency with the birth of Reformed religion. Literary jesting implicated friars in a range of ugly behavior: they seduced women, wheedled money out of the unsuspecting, sold counterfeit dispensations and indulgences to a gullible public desperate to save their own souls or those of loved ones, and dispensed unauthorized sacraments. On the extreme end, they consorted with murderers, witches, regicides, and Satan himself.[124]

Still, some Englishmen in New England thought they would do well to emulate at least some of the missionary successes of the so-called friars of the Maine frontier. To do so, however, they needed to build up their own credibility. Like the Jesuits decades before, Joseph Baxter and the layman John Gyles both labored to discredit the "shaman"—in this case, the Jesuit—by ripping down the latter's framework and building their own, which emphasized similarities, in its place. Sebastien Rale complained bitterly that Joseph Baxter "turned to ridicule the Sacraments, Purgatory, the Invocation of Saints, the Beads, the Crosses & Images, the lighting of our Churches, & all the pious customs so sacredly observed in the Catholic Religion."[125] But he also no doubt realized that the minister sought to adopt those successful missionary techniques that crossed the boundaries of faith.

And indeed Baxter did, in his use of objects to attract children, in gathering places, and in discrediting preexisting religious leaders. It was only on the entangled frontiers of religious culture that such techniques could be observed firsthand, and put into use.

Heaven and hell, saints and devils intermingled in the frontier missions of both Catholics and Protestants. But so did the intellectualism and true piety prized so highly by Jesuit and minister alike. Ironically, one of Rale's most enduring achievements as the Norridgewock missionary was not in the field of piety or politics but in a work of scholarship — his Wabanaki lexicon. Rale created the lexicon as a tool for his fellow Jesuits to use for communicating effectively in Wabanaki vernacular. This, in turn, would make it possible to teach effectively the prayers, meditations, and other pious practices of reformed Catholicism. Such peaceful spiritual endeavors were more consistent with the actions of the zealous yet patient Francis Xavier than the warrior-saint Loyola. And it was Xavier, after all, who rose to prominence as the saintly guiding light for the Jesuit's New World missions, lending his name to the settlements and their churches, and his image to church decoration more than any other Jesuit saint.[126] In a final irony, Rale's Wabanaki lexicon, a tool of peace, piety, and cultural learning, now resides at Harvard University, which trained so many Puritan ministers — including Joseph Baxter.

CHAPTER FIVE

Protestant Ornaments and Popish Relics

Maine's Material Culture of Lived Religion

With Norridgewock destroyed and Sebastien Rale dead, 1724 was a transitional year for Christian religious culture in colonial Maine. By 1727 the effective end of Dummer's War signaled a turn of the tide favoring the English, who now possessed the means, in times of peace and war, to pressure, subdue, or placate the Eastern Indians.[1] As the pace of conflict slowed and then stopped altogether, Maine's ever-growing Protestant settler population became more capable of un-ambiguously creating and defending its geographical borders. Peace was also secured through the world of frontier trade, with "truck-houses" appearing at the St. George's, Kennebec, and Saco rivers after a peace treaty was signed at Casco Bay in 1726.[2]

Religious borders also became more clearly defined as, after Dum-mer's War, the religious culture of Maine's English settlements came to be more predictably and recognizably Protestant. This represented a shift from the years between 1688 through 1727, when religious culture was shaped by an eclectic heritage, warfare between Chris-tians, and geographically entangled borders and New World empires. During those years, Maine's Protestant Christians were exposed to an alternative religious physical and material culture, which included

211

pious objects and practices, different forms of worship, and different ways of viewing the role Christianity played in lived lives. Sometimes, these encounters elicited hostile reactions from frontier Protestants, who knew "the spice of popery" in object and worship when they saw it. Other Maine settlers recognized the power of sacred objects in ways that transcended confessional boundaries. Other Protestants, however, used these objects to make common cause with Native Americans or reimagined them to render them suitable for their own spiritual needs.

The Protestant encounter with Catholic religious material culture illustrates the connections these observers made, consciously or otherwise, to a pre-Reformation European Christian culture that predated the establishment of Protestant New World communities, as well as Protestantism itself. Recognizing the importance that pious objects held for Catholics, Protestants could relay powerful messages of local influence and control by destroying such objects and openly ridiculing religious practices. Accounts of such acts demonstrate Protestant awareness of objects that were explicitly Catholic when they saw them, suggesting that frontier encounter reinforced the mnemonic power of a Catholic past that still shadowed even orthodox Puritans. Furthermore, knowledge of the world of Catholic material culture, works, and religious gestures could be put to use by frontier Protestants, who, far from dismissing it all as so much "popish trash," used this knowledge at times for personal gain or, more cannily, to comprehend the nature of Catholicism's persistent appeal to Native Americans, and to suggest ways to appropriate and subvert it in the service of Protestant frontiers well defended.

The encounter with Catholic material culture was an omnipresent feature and took many forms in the life of Protestant John Gyles, a native of Pemaquid who spent nine years in captivity before returning to New England and becoming a prominent frontier culture broker and politician. Gyles's account of his childhood captivity among the Maliseet Indians, "Memoirs of Odd Adventures, Strange Deliverances, &c," describes some of these encounters. Records of his work as a culture broker (as a provincial representative of English interests to the Maine Indians) contain more. Taken together, the texts that document Gyles's interactions with material and physical Catholicism cover almost every angle of the Protestant perspective on this encounter.

For John Gyles, fear of Catholicism and its associated influences hung heavily over the Pemaquid of his childhood. The community was poor, remote, and loosely organized in terms of its Christian culture. At a time when even ministers and officials far from the frontier recognized the successes French missionaries enjoyed among the Eastern Indians, the colonists who were struggling to eke out a living in a settlement as far east as Pemaquid were subject to regular reminders of these successes. Sometimes they witnessed them in action. In the "Memoirs," Gyles tells of settlers of this notoriously unchurched town who had their own vaguely anti-Catholic defenses, warning each other against the "snares and traps" of popery.[3] The anti-Catholic aspects of Gyles's early religious training, which focused on supernatural suspicions, came to a head in the final exchange the captive had with his mother before they parted for good in the wake of a French and Indian raid on the settlement. As they were separated, Margaret warned the young John, "If it were God's will, I had rather follow you to your grave than you should be sold to a Jesuit, for a Jesuit will ruin you, body and soul."[4] Such attitudes toward Catholics were normal to the young Gyles, who himself relates, "I was very young and had heard much of Papists torturing the Protestants, etc."[5] Armed with this early religious training, his mother's warning, a body of terrifying religious lore, and the evidence of his own eyes during the trauma of the raid, Gyles describes resisting Catholic overtures to change his religion wherever he encountered them during his years in captivity.[6] As described by her son, Margaret Gyles's beliefs about Jesuit connections to the dark arts were steeped in folklore, popular magic, and anti-Catholic stereotypes commonly found among English men and women.[7] Pemaquid was a rough frontier settlement that lacked a firm religious identity of its own. Beliefs and folklore like those shared among the Gyles family suggest that Protestant identify found a way to assert itself even in the absence of an established orthodox religious culture. This amalgamation of anti-Catholicism, occult beliefs, and perhaps deep-seated cultural memories of religious practices that predated the English Reformation were part of the frontier religious experience.[8]

Once held captive by Catholics and their allies, Gyles experienced for himself the beliefs of Catholics in action, as well as their religious culture. The events surrounding his captivity did little to alter the ideas passed on by his mother. He witnessed the brutal death of his father, endured violent separation from his mother and other siblings, and later discovered that a brother had been brutally tortured and killed for trying to escape his captors.[9] Such violent encounters only reinforced notions that torturing Protestants was a common Catholic practice. Even more fear inspiring to the young Gyles were the priests, whose coercive powers extended in particular to vulnerable Protestant children. The first priest Gyles described was encountered at the coastal trading post of French trader Jean-Vincent d'Abbadie de Saint-Castin. "The Jesuit," as Gyles called him, hoped to purchase the boy from his Indian captors.[10] Terrified of bewitchment, the boy (who was likely suffering from extreme hunger, a state about which all captives complained) even refused the priest's offer of food. As he put it, "The Jesuit gave me a biscuit which I put into my pocket and dare not eat but buried it under a log, fearing that he had put something in it to make me love him. . . . I hated the sight of a Jesuit."[11]

Gyles's assumption that he was dealing with a Jesuit (he probably was not) is tied to earlier English perceptions about the members of the Society of Jesus. Antipopery thrived in English popular literature in the late fifteenth and sixteenth centuries.[12] Its tropes were powerful enough to penetrate the remote Maine frontier and were considered sufficiently important to be passed from parent to child. More importantly, Gyles invests great significance in a material object (a biscuit) to establish the depths of his aversion to Catholicism. The simple object of a biscuit, which might have been anything from a consecrated host to hardtack, became for Gyles an object of religious manipulation turned to this evil purpose by the dark arts of "the Jesuit." It also suggestively parallels the importance of transubstantiation in Catholic belief, which posits that consecration turns bread

into the literal body of Christ, a belief that Protestants largely es-
chewed. Popular literature and lore in England, particularly after the
Gunpowder Plot in 1606, held that the priests were well practiced
in the arts of witchcraft and could even apply their arts to shape-
shifting. English poet Thomas Dekker encapsulated this belief in
his anti-Catholic poem "The Double P": "He's brown, he's grey, he's
black, he's white — He's anything! A Jesuite!"[13] Anti-Catholic and
anti-Jesuit literature was full of Jesuits putting ordinary objects, including their own bodies, to uses that destroyed Protestants "body
and soul," as Margaret Gyles reportedly said. Even marginally literate New World Protestant Christians were aware of the trope and
gave it credence.

As a child, John Gyles was privy to English superstition about
Catholics and their practices. But by the time he wrote his "Memoirs"
nearly four decades later, the onetime captive had become a worldly
frontier defender. Wise in the ways of intercolonial and intercultural
politics (as evinced by the critical role he played at the Indian conferences during Dummer's War), he had become a more militant Protestant of the type envisioned by Fort Loyal commander Sylvanus Davis.
He had also become more knowledgeable about Protestantism itself, a faith identity he claimed to retain throughout his captivity and
one that he embraced, apparently with vigor, upon his release. As the
"Memoirs" show, the seeds of Gyles's spiritual maturation had been
planted while he lived among Catholics. Gyles described an encounter with Catholicism that, for him, became a "disenchanted" religion,
full of superstitious priests, ineffectual rituals, and passive laypeople
who, far from wanting to torment Protestants in principle, preferred
to accept them as fellow Christians and be left to live in peace.[14] Reporting that he witnessed these Catholic vulnerabilities, Gyles applied the lessons he learned from his religious adversaries to bring
about peaceful religious transformations among the Wabanakis. He
counseled that physically attacking Catholic missions, objects, and
people would create anger at the iconoclasts and make martyrs of the
dead, and would therefore inspire resistance. Diplomacy and religious
substitution became his tools of choice. This strategy also relied on

synthesizing aspects of belief and religious culture that Protestantism had retained from its Catholic roots and which it was believed to have perfected. Frontier people, by their very nature, often had sufficient experience with and knowledge of Catholicism at least to attempt to bring these new understandings to Christian Indians with the hope of instilling in them a more perfect Christian vision that was compatible and sympathetic to Protestant interests. Religious material culture would play a key role in this effort.

Four decades of nearly constant warfare, and inbound and outbound human movement, made the Province of Maine a place where various Christianities encountered one another, converged, competed, and overlapped. These encounters reminded settlers that Catholics and Protestants shared common elements of the material culture of New World Christianity. While some of these elements went unacknowledged, others became effective tools in helping bring about religious conversions, enhancing diplomatic measures between Native Americans and Euro-Americans, and explaining (if not tolerating) divergent Christian cultural perspectives. Though Maine's Protestants most often claimed that Reformed religion rejected many of these commonalities, they were forced to grapple with the uncomfortable reality that there were common threads in the Christian past that they shared with local Catholics.

Religious Material Culture:
Common Origins, Multiple Dimensions

By 1727 John Gyles had had numerous opportunities to use his early encounters with Catholicism to challenge its hold among the Wabanakis. The Maine of Gyles's adulthood was in the process of major transformations, wrought by the solidification of colonization initiatives, significant English victories in the province, and new difficulties for the French in retaining their influential hold on the Wabanakis. Still, problems for the English persisted. The "ancient boundaries" identified by the Treaty of Utrecht were still hotly contested. The Arrowsic Conference of 1717 failed to answer questions about the degree to which Maine's Wabanakis would tolerate English settlement in the Kennebec region. The encroachment of the English settlements in the Kennebec and Androscoggin valleys, accompanied by the building of forts in those areas, sparked Dummer's War. This conflict raged throughout Maine between 1722 and 1724, then continued sporadically until truces were secured at Casco Bay in 1726 and at the St. George's River at 1727, with isolated fighting that lasted even longer.[15] The death of the influential Jesuit Sebastien Rale and its implications for continued French influence, however, created opportunities to test the Indians' commitment to Catholic Christianity.

John Gyles was among those who assumed the challenge. Shortly after the St. George's River Conference, Gyles wrote Massachusetts governor William Dummer that the Eastern Indians were open to "true religion," and that efforts to bring it to the frontier were worthy of support. Gyles asserted he had evidence of the Wabanakis' sincere interest in Protestantism in the form of a conversation he had had with a Catholic "Machies" (most likely Penobscot) Indian. The unnamed Indian allegedly confided to Gyles his belief that the English knew how to keep the Sabbath better than the French. Gyles described to Dummer how he seized the opportunity to agree, taking the opportunity to summarize Protestant views on the scriptural mandate to keep the Sabbath, a mandate from God that transcended any other Christian concern: "I find Gods word, (in his Book) whear God Commands us to keep ye Sabbath Day holy which is ye Seventh Part of time, Set a Part to worship ye only true & Liveing God, that made ye heavens ye Earth ye Sea & all Creaturs, and man in six days, and on ye Seventh Day (which is the Sabbath) to his service to Praise him."[16]

Using the literal biblical mandate as evidence, Gyles confirmed for his Indian companion his perspective on Catholicism's inadequacies. New Englanders practiced the simplicity of a scriptural Sabbath. In contrast, a catechist like the "Machies" Indian would have been familiar with Catholicism's censorial celebration of Sunday liturgy. Protestants, Gyles asserted, took care to obey God's commandment "to have no other Gods which are images & ye worke of mens hands, they Can neither hear See not smell nor Do us any Good, but that only true & Living God, Knows all our thoughts & Actions & tis of

him we Live move & have our being, our health Breath meet Drink
& Clothing & all we Enjoy is from him &c."[17] In short, Gyles, the
sympathetic Protestant and true Christian (at least in his telling of
events), advocated that the Indian trade Catholicism's appeals to
the senses for those of the heart and head. Reportedly, the Indian
agreed, at least in principle, that Protestantism was indeed a superior
form of Christianity to Catholicism.

In Gyles's writings to his superiors in Boston and elsewhere, this
Christian Wabanaki and others appear not as the gullible, superstitious dupes of French Catholics but as morally and spiritually superior versions of them, capable of identifying the perceived defects
of Catholicism and turning their hearts and minds to true religion.
Gyles's reported exchange with the Machies Indian, however, underscored a strange reality for zealous defenders of the New World's
godly societies: what made Gyles so capable in countering Catholicism effectively was the fact that he had had real exposure to it,
living among Catholic people and observing the ways of their faith
for years. Other Protestant frontier dwellers had done the same, and
some, as opposed to the Machies Indian, had even found Catholicism preferable.

Frontiers, with their proximity to dangerous forms of Christianity,
provided opportunities for religious intermingling that demonstrated
basic Christian commonalities and revealed that the Reformation and
all its spiritual innovations had not been able to eradicate completely
the shadowy memory from the consciousness of Maine's English
settlers.[18] The mnemonic power of a pre-Reformation, shared Christian past was not excusive to Maine; it persisted in many forms of
New World Protestant religious expression. Charles Hambrick-Stowe
has shown that even the most zealous New England Puritans valued
the writings of pre-Reformation Christian authors who met their
standards for appropriate Christian spiritual expression. Chief among
these were the writings of Saint Augustine, a critical influence on
the development of Puritan theology.[19] Thomas à Kempis's *Imitatio
Christi* was influential as well, though it sparked a Puritan controversy: when the General Court of Massachusetts tried to prevent its

printing by the press at Cambridge, arguing that it was "wrote by a popish minister, and containing some things less safe to be infused among the people," the Cambridge press printed and distributed the book anyway.[20] Even Cotton Mather penned meditations on works of pre-Reformation theologians.[21] Ironically, the same works that in - fluenced Mather also profoundly influenced the spiritual writings of Ignatius of Loyola, founder of the Society of Jesus. Common theological roots made for strange bedfellows among Christians in Old and New worlds.[22]

As the seventeenth century gave way to the eighteenth, and the line of English settlement moved ever closer to the places in Maine with a sustained Catholic influence, both religions struggled to establish or maintain the legitimacy of their version of Christian truth by emphasizing religious differences. In the process, however, they often unwittingly demonstrated commonalities of religious life and practices. In New England, keeping the Sabbath was a key public expression of Reformed religion. It was protected by law and enforced by civilians and ministers, who kept an eye out for infractions. The Sabbath took on added importance because it was the *only* day in Puritan theology specifically ordained by God. Protestant critics asserted that the holy days and feast days embedded in the Catholic liturgical calendar had no biblical mandate. They condemned the liturgical calendar's implication that only certain times of the year, in lieu of all times, belonged to God.[23] Thus many Protestants tended to tar Catholics with the "holy day" brush, intimating that yet another of the religion's flaws was its unscriptural separation of sacred time from profane time.

Despite Protestant claims to the contrary, the simple mandate to keep Sunday sacred was of great importance for Catholics as well. The Fourth Lateran Council of 1215 reinforced the importance of reserving the Lord's Day for prayer and other acts of piety. Ideally, the pre-Reformation Sabbath was to begin the night before, and the day itself would be reserved for religious observances and abstinence from using sacred spaces for play.[24] The nature of the Sabbath for post-Reformation Catholics was codified by the Council of Trent, which set new standards for the Universal Church and reinforced old ones. The council reaffirmed the need to keep the Sabbath holy, stipulating that "the faithful are bound to assemble in the church and hear the Word of God. . . . Rulers and magistrates should be admonished and exhorted to lend the sanction and support of their authority to the pastors of the Church, particularly in the upholding and extending the worship of God."[25] Regardless of the efficacy of its enforcement in New France, or in any other places where adherents of Reformed religion heard stories of or viewed Catholics at play on Sunday, reverence for the Sabbath was an immutable part of Catholic doctrine and had been for centuries.

Like their Protestant counterparts in Massachusetts, Maine's Catholic missionaries sought to create Catholicism anew. They idealized the role that eager souls, newly exposed to Christianity, would play in the process. Missions, in particular those founded by the Jesuits, were meant to be showplaces of Catholic Reformation reforms. Their missionaries took pains to infuse both ancient and post-Reformation pious practices into the daily lives of the proselytes. They succeeded among many of their converts, for whom solemn Sabbath observance became a point of pride and a badge of Christian identification. Mission Wabanakis were insulted when outsiders to their Christian customs assumed otherwise. This was clear at the Georgetown Conference of 1717 whose attendees included John Gyles and prominent Puritan minister Samuel Sewall. After haggling over property claims that ran late into a Saturday, a frustrated and peevish William Dummer, lieutenant governor of Massachusetts, closed the proceedings by abruptly stating: "To Morrow is the Lord's Day, upon which we do no Business. On Monday we will give you an Answer to what you have said; and we will Order the same Signal when we are ready as we did today." Disliking the assumption that others were open to profaning the Sabbath with business, Loron, a Catholic Penobscot sachem, tersely reminded Dummer, "To Morrow is our Sabbath-day, and we also keep the Day."[26] In defending his Sabbath practices, the sachem also reminded the Protestants with whom he dealt of common claims to Christian rectitude. Protestants had reasons for believing a different story. John Gyles's Machies Indian reportedly claimed mission priests failed to enforce the sacred nature of the day. The Indian told Gyles, "I tould ye Jesuitt that I believed the English kept the Sabbath best for they Praied all Day, but the French Shott Guns and Go to Play, but ye Jesuitt tells me I am above ye English which are not Good."[27] The Jesuit Sebastien Rale was blamed by Samuel Shute for profaning the Sabbath by inciting a ruckus in Brunswick, during which a Wabanaki was detained for public drunkenness. "I must needs Desire you in your Religious Instructions to the Indians to Observe and press upon them how very necessary it is for them and all Christians to Sanctify the Lords day Sabbath," Shute scolded the priest.[28]

The Machies Indian assented to Gyles's reasoning that Protestantism was superior to Catholicism. But his assent might have been driven by other considerations as well. In an effort to end Dummer's War on favorable terms for New England, the General Court agreed to provide trading houses at the St. George's, Kennebec, and Saco rivers which offered goods priced to undercut those of the French.[29] Was Gyles explicitly linking empathy for Protestantism with greater access to English-supplied goods? Or did the Machies Indian tell the interpreter that he sided with the English on matters of worship to secure favorable trade terms for himself and his people?

Of course, it is also possible that the Machies Indian had no secondary motives and had observed violations of the Sabbath by the French firsthand. Catholic Wabanakis were frequent visitors to New France, especially during key phases of the liturgical year, when pilgrimages, processions, sacraments and sacramentals brought them to the churches of Montreal and Quebec. The flouting of Sabbath observances among New France's Euro-American settlers was sufficiently common that Bishops Laval and Saint-Vallier complained about it. Saint-Vallier was particularly appalled when *habitants* retorted that masses and sermons cut too deeply into the usable hours of the day, leaving little time for playing cards, gambling in the cabarets, and visiting with friends and family in the countryside. The pursuit of pleasure even followed the settlers into mass: some thought nothing of leaving the church building during the sermon for a quick drink, smoke, or chat with a fellow parishioner.[30]

But the Machies Indian's comments on Sabbath-breaking in New France were perhaps less of a reflection on the failure of Catholics to respect the day than a commentary on the failure of colonists in many corners of the New World to abide by mandated religious devotions. Greater exposure to New England might have disabused him of the notion that Catholics and their priests were the only Sabbath-breaking malefactors. While Gyles might have faithfully marked every Sabbath, many of his borderland coreligionists indeed failed in their sacred duty to honor God's day. Seventeenth- and eighteenth-century Maine set the stage for numerous cases pressed in Maine courts. The threat of French and Indian ambush on the way to distant meeting-houses accounts for some of these infractions, for the wars of empire tore apart Protestant congregations and sent settlers and their ministers fleeing for safety. But even in times of peace, attendance at services, and the orthodoxy such attendance was meant to impress upon the faithful, was frequently flouted. Like the bishops of New France, the Massachusetts Court of General Sessions of the Peace augmented its preexisting Sabbatarian legislation in 1717 with "An Act in Addition to the Act for Better Keeping of the Lord's Day." Like their counterparts in New France, Mainers also frequently stood accused of "'Playing and rudeness' on the Lord's day, [creating] disturbances during religious services, [and] the publishing of 'filthy, obscene or profane songs, pamphlets or mock-sermons.'"[31] Maine's English settlers persisted in bringing their dogs into the meetinghouse with them well into the eighteenth century. Outrage over the sacrilegious overtones, the persistent belief that Satan sometimes took canine form, and the solid waste left by canine visitors eventually led to a York law banishing dogs from meetinghouses.[32]

For both Protestants and Catholics, keeping Sunday sacred was a physical and cerebral experience, requiring a weekly set of proscribed behaviors. For New World Catholics, the physicality of religious culture changed according to the seasons, emphasizing the use of a bifurcated calendar that demarked (as it continues to do) sacred from ordinary time. In the early modern world, the calendar molded diets, determined patterns of work, dictated public activities, and informed times for celebration for Native American and Euro-American Catholics. The tradition of keeping these days crossed the Atlantic with the French and their missionaries and, to a certain extent, also continued to shape the religious lives of Protestant English Anglicans. It became a defining feature of colonial Catholic life.

For the most part, Reformed churches repudiated the old church calendar and obliterated almost all of its feast and fast days.[33] Puritans in particular found the implications of the Catholic liturgical calendar—that some parts of the year required less time for God than others—offensive.[34] As English Protestants sought to cultivate Maine's Catholic Indians, however, they were also forced to recognize that the Indians operated on a yearly schedule that coincided with the religious calendar of the French (and therefore varied greatly from their own). This, in turn, sometimes hindered and even thwarted English attempts to create a fully realized Reformed Protestant society untainted by the memory of the Catholic liturgical calendar. Instead, Protestants on the frontiers learned that dealing with the Wabanakis meant acknowledging their sense of sacred time, set forth by numerous feast days throughout the year. Throughout the seventeenth and eighteenth centuries, Eastern Indians showed their commitment to this calendar by traversing Maine and the St. Lawrence Valley to partake in regular cycles of religious holidays. Some of these holidays were spent in the missions; others required seasonal trips farther afield for rites and celebrations that were part of Catholic sacred time.[35] Until the middle of the eighteenth century, Catholics and Protestants used different calendars, which forced a literal separation of the two faiths for part of each year. The disjuncture between the Julian and Gregorian calendars corresponded to the holiest time of the Catholic sacred calendar: the period between Christmas and Easter. Though no saints' days, and virtually nothing from the Catholic tradition of sacred time, survived in Puritan New England, even the most orthodox Puritans (let alone less exacting borderland Protestants) were reminded of or forced to acknowledge the complex reality of the Catholic calendar when they sought to do business with other borderland Christians. When one John Parker purchased access to land from Nanriddemance, a Wabanaki sachem, the seller requested payment in "the rent of one bushel of Corne, and a quart of

Liquor to be paid unto Nanriddemance and his heyres for ever at or before every five and Twentieth day of December yt being Christmass Day."[36] Not only was the date easy to remember, but the coordination of payment acted as a reminder to the lessee that the Indian planned to commemorate the day. Thus an English Protestant was put in the potentially uncomfortable position of providing cheer for Christmas, a holiday that for Puritans epitomized Catholic rejection of Scripture like no other. Parker's own form of Protestantism is unknown, and if he were an Anglican, such an exchange would have come with little personal recrimination. If Puritan, however, the exchange would have had the ironic effect of subsidizing a Christmas celebration that was illegal in Massachusetts during part of the seventeenth century, and strongly discouraged for much of the next.[37] Another cushion against Christmas, the gap in days that separated the Julian and Gregorian calendars, was also compressed by borderland realities. Despite the calendar gap, the Christmas season in general remained a convenient annual benchmark for other activities for Protestants and Catholics alike. Joseph Dudley, the governor of Massachusetts, reported to the Board of Trade his plans for military maneuvers at Casco "about Christmas."[38] In another missive, Shadrach Walton noted with relief that outbreaks of violence early in Queen Anne's War had ceased as the Wabanakis made their way "to the Eastward" and the Penobscot mission there, to observe Advent and Christmas.[39] Others, like Joseph Baxter and John Gyles, feared the solidarity that such holy day gatherings could inspire. In January 1717/18, Baxter reported that over one hundred Kennebecs had used the opportunity of "ye Romish Christmas" (December 14 on the Julian calendar) to congregate near Pemaquid and discuss their relations with the nearby English—a conversation that could bode well or ill for Baxter and his company.[40]

The English were forced to accommodate further the Catholic liturgical calendar through the seasonal travel it dictated to Catholic Wabanakis. Many of Maine's Native Americans integrated seasonal travel patterns that predated the arrival of Europeans with seasonal religious duties of the Catholic liturgical calendar. English observers describe these practices as persisting well into the eighteenth century, lasting even after Quebec fell to the British. Though meant to reinforce religious commonalities among New World Catholics, these travels also provided convenient opportunities to maintain decades-old trade relationships, bringing cash for pelts and ready markets for the sale of other goods.[41] Saints' days also became opportunities for the French to count on numerous Indian allies to visit the established centers of la Nouvelle France. Taken together, these sacred times provided for Catholics, Indian and French, a convenient pretext for the French government to make its political wishes known, and to learn for itself what the Indians demanded in return. Governor Vaudreuil recognized the explicit connection between the liturgical calendar and the opportunities to conduct business with the Wabanakis when he wrote Sebastien Rale requesting a meeting with mission Indians when they arrived in Quebec for All Saints' Day.[42] As late as 1741, the Massachusetts government took note of the liturgical travels of the Wabanakis, and was well aware that the Eastern Indians used this time for political discussion as well as piety.[43] By extension, they too were made aware of the continued presence of All Saints' Day on the doorstep of the Puritan New World.

All Saints' Day was one of many Catholic observances throughout the year that honored those the church identified for special recognition. Just as they had throughout Europe before and after the Reformation, Catholic devotions to certain saints took a politicized form, and these forms of veneration were passed on to, or adapted by, the Eastern Indians.[44] The most overtly policized of these was the Virgin Mary, whom Catholics placed head and halo above the rest of the communion of saints. Most Protestants rejected the Virgin Mary's prominence in relationship to God the Father or Christ, but New France's Catholics revered her as the colony's protector and intercessor.[45] Though the Jesuit Charlevoix was glad to see that no Canadian children credited Mary as the creator of heaven and earth (as their peers in Brittany did), he did note that *canadiens* of all ages were likely to seek Mary's intercession in worldly matters before invoking the Trinity. French colonists further believed the Virgin Mary's direct intervention had protected Quebec from English assault not once but twice between 1688 and 1727.[46] A church in Quebec's *basse-ville* paid homage to this intercession and was reconsecrated, in honor of the Virgin, as Notre-Dame des Victoires in 1691. A popular song, "Cantique sur la retraitte des Anglois," which celebrated the failed 1711 attempt to take the city, credited the Virgin with a special ability to beat back the English. Proclaiming "Vous triomphez, Vierge!" the canticle's lyrics left little doubt that the composer, known as "a Lady of Quebec," saw the hand of the Virgin Mary in the destruction of Vetch and Walker's flotilla.[47] As one of the three members of the Holy Family, Mary was also a divine patron of the Holy Family Militia, which protected the colony from Indian and Euro-American threats. It counted among its members Jacques Le Ber, the Montreal merchant who became deeply involved in the lives of many converted Maine captives.[48] Common soldiers were united with elite persons like Le Ber in their veneration of Mary. Observing them while he visited Canada, Peter Kalm noted that "every morning . . . [soldiers read] the litany of the Blessed Virgin Mary; . . . this was never overlooked."[49]

Like other elements of Catholic religious culture, the Virgin Mary crossed over into New England and was made known through French intermediaries, Christianized Native Americans, and converted captives. New Englanders were as likely to experience Marian devotions focused on the Virgin as a warrior queen of heaven, an active intercessor in protecting righteous Catholics from heretics, as they were the model for obedience, submission, duty, patience. Cotton Mather found it particularly disturbing that Bomazeen, a Wabanaki sachem and close associate of the Jesuit Rale detained in a Boston jail, threatened, "the Lord Jesus Christ was of the *French Nation*; that his mother, the virgin *Mary,* was a *French Lady*; that they were the English who murdered him and that whereas he rose from the dead, and went up to the Heavens, all that would recommend themselves unto his favour, must revenge his quarrel upon the *English* as far as they can."[50] Mather likely knew well that both Christ and His mother demanded veneration from the Catholic faithful. English denial of the Virgin Mary's intercessory power in many spiritual matters was, to a Catholic, irreverent. Though Mather and other Puritans disavowed the importance of Mary as Christ's mother, they knew the Wabanakis did not, and could use a defense of the Virgin as a powerful spiritual motivator against those who derided her. The evidence of Indian reverence was reinforced for Protestants who traveled throughout Wabanakia, where chapels were consecrated to her many incarnations and her image graced walls, niches, and alters.[51] Christian Indians reported that they had learned from experience that Mary provided special protection to Native believers. In his North American journal, Charlevoix told the story of an Indian in the *pays d'en haut* who asked the Virgin Mary to protect his own gun and cause his enemy's weapon to misfire. The Indian told Charlevoix that the prayer had worked.[52] The Virgin Mary's role as patron-protector for those who went to battle in her name extended over Maine, and was considered to be a powerful source of spiritual support for borderland Catholics. Though most Maine Protestants had long ago stripped her of her importance to Christianity because of her lack of scriptural credentials, they *knew* that she remained a powerful symbol for Catholics. Veneration of the Virgin Mary affected both faith groups: one that believed in her efficacy and importance, the other that feared her power as a symbol of unity.

The Virgin Mary became a potential protector to women who had survived the captivity ordeal. Some, like New Hampshire captive Grizel Otis Robitaille, were enthusiastic participants in Marian devotions.[53] So too, of course, were the eight New England–born captives who became nuns. For these women, Mary's virgin life legitimized female celibacy (not commonly found among Protestants). Captors attempted to couch the Virgin's importance in terms that Bible-reading Protestants could understand: namely, in Holy Scripture. Put into Casco captive Hannah Swarton's mouth by Cotton Mather, the argument against the Virgin Mary's primacy was a debate worth having. Though she bemoaned that it was "bootless" of her, "a poor woman, to acquaint the world with what arguments I used if I could now remember them," she did remember with certainty that she countered the Catholics' Luke-based arguments supporting veneration with references to Revelation 19:10 and 22:9, which commanded believers simply to "worship God."[54]

In the contest for religious hegemony, the Virgin Mary served as a powerful symbol for both Christianities, representing both triumphal, militant Catholicism and, for Protestants, the worst and perhaps most dangerous hallmarks of popery. Mary's detractors dotted Maine. But so did her *dévotes*. And though New Englanders did not venerate the Virgin Mary, they were forced to recognize her power to mobilize and inspire borderland Catholics.

Holy Books and Sacred Structures

As the English began to gain an upper hand in establishing a Protestant religious culture in Maine, they attempted to supplant the pious materials of Catholicism with comparable Protestant ones. An easy starting place was religious texts, which were small and portable, and contained content that was more often than not subject to Euro-American Christian interpreters.

Catholic Wabanakis were catechized in an environment that emphasized oral traditions and sacred spaces decorated with spiritual iconography that was meant to be "read" by the often illiterate faithful. Even the most rustic mission churches contained statues of saints and religious paintings, which for Catholic missionaries facilitated the teaching process.[55] In addition, the Jesuits and members of other religious orders, men and women both, often worked to educate indigenous people in the basics of French and, under ideal circumstances, Latin, the language of Catholic liturgy. These efforts were subject to constraints of time and tools.

English Protestants had a more entrenched culture of what can be termed "religious literacy" than the French in Canada did. It was through literacy that they hoped to woo Christian Indians away from the Catholics. As noted before, New England Protestants like John Gyles and Joseph Baxter came to recognize that destroying and discrediting Catholic objects and spaces was more likely to incur anger than attract Catholics to Protestantism. So they took a different tack by offering Scripture, in its object form as a book, as an alternative. This swapping of pious materials unfolded in a particularly public way at the Arrowsic Conference of 1717, when Massachusetts governor Samuel Shute addressed the gathered sachems through interpreters, who included several ex-captives who had spent time among the Wabanakis and French. Included in this group were John Gyles and Samuel Jordan, grandson of the notorious Anglican priest of Scarborough, Robert Jordan. Related through birth and marriage to two women who spent the remainder of their lives in Canadian convents, Jordan, like Gyles, likely had a particularly compelling reason for luring some Catholic souls to his own faith.[56] Through these interpret - ers, Shute told the English and Indian attendees that

> KING *GEORGE,* and the *British Nation,* are Christian of the Reformed Protestant Religion; That the great and only Rule of their Faith and Worship, and Life, is contained in the BIBLE . . . here in this Book which is the Word of GOD . . . is contained our Holy Religion; and we would gladly, have you of the same Religion with us, and therefore we have agreed, to be at the Charge of a Protestant Missionary among you to instruct you. . . . And I hope also in a little Time to appoint a Schoolmaster among you to teach your Children, and that I hope and expect that they Treat this Protestant Missionary with all affection and respect, not only for the sake of the King's Government, but of his own Character, He being a minister of *Jesus Christ* our only Lord and Saviour, who will Judge them and us at the last Day.[57]

As he spoke, Shute raised the Bible in his hands, over his head, a gesture that seemed calculated to evoke the elevation of the Eucharist by a priest in a Catholic mass. Thus would the message have been clear: the Word should become the focal point of neophyte spirituality and supplant the transubstantiated Host. The sacramental replacement was enhanced when copies of "Indian Bibles" were passed out to the participants—another evocation of the sacramental practice of a priest sharing Eucharist with a congregation.

The Bibles—and the offer of minister Joseph Baxter's services to acclimate them to reading the text—were politely declined. Wiwurna, a Norridgewock sachem, explained to the delegation, "We desire to be Excused on that Point. GOD has given us Teaching already, and if we should go from that, we should displease GOD. We are not capable to make any Judgment about Religion."[58] With this refusal, the English believed they had seen proof of the notion that lay Catholics were forbidden to read Scripture for themselves. Samuel Shute had this idea in mind when he chastised Sebastien Rale, "Must it not seem Strange even to our Self, That a People whom you pretend to have Instructed in the Christian Religion and Even Proselyted thereunto, Should Disclaim the holy Scriptures which Contain the Entire Rudiments of the Christian Religion and are the Only Rule of Faith, Worship and Manners."[59] This perceived dismissal of Scripture was almost incomprehensible to the English, who considered Scripture a spiritual necessity to all professed Christians. As Nicholas Beasley has shown, even the roughest, crudest, and most violent of English mariners, the corsairs who prowled the Caribbean for New World treasure extracted by the Catholic Spanish, took the Catholics they attacked to task for not reading Scripture. This was evident in the sack of the Spanish island of Chapera in 1576. When a group of privateers under John Oxham found a stash of pious books "they threw [them] on the floor and trampled on them and tore them up."[60] Finding among the offending material a New Testament in Spanish, the corsairs commanded the Spanish victim to "read that book, because it was a good book . . . in as much as the others were fabrications and lies."[61] Destroying the books of an enemy faith was a common form of early modern iconoclasm, spanning from this English-Spanish anecdote to the Spanish soldiers and clergy who defaced and burned countless Native American texts. But the spiritual self-righteousness of such a tough band of seafarers, who were notoriously lax in their own religious practices, suggests that such men created in the Protestant reliance on Scripture a tool for spiritual superiority.

There is another perspective to be gleaned from this story, however, in the fact that an officer in a remote Spanish imperial outpost had a copy of Scripture in his native tongue with him. In the entangled world of borderland religious culture, violent encounters could reveal underlying commonalities between religious enemies which remained hidden during times of peace and separation. In this case, the presence of the "offending material" subverted the common belief among Protestants that Catholics were forbidden to read Scripture for personal edification and spiritual fulfillment, and without the interference of a clerical intermediary. Clearly there is precedent for Spanish lay colonists doing it. Other Europeans did as well. In seventeenth-century Maryland, for example, Catholic settler Robert Cole educated both his sons and daughters to read the Bible, confirming that lay reading of Scripture was not a phenomenon exclusive to the Spanish.[62]

A tradition of clerically controlled access to Bibles, as well as low literacy rates in French Canada, meant copies of the holy book were still largely in the hands of the literate Catholic clergy and religious. But pious books and catechisms were widely accessible to the literate throughout the French colony, and it was expected that pious people would want to own them. They were available enough that Bishop Saint-Vallier issued a list of books every family in the colony should own, including, among other works, a collection of saints' lives. This text had a Protestant corollary in Foxe's *Book of Martyrs,* which drew heavily on pre-Reformation Christian sources for tropes of piety, sacrifice, and martyrdom. Another form in pious literature, the *livret bleu,* cataloged for French Catholics similar signs, wonders, and portents and contained strong parallels to the collections of "wonder stories" that circulated throughout Protestant New England.[63] Like other Atlantic World Protestants, those on the Maine frontier treated most Catholic books, or at least books with recognizable religious symbolism written in French or Latin, with suspicion. In one case, a Catholic devotional manual that was shown to some New England prisoners in the early years of their captivity during King William's War was transformed into a tool of Satan at the Essex County witch trials.[64] In fundamentals, however, the spiritual exercises and meditations contained in these books closely paralleled manuals that were used by Anglicans and Puritans.[65] Pious literature common to Catholics and Prot-estants did little to engender tolerance or coexistence, but it did provide a body of religiously based anecdotes and tropes that shaped their perceptions of the wonder-working of Providence and the presence of the spiritual in the world around them.

Why would such books cause alarm, especially in light of the fact that Protestants who encountered Bibles in the hands of Catholics assumed that they were, by their very nature, "Protestant"? In an area like colonial Maine, where books were in short supply, settlers were possibly not aware of the similarities these books shared with material that was flowing from Puritan printing presses. Puritan and Catholic printing houses (both abroad and later, in the colonies) produced the works of pre-Reformation writers such as Augustine, Bernard of Clairvaux, and Thomas à Kempis. They also produced meditative emblem books, complete with illustrations that served both faiths.[66] One of these, Francis Quarles's *Emblemes, Divine and Moral,* an extremely popular text with Puritan readers, had been copied from nearly identical Jesuit sources.[67] To borderland Protestants, who in general lacked a full range of written materials with which to engage their faiths, these little books with French and Latin inscriptions and iconography must have appeared uncompromisingly alien, full of the worst distortions of Christianity that Catholicism could deliver.

The events at Arrowsic indicate that the English representatives clung to the old idea that Catholicism kept the faithful from the printed word of God. Maine's Native American Catholics—and its ex-captives—often knew differently. During their captivity, Hannah Swarton and John Williams both expressed surprise over the availability of English-language Bibles in New France.[68] Joseph Bartlett, a captive from northern Massachusetts, engaged in lively disputations over scriptural meanings with Père Meriel, with the help of an English-language Bible. While it is possible that these captives were given Bibles looted from English settlements, they also might well have been given Douai, or "Catholic," Bibles, which had been in print in English since the end of the sixteenth century and were likely available in Catholic Europe for purchase by England's refugee recu-sant population on the Continent.[69]

Ultimately, Holy Scripture was the primary literary source that bridged Catholicism and Protestantism. Available in both cultures, it served as an important tool for religious communication in challenging circumstances. Such communication could be truculent or peaceful, but either way it reinforced the idea that all New World Christians held the seminal work of Christianity in common.

The cult of saints, holy days, and liturgical calendars, and books had some commonalities that crossed faith-based lines. So too did houses of worship. Euro-American Catholics and Protestants harbored different understandings of the spaces in which religious services were conducted. But both faiths recognized that structures for worship were meeting spaces for their respective communities that reinforced what Nancy Shoemaker terms a "sentimental or nationalist bond between people." This perspective on houses of worship resonated with Native people, who revered specific places and landmarks of their tribal territories because of the events in tribal history that had unfolded there, or the role the place or landmark played in Native creation stories.[70]

Euro-Americans also used these spaces for community-building activities, such as spreading news and building community support for common enterprises. When Maine's punishing climate permitted, Native Americans regarded certain exterior spaces as sacred as well. After contact with Christians, these provided a point of religious commonality that Catholics in particular could exploit and emphasize.[71] As commonly found elements of built or manipulated environments, religious places and religiously charged exterior spaces were centrally located within communities, where they reminded members of the omnipresence of the divine in all aspects of human enterprise. Sebastien Rale emphasized this connection when he built two of Norridgewock's chapels "on the path that leads either to the woods or to the fields." The priest confirmed that sacred landmarks were a revered feature of the landscape when he wrote his nephew in France, "The Savages never pass them without offering prayers therein."[72]

It comes as no surprise that, in times of war, these large-scale landmarks of religious culture, along with their contents, were often the first targets of enthusiastic iconoclasts. The Protestants who attacked Catholic communities throughout the Atlantic World singled out their places of worship for particular degradation, burning churches and chapels, smashing crucifixes and statues, shredding priestly vestments, and stealing movable items of value.[73] Even on the Maine frontier, Sebastien Rale clearly knew of this trend. In 1722, as English forces under Thomas Westbrook approached the mission, Rale sensed his church would likely be targeted. The fleeing Jesuit took time to nail a note to its door stating that the structure was "ill built, because the English dont work well," suggesting the English would be doing the mission a favor if they burned it down.[74]

Catholics were not averse to iconoclasm, but Catholic-led violence against the material culture of Protestantism required a reorientation of object-centered violence based on differing Protestant senses of sacred space. Natalie Zemon Davis and Edward Muir have observed that Catholics and Protestants developed different perceptions of spirituality in space. Muir notes "the contrast . . . between a Catholic appreciation of the variability of spiritual presences in the created world and a Protestant caution about measuring and therefore containing the spiritual, but the difference between them was more of degree than kind."[75] New World Calvinists took this distinction further: instead of remodeling existing structures, which still were likely to carry associations (if not their furnishings) with pre-Reformation Christianity, they built new ones that had no historical or visual baggage. Frontier worship spaces were even more removed from those in the Reformed communities of either Europe or urban America, who built their meetinghouses from the ground up with few, if any, church-specific architecture elements or furnishings aside from the pulpit and pews. A New England meetinghouse was characterized less by its architectural features and fittings and more by its function. As the space in which the sermon was read and the sacraments dispensed, the interior accommodated the practical, physical needs of the congregation.[76] The Catholics who attacked Maine's English settlements were usually indiscriminate in what they targeted. Chances were, with an entire community ablaze, the meetinghouse with its lack of defining religious features simply went up with it.

Catholic reliance on churches as sacred space for liturgy and sacrament presented Protestants with chips in diplomatic negotiations. In Maine, the concept of religious space as bargaining tool emerges clearly in the proceedings of a 1711 English-Wabanaki conference. It was there that the English agreed to an unusual concession: in exchange for the right to build a new trading house at New Harbor, they would build the Christian Wabanakis a church, which would replace the structure destroyed by Winthrop Hilton's and Shadrach Walton's forces in 1705.[77] The destruction of the church had been touted as a symbolic blow against popery and even heralded in the *Boston News-Letter*, which crowed that the "Meeting-house" had contained "only a few old Popish relics" which were quickly dispatched by "our men, hail and lusty."[78] Catholic Wabanakis, however, neither forgot nor forgave the assault. When the English approached them to negotiate for trade several years later, the Wabanakis named rebuilding their church as one of their conditions.[79] The Massachusetts government understandably did not want to engage in the business of building popish churches for Indians, so instead, negotiators suggested an artful compromise, offering to build a suggestively termed "meeting house" if it could be staffed with one of their own ministers.[80] The Norridgewocks pondered the plan, but, as they would do later with the Bibles, ultimately rejected it. They continued to insist, however, that the English provide then with a replacement structure suitable for Catholic worship. The issue was not resolved until 1720, when the English grudgingly agreed to build the chapel the Indians wanted. The English workers assigned to the job clearly resented being put to work on a papist chapel. The Wabanakis were also dissatisfied with their work, and lodged complaint after complaint to the Massachusetts Assembly about the quality of the workmanship, the chronically drunk and surly workers, and the propensity of Jabez Bradbury (called "Jebis" by the Wabanakis), the militia captain who oversaw the work, to threaten to leave the job undone unless he received additional money and goods from the Wabanakis themselves.[81]

To the Wabanakis and their missionary, the long battle to replace the church was also a test of English respect for the religious prerogatives of their would-be trading partners. Given the fact that the English-built church was not the only one in the mission, the point of seeing it rebuilt seemed to privilege principle over practical need.

The mission had at least two other consecrated spaces that were suitable for Catholic liturgy. In addition, logic dictated waiting until tensions had ended to get on with rebuilding something that had already been a target. For Sebastien Rale, the absence of a sacred space that had hitherto served as the centerpiece of Catholic life at Norridgewock, was a convenient reminder of English perfidy contrasted with French promises, and also kept—as the priest desired—anti-English tensions high. Another, perhaps more powerful function was served by the fact that it needed to be rebuilt in the first place. As Jon Butler has noted, "Even destroyed church buildings could be made to proclaim Christianity, at least the kind demanded of the state."[82] Norridgewock's age, size, and the sheer number of its sacred structures amplified the significance of periodic destruction. Even the act of targeting the mission underscored its importance as a material testament to French claims on the province. New Englander Thomas Coram understood this when he wrote to the Board of Trade in London, "The Jesuits of Canada built a great Church at Norridgewock near the River Kenebek as a Standing Proof of the French Right and Possession."[83]

Staking out the parameters of sacred space was not specific to Catholic missions on volatile, entangled frontiers; it was a common feature to identity and community formation among Europeans as well, even those who, as in New France, lived in homogenously Catholic colonies. Like their counterparts in France and other parts of Europe, French colonists viewed church structures and established parish boundaries as personal affiliations that tied them to the surrounding land, their families, and their neighbors.[84] An extreme example of this commitment was witnessed by the colonists in 1714, when Bishop Saint-Vallier attempted to redraw a parish line in the village of St. Léonard, near Montreal. Incensed by the proposed change, a group of parish women confronted the official sent to report on the situation and threatened to kill him and throw his body into a swamp if he implemented the change.[85] Churches were ubiquitous reminders of religious identity which also held significance for those who lived around them and, in the case of the colonial world, protected them from abusive enemies—even when those enemies came from within. The ability to destroy a church implied the ability to destroy a community as well. As such, they were worth protecting.

Equally important was defending the right to build a religious marker on the landscape. The destruction of a church was particularly egregious and sent a powerful message to believers about both the religious past and the religious future of place. By desecrating the church at Norridgewock in 1705, Hilton and his men demonstrated that religious practice in Maine was ultimately subject to the sufferance of local governments and the monarchs they represented.[86] Among his many threats to the rival New Englanders, Rale swore "upon my Land thou mayest depend upon it, That I will Revenge myself also and that upon thy Land in such manner as will be more sensible and more Disadvantageous to thee, for one of the Meeting houses or Temples, is of more value beyond Compare than our Church." Rale's additional threat, "I shall not be satisfied with Burning only one or two of thine, but many; I know where they are," emphasized that the Jesuit was familiar with the English settlements in Norridgewock's vicinity.

Throughout the wars of empire, religious buildings remained popular targets for settling scores in the secular world. Looting and iconoclasm were common features of these attacks and served multiple purposes. When forces under Maine-born Sir William Phips attacked Port Royal in 1690, the troops sacked the church as much to demonstrate their commitment to Boston's theological opposition to idolatry as to gain treasure.[87] By supporting the looting and desecration, Phips behaved like any other English fighting man with proper priorities, but he might also have been trying to avoid the fate of the recently deposed Edmund Andros, whose downfall came in part from his reluctance to destroy the Catholic symbols, which in turn fed suspicions that he was a crypto-papist.[88] Perhaps the critics were right: Andros did indeed fail to dismantle a building that was obviously a chapel when he assaulted French trader Jean-Vincent d'Abbadie de Saint-Castin's Pentagoët fort. The failure to act against overt symbols of an enemy religion carried its own meanings.

Often taking a leading role in destroying specifically Catholic targets were the rank-and-file fighters, who frequently took to their work with gusto. As historian John Walter has shown, it was common for iconoclasts throughout the English-speaking world to come from society's middle and lower ranks. These, of course, constituted the largest percentage of English men to join the army. Their actions against Catholic material culture were consistent with well-established iconoclastic behaviors in England, especially in the prelude to the English Civil War, when grassroots agitation against the highly unpopular Archbishop Laud was frequently manifested in iconoclastic terms.[89] Puritans in particular were acting in accord with Calvinist principles when they destroyed objects that they saw as detracting from the "living icons" of the congregation and providing visual obstacles to the "clear visual space" mandated by reformed churches.[90]

The Maine men and their allies who attacked Port Royal with Phips sometimes resisted the impulse to destroy Catholic liturgy-specific objects, reserving these prizes for a more important display of Protestant triumph over Catholic communities. Some were carried to Boston by Phips's returning troops, who did this, as Emerson Baker notes, because such items offered clear proof of "the religious significance of the expedition's success."[91] But herein was also proof that Maine's Protestants lived in closer intimacy with Catholics, who, as the items demonstrated, freely practiced their rituals in close proximity to New England itself. Such objects satisfied a certain amount of curiosity about other Christians and their practices, to which colonists in the New England metropole would have had virtually no exposure.

The Maine settlers in the fighting contingent had a good deal of experience with such objects, which were less avowedly alien than even the most orthodox Puritans would admit. As Joyce Chaplin contends, post-Reformation English men and women still acknowledged, albeit with unease, that their form of Christianity had a connection to material symbols.[92] Puritan New Englanders struggled to separate appropriate from inappropriate uses of Christian symbols. The best known example of this struggle happened in early seventeenth-century Massachusetts when Captain John Endecott sought to remove the red cross on the king's colors that flew over Salem. This led to a heated debate among Puritans over the use of such a transcendent Christian symbol. On one hand, John Winthrop argued that Endecott acted righteously because "the red cross was given to the king of England by the pope, as an ensign of victory, and as a superstitious thing, and a relique of the antichrist."[93] Other Puritan leaders disagreed, and questioned the legality, and even the legitimacy, of Endecott's actions. From a religious standpoint, the move was legitimate, as the Assistants acknowledged they were "doubtful of the lawful use of the cross in the ensign."[94] Still, the debate erupted in the first place because the Massachusetts Bay authorities were worried about the political repercussions the act might carry. Thus they sublimated their rejection of religious symbols to political concerns that were, at the time, seen as possessing greater importance. Some Puritans even supported the use of religious symbols, provided they were employed in the appropriate spirit. Connecticut founder and Puritan minister Thomas Hooker believed that superstitious abuses of the past should not deny the cross its appropriate uses. He thought it appropriate for Christians to use the cross for civil purposes, provided they avoided investing it with any inappropriate meanings.[95]

Destruction of churches and the tools of religion and the display of religious trophies were common phenomena wherever Old and New World Catholics and Protestants took up arms against one another. Converging Christians in and around Maine, however, were just as likely to adapt religious objects to new uses. This, in part, reflects the region's poverty. In Maine and other frontier regions, the value of a bell, a musical instrument, or an altar made it a likely candidate for spiritual reuse rather than destruction. Catholics and Protestants both engaged in a frontier recycling program of religious material culture. Both appropriated items that would develop their worship spaces more fully, at little or no expense to themselves. The looting that conflict fostered provided opportunities to gain some of these desirable items.

Anglicanism in particular had many church fittings in common with Catholicism. Recognizing these commonalities, Anglicans who raided Catholic churches conducted a lively trade in church objects with other non-Catholics who knew their value. St. John's Anglican

Figure 10. Baptismal font, St. John's Church, Portsmouth. Originally intended for a Catholic church in New France, this font was looted by the English for sacramental duty in an Anglican church. Courtesy of St. John's Church, Portsmouth. Photo by Landya McCafferty.

Church in Portsmouth, New Hampshire, boasted a marble baptismal font that had been crafted in Senegal and was intended for a Catholic church in Canada. It was seized off the Maine coast by a New England privateer during the Seven Years' War. The same church called its faithful to worship with a bell taken from Louisbourg in 1745 by forces led by Kittery native William Pepperrell. Though Pepperrell's troops apparently reveled in destroying the rest of the chapel, the bell was too difficult to destroy, and too valuable to be wasted.[96] Some of these war trophies found their way to the heart of Boston itself. Decorative cherubim flanking the organ at Christ Church were reputed to have come from a looted Quebec convent. A decidedly less sacred relic was a chandelier crafted from the ribs of a French vessel destroyed during a war of empire.[97]

Large-scale objects like the Louisbourg/Portsmouth bell were of particular interest to raiders. Aside from their size and value as large metal objects, bells added a sensory experience to religious communities. Their "voices" became an identifiable part of essential religious practice. They called congregations together, and, for Catholics, they were valued as markers of both sacred and secular time. And they added a literal religious voice to a community that linked aural experience and communal worship with a specific landscape. It is little wonder that they were highly regarded as both symbolic and valuable prizes.

Frontier Catholics, whose liturgical needs demanded a greater number of objects than did most Protestant denominations, also took part in religious looting and adaptive reuse.[98] In her study of identity and narrative in the early St. Lawrence Valley, Linda Breuer Gray discusses the oral legend that linked the 1703 attack on Deerfield to the theft of a bell that was intended for the Mohawk mission of Kahnawake, outside Montreal. The residents felt the bell should not be allowed to "sing" for Protestants and decided to get it back in 1703, which they did.[99] A less fanciful, Maine-based legend has a similar twist. Not wanting the Protestant attackers to appropriate the mission's "voice" as their own, a group of Norridgewock survivors buried the modestly sized chapel bell to keep it out of the hands of marauding Protestants.[100] It was found again in 1808, quieted by the roots of a hemlock tree, at a time when the old religious hostilities had been softened by time into romances of the forest.

✦ ✦ ✦

Early Maine's material culture of religion reflected the region's multiple influences. Objects, icons, buildings, books, and even more ethereal concepts that affected the material world, such as the liturgical calendar and its feast days, were forms of tangible interfaith contact in themselves, which, though they often reminded Protestants and Catholics of their intrinsic differences, also provided potent reminders of their shared heritage and persisting commonalities. In addition, they afforded Maine's settlers the opportunity to experience other Christian expressions holistically, in ways that only their counterparts in the most religiously diverse areas of Europe did. Though they rarely, if ever, led to interfaith coexistence or tolerance, the physical manifestations of frontier religious culture open a window onto a world of shared Christian understandings. Some of these understandings were put to use in exploitative situations; others served to prop up the geopolitical objectives of one of the competing groups. Nevertheless, they hint at a world of shared experiences and memories of a common religious heritage that colonial borders, ideological or literal, could not divide.

CHAPTER SIX

"The Lord . . . Will Greatly Reward Me"

The Religious Dimensions of Worldly Goods

In Maine's contest to establish a dominant Christian culture, even commonplace objects were recast for religious purposes. The elevation of the mundane into the sacred, in the form of inherited land and goods, was one of the few practical measures to curb persisting religious incursions that Maine's English settlers could control. In their hands, this control moved from the purely reactive into the proactive by offering goods to Catholic convert children who renounced their new religion and returned to live out their lives as Protestants. Applying strictly religious eligibility tests for receiving property and goods via inheritance was a prerogative of Maine parents, or, in their absence, male siblings. The province's Protestants used inheritances to save souls from religious corruption, reconstitute families and their associated God-ordained hierarchies, and exercise whatever power they could to ensure that the land of the Province of Maine, as claimed by Massachusetts, flourished in the name of Protestant kings. Still, as with many other elements of frontier religious culture, the approaches and outcomes varied. Many colonists made the distribution of family wealth contingent not only on return to New England, but on a renewed commitment to Protestantism. Others had a more complex

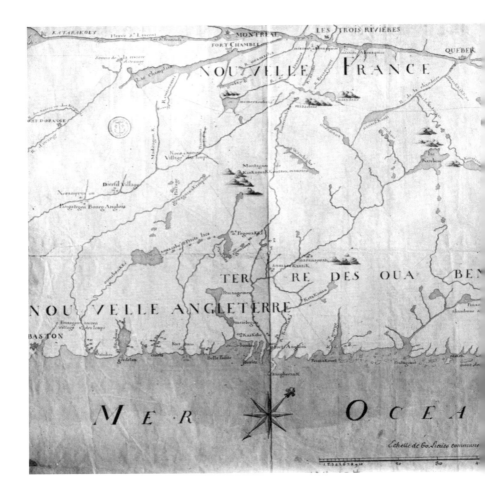

response that took into account not only their own religious scruples but the wishes of their religiously errant loved ones and their particular life situations. The religious culture of Maine was imprinted with vast and varied experiences and circumstances that contextualize a complicated world where religious identity and belief extended beyond faith-based identities, religious objects and places, and imperial boundaries established by European religious rivalries.

The impulse to extend sacred significance to worldly goods such as land and money was born of an ongoing post-Reformation im-

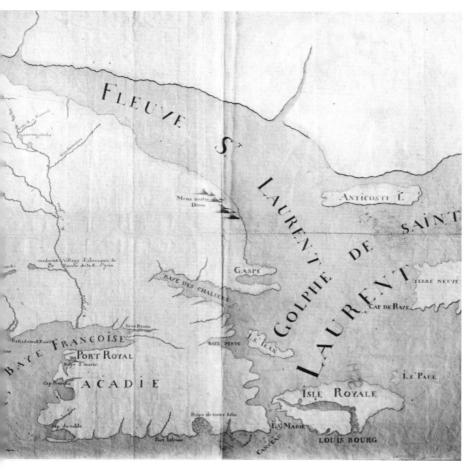

Figure 11. Jesuit Joseph Aubery's 1713 map shows Maine from the perspective of Wabanaki settlement and French religious influence. Courtesy of the Newberry Library.

pulse described by Robert Scribner, who observed that "evangelical forms of consecration reemerged and multiplied, and were applied to a wide variety of objects: church foundation stones, new or restored churches, pulpits, fonts, organs, alters, bells, [and] cemeteries."[1] In this formulation, land took on particular religious importance. Christian explorers and would-be colonizers marked the regions of the New

World they claimed by erecting crosses, which, despite Protestant disdain for religious symbols, stood as universally understood icons of European presence and intentions. As Christian settlements progressed, the land became marked with more overt religious symbols. The most apparent were church structures, church yards, and cemeteries, which sacralized the landscape by involving, as Scribner points out, "the dead as well as the living" in the colonial enterprise.[2] The Jesuit Joseph Aubery recognized the powerful interplay between spirit and landscape when he mapped Maine from the French colonial perspective to press post-Utrecht land claims that favored their interests.[3] Aubery's cartographical interpretation of Maine is conspicuous for its overt Catholic symbolism infused in the visualized landscape, which the Jesuit considered to be sacralized by the presence of Catholic missions. The pictorial representations of the missions themselves, which depict the Maine settlements as peripheral to Abenaki country, loom large in comparison to the small dots representing the English settlements of Kittery, York, Wells, and Falmouth.[4] Tellingly, Aubery's depiction of the English settlements shows no buildings at all, let alone those connected to religion. Lacking the exterior symbolism of Catholicism, meetinghouses would not have stood out as particularly "churchlike" to a Jesuit (except, of course, Sebastien Rale, who knew the settlements firsthand) or any Catholic who had never seen the community. From a Catholic perspective, they lacked the overt sacred connections between land and structure.

Maine Protestants, however, had their own concepts of land's ties to God. For Puritans in particular, land was made sacred through its connection to the God-ordained family patriarchy and hierarchy. The acquisition, mastering, and passing on of land to new generations were also indications of Providence's favor. Thus inherited lands and property became sacred in their own right, passing from one generation to the next, and allowing families to follow divine mandates to thrive, multiply, and use settlement of the land to spread their influ-ence. In Maine, however, family members lost to captivity and other borderland vagaries challenged the established inheritance customs that were rooted in English common law and Puritan beliefs that de-fined the smooth running of God's microcosm of heavenly order, the so-called Little Commonwealth. The experience of Aaron Littlefield of Wells provides a detailed example of how the province's unsettled religious state disrupted the smooth and godly transmission of property within Protestant frontier families. Littlefield's case further challenged the very concept of who, and under what circumstances, could claim the right of land ownership. To some in the growing, increasingly secure Province of Maine of the mid-eighteenth century, the determination of religious allegiance and its ties to land ownership transcended the need for bodies to populate and develop it, forcing a new definition of who could settle in the province, and under what terms.

Protestants for the most part differed from Catholics in their views of the sacredness of land. Nevertheless, a concept that has often been associated with Catholicism and, to a certain extent, Anglicanism is apparent when one examines the connections between inheritance and religion. On this entangled frontier, interests of land and goods took on a spiritual significance, extending the concept of religious culture to the most unlikely places.

The Spiritual Implications of Early American Property

Aaron Littlefield was born into a large and particularly fecund Puritan family. The Littlefields were among the first English men and women to come to the province. Aaron's great-grandfather, Edmund, received a land grant from the Puritan-leaning Thomas Gorges in 1643.[5] Like other families to the Eastward, the Littlefields suffered terribly from frontier violence. Particularly notable was the ordeal of Aaron's cousin, Lieutenant Josiah Littlefield, whose wife and son were killed during Queen Anne's War. Shortly after remarrying, Josiah himself was taken captive and lived in Canada for two years. Two years after his redemption in 1710, he was killed in another raid by local Indians.[6] Aaron's frontier odyssey, though far less tragic, was ultimately far stranger. By the time he died sometime after 1751, Aaron Littlefield had been known for decades as Pierre-Augustin Litrefils, *agriculteur*. And when he made the unusual move of suing his Protestant birth family for his rightful inheritance, this unrepentant acculturated French Catholic from a remote corner of the British empire raised important issues regarding the relationship of religion to land ownership in the king's dominions and the ability of Maine's Protestants to keep Catholic family members from claiming what appeared to be lawfully theirs.

Aaron Littlefield was a member of the party that brought Mary Storer and Esther Sayward home to visit in 1725. By that year he was a farmer at Saint-Mathias, outside Montreal. As he was coming only for a visit and not to resettle, Littlefield undertook the journey without his wife and children, who remained behind in Canada. Perhaps his lifelong connection with Mary Storer informed his decision to travel with her. In Maine, the Littlefields and Storers had been longtime neighbors who shared family connections and friends. These two captives carried on the family connections even in New France, where they maintained contact throughout their lives in New France.[7]

Similar to that of Mary Storer, Aaron's *congé* stated that his reason for returning to Maine was to see his family and to sort out his personal affairs. There might have been some urgency to do so while his aging mother, Martha Lord Littlefield, still lived (she had outlived Aaron's father, Moses, by a decade and was now married to her third husband). At stake in the visit was the fate of Littlefield and Lord property in Wells and elsewhere in the province. As the only surviving son of a once larger family, Aaron no doubt wanted to secure what tradition and custom dictated would be his: family-owned lands and movable goods. Firstborn New England males enjoyed the right, secured by gender and birth order, to inherit the property of their parents. The fact that he had lived for almost two decades near Montreal as Pierre-Augustin Litrefils, a culturally French husband, father, and Catholic, was, for the ex-captive at least, immaterial.[8] It was, after all, a cruel twist of fate, and not an act of will, that had carried him away from his parents and resulted in his cultural transformation.

Like Mary Storer's, Aaron's visit to Wells resulted from both an interest in reconnecting with his family and a desire to reap material gains. In pressing their respective claims for inheritance, Mary and Aaron did not see themselves as intrinsically different from their Protestant siblings. They were now Catholic and had married without engaging their families' approval. Nevertheless, they were still Maine Littlefields and Storers, leading respectable lives—farming, trading, raising children, worshipping the same God—and doing most of the other things that people of their class, status, and religion were expected to do in New England. Interactions with their Protestant relatives, however, suggest that the latter believed conversion and marriage fundamentally transformed their loved ones. New and undesirable religious affinities wrought under the crisis of captivity would have been met with compassion, but persistent commitment to these into adulthood and times of peace between Britain and France stoked suspicions in such families that their Catholic kin possessed spiritual defects that only a return to New England could undo. It was under this pretext that Joseph Storer denied his daughter Mary her fifty pounds; the stakes for Aaron, as a firstborn son and heir to a New England property, were much higher. While the transfer of patrimony was often a private family issue, Aaron's became an issue of public contention when his claims were challenged by Protestant cousins, Benjamin and Nathan Lord, who themselves wanted properties that had passed to Aaron from his mother's family. The Lords based their opposition to their cousin on the grounds that he had "turned papist," and as such, had lost his right to lands claimed by a Protestant king. Given the long history of undesired papists on Maine's soil, this argument fell on fertile ground, and the Maine courts ruled against Aaron and for his Protestant cousins.

Aaron Littlefield likely had little choice when he "turned papist." He was taken in the same raid on Wells that brought the Storers, the Wells-born Ursuline nun Esther Wheelwright, and numerous others, through Wabanakia and into Canada. Though Aaron's captive mother soon returned, her three children remained in captivity and never returned. These included Aaron's younger sister, Ruth, who in her teens entered the convent of the Hôtel-Dieu in Montreal and took the name Soeur Angelique. Supposedly there was another daughter, Tabitha, an acculturated Wabanaki whose story is recorded in family tradition but cannot be corroborated by records. Like other Wabanakis, Tabitha made her way to Wells from time to time, making herself known to family and friends before retreating back to her new

Indian kin. Family lore also asserts that a third daughter, Josephine, was lost to the French. While records related to Josephine have yet to be uncovered, both Canadians and New Englanders have claimed to be her descendants.[9] The loss of these children to captivity devastated Moses and Martha Littlefield's family, which had once been large. And when their sole surviving son and heir died, he cleared the way for his older brother in Canada to inherit his parents' entire estate.[10]

The intervening years had seen Aaron struggle against new religion in his involuntarily adopted culture. Like many of the captives of Queen Anne's War, Aaron was quickly ransomed from his Indian captors by the French.[11] Within five months, he was already working as a *domestique* for the curé of Boucherville. He was also baptized by the ubiquitous Père Meriel, who gave the boy the highly suggestive name of Pierre Augustine.[12] Both Protestants and Catholics honored the apostle Peter and Augustine, two saints revered for their tireless labors to spread Christianity. Applying this combination of names might have been the priest's way of demonstrating that baptisms like Aaron's, which brought a soul out of a heretical Reformed church and back to the true faith, symbolically recreated a single Christian vision (albeit on Roman Catholic terms). Baptism and symbolic names notwithstanding, statistics show that most captive males like Aaron could expect to return to New England, where Catholic baptism would be rendered meaningless.[13] Because both cultures wanted to retain their young men, Aaron's redemption became the object of heated negotiations in 1714. The New England mission sent to secure his return was so confident he would be released that they took the advance step of buying him new clothes for the journey to New England.[14] But the curé with whom the boy lived was determined to keep Aaron's person and soul for Catholic New France. As John Stoddard later explained, the priest bought time to convince the boy to stay by hiding the new travel clothes.[15] To Stoddard, the curé's actions were "barbarous and inhumane," underhanded tactics by a supposed man of God who combined corporal deprivations with threats of "the danger of perdition" that returning to New England and its heresies would bring to the neophyte's soul.[16] The French priest, however, saw things differently. Priests, nuns, and laypeople were all witness to the fickleness of New England males who agreed to convert but then promptly left the colony when the chance arose. Retaining these uncertain converts was not simply a matter of imperial triumph. To the clergy and religious, it meant preventing captives from sliding back into what to them was heresy. To early modern Christians, the stakes could get no higher than the preservation of the soul for true religion, and even deceitful tactics had merit if they reached the desired goal.

Since Aaron was twenty years old when these events unfolded and had, at this point, spent half his life in Boucherville, it is possible that Stoddard and Williams were working from outdated intelligence describing his wish to return. Aaron's transition to adulthood was already unfolding in New France, where he was likely already learning key skills to earn a living and thinking, at least in theoretical terms, about raising his own family. More importantly, and perhaps under the tutelage of the canny priest who sheltered him, Aaron had requested and received French citizenship in 1710. This required him to abide by the laws of the colony, where naturalized French subjects did not have unrestricted rights of movement within territory claimed by the French to move beyond its borders. It was therefore not as a captive but as a *French subject* that Aaron "could not have liberty to return."[17] Had he not become naturalized, no French civil impediment to his return would have existed.

Though Governor Vaudreuil would later accede to English demands that underage subjects be free to leave New France, Aaron did not qualify.[18] Still, after persistent pressure from Williams and Stoddard, Vaudreuil assented to the youth's return, and ordered the curé to bring Aaron to Quebec. By that time, however, the young man's mind had changed. John Stoddard was left to complain bitterly, "[The curé] had made too thorough work with his proselyte." It is not clear whether Aaron's choice was shaped by the lack of proper travel clothes; the curé's warnings about his imminent damnation if he resumed practicing the faith of Calvinist heretics; appeals for gratitude extended by the government that had redeemed him from Wabanaki hands; or his own wishes as a colonial man who had matured among the Canadians and had come to like his life in Canada. In any case, three years later, he was married to Marie Brunet, with whom he had six daughters and a son.[19] Now Pierre-Augustin Litrefils, he settled into life as a Canadian farmer in Chambly on a *concession* granted to him by the Frères Hospitaliers, who operated the Hôpital-Général de Montreal.[20] He remained a French Catholic for the rest of his life.

Still, Aaron Littlefield appeared to be drawn to the people who shared his origins. Like other onetime captive New Englanders, he played an active role in the community of New France's Catholic converts. They in turn played important roles in Aaron's own religious life. One of these was Daniel Maddox, an immigrant from England who had become a naturalized French citizen and Catholic convert, who was witness to Aaron's 1717 marriage to Marie Brunet.[21] Aaron's sister Ruth, now professed as Soeur Angelique, was cloistered at the Hôtel-Dieu in Montreal yet like her brother managed to see other New England–born Catholics from time to time.[22] Among her acquaintances was Christine Otis Le Beau Baker, a captive from Dover, New Hampshire, who knew both Littlefields before her return to New England in 1714. Aaron's friendship with Mary Storer and her family was particularly strong and durable. Both had lived in Boucherville for some time after their redemption from the Wabanakis and shared *marraines* and *parrains* drawn from the powerful Boucher family. Several members of Mary's extended family served as godparents to Aaron's children.[23] The friendship continued after the critical visit to New England, for in 1728 Mary wrote her brother Ebenezer that "aron Litelfielde is well and his familie he remembers his love to you."[24]

As an acculturated male captive, Aaron was an anomaly in New France, with the vast majority of acculturated captives from Maine and elsewhere in New England being girls and young women when taken.[25] He was among only nine male captives from Maine of any age taken between 1688 and 1727 who remained permanently within the captor culture (French or Indian) for life. On October 8, 1746, the Reverend John Norton wrote in his captivity journal that "this morning there came an Englishman to see me, his name Littlefield: He was taken as a Lad from Piscataqua, and so continued with the French, having a Family, at Champlain: we had considerable Discourse together."[26] Norton, unfortunately, gave no further details of the conversation, leaving historians to wonder whether Aaron impressed the minister as a bit too content with how his life, spiritual and material, had evolved. Young male captives who showed an inclination to stay were clearly prized by the French and subjected to forms of enticement, mostly gifts of land, that were never offered to women and girls. This suggests that the French knew that males might be lured home by the promise of inheriting land in New England. As significant landlords in New France, religious orders such as the Frères Hospitaliers (Aaron's *concession* came from them) and the Sulpicians (who gave one to acculturated Kittery captive Joseph Fry) did their part to encourage Maine captives to remain through both evangelization and land grants. Furthermore, they seemed to recognize, as New Englanders had, that land and religion were intertwined, not simply on maps and in terms of imperial definitions, but in discrete, tangible ways. Giving *concessions* to converts like Aaron validated not only their choice to remain Catholic but also their perceived value to the whole colonial endeavor. With generous land holdings in their own right, these religious orders were situated to play an important role in a colonial enterprise that welcomed Catholics only. As will be seen, the Court of Common Pleas that heard Aaron's case, as well as his Protestant family, played a related role, yet in reverse. Their chief duty, as they saw it, was to keep Protestant land in Protestant hands.

Spirituality and material goods were intimately intertwined elements of the cross-cultural traveler's experience. French captors strove to create a level of enticement that secured the body for New France and the soul for Rome. After the Treaty of Utrecht created the possibility of the return of many New England Protestant captives, the desire to secure those who had undergone spiritual and cultural "conversions" took on an added urgency. But material enticements could go only so far, and were dependent on the means and inclinations of those in the captor colony who had a vested interest in bestowing them. In granting Mary Storer St. Germaine and Aaron Littlefield each a *pérmis "pour aller à la Nouvelle-Angleterre y voir ses parents et régler ses affaires domestiques,"* the French government simultaneously expressed confidence in a completed acculturation process and indicated that its pockets, while deep, were finite. Allowing captives to see their parents was an important part of the mission, but it was only half of its purpose. Those who succeeded in securing their patrimo - nies could then tie New England lands to the rival French colony.

Aaron had more reason to anticipate success in securing his inheritance than Mary Storer did. English common law privileged the passing of money, real estate and goods to males. For the most part, it maintained that gender-based bias for captive sons. As Ann M. Little has shown, male captives were much more likely to press successfully for their inheritance than females. Little cites the case of New En - gland siblings William and Mary Moore, which demonstrates the differences in the ways parents of captives viewed male and female heirs. William only had to be alive and ask for his inheritance; Mary, however, was required to return from captivity or else she would lose her portion to other siblings.[27] Even when male captives encountered birth families unwilling to acknowledge them through bestowing an inheritance, the courts ultimately favored them, and in the process en - sured that the passing of real property from fathers to sons remained free from the taint of religious difference.

Still, the process of coming to New England to claim an inheri - tance was fraught with potential trouble. Events in the life of Wil - liam Hutchins underscore the lengths to which some Maine captives went to press their claims. Hutchins, who was taken from Berwick with his mother and siblings during Queen Anne's War, was the only member of his family who did not return. When he did so unexpect - edly decades later, his brothers, who now controlled the estate, claimed he was an imposter. A court case ensued, and it was settled (in Hutch - ins's favor) only when his mother swore before the Maine Court of Common Pleas that scars on his body matched those of the child she had not seen for years.[28]

Returning to the Maine of his childhood in 1725 to see his mother, Aaron likely foresaw no religiously based impediments to securing his inheritance. The visit lasted three weeks, long enough for Aaron to learn the details of his inheritance, which was signifi - cant, including land in Wells and, through a maternal connection, lots in Berwick. Legally, Aaron had already come into two-thirds of the estate of his father. But as a widow who lacked access to her liv -

ing children, Martha retained control over all of her deceased husband's estate. No one knows what transpired between mother and son, but the visit ended with Aaron clearly assuming that he was executor of his mother's estate as well as her heir.[29]

But there was a peculiar glitch in this arrangement. Martha Littlefield died without a will in 1726—a curious thing, since she knew her son was alive and well in Canada.[30] Perhaps she assumed that her son would simply assume his right to the estate in accordance with the laws of Massachusetts. But the estate's disparate parts were governed by equally disparate laws, leaving the inheritance of her Berwick property in question. It is tempting to speculate that Martha hoped the ambiguity about the state of her property might coax Aaron home again to sort out the myriad details. Perhaps she wanted the absence of a will to act as a form of rebuke to her son for his abandonment of family and Protestantism. Or, conflicted about the son she had borne but barely knew, did she leave the inheritance question for others to sort out after she was gone? It is impossible to know the answers to these questions, but it is important to note that this single act created knots in a smooth transition of property that only Aaron's return could untangle.

Adding to the list of questions is the fact that Aaron waited until ten years after the death of his mother to press his claims to the Berwick land. The timing was suggestive: 1738 was a deeply difficult year for Canada's agricultural families, who were suffering the effects of a severe famine. From the relative comfort of the Quebec Hospital, Mother de Sainte-Hélène noted sympathetically that "wheat was lacking, and the poor inhabitants were reduced to eating tree buds, potatoes, and other things unsuitable for the nourishment of mankind."[31] As late as 1746, John Norton noted that the land in the vicinity of Aaron's home was "very poor, it being cold, sour land" and that its inhabitants lived in "generally but poor Hutts."[32] He did not describe this as Aaron's particular situation, however, which suggests that the ex-captive might have been better off than some of his neighbors. Still, in 1738 the survival of Aaron's family might have depended on securing his inheritance and the income it stood to produce. Tellingly, and despite these hard times, Aaron seemed to have had no inclination to leave Canada permanently, even if removing to Berwick would have afforded a more comfortable existence for his family.

At this time Aaron's religious conversion became a fully realized source of family controversy involving the maternal Lord cousins, who must have refused the returned captive access to the Berwick land. Aaron sued for title, and the Lords countersued. In the process, the cousins claimed for the record (though critically, not in the plea) that Aaron's Catholicism disqualified him from claiming land in a jurisdiction controlled by Protestants. Whether they truly believed that papists could not own property in the Protestant British king's dominions or were just cynically manipulating religious fears to claim the property for themselves is not known. But after so many years of interfaith conflict on the Maine frontier, the fundamentals of the argument no doubt carried weight.

The Court of Common Pleas gave credence to these fears by affirming the perspective of the Lords on the basis that Aaron, a papist, did not even possess the right to use Maine's courts to press his case. The judges concluded that Aaron, "if a Papist, by Law Debarr'd from maintaining an action for a Real Estat then Cost for the ye Defts but if not the Jury find for the Plt ye Land Sued for & Cost upon wch Verdict of Court have maturel Considered and advised is of the opinion that a Papist Cannot by Law maintain an action for ye Recovery of a real Estate. It's therefore Considered by the Court that the Defts Shall recover against the Plt Cost of Court."[33]

Thus denied his plea, and stuck with additional fees related to the case, Aaron appealed to the Court of Common Pleas of Suffolk County, Massachusetts, and engaged Noah Emery, a Maine-born Protestant lawyer, to represent him. To win the case, Emery took an unanticipated tack. Instead of insisting that common law and tradition guaranteed the transition of property from one generation to another unless an individual was specifically disinherited by the parents, Emery presented a group of counterarguments that encouraged the court to consider the broader implications of borderland religious identities and the application of English laws on the American continent. He wrote to the Court of Common Pleas that his client deserved the property based on the following grounds:

1. Because Judgment ought to have been for ye Plt to recover against ye defts ye Premises sued for & Costs.
2. the Plts being a Papist or not a papist was not mentioned in the Issuable Plea & so not proper or Lawfull for the Jury to give a Verdict upon nor Could they lawfully take notice of ye Pleas made in abatement but only ye issuable Pleas.
3. there is no Euidence to proue that ye Plt is a papist nor ought any deposition of any Person be deem'd as sufficient Evidence to prove it and ye Plt ought not to Loose his Inheritance (if there was such a Law) before he be Convict of Papish Recusancy in a Court proper to try the Same for ye Pet is now a Protestant for aught that now appears to the contrary and may settle on ye land himself.
4. This shows that he has proved his descent and rights.
5. Many of ye Kings Subjects in many parts of his dominion are Papists yet enjoy their estates altho they may not bear any office & there is no Law that does Debarr ye Pet. from maintaining this action if he was a Papist.[34]

According to Emery's legal reckoning, Aaron's right to claim the property was based less on the fact that Catholics were not explicitly barred from owning property (a relatively straightforward, incontrovertible argument) than on the fact that no one involved in the case knew for certain that Aaron had indeed renounced Protestantism and adopted in its place an active Catholicism. This was a cunning strategy, given that it would have been virtually impossible for Aaron to live as an active Protestant in New France. Protestantism in any form was specifically prohibited in France's New World possessions. While some Protestants were permitted to reside in the colony *"comme des catho - liques sans scandale,"* the formation of Protestant worship groups was strictly outlawed.[35] Since prayer and the reading of pious texts were common among illiterate and literate Catholics alike, these signature Protestant devotional practices were largely private endeavors and unlikely to arouse the suspicion of religious authorities. In short, it was technically possible to remain true to one's Protestant religious identity while living in New France. Still, the flimsy argument that Aaron was perhaps not a Catholic after all attests to the continued abhorrence with which New England Protestants viewed Catholics. The more potent argument, that papists throughout territory claimed by a Protestant Britain enjoyed the protection of property in local courts, was by necessity downplayed in the religiously fractious environment.

For Noah Emery, the more important case to prove was whether Aaron had actually converted to Catholicism. To bolster his arguments about the lack of compelling proof that Aaron was a Catholic, the lawyer called Christine Baker, Grizel Otis Robitaille's redeemed and reconverted daughter, to testify about Protestant captives and religious life in New France. Though Christine had little affection for the Catholic Church, she admitted "that she was not present not ever saw Peter Littlefield baptized in Canada nor any Priest ever tell her that he was baptized but she only concluded he was from ye Custom of ye Papists & that he always went by the name of Peter after she was acquainted with him."[36]

To settle Aaron Littlefield's case, the court at Suffolk took a more liberal view of the ability of Catholics to function within New England. Aaron won his case — but he then disappears from the historical record again until John Norton's meeting in 1751.

The details of Aaron Littlefield's struggle to disengage property ownership from early religious litmus tests open a window onto another element of Maine's complex religious culture, which was becoming more denominationally rigid and stable. The 1730s and 1740s bore witness to the full fruition of the results of captivity in a religiously foreign land, the willingness or pragmatism behind adopting the religion of the captors, and the end products of persisting in contact and the hope it engendered. While English law did not bar Catholics from enjoying private property, Maine Protestants worked to protect local needs by placing appropriate limits on colonists who failed to conform to religious norms. In some cases, those who were bound by these limitations were actually blood relations.

Aaron's case reveals one way in which Maine colonists applied their own understandings of sacred landscape to their own corner of New England. Keeping Maine Protestant, particularly after the wars of empire had proved so devastating and disruptive, was a way to ensure cohesion among coreligionists.

The Clash of Wills: Religion, Family, and Inheritance

Aaron's quest to claim his inheritance had the odd and undesirable consequence, at least on the local level, of affirming the rights of a papist to hold or benefit from the sale of a piece of the Province of Maine. The case also demonstrated how everyday material realities became tools of religious and family control. For Maine frontier families who were now mixed in terms of faith, crafting wills and arranging terms for the transfer of real property from one generation to the next became a religiously symbolic act. Many acculturated captives were provided for by their parents or siblings, who confirmed this remembrance by leaving their apostate kin money and goods in their wills. These bequests, however, came with religiously tinged demands that meant forfeit of the bequest if they were not met. For mixed-faith families, bequests could be tools to win captives back into the God-ordained family covenant, and by extension, back to Protestantism.[37] Thus the stuff of inheritance was transformed into sacred material, requiring the heir to come to terms with family obligations that included proper religious behavior.

In the cases of Mary Storer St. Germaine, Priscilla Storer Dagueil, and Rachel Storer Berger, the wills of their fathers show how the status of women within colonial families was shaped by religious behavior. Joseph and Jeremiah Storer both used the instrument of the will to try to enforce the dual priorities of return to New England and recommitment to Protestantism by rewarding returned daughters and disinheriting disobedient ones. In this, the Storer fathers were not alone: Maine families often attempted to affect this process by requiring the errant heir to resettle permanently in New England as a condition of claiming the bequest. In setting this requirement, they aimed to lure captives away from their new religions, and new families, which the captives themselves had constructed in accordance with Catholic forms of fictive kinship like the sacrament of marriage.

Since communication across colonial borders became increasingly easy in times of peace, some Maine captives were aware that they were poised to inherit from their Protestant natal families. It was logical to assume that the promised bequests would be distributed after the family wills were probated. What Aaron Littlefield, Mary Storer, and various other acculturated captives seem to have failed to anticipate was that their Catholicism would—and could—be used in an attempt to force them to reconfigure their adult lives radically. Property, which for New Englanders was a critical tool for the implementation of godly prerogatives of family care and stability, adopted a distinctly religious context.

Though the desired ends were the same, the strategies used to bring well-established, adult Catholics back to New England varied and had mixed results. Martha Lord Littlefield's possible strategy of encouraging her son to return after her death by refusing to structure her own inheritance wishes is one of the most sophisticated. The *lack* of a will would have forced an heir, particularly a male one, to re-think his choices. But it would also have spared the parent from having to pen written condemnations that would humble and humiliate the children. Such a strategy would actually free a Catholic convert's parents from a moral imperative to condemn the acts of their children and would promote memories of a loving bond over the irreparable break of affection that death would inevitably bring.

In some cases, these carefully worded bequests encouraged captives to return to Protestant New England and break their attachment to the Catholic captor culture altogether. As it was in New France for Protestants, it was virtually impossible for a person to live in a European settlement of New England and practice Catholicism. Catholi-cism relied heavily on the accessibility of the sacraments, which in turn required access to a sacramental "technician" in the form of an ordained priest. With priests excluded from New England by law on pain of imprisonment or death, *practicing* Catholicism there in the early eighteenth century was all but impossible. A captive's permanent return to New England was therefore a repudiation of the Catholic baptism he or she had received while among the Catholic Waba-nakis or the French and an implicit re-embrace of a Protestant past.

Some captives were audacious enough to respond to these restrictions with demands of their own. Mary Storer went around her brother Ebenezer, the executor of their father's will, to appeal to her mother to find the means to give her the bequest of fifty pounds to which she clearly thought she was entitled. Aaron Littlefield and William Hutchins also used the New England courts to assert their rights to property and, at the same time, reinforce their status within their birth families, even in the face of family repudiation.

There were some, however, who simply left the matter alone. Others seemingly neither knew nor cared that provisions had been made for them in the wills of family members because their lives had taken them in directions that made their patrimony inconsequential. Esther Wheelwright, or Soeur Marie-Joseph de l'Enfant Jesus, was likely unaware that she was slated to receive equal treatment under the terms of her father's estate. Upon entering the Ursuline order, she ostensibly rejected worldly possessions by virtue of religious vows that placed all her personal property in community hands. Goods that came to sisters came into the community as a whole and were shared by the sisters according to their status within the order.[38] If Esther had decided to pursue her patrimony, inherited Wheelwright goods and money would have served the highly unusual role of funding a Catholic institution. In the early eighteenth century, Maine was the kind of place where the legacy linked to the radical Puritanism of Anne Hutchinson could find its way to the coffers of a Catholic convent.

According to John Demos, bequests with conditions attached were used to discipline children who failed to please and honor their parents and fulfill their appropriate role in their families. Thus inheritance was "made contingent on their maintaining a proper sort of obedience."[39] Obedience, in the case of Maine's mixed-faith families, was recreating a religiously homogeneous family. If this strategy had worked, the logical results would have had interesting implications for Maine families, prodding them toward full acceptance of their sons-in-law and grandchildren, who would come to Maine speaking an alien tongue, worshipping the Christian God in ways that deviated significantly from their own, and still clinging to their own set of cultural expectations. Certainly Maine-born captives reestablished at least parts of their identities. Post-captivity records show Rachel Storer using the first name of her birth, not the one she took in Catholic baptism, coupled with her married name, "Berger." In his struggles with his New England family, Aaron Littlefield persisted in using the name given to him in Catholic baptism, which in part constituted the case against him. Even while visiting New England, the captive persisted in using the anglicized version of his Catholic baptismal name. When Christine Baker testified that she "Very well knew [Aaron] in Canada and that he was baptized Peter, & that he was a Papist by Profession and Living & his Marriage Was in a Place Called Boshervell in Canada nine miles from mount Royal and that I See his Sister in the Nunnery in Canaday," she saw Aaron's persistent use of "Peter" as an indication of his commitment to Catholicism.[40] Martha Littlefield rejected her son's new name altogether by reverting to "Aaron." It is tempting to speculate that she did so not only to reassert a mother's prerogative to name her children, but also to reintroduce his Protestant identity through use of his Old Testament name.

To some Maine families, however, the religious affinities and Catholic kinship ties that captivity often brought about were not suffi-cient grounds for reinterpreting New England inheritance patterns. The case of Jabez Simpson, Aaron Littlefield's cousin, illustrates this point. Along with his mother and brother Henry, Jabez was taken from Maine in the Candlemas raid of 1691/2. Mother and brother returned to New England; Jabez did not. Almost two decades later, he still remained in Canada.[41] His surviving siblings argued among themselves as to how the estate of their father, who died in 1702, was to be apportioned, a quarrel that spilled into the York Court of Common Pleas.[42] Though the court devised portions for the Simpson siblings, all parties involved agreed that "upon the Return of Jabez Sympson from Captivity: he shall have the Equall proportion of the Estate with his brethren: he allowing his part & portion of charges with the rest."[43] While other family members doubtless benefited from Jabez's share of land by continuing to improve it in his absence, it did remain, in a legal sense, his for the claiming. Such claiming was known to happen, as in the case of York captive Charles Trafton. Taken as an adult, Trafton accepted Catholic baptism and seemed to embrace his new faith with enthusiasm, serving as godfather to both Bonaventure LaForge, a Huguenot captive from York, and the daughter of an anonymous Maine captive, and also witnessing to the deathbed conversions of both Esther Ingersoll, a Northampton, Massachusetts, captive, and Abigail Cass Turbet.[44] Such evidence suggests Trafton was an active churchman while in captivity. But upon the death of his father in 1716, Trafton had a change of heart, soul, purse, or all three, and abruptly left Canada and the life he had known there. Shedding his French baptismal identity of Louis-Marie, Charles joined his brother Zaccheas, whom he had likely not seen for decades, in several ventures in land speculation.[45] Dying without children, Trafton left the bulk of his sizable estate to his wife and his brothers. Tellingly, his will was witnessed by Kittery's Congregational minister, John Newmarch.[46]

Some parents wanted to remember their children regardless of religious complications. One was Deborah Webber of York, who left her captive daughter Barsheba, taken in an unspecified raid, a share of her tiny estate equal to that of her siblings, with none of the common strings of repatriation or readaptation to Protestantism attached.[47] Barsheba's father, however, might have lodged his own disapproval by leaving her out of his will.[48] Though Dominicus Jordan set no formal conditions on inheritance for his captive sister, Mary Ann, her patrimony in land would be, as Aaron Littlefield also learned, difficult to claim without resettlement and cultural and religious reconversion.[49] Nevertheless, Mary Ann did manage to sell her portion of her father's estate in 1761, years after Dominicus's death. Mary Ann most likely never married, but she led her life as a laywoman with the Ursuline sisters at Trois-Rivières and provided them with financial support that more than likely came from her Jordan family patrimony. This inheritance, which had roots stretching back to the troublesome grandfather, Robert, whose repeated nips at the heels of Puritan authorities frequently landed him in trouble, was in the end used to subsidize the income of a Catholic women's religious order.[50]

When Charles Trafton and another late-returning ex-captive, William Hutchins, came home to claim property, they stayed. Some settlers in the province thought all returning captives needed to make the same commitment. For example, Aaron Littlefield's brief forays into Maine became part of the case against him. To his Lord cousins and other observers, winning the case against Aaron would result in material gain for them, as family lands skipped over the religiously unqualified and passed into the hands of those whose religious identifications were clear. In some cases, these beneficiaries were not even blood relations. In the case of Captain Roger Dearing, his church and nonrelated, though "religious," people were substituted for blood kin once Protestant family members were lost to captivity. In an attack near Scarborough in 1723, Dearing lost his wife and other relatives to the French and Indians. In the wake of these tragedies, the grieving Dearing moved throughout New England, seemingly bereft of his moorings. Resettlement in Scarborough decades later, however, brought a new commitment to community, and Dearing became a local leader in both civic and militia affairs.[51] He also remarried, though he remained childless. The captive members of his family, though, seem never to have returned. Records are silent on their whereabouts, and Dearing did not include them, or any conditions under which they could inherit, in his will. After providing for his second wife, Dearing gave the bulk of his estate to two additional beneficiaries: his local Congregational church, and "the religious industrious poor of ye Town of Scarborough."[52] Thus, this settler who had suffered so much during Dummer's War used the worldly instrument of his will to reinforce Protestant institutions and people in his frontier town, forming a religiously based fictive kinship.

One of the richest examples of the intermingling of religious culture and inheritance brings this story back to the Wheelwright family, whose daughter Esther eventually became superior of the Ursuline convent in Quebec. Colonel John Wheelwright did not leave Esther, whom he knew to be alive, the same share as his other daughters. Instead, he stipulated that his four sons would be responsible for providing for her should she return, stating, "If it Should please God that [Esther] return to this country and Settle here then my Will is that my Four Sons vizt Iohn Samuel Ieremiah and Nathaniel each of them pay her Twenty five pounds it being in the whole One Hundred pounds within Six Months after her return and settlement."[53] When Esther, unwilling or unaware, did not return to collect her inheritance, her mother, who outlived Esther's father by a number of years, submitted her own will-based plea:

> Provided my beloved Daughter Esther Wheelwright who has been many Years in Canada is yet living, and Should by the wonder working of Providence of God be returned to her native Land and tarry and dwell in it, I give and bequeath unto her one fifth part of my Estate which I have already by this instrument will'd Should be divided to & among my aforesd Daughters & Grand Daughters to be paid to them in Proportion to their respective Share in the abovementioned Division unto her my Said Daughter Esther Wheelwright within one year after my Decease.[54]

Having reestablished contact with her mother before Mary Snell Wheelwright's death, Esther might have known about this stipulation, which would have left her well provided for as a single woman in New England. Yet this member of a religious family could not be swayed by the promise of these gifts, or, for that matter, by the assurance of loving and supportive reintegration into her Protestant family. As she explained to her mother, the joy of reunion would have to wait until the next life, where, Esther hoped, "the Lord to whom I have devoted myself will greatly reward me from his infinite goodness, since he himself assures us in his holy word that he who leaves for his sake, Father, Mother, Brothers, and Sisters, shall have an hundred fold in this life, and Life eternal in the next."[55] Aware of the disappointment her preference for Catholic religious life caused for both her parents, Esther sought to soften the realities of her life choices by assuring her mother that the Wheelwright family was at once Protestant and Catholic, heirs to the historical legacy of their connection with England. She enthused, "Oh, what joy, what pleasure, what consolation would it give me, my dear Mother if you had the happiness of knowing this holy religion which a kind providence hath made me embrace since I left you. [It is] an established religion which our Forefathers professed for a long time with much need and fervour."[56] By appealing to the "forefathers," Esther evoked the commonalities

Figure 12.
Esther Wheelwright,
by an unidentified artist
(ca. 1763). Courtesy
of the Massachusetts
Historical Society.

of New World Protestantism and Catholicism. In so doing, she likewise suggested that her mother *might* know the same religion, and perhaps be swayed to her daughter's way of thinking.

For the rest of her days, Esther Wheelwright remained a committed Catholic. Likewise, Mary Snell Wheelwright remained a committed Protestant. Yet mother and daughter continued to exchange loving and sensitive tokens until Mary's death parted them. Esther also received a set of silver vessels, items that would have represented significant expense for any eighteenth-century family. Incised with the Wheelwright family crest, these costly items were put into service in the convent's liturgies.[57] But this valuable gift of silver carried perhaps the greatest significance for the family that gave it. As Barbara and Gerald Ward note, gifts and bequests of silver passed through New England families and "acted as a vehicle for communicating family prestige and honor and transmitting these qualities to the next generation."[58] Already several generations removed from the practices of the Catholic Church, the Calvinist Wheelwrights were unlikely to know, or have much concern for, the important role such vessels played in Catholic liturgical practices. Gifts of silver objects like these passed from New England parents to their daughters were demonstrations of a prestigious lineage and were commonly given to women who were about to leave the family name behind as they married. Resisting return to New England for decades, Esther had ably demonstrated her spiritual marriage to the Church of Rome. The vessels took their place in her new home, to be used with her new family, created from the fictive kinships engendered by convent walls. Intentionally or otherwise, the silver fulfilled its intended role both in the context of Protestant inheritance patterns, while also serving as a tool to help Esther in her future life, which in this case was a long and happy marriage to the Church of Rome.

In general, New England parents did not seek to exert posthumous control over the spiritual lives of their children. But this changed for religiously acculturated children of frontier families who remained in French Canada. The parents of Maine's captives set conditions on worldly goods in the form of bequests to these children because they clearly persisted in the hope that the promise of worldly gifts would eventually change the course of their children's spiritual lives. Wills therefore became tools that used items of real, calculable value—money and household goods—to demonstrate to children what they had to gain through spiritual obedience. Inheritances therefore crossed the boundary that separated the worldly from the spiritual, becoming *religious* objects in and of themselves, and contingent on religion, properly professed. Thus the timing of these gifts became insignificant: a captive's redemption, even if it happened long after a parent's death, was better than no return at all. In death, parents continued to press the hope that had failed them when they lived and used any means at their disposal. In this way, the most worldly items appropriated sacred meanings and became possible tools of spiritual redemption.

But most captives found that becoming active, baptized Catholics who backed up their convictions with sacramental marriages and parented baptized children brought with it worldly successes, through *concessions* of land from religious orders or well-arranged marriages to well-placed colonial Frenchmen. Thus the religious demands of parents that bounded the bequests from still often-humble Maine parents were drained of their significance. Many captives continued to enjoy the ample evidence that conversion to Catholicism brought physical comfort and spiritual acceptance—two things the wills with Protestant caveats also promised, albeit with more questions than assurances.

In the years following the wars of empire, Maine's Protestants were more concerned than ever to develop their own concept of a sacred landscape. Echoing the concerns about the need for spiritual unity expressed by Sylvanus Davis in 1690, the Maine-based phase of Aaron Littlefield's inheritance case was predicated on the assumption that Maine needed to be made safe for the growth of Protestant communities, that the land should be worked and the waters fished by Protestant hands, and that Maine's Native peoples should be brought to a Protestant form of Christianity.

More than four decades separated the initial captivities of Sylvanus Davis and Aaron Littlefield. This period was a time in Maine history when geography, war, and religious encounter challenged and complicated any hope of extending the New England Way throughout the province. By the end of Dummer's War, the by-products of Catholic encounter in Maine had produced a mixed religious culture with deep roots. Though the words of New World Christianity often emphasized ideological separation, a Christian religious culture was developed, challenged, and shaped by the Protestants and Catholics whose paths converged in places like the early Maine frontier.

Afterword

When Benedict Fenwick, the Catholic bishop of Baltimore, proposed to construct a memorial to the slain Jesuit Sebastian Rale, he found an unlikely supporter for the project in the person of William Allen, Jr., the president of Bowdoin College and a devout Congregationalist. The intermediary between the two men was Edward Kavanaugh, the proprietor of the mills at Damariscotta, the place where Sylvanus Davis had first purchased Maine property. A native of Ireland, Kavanaugh was the most prominent Catholic layperson in Maine in 1832. But though a strong supporter of Fenwick's proposed monument, Kavanaugh wisely recognized that such a project would never be built without the assistance and support of the most influential families in Maine, who, like Allen's, had lived in the province for generations.

Seeking to cultivate Allen, Kavanaugh asserted that Bishop Fenwick was a true American who had "the advantage not hitherto enjoyed by most of the Catholic clergy in the northern states of being an American by birth and he yields to no one in the ardor of national feelings; until his promotion to the episcopal dignity he belonged to the order of Jesuits of which his profound erudition made him a conspicuous member."[1] Fenwick's manners, erudition (he had been a

member of the newly reconstituted Society of Jesus before his elevation to bishop), and patriotism appealed to Allen.

Before long, the two men were corresponding enthusiastically
about the proposed memorial. Allen even offered to act as the proxy
for the Diocese of Boston to the purchase of the property on which the
monument was to be erected. Allen's support for the project amazed
Fenwick, who probably assumed that a Maine Calvinist of old family
would have heard the story of the Norridgewock mission from the
New England perspective alone. The bishop marveled

> I cannot but admire, my dear Sir, the generous interest you have
> taken in this affair—and your endeavors to do justice to the
> memory of the long injured Rasle [*sic*] in spite of the infamous
> aspersions of a host of prejudiced historians upon his character.
> It is indeed the more remarkable considering the few opportuni-
> ties you have had at ascertaining the true history of that great
> man from authentic documents, which with the blessing of God,
> I shall present to the public next summer, if you are so happy as
> to succeed in the purchase of that lot.[2]

Fenwick's design for the monument called for a granite obelisk,
eight feet square at the base and thirty-two feet high, topped with a
large cross. Each of the monument's four sides would contain the
same epitaph in a different language—Wabanaki, French, English,
and Rale's beloved Latin—inscribed on four white marble slabs.[3]
Though an obelisk was a common form for a monument, the inspi-
ration for Fenwick's particular design was a monument at Harvard,
the college that had brought forth so many of the Protestant ministers who attempted to counter Jesuit successes among the Wabanakis and other indigenous Americans. The Harvard obelisk honored its founder, John Harvard, and in borrowing its design and
grandeur for Rale, Fenwick implied that the Jesuit deserved a similar
place in history not as a warrior but as a scholar, an intellectual, a pro-
ponent of early American spiritual education, and a founder of the
state of Maine. For Fenwick, the key difference between Sebastien
Rale and John Harvard—their professed forms of Christianity—

was irrelevant. When the Rale monument was unveiled in 1833, it attracted such a large crowd that part of the opening ceremony had to be omitted. The event attracted both the faithful and the curious. In all, six thousand people attended, including a group of Penobscot Indians, whom the *American Advocate* described as "standing on the ground which had been consecrated by the blood of their countrymen."[4]

Benedict Fenwick's design for the monument might not have been original, but his singling out of Sebastien Rale for a public memorial certainly was. For decades following his death, the Jesuit remained a reviled figure in Maine. The Jesuit missions, and the French in Canada and Acadia were remembered with anger and fear. The anti-Catholicism they inflamed helped inspire Maine colonists to take a leading role in the attacks on the fortress at Louisbourg, the expulsion of the Acadians from Nova Scotia, and the American attack on Canada during the American Revolution—all events with implicit anti-Catholic components.

Events in Europe during the century that separated Rale's death and Fenwick and Allen's efforts to memorialize him fostered the growth of antipopery and a unified Protestant identity.[5] Protestant and Catholic Europeans continued to wage war against each other throughout the eighteenth century, and these conflicts continued to spill over into the British colonial arena. In North America, the Quebec Act, one of the major catalysts of the American Revolution, was seen as an insult to American Protestantism and created fears of a papist resurgence on the northern borders.

Also changing were attitudes among the settlers themselves on New England's once-derided "pagan skirts" who had once desired a critical mass of Protestants for frontiers well defended. In the years following Dummer's War, the growing population in Maine's English settlements and their steady northward march solidified the region's Protestant identity. The days when ministers could aggressively condemn popery, yet still encounter and borrow proselytization techniques from one of its practitioners, came to an end. New Protestant groups came to the region, and the Puritans (now Congregationalists) were increasingly disliked and distrusted by the newcomers. One angry newcomer, a Presbyterian named William McClenachan, denounced as "papists" the Puritan land speculators who fought to keep fellow Protestants from settling on land they claimed to own.[6] For their part, older Protestant settlers continued to be wary of newcomers, even coreligionists, suggesting a diminished sense of urgency about the importance of religious identity in the once-volatile region. Evidence of this transition began to appear as early as 1730, when the government of Massachusetts was petitioned to assist in the removal of some Irish Protestants who had moved into the area near what had been Pemaquid by Colonel Jeremiah Dunbar, a British officer. Though they were coreligionists, they were still squatting and were thus unwelcome.[7] Based on the events of the previous century, Massachusetts had good reasons to want to control who settled where. But there were other issues at stake, including property rights, revenue collection, and access to Maine's rich resources.

By 1773 the line of entrenched English settlement had moved as far north as what had been Norridgewock (now Madison, Maine).[8] In that same year, the Society of Jesus, to which Gabriel Druillettes, Jacques and Vincent Bigot, and Sebastien Rale had all belonged, was suppressed by papal order and its communities of its priests dispersed.

✦ ✦ ✦

As the title of this book indicates, Catholicism was the "spice" that lingered on Maine's palate. Other North American English colonies had Catholic colonists. But none, with the possible exceptions of Maryland and Pennsylvania, had a fully realized Catholic colonial subculture within their perceived boundaries. In Maryland's case, its Catholic past was fundamental to its seventeenth-century identity, being neither underground nor countercultural, but an intrinsic part of what the colony fundamentally was founded to be. Pennsylvania's religious origins likewise deviate from the British colonies overall. Maine was different. An outpost of New England, the province should have shared in the region's Protestant identity. But Maine's proximity to French New World possessions, and the seeping influence of those possessions on the region's indigenous people, its landscape, and its

New England–oriented settlers, led to a period in its history when its religious fate was anyone's guess.

Maine's English settlers were resilient and inventive. In some instances, these colonists countered their religious adversaries by deploying their own tools against them. In other cases, they sought safety in numbers through increased regional cohesion. But they were also frequently on the losing end in conflicts with the French. Many children, spouses, and extended family members, by going to Canada, converting to Catholicism, and creating their own Catholic families, were bound to the French colony by sacrament, law. and affection. This left an indelible print of popery on some of the region's most prestigious families. In this sense, the borderland experience brought remote frontier dwellers into the same state as many Protestants in Europe, where mixed-faith families were not anomalies. The desire behind immigration to the New World came from the effort to diminish the possibilities of such fissures among Calvinist families. As James Axtell notes, "New England was a different land, and Puritans were a different breed. There a sterner environment and an aggressive religious zeal would unite to eradicate the idleness of the Old World while reducing the godforsaken wilderness to a garden divinely favored with moderate but wholesome abundance."[9] At various points in time, the inhabitants of the more thickly settled parts of New England seem to have achieved this goal. But the Protestants of Maine between1688 and 1727 did not. Geography, the probability of encounter, warfare, and the pool of settlers themselves were all factors that undermined this goal. But by the time the Province of Maine was sufficiently secure to attempt to realize this vision, its urgency was quickly passing.[10]

Subsequent generations of Mainers romanticized its fractious religious past. John Greenleaf Whittier's poem "Mogg Megone" cele - brates one of the Wabanaki sachems who attacked English settlements in Maine during King Philip's War. Another Whittier poem, "Norumbega," gives Maine an explicitly Catholic past where the heroes of exploration are French (Samuel de Champlain), not English. In Whittier's poem Champlain comes across an ancient cross planted long ago by unknown hands, similar to those the French would literally "plant" to consecrate the land to France and mark the parameters of their territorial claims, during his own explorations of Norumbega.[11]

Whittier had good literary company when it came to sentimentalizing New England's complicated Christian heritage. Maine native Henry Wadsworth Longfellow's epic poem "Evangeline" immortalizes the involuntary odyssey of New World French Catholics who became victims of imperial politics and religious bigotry at the hands of intolerant Protestant Englishmen. Produced less than one hundred years after the actual expulsion of the Acadians in 1755, Longfellow's work helped craft an image of these French New World peasants as peaceful and devout farmers and tragic victims of larger political circumstances rather than borderland dwellers who hedged a bad bet.

Entranced by the same spirit and under the influence of William Allen, who had been a popular instructor at his Maine alma mater, Bowdoin College, Nathaniel Hawthorne memorialized the controversial Sebastien Rale in his "Bell" sketches.[12] The trials and triumphs of Maine families' fortunes won and lost during the wars of empire surface in *The House of Seven Gables*. Maine ministers of the colonial period receive less than favorable treatment in "The Minister's Black Veil," a story of the tragically demented minister grandson of York's "Father" Samuel Moody.[13] Years later, even marginally educated readers of Hawthorne's *The Scarlet Letter* were unlikely to miss what one scholar has termed "certain obviously Catholic features" of the novel's main characters.[14]

Perhaps the most flamboyant recasting of Maine's past by a native Protestant New Englander is Nathaniel Deering's play *Carabassett*. The real Carabassett was a Wabanaki sachem with a flair for the ceremonial. He was known for sporting "a blue lace coat and a silver Medal" (or *justaucorps*, a French gentleman's coat), given to him by a governor of New France. Nathaniel Deering, however, transformed this borderland popinjay into a noble savage of Byronic proportions.[15] Since he was of the same family as Roger Dearing, the Scarborough settler who lost his family in Dummer's War, Deering had chosen a poignant focus for his drama.[16] But he harbored far more sympathy for the subjects of his play (the Wabanakis and their French priests)

Figure 13. Evangeline, by James Faed (1854). Henry Wadsworth Longfellow gave this engraving of his tragic Acadian heroine to his sister, Anne Longfellow Pierce. It hung in the parlor of the author's home. Courtesy of the Maine Historical Society.

than he did for his suffering ancestors. In the preface to *Carabassett,* Deering explains this sympathy as the by-product of French sources combined with his own historical imagination, writing, "In the portrait of Rallé [*sic*], I have followed the French writers, rather than the English; it being the object of the latter to place him in an unfavorable light, to palliate [Rale's killing] which must ever be a blot on our history."[17] For the character of Carabassett, Deering constructed a narrative of loss and victimization. At one point in the dialogue, the Indian tells the Jesuit that "I too have lov'd, and those I lov'd were murdered."[18] The murderers were New England militiamen, defenders of the region's Protestant identity.

The air of Catholic sentimentalism that crept into American arts and literature in the early decades of the nineteenth century did not last. In 1836 a Protestant mob burned to the ground the Catholic girls school and convent at Charlestown, outside of Boston. Firefight - ers who were called to the scene refused to interfere with the work of the arsonists. The Ursuline nuns who had staffed the school were originally from the same Quebec community that Esther Wheelwright had joined over a century before.[19] As dislike of Catholics grew, it fueled nativism, a nationwide political movement. Mainers still harbored their own smoldering hostilities toward their complex and often tragic religious past, and the creation of a monument to Sebastien Rale only fanned the flames. On September 27, 1836, William Allen wrote to Fenwick that the newly erected monument to Rale had been destroyed under mysterious circumstances. Local newspapers considered the destruction a copycat incident and a sad sign of the times. The editors of the *Bangor Commercial* expressed both sympathy for the Jesuit's story ("No one could visit [Old Point, the site of the monument] and read the classic inscriptions that spoke of Father Ralle's virtues and his sufferings and the destruction of the whole tribe, without his feelings touched by the tale of sorrow") and disgust over the implicit act of religious intolerance ("This disgraceful outrage reminds one of those acts of the early Christians who destroyed with such holy zeal the temples of the gods filled with the most exquisite works of Painters and Sculpters—and the intolerant ignorance of the Cove - nentors in destroying the Churches of the Episcopalians").[20] That

Figure 14. The "Old Point Monument" in Madison, Maine. A view of the restored monument to Sebastien Rale as it looked at the beginning of the twentieth century.

news of the desecration was reported and condemned in newspapers as far south as Pennsylvania suggests that knowledge of Rale and his work had become relatively widespread by the early nineteenth century. Like its counterparts in Portland, the *Philadelphia Public Ledger* reported, "*Father Ralle's Grave*—The monument erected over the remains of this benevolent and excellent missionary on the bank of the Kennebeck, has been destroyed by some miscreants. Miscreants indeed they were; but the world is full of such. Religious fanaticism, of whatever creed, always makes the malignant ten times worse."[21] Ten years later, the malignant were still at work, this time in Philadelphia, where scores of Catholic and Protestant working men rioted in the streets of the suburb of Southwark.

The monument's attackers were never caught. And though its creators shared the conviction that the act would be condemned "by every respectable paper in the United States," Allen, Fenwick, and Kavanaugh, who would later see the monument restored, perhaps neglected to account for Maine's heritage of suffering during the wars of empire. This was, at very least, equal to the more constructive elements of its cross-cultural encounters.[22] The power of Maine's past lay in its range of experience and, for ill or good, carried with it long-term consequences that evolving in religious culture, and the passage of time itself, could do little to change.

Abbreviations

ANB	Garrity, John A., and Mark C. Carnes, general eds. *American National Biography*. 24 vols. New York: Oxford University Press, 1999.
CDRNF	*Collection de manscrits contenant lettres, mémoires, et autres documents historiques relatifs à la Nouvelle France*. 4 vols. Quebec: Côté et Cie, 1884.
Coll MeHS	*Collections of the Maine Historical Society*. Series 1, 2, and 3. Portland: Maine Historical Society, 1831–1916.
DCB	*Dictionary of Canadian Biography*. 13 vols. Toronto: University of Toronto Press, 1966–.
DHSM	Baxter, James Phinney, ed. *Documentary History of the State of Maine*. In *Collections of the Maine Historical Society*, 2nd ser., 24 vols. Portland: Maine Historical Society, 1869–1916.
GDMNH	Noyes, Sybil, Charles Thornton Libby, and Walter Goodwin Davis. *Genealogical Dictionary of Maine and New Hampshire*. Portland, ME, 1928–35. Reprint, Baltimore: Genealogical Publishing Co., 1972.
JR	Thwaites, Reuben Gold, ed. *The Jesuit Relations and Allied Documents*. 73 vols. Cleveland: Burrows Brothers, 1896–1901.

MeHS   Maine Historical Society, Portland.

MHS   Massachusetts Historical Society, Boston.

MPCR   Libby, Charles Thorton, Robert E. Moody, and Neal W. Allen, Jr., eds. *Province and Court Records of Maine.* 6 vols. Portland: Maine Historical Society, 1928–75.

MSA   Massachusetts State Archives, Boston.

MW   Sargent, William A., ed. *Maine Wills, 1640–1760.* Portland: Brown Thurston, 1887.

NAC   National Archives of Canada, Ottawa.

NEC   Coleman, Emma Lewis. *New England Captives Carried to Canada between 1677 and 1760 during the French and Indian Wars.* 2 vols. Portland, ME: Southworth Press, 1925. Reprint, Bowie, MD: Heritage Classics, 1989.

NEHGR   *New England Historical and Genealogical Register.* New England Historic, Genealogical Society. 101 vols. Boston: NEHGS, 1880–1947.

YD   Sargent, William, ed. *York Deeds.* 18 vols. Portland, ME: John T. Hull, 1887.

Notes

Introduction

1. Sybil Noyes, Charles Thornton Libby, and Walter Goodwin Davis, *Genealogical Dictionary of Maine and New Hampshire* (hereafter *GDMNH*) (Portland, ME, 1928–35; repr., Baltimore: Genealogical Publishing Co., 1972), 743.

2. Nathaniel Wheelwright Diary (hereafter Wheelwright), 26 Jan. 1754. Collections, Massachusetts Historical Society, Boston (hereafter MHS). On New England suspicions of Catholic convents and the women who lived within their walls, see Ann M. Little, "Cloistered Bodies: Convents in the Anglo-American Imagination in the British Conquest of Canada," *Eighteenth-Century Studies* 39:2 (2006): 187, 191, 197.

3. Esther was elected superior in 1760, which coincided with the British conquest of Quebec. Historians interpret this as the Ursulines' attempt to cultivate positive relations with their new conquerors. In her article "The Life of Mother Marie-Joseph de l'Enfant Jesus," Ann M. Little examines this and other gendered and political implications of the key events in Soeur (later Mère) Esther's life. Ann M. Little, "The Life of Mother Marie-Joseph de l'Enfant Jesus, or, How a Little English Girl from Wells Became a Big French Politician," *Maine History* 40:4 (Winter 2001–02): 279–308. Details of her life also come from James Axtell, *The Invasion Within: The*

281

Contest of Cultures in Colonial North America (New York: Oxford University Press, 1985), 297–300, and Gerald Kelly, "Esther Wheelwright," *Dictionary of Canadian Biography* (hereafter *DCB*) (Toronto: University of Toronto Press, 1966), 4:764–66.

4. Cotton Mather, *The Present State of New England Considered in a Discourse on the Necessities and Advantages of a Public Spirit in Every Man* (Boston: Samuel Green, 1690), 52. Maine's character as a cultural crossroads is examined by Alan Taylor in his article "Centers and Peripheries: Locating Maine's History," *Maine History* 39:1 (2000): passim.

5. W. H. Whitmore, ed., *The Andros Tracts*, 3 vols. (Boston: The Prince Society, 1868–74), 2:22.

6. Richard P. Gildrie, *The Profane, the Civil, and the Godly: The Reformation of Manners in Orthodox New England, 1679–1749* (University Park: Pennsylvania State University Press, 1994), 196.

7. A list of the works that most influenced my own scholarly trajectory includes Axtell, *The Invasion Within* and *The European and the Indian: Essays in the Ethnohistory of Colonial North America* (New York: Oxford University Press, 1981); Colin Calloway, *New Worlds for All: Indians, Europeans, and the Remaking of Early America* (Baltimore: Johns Hopkins University Press, 1998), and *After King Philip's War: Presence and Persistence in Indian New England* (Hanover, NH: University Press of New England, 1997); John Demos, *The Unredeemed Captive: A Family Story from Early America* (New York: Knopf, 1994); Nicholas Griffiths and Fernando Cervantes, eds., *Spiritual Encounters: Interactions between Christianity and Native Religions in Colonial America* (Lincoln: University of Nebraska, 1999); Eric Hinderaker and Peter C. Mancall, *At the Edge of Empire: The Backcountry in British North America* (Baltimore: Johns Hopkins University Press, 2003); Jill Lepore, *The Name of War: King Philip's War and the Origins of American Identity* (New York: Vintage, 1999); Kenneth M. Morrison, *The Embattled Northeast: The Elusive Ideal of Alliance in Abenaki-Euroamerican Relations* (Berkeley: University of California Press, 1984); Daniel K. Richter, *The Ordeal of the Longhouse: The Peoples of the Iroquois League in the Era of European Colonization* (Chapel Hill: University of North Carolina Press, 1992); Neal Salisbury, *Manitou and Providence: Indians, Europeans, and the Making of New England, 1500–1643* (New York: Oxford University Press, 1982); Taylor, "Centers and Peripheries"; Daniel Usner, *Indians, Settlers and Slaves in a Frontier Exchange Economy: The Lower Mississippi Valley before 1783* (Chapel Hill: University of North Carolina Press, 1992); and Richard White, *The Middle Ground: Indians, Empires, and the Republics in the Great*

Lakes Region, 1650–1815 (Cambridge: Cambridge University Press, 1991). Though this list contains many titles that set new standards for the study of early American frontier interactions, the list is far from comprehensive of the genre as a whole.

8. Jon Butler, *Awash in a Sea of Faith: Christianizing the American People* (Cambridge: Harvard University Press, 1990), 2.

9. Thomas S. Kidd identifies and describes "the Protestant Interest" as a unifying ideology that replaced Puritanism in New England after 1689. *The Protestant Interest: New England after Puritanism* (New Haven: Yale University Press, 2004). In *No King, No Popery: Anti-Catholicism in Revolutionary New England* (Westport, CT: Greenwood Press, 1995), Francis Cogliano explores the roots of New England's anti-Catholicism, as does Charles P. Hanson in *Necessary Virtue: The Pragmatic Origins of Religious Liberty in New England* (Charlottesville: University Press of Virginia, 1998). For an older yet solid treatment of this topic, see Mary Augustine Ray, *American Opinion of Roman Catholicism in the Eighteenth Century* (New York: Columbia University Press, 1936).

10. Ray, *Opinions of Roman Catholicism,* 66.

11. Adhering to the directives of Armand-Jean du Plessis, Cardinal Richelieu and founding member of the Company of One Hundred Associates, only Roman Catholics were permitted to settle in the colony after 1627. Louis XIV's 1685 revocation of the Edict of Nantes, which had hitherto granted limited toleration to French Protestants, reinforced this restriction. On the official status of Protestants in the French North American colonies and some of its consequences, see William Eccles, *The Canadian Frontier: 1534–1760* (Albuquerque: University of New Mexico Press, 1983), 32–33; Cornelius Jaenen, *The Role of the Church in New France* (Toronto: McGraw-Hill Ryerson, 1976), 66–67; Peter Moogk, *La Nouvelle France: The Making of French Canada—A Cultural History* (East Lansing: Michigan State University Press, 2000), 60.

12. Kidd, *Protestant Interest,* 18.

13. Emerson W. Baker adopts a similar approach in *The Devil of Great Island: Witchcraft and Conflict in Early New England* (New York: Palgrave Macmillan, 2007), a work that significantly influenced my own.

14. In *The New England Soul: Preaching and Religious Culture in Early New England* (New York: Oxford University Press, 1986), Harry Stout defines religious culture as primarily written, oral, and aural. My study adopts a broader view to include the artifacts of religious life—buildings, objects, and religious folklore—in an attempt to develop a rough parity of lived

religion among borderland dwellers. In *The Invasion Within*, James Axtell was one of the first scholars to assert that, for a variety of reasons, French religious orders produced more successful missionaries to the Native Americans, in large part because they eventually adopted a policy of cultural adaptability. Evidence of these attitudes remains in the artifactual record, as well as period descriptions of missions. Additional works that add structure to the concept of lived religion and religious culture are David Hall, *Worlds of Wonder, Days of Judgment: Popular Religious Belief in Early New England* (Cambridge: Harvard University Press, 1989); Robert Scribner, "The Reformation, Popular Magic, and the 'Disenchantment of the World,'" *Journal of Interdisciplinary History* 23:3 (Winter 1993): 475–94; Charles Hambrick-Stowe, *The Practice of Piety: Puritan Devotional Disciplines in Seventeenth-Century New England* (Chapel Hill: University of North Carolina Press, 1982); Gildrie, *The Profane, the Civil, and the Godly.* For encounters between Euro-American Protestants and Catholics in both the colonial and revolutionary periods, see Cogliano, *No King, No Popery,* and Hanson, *Necessary Virtue.*

15. Allan Greer discusses the drive to create a pure version of post-Reformation Catholicism in *The People of New France* (Toronto: University of Toronto Press, 1999), 150. In *The Role of the Church in New France,* Cornelius J. Jaenen explores the role that Catholic Reformation religious orders played in early Canada ("The Missionary Church," passim). Richard Gildrie demonstrates how this vision failed in numerous corners of "Puritan" North America. See *The Profane, the Civil, and the Godly,* passim. In "The Revolt[ing] Welch: Milton and the 'Dark Corners of the Land,'" Hugh Jenkins observes that learned Englishmen of the seventeenth century were using the term *dark corner* to describe any place that resisted Puritan orthodoxy or what had become standard Protestant mores. See Kristin Pruitt and Charles Dunham, eds., *Milton's Legacy* (Selinsgrove, PA: Susquehanna University Press, 2005), 103. The term was popularized by Christopher Hill in his landmark essay "Puritans and the 'Dark Corners of the Land,'" in *Change and Continuity in Seventeenth Century England* (New Haven: Yale University Press, 1991), 16, 20.

16. In addition to Butler, *Awash in a Sea of Faith,* see Patricia U. Bonomi, *Under the Cope of Heaven: Religion, Society and Politics in Colonial America* (New York: Oxford University Press, 1986), passim.

17. Taylor, "Centers and Peripheries," 13.

18. More recent studies that focus on Indian/Euro-American relations to develop this perspective in Maine and throughout the Atlantic World in

general include Emerson Baker and John G. Reid, "Amerindian Power in the Early Modern Northeast: A Reappraisal," *William and Mary Quarterly* 61:1 (Jan. 2004): 77–106; Juliana Barr, *Peace Came in the Form of a Woman: Indians and Spaniards in the Texas Borderlands* (Chapel Hill: University of North Carolina Press, 2007); Allan Greer and Jodi Bilinkoff, eds., *Colonial Saints: Discovering the Holy in the Americas, 1500–1800* (New York: Routledge, 2003); William Cronon, George Miles, and Jay Gitlin, eds., *Under an Open Sky: Rethinking America's Western Past* (New York: Norton, 1993); Christine Daniels and Michael V. Kennedy, eds., *Negotiated Empires: Centers and Peripheries in the Americas, 1500–1820* (New York: Routledge, 2002); Kathleen DuVal, *The Native Ground: Indians and Colonists in the Heart of the Continent* (Philadelphia: University of Pennsylvania Press, 2006); Allan Greer: *Mohawk Saint: Catherine Tekakwitha and the Jesuits* (New York: Oxford University Press, 2005); Griffiths and Cervantes, *Spiritual Encounters*; Steven W. Hackel, *Children of Coyote, Missionaries of Saint Francis: Indian-Spanish Relations in California, 1769–1850* (Chapel Hill: University of North Carolina Press, 2005); Evan Haefeli and Kevin Sweeney, *Captors and Captives: The 1704 French and Indian Raid on Deerfield* (Amherst: University of Massachusetts Press, 2003); Hinderaker and Mancall, *At the Edge of Empire*; A. G. Roeber, ed., *Ethnographies and Exchanges: Native Americans, Moravians, and Catholics in Early North America* (College Park: Pennsylvania State University Press, 2008); Ann Marie Plane, *Colonial Intimacies: Indian Marriage in Colonial New England* (Ithaca: Cornell University Press, 2000); Nancy Shoemaker, *A Strange Likeness: Becoming Red and White in Eighteenth-Century North America* (New York: Oxford University Press, 2004); Susan Sleeper-Smith, *Indian Women and French Men: Rethinking Cultural Encounters in the Western Great Lakes Region* (Amherst: University of Massachusetts Press, 2001); Claudio Saunt, "Go West: Mapping Early American Historiography," *William and Mary Quarterly* 65:4 (2008): 745–78; Taylor, "Centers and Peripheries"; Usner, *Indians, Settlers and Slaves*. I am grateful to Ann M. Little for calling my attention to some of these titles.

19. Eliga Gould, "Entangled Histories, Entangled Worlds: The English-Speaking Atlantic as a Spanish Periphery," *American Historical Review* 112:3 (2007): 765.

20. Saunt, "Go West," 746.

21. Taylor, "Centers and Peripheries," 12, 14.

22. The Irish Edmunds family settled in Pemaquid and was taken to Canada in 1695. While John and Marie Kelly Edmunds were most likely already baptized Catholics, their children, who were very young at the time

of captivity and probably born in Pemaquid, most likely were not. Antonio Fortado/Hurtado, a fisherman and native of Portugal, married a Maine woman in 1683. Given that Portugal was dominated by Spain throughout the seventeenth century and had virtually no Reformed Christian tradition, it is highly unlikely that Fortado/Hurtado settled in New England for the sake of Protestantism. Emma Lewis Coleman, *New England Captives Carried to Canada between 1677 and 1760 during the French and Indian Wars,* 2 vols. (Bowie, MD: Heritage Classics, 1989), 1:188, 2:391–92 (hereafter *NEC*). For a brief overview of the migration of the diverse Europeans outside of their homelands, see Euan Cameron, ed., *Early Modern Europe* (New York: Oxford University Press, 1999), 188, 289. On the Portuguese in northern New England, see Baker, *Devil of Great Island,* 157.

23. For fears of crypto-Catholicism in early New England, see Mary Beth Norton, *In the Devil's Snare: The Salem Witchcraft Crisis of 1692* (New York: Knopf, 2002), and Louise A. Breen, *Transgressing the Bounds: Subversive Enterprise among the Puritan Elite, 1630–1692* (New York: Oxford University Press, 2001). For pervasive fears of popery in general and the pan-Protestant initiatives it inspired, see Kidd, *Protestant Interest,* and Cogliano, *No King, No Popery.*

24. Mary R. Calvert, *Black Robe on the Kennebec* (Monmouth, ME: Monmouth Press, 1991), 172–73.

25. For the variety and ramifications of religious experimentation in England in the era of the English Civil War, see Christopher Hill's classic study *The World Turned Upside Down: Radical Ideas during the English Revolution* (New York: Penguin, 1972).

26. Emerson Baker describes some of the religious complications of early Maine in *Devil of Great Island,* 157–62.

27. The most comprehensive treatment of all aspects of Maine's early development remains Charles Clark's synthesis *The Eastern Frontier: The Settlement of Northern New England, 1610–1763* (New York: Knopf, 1970).

28. Axtell, *Invasion Within,* 247.

29. Numerous book-length treatments cover the Native American encounter with Catholicism as a stand-alone issue. This takes into account not only the theological implications of this encounter, but the political and cultural ones as well. The titles that were particularly helpful for this study include Axtell, *The European and the Indian,* and *The Invasion Within*; Christopher Bilodeau, "Policing Wabanaki Missions in the Seventeenth Century," in Roeber, *Ethnographies and Exchanges*; Demos, *Unredeemed Captive*; Greer,

Mohawk Saint; Haefeli and Sweeney, *Captors and Captives*; James T. Moore, *Indian and Jesuit: A Seventeenth Century Encounter* (Chicago: Loyola University Press, 1982); Morrison, *The Embattled Northeast*; Alice N. Nash, "The Abiding Frontier: Family, Gender and Religion in Wabanaki History, 1600–1763" (Ph.D. diss., Columbia University, 1997); Norton, *In the Devil's Snare*; and Sleeper-Smith, *Indian Women and French Men*. For a concise description of the dissonances and compatibilities between Native American religions and European Christianity, see Daniel Richter, *Facing East from Indian Country: A Native History of Early America* (Cambridge: Harvard University Press, 2003), especially chap. 3. In *Ordeal of the Longhouse*, Richter explores this issue as it relates specifically to the Iroquois Confederacy.

30. Sleeper-Smith, *Indian Women and French Men*, 1–3.

31. Notable studies of northeastern Indian alliances and political adaptability include Francis Jennings, *The Invasion of America: Indians, Colonialism, and the Cant of Conquest* (New York: W. W. Norton, 1976). For more recent treatments, see Denys Delâge, *Bitter Feast: Amerindians and Europeans in Northern North America, 1600–64*, trans. Jane Brierley (Vancouver: University of British Columbia Press, 1993); Haefeli and Sweeney, *Captors and Captives*; Morrison, *Embattled Northeast*; Richter, *Facing East from Indian Country*.

32. Notable Maine captives include Hannah Swarton and John Gyles, whose experiences were recorded in stylized narrative treatments with strong didactic overtones. Captives from other parts of New England, such as Quentin Stockwell and the Reverend John Williams, reported on the state of Maine captives during their confinement. Swarton's, Gyles's, Stockwell's and Williams's narratives all appear in Alden T. Vaughan and Edward W. Clark, eds., *Puritans Among the Indians: Accounts of Captivity and Redemption, 1676–1724* (Cambridge: Harvard University Press, 1981). Recent scholarly studies that examine the literary conventions and cultural implications of captivity narratives, especially in terms of constructions of gender, include Lorrayne Anne Carroll, *Rhetorical Drag: Impersonation, Captivity, and the Writing of History* (Kent: Ohio State University Press, 2007); Christopher Castiglia, *Bound and Determined: Captivity, Culture-Crossing, and White Womanhood from Mary Rowlandson to Patty Hearst* (Chicago: University of Chicago Press, 1996); Rebecca Blevins Faery, *Cartographies of Desire: Captivity, Race, and Sex in the Shaping of the American Nation* (Norman: University of Oklahoma Press, 1999); Annette Kolodny, *The Land before Her: Fantasy and Experience of the American Frontiers* (Chapel Hill:

University of North Carolina Press, 1984); Ann M. Little, *Abraham in Arms: War and Gender in Colonial New England* (Philadelphia: University of Pennsylvania, 2006); June Namais, *White Captives: Gender and Ethnicity on the American Frontier* (Chapel Hill: University of North Carolina Press, 1993); and Teresa A. Toulouse, *The Captive's Position: Female Narrative, Male Identity, and Royal Authority in Colonial New England* (Philadelphia: University of Pennsylvania Press, 2007). A hefty body of historical scholarship on the New England captives themselves has appeared in recent decades. Many of these studies rely on two classic, exhaustively researched antiquarian works, Charlotte Alice Baker's *True Stories of the New England Captives during the Old French and Indian Wars* (Portland, ME: Southworth Press, 1897; repr., Bowie, MD: Heritage Books, 1990), and Coleman's *NEC.* Using Coleman's work, Alden Vaughan and Daniel Richter started the trend toward demographic and cliometric studies of captives in their seminal article "Crossing the Cultural Divide: Indians and New Englanders, 1605–1763," *Proceedings of the American Antiquarian Society* 90:1 (1980): 23–99. Other studies that rely heavily on Baker's and Coleman's works include John Demos, *Unredeemed Captive*; William H. Foster, *The Captor's Narrative: Catholic Women and Their Puritan Men on the Early American Frontier* (Ithaca: Cornell University Press, 2003); Barbara E. Austen, "Captured . . . Never Came Back: Social Networks among New England Female Captives in Canada, 1689–1763," and Alice N. Nash, "Two Stories of New England Captives: Grizel and Christine Otis of Dover, New Hampshire," essays in Peter Benes, ed., *New England/New France 1600–1850*, Annual Proceedings of the Dublin Seminar for New England Folklife, vol. 14 (Boston: Boston University, 1992); Linda Breuer Gray, "Narratives and Identities in the Saint Lawrence Valley, 1667–1720" (Ph.D. diss., McGill University, 1999). An essential reference source for the French side of the encounter is Marcel Fournier's *De la Nouvelle-Angleterre à la Nouvelle-France: L'histoire des captifs anglo-américains au Canada entre 1675 et 1760* (Montreal: Société Généalogique Canadienne-Française, 1992). Additional important works that focus on the expanded experiences of specific demographic groups or individual captive stories include Evan Haefeli, "Ransoming New England Captives in New France," *French Colonial History* 1 (2002): 113–27; Haefeli and Sweeney, *Captors and Captives*; and Little, *Abraham in Arms.*

33. The most recent analyses of the complexities of captor/redeemer relations are Haefeli and Sweeney, *Captors and Captives,* Foster, *Captor's Narrative,* and Little, *Abraham in Arms.*

34. Alden Vaughan and Daniel Richter demonstrate that the captives most likely to resist return to New England were those who had become acculturated French Catholics, not transculturated Native Americans. See "Crossing the Cultural Divide," passim.

35. See Little, "Life of Mother Marie-Joseph de l'Enfant Jesus," and Foster, *The Captor's Narrative.*

36. For critical transition points in Wabanaki/French relations through 1760, see Morrison, *The Embattled Northeast.*

37. Jay Gitlin, "On the Boundaries of Empire: Connecting the West to Its Imperial Past," in Cronon, Miles, and Gitliu, *Under an Open Sky.* See also David J. Weber, *The Spanish Frontier in North America* (New Haven: Yale University Press, 1992); Gordon M. Sayre, *Les Sauvages Américains: Representations of Native Americans in French and English Colonial Literature* (Chapel Hill: University of North Carolina Press, 1997); and Axtell, *Invasion Within.*

38. Wheelwright, 31 Dec. 1753. Collections, MHS, Boston.

Chapter 1. *"The Land That Was Desolate . . . Shall Flourish Like the Lily"*

1. J. Money, "Noel Negabamat," *DCB* 7:516.

2. The English ban against selling liquor to the Wabanakis carried strict penalties for malefactors but was virtually unenforceable. Morrison, *Embattled Northeast,* 77, 80.

3. Ibid., 81.

4. Winslow's brother, Edward, was one of the founders of the colony and had served a prison term in England for preaching opposition to England's High Church archbishop, William Laud. Richard Gildrie, "Edward Winslow," *American National Biography* (hereafter *ANB*), 23:648.

5. Francis Parkman, *The Jesuits in North America in the Seventeenth Century* (Boston: Little, Brown, 1867; repr., Lincoln: University of Nebraska Press, 1997), 422.

6. Reuben Gold Thwaites, ed., *The Jesuit Relations and Allied Documents: Travels and Explorations of the Jesuit Missionaries in New France, 1610–1791,* 73 vols. (hereafter *JR*) (Cleveland: Burrows Brothers, 1896–1901), 36:85.

7. Ibid.

8. Quoted in Parkman, *Jesuits in North America,* 422.

9. Cogliano, *No King, No Popery,* 84.

10. Quoted in Morrison, *Embattled Northeast*, 81.

11. *JR* 36:86.

12. For a description of a Catholic mass adapted to "wilderness" celebration, or other locations where consecrated spaces to celebrate the mass were unavailable, see "Missions of the Montagnais or Lower Algonquians during the Years 1673 and 1674," *JR* 59:33.

13. Parkman, *Jesuits in North America*, 423.

14. *JR* 36:91. The role of North American seafood in New England dietary practices during the colonial period is described in Peter Benes, ed., *Foodways in the Northeast*, Annual Proceedings of the Dublin Seminar for New England Folklife, 1982 (Boston: Boston University Press, 1984), passim.

15. *JR* 36:91.

16. Ibid., 36:89.

17. Ibid., 36:109.

18. Ibid., 36:105.

19. Ibid., 36:107; for population statistics, see Thomas L. Purvis, *Colonial America to 1763*, Almanacs of American Life (New York: Facts on File, 1999), 129.

20. Parkman, *Jesuits in North America*, 429.

21. Ibid.

22. Richard Middleton, *Colonial America: A History, 1607–1760* (Oxford: Blackwell, 1992), 67.

23. I am indebted to Ann M. Little for this insight. Communication from Ann M. Little to author via University of Notre Dame Press, Nov. 29, 2008.

24. A brief description of the Eastern Wabanakis at the time of European contact and settlement can be found in Colin Calloway's introduction to a collection of primary sources on the topic that constitute *Dawnland Encounters: Indians and Europeans in Northern New England* (Hanover, NH: University Press of New England, 1991). For the range of Eastern Wabanaki settlement and influence, see *Dawnland Encounters*, 3, 5.

25. Based on linguistic and cultural similarities, some anthropologists classify the Passamaquoddy Indians as Eastern Wabanakis. Ibid., 5.

26. Ibid., 8; Baker and Reid, "Amerindian Power in the Early Modern Northeast," passim; Morrison, *Embattled Northeast*, chaps. 4, 5, and 6.

27. Eccles, *Canadian Frontier*, 20–22; Clark, *Eastern Frontier*, 16.

28. As early as 1602, Englishmen Bartholomew Gosnold and Martin Pring were promoting the Maine coast as an ideal place to establish a settlement to develop the cod and fur trades. See Brian Fagan, *Fish on Friday:*

Feasting, Fasting and the Discovery of the New World (New York: Basic Books, 2006), 261.

29. Ibid., 268.

30. Clark, *Eastern Frontier*, 16–17.

31. Ibid., 14.

32. Cotton Mather, *Magnalia Christi Americana* (London: Thomas Parkhurst, 1702; repr. New York: Arno Press, 1972), 15; Clark, *Eastern Frontier*, 19.

33. Clark, *Eastern Frontier*, 19–20.

34. Ibid., 11; Maxine Lurie, "Robert Gorges, William Gorges, and Thomas Gorges," *ANB* 9:302.

35. Clark, *Eastern Frontier*, 47.

36. Ibid., 47–48; *GDMNH* 268.

37. Clark, *Eastern Frontier*, 51.

38. Quoted in Clark, *Eastern Frontier*, 25.

39. Moogk, *La Nouvelle France*, 14.

40. Eccles, *Canadian Frontier*, 25–26.

41. Ibid., 32.

42. Ibid., 35–36.

43. Marie-Claire Daveluy, "Jeanne Mance," *DCB* 1:483.

44. Ibid., 1:60; Moogk, *La Nouvelle France*, 21.

45. Quoted in Moogk, *La Nouvelle France*, 21.

46. Emerson W. Baker and John G. Reid, *The New England Knight, Sir William Phips, 1651–1695* (Toronto: University of Toronto Press, 1998), 18, 135–36.

47. Axtell, *Invasion Within*, 297.

48. Mather, *Magnalia Christi Americana*, 15.

49. Clark, *Eastern Frontier*, 66.

50. I am indebted to Emerson W. Baker for this insight. Personal correspondence, Sept. 3, 2004.

51. Francis Cogliano provides a detailed analysis of the cultural origins of the numerous derogatory terms used by Protestant colonists to describe Catholics and Catholicism. Cogliano, *No King, No Popery*, 5–18.

52. Hambrick-Stowe, *Practice of Piety*, 27. Also see Henry Outram Evennett's discussion of post–Counter Reformation Catholic education in *The Spirit of the Counter-Reformation* (Notre Dame, IN: University of Notre Dame Press, 1968), 78–79.

53. Edmund S. Morgan, *Visible Saints: The History of a Puritan Idea* (Ithaca: Cornell University Press, 1963), 53.

54. Axtell, *Invasion Within,* 71, 77, 80.

55. David Murray, "Spreading the Word: Missionaries, Conversion, and Circulation in the Northeast," in Griffiths and Cervantes, *Spiritual Encounters,* 43–60.

56. This popular theme managed to work its way into the homes of prominent northern New Englanders. The reception space of the home of nearby Portsmouth, New Hampshire, merchant Alexander Macphaedris was decorated with a mural showing the symbolic triumph of Protestantism over Catholicism in Ireland. Laurel Thatcher Ulrich, *The Age of Homespun: Objects and Stories in the Creation of an American Myth* (New York: Knopf, 2001), 95–98.

57. Ray, *American Opinion of Roman Catholicism,* 211.

58. Cotton Mather, *Decennium Luctuosum: An history of remarkable occurrences, in the long war, which New-England hath had with the Indian salvages, from the year, 1688* (Boston: B. Green and J. Allen, 1699), 62.

59. Morgan, *Visible Saints,* 53.

60. Clark, *Eastern Frontier,* 4.

61. "Jouvency's Account of the Canadian Mission," *JR* 1:227.

62. This was the Popham Colony at the mouth of the Kennebec River, the brainchild of Sir John Popham, whose partner, Sir Ferdinando Gorges, chose to encourage settlement farther to the south. Clark, *Eastern Frontier,* 5, 16.

63. *JR* 2:247.

64. Ibid., 2:247–49.

65. Patricia Seed, *Ceremonies of Possession in Europe's Conquest of the New World, 1492–1640* (London: Cambridge University Press, 1995), 56.

66. Joyce Chaplin, *Subject Matter: Technology, the Body, and the Anglo-American Frontier, 1500–1676* (Cambridge: Harvard University Press, 2001), 58, 66; James Rosier, "A True Relation of the Most prosperous voyage made this present yeere of 1605, by Captaine George Weymouth, in the Discovery of the Land of Virginia," in Andrew J. Wahll, ed., *Sabino: Popham Colony Reader, 1602–2000* (Bowie, MD: Heritage Books, 2000), 52.

67. Quoted in David Hackett Fischer, *Champlain's Dream: The European Founding of North America* (New York: Simon & Schuster, 2008), 239.

68. Seed, *Ceremonies of Possession,* 41–42.

69. *JR* 1:193.

70. Ibid., 1:227; Vincent A. Lapomarda, *The Jesuit Heritage in New England* (Worcester, MA: College of the Holy Cross, 1977), 1–3.

71. Chaplin, *Subject Matter,* 3.

72. Nathaniel Saltonstall, *A new and further narrative of the State of New-England*, 98–99. Quoted in Lepore, *Name of War*, 72.

73. See Lepore, *Name of War*, chap. 3.

74. The historical dynamics of this relationship are discussed extensively in Morrison, *Embattled Northeast*, and "Sebastien Rale vs. New England: A Case Study of Frontier Conflict" (M.A. thesis, University of Maine at Orono, 1970). See also Nash, "Abiding Frontier," and Christopher Bilodeau, "Policing the Wabanaki Missions in the Seventeenth Century," in Roeber, *Ethnographies and Exchanges*.

75. "Rerum Gestarum," *JR* 2:207–9.

76. *JR* 2:213.

77. Ibid.

78. Ibid., 3:223.

79. Clark, *Eastern Frontier*, 16.

80. *JR* 2:257.

81. Ibid., 2:253, 255.

82. Ibid., 2:259.

83. Ibid., 2:267.

84. Ibid., 2:265.

85. Ibid., 2:267, 271.

86. Morrison, *Embattled Northeast*, 80.

87. *JR* 51:71.

88. Ibid., 51:72.

89. Ibid., 51:72.

90. Philip F. Gura, *A Glimpse of Sion's Glory: Puritan Radicalism in New England, 1620–1660* (Middletown, CT: Wesleyan University Press, 1984), 203.

91. John Cannon and Ralph Griffiths, *Oxford History of the British Monarchy* (New York: Oxford University Press, 1988), 408–9.

92. For examples of ethnic diversity among Maine's early Euro-American inhabitants, see *GDMNH* 64, 83, 93, 90, 101, 121, 133, 140, 148, 212, 290.

93. Jon Butler, "Historiographical Heresy: Catholicism as a Model for American Religious History," in Thomas Kselman, ed., *Belief in History: Innovative Approaches to European and American Religion* (Notre Dame, IN: University of Notre Dame Press, 1991), 296.

94. Clark, *Eastern Frontier*, 20.

95. Emerson W. Baker, "The World of Thomas Gorges" in Emerson W. Baker, ed., *American Beginnings: Exploration, Culture and Cartography*

in the Land of Norumbega (Lincoln: University of Nebraska Press, 1994), 262–63.

96. Ibid., 276.

97. Ibid.

98. Lurie, "Robert Gorges, William Gorges and Thomas Gorges," *ANB* 9:302.

99. George Francis Marlowe, *Churches of Old New England: Their Architecture and Their Architects, Their Pastors and Their People* (New York: Macmillan, 1947), 207.

100. *GDMNH* 705–6; Marlowe, *Churches,* 210.

101. *GDMNH* 136–37.

102. *GDMNH* 391; James Phinney Baxter, ed., *Documentary History of the State of Maine,* 24 vols. (hereafter *DHSM*) (Portland: Maine Historical Society, 1869–1916), 4:151.

103. *GDMNH* 391; Bourne, *History of Wells and Kennebunk,* 66.

104. Alden was the grandson of Plymouth settler John Alden and son of Captain John. He was related through marriage to Anne Hutchinson. Breen, *Transgressing the Bounds,* 197–98.

105. Ibid., 80.

106. *GDMNH* 624.

107. Emerson W. Baker, "Lithobolia: Frontier Prelude to Witchcraft in Salem," paper presented at the American Historical Association Annual Meeting, Boston, Massachusetts, Jan. 2001, 2. This paper has been integrated into the book *The Devil of Great Island.* My thanks to the author for graciously sharing this work in progress with me.

108. This was Richard Nason, a trustee for the Gorges family and Kittery selectman. *GDMNH* 505.

109. "Joseph Dudley to the Board of Trade," March 1, 1708/9, *DHSM* 9:264.

110. Baker, *Devil of Great Island,* 121–22.

111. Clark, *Eastern Frontier,* 81.

112. Bourne, *History of Wells and Kennebunk,* 176.

113. Ibid., 61; John G. Reid, *Acadia, Maine and New Scotland: Marginal Colonies in the Seventeenth Century* (Toronto: University of Toronto Press, 1981), 13.

114. Charles Thornton Libby, Robert E. Moody, and Neal W. Allen, Jr., eds. *Province and Court Records of Maine,* 6 vols. (hereafter *MPCR*) (Portland: Maine Historical Society, 1928–75), 1:136.

115. Clark, *Eastern Frontier,* 48.

116. In many Anglican churches, *Actes and Monuments* (more commonly known as *The Book of Martyrs*) had a place on the lectern next to the Bible. Cogliano, *No King, No Popery*, 6–7; Hambrick-Stowe, *Practice of Piety*, 117.

117. Quoted in Stout, *New England Soul*, 49. In *Popular Culture in Early Modern Europe*, Peter Burke identifies the basic assumptions regarding literacy as "more [Europeans] could read in 1800 than in 1500; that craftsmen were generally much more literate than peasants, men than women, Protestants than Catholics, and Western Europeans than Eastern Europeans." Burke asserts that this evidence is "precise, yet fragmentary" and relies on "signature literacy," a riskily inaccurate assessment tool that relies on one task alone—the ability to sign one's name. Nevertheless, the author notes that rising rates of literacy throughout Western Europe started to transcend sectarian lines once Protestantism became deeply rooted and Catholicism responded to some of its more challenging initiatives. Burke, *Popular Culture in Early Modern Europe* (New York: Harper, 1978), 38.

118. Though the Jesuits repeatedly requested a printing press to aid in the teaching of Indian languages, New France was prohibited from having one of its own for fear that local book production would undermine the mother country's lucrative trade in supplying print material to its colonies. Roger Magnuson, *Education in New France* (Montreal: McGill-Queen's University Press, 1992), 107–8.

119. Ibid., 107.

120. Ibid.

121. Ibid., 105.

122. Assessment made by author using vol. 3 of William A. Sargent, ed. *York Deeds*, 18 vols. (hereafter *YD*) (Portland: John T. Hull, 1887–1910).

123. William A. Sargent, *Maine Wills, 1640–1760* (hereafter *MW*) (Portland: Brown, Thurston, 1887), 131.

124. The ability of New England males to sign their names to legal documents ("signature literacy"), hovered around 61 percent in 1660; for women, the figure was considerably lower (31 percent). Theorists of the history of literacy use these figures as benchmarks, determining from them that at the very least, this percentage of the population could also read, but some scholars challenge this assumption. See Magnuson, *Education in New France*, 87–88n198; Purvis, *Colonial America to 1763*, 248.

125. Hall, *Worlds of Wonder*, 35.

126. J. T. Champlin, "Educational Institutions in Maine While a District of Massachusetts," *Collections of the Maine Historical Society* ser. 1, 9 vols. (hereafter *Coll MeHS*) (Portland: Maine Historical Society, 1831–87),

8:158. Known as the "Old Deluder Satan" act, the movement was intended to create mandatory schools throughout New England and compel children to attend them, "it being one chief project of the old deluder Satan to keep men from the knowledge of the Scriptures." Quoted in Magnuson, *Education in New France,* 111.

127. Joseph Dudley to the Board of Trade, Dec. 2, 1712, *DHSM* 9:336.

128. There are several recent scholarly treatments that study this subject in detail. They include Norton, *In the Devil's Snare,* and "George Burroughs and the Girls from Casco: The Maine Roots of Salem Witchcraft," *Maine History* 40:4 (Winter 2001–2): 259–77, Breen; *Transgressing the Bounds*; Emerson W. Baker and James Kences, "Maine, Indian Land Speculation, and the Essex County Witchcraft Outbreak of 1692," *Maine History* 40:3 (Fall 2001): 159–89; and Baker, *The Devil of Great Island.*

129. *GDMNH* 187–88.

130. Alice R. Stewart, "Sylvanus Davis," *DCB* 2:172.

131. Baker and Reid, *New England Knight,* 18, Alvin Hamblen Morrison argued for the same usage in "Dawnland Decisions: Seventeenth-Century Wabanaki Leaders and Their Responses to the Differential Contact Stimuli in the Overlap Area of New France and New England" (Ph.D. diss., State University of New York at Buffalo, 1975). I am indebted to Emerson Baker for pointing me toward this reference.

132. "Sylvanus Davis et al. to General Council," July 15, 1689, *DHSM* 9:14–15.

133. Falmouth's first meetinghouse was still unfinished as late as 1728. William Willis, *The History of Portland,* 2 vols. (Portland: Day, Fraser, 1831), 2:97.

134. Stout, *New England Soul,* 14.

135. "Sylvanus Davis to General Council," Sept. 11, 1689, *DHSM* 9:48.

136. Samuel Sewall, *The Diary of Samuel Sewall,* 2 vols., ed. M. Halsey Thomas (New York: Farrar, Straus and Giroux, 1973), 1:259.

137. Davis, who had served as a militia captain during King Philip's War, was an obvious choice to lead the militia at Fort Loyal despite the ill-will he may have incurred over the land patents issue. He played a role in redeeming captives at Cocheco several months before the attack on Casco Bay, and it therefore seems unlikely that he would be ignorant of the profits attached to the ransoming of captives. "Davis," *DCB* 2:172; *NEC* 1:142; *DHSM* 5:145–46.

138. *NEC* 1:198.

139. For a thorough recent treatment of France's wars of religion and their effects on the founding of New France, see Fischer, *Champlain's Dream*, 49–60.

140. R. Po-chia Hsia, *The World of Catholic Renewal, 1540–1770* (New York: Cambridge University Press, 1998), 70–71.

141. "Declaration of Sylvanus Davis," n.d., *DHSM* 5:145–46. Étienne Taillemite suggests that Robinau de Portneuf may have been powerless to stop his Wabanaki allies from seizing and killing some of the Casco captives— a common though sometimes unsubstantiated claim by French forces in almost every war of empire. Étienne Taillemite, "René Robinau de Portneuf," *DCB* 2:441.

142. *GDMNH* 188; Baker and Reid, *New England Knight*, 171–72.

143. "Davis," *DCB* 2:172.

144. "Captain Sylvanus Davis: His Narrative at his Return from Canada, November 1690," Massachusetts State Archives (hereafter MSA), 36:212.

145. Ibid.

146. Ibid., 36:216.

Chapter 2. *"Satan's Prey" or* "L'esclavage de l'hérésie calviniste"

1. Quoted in Axtell, *The European and the Indian*, 276.

2. By the 1670s Beverly already had few options for newcomers and those on the lower end of the economic scale. John Swarton's experience clearly falls into the occupational patterns of such newcomers. Daniel Vickers, *Farmers and Fishermen: Two Centuries of Work in Essex County, Massachusetts, 1630–1850* (Chapel Hill: University of North Carolina Press, 1994), 55.

3. Hannah Swarton, "A Narrative of Hannah Swarton Containing Wonderful Passages Relating to Her Captivity and Deliverance," in Vaughan and Clark, eds., *Puritans among the Indians*, 150.

4. Ibid., 148.

5. The nineteenth-century editor likely changed the family surname from Swarton to the more lyrical and allegorically suggestive "Swanton."

6. His return was Jasper Swarton's last entry in the historical record as well. It is possible that the boy died young, probably shortly after his return. *NEC* 1:204.

7. *New England Historical and Genealogical Register* (hereafter *NEHGR*), 5:122.

8. The name Hibbard and all its variations appears frequently in vital records of Essex County well into the nineteenth century. Several accused witches were from Beverly, and town residents were part of the greater "chain of gossip" that helped spread the hysteria throughout Essex County. *Vital Records of Beverly Massachusetts to the End of the Year 1849*, vol. 2 (Topsfield, MA: Topsfield Historical Society, 1906–7), 160–1; Norton, *In the Devil's Snare*, 113, 146.

9. Mary's husband, the Ireland-born John Lahey, was born a Catholic but became a Protestant after he migrated to the English North American colonies. He returned to Catholicism while in the captive service of Jacques Le Ber and soon afterward was freed, settling in the St. Lawrence Valley permanently. John and Mary, who in marriage became "Marie-Madeleine Lahé," had thirteen children. Foster, *Captor's Narrative*, 31; *NEC* 1:206.

10. Gildrie, *The Profane, the Civil, and the Godly*, 135.

11. Kidd, *Protestant Interest*, 18, 139.

12. Thanks to Emerson Baker for this insight. Personal correspondence, July 22, 2004.

13. Richard Gildrie contends that the structure of Catholic liturgy "exercised a strong pull on those captive English who experienced the demoralization of a collapsing frontier from 1675 to 1725." *The Profane, the Civil, and the Godly*, 139.

14. Alan Gallay, ed., *The Colonial Wars of North America, 1512–1763* (New York: Garland, 1996), 343.

15. Ibid., 342.

16. Samuel Adams Drake, *The Border Wars of New England* (New York: Charles Scribner's Sons, 1897), 67–69.

17. Baker and Reid, *New England Knight*, 96–97.

18. Drake, *Border Wars of New England*, 65; Gallay, *Colonial Wars of North America*, 346.

19. The dates listed here reflect the differences in the way English and French colonists dated colonial events. The English retained the "old-style" Julian calendar, while, after 1582, Catholic Europe adopted the calendar reforms of Pope Gregory XIII. Among other things, the two calendars recognized different beginnings of the New Year (January 1 for the Gregorian; March 25 for the Julian), leading to an overlap in the way the years were recorded.

20. Gallay, *The Colonial Wars of North America*, 348.

21. Ibid., 349.

22. Ibid., 351.

23. The Mather–Hannah Swarton connection is pinpointed and described in recent works, including Carroll, *Rhetorical Drag,* and Toulouse, *The Captive's Position.* Carroll in particular shows how gender conventions and religious propriety were tied to gender impersonation of female protagonists by clerical male authors. *Rhetorical Drag,* 11, 36–39.

24. Tara Fitzpatrick, "The Figure of Captivity: The Cultural Work of the Puritan Captivity Narrative," *American Literary History* 3:1 (Spring 1991): 9.

25. Carroll, *Rhetorical Drag,* 11, 36–39. In *The Land before Her* (24–27), Annette Kolodny suggests the Mather-Swarton literary connection was more collaborative in nature.

26. Puritan marriages were covenants, in which each person had responsibilities, often governed by law, toward the other. Still, Puritan women were expected to "guid the house &c. not guid the Husband," suggesting that major decisions were the demesne of males. Quoted in Edmund Morgan, *The Puritan Family: Religion and Domestic Relations in Seventeenth-Century New England* (New York: Harper & Row, 1966), 43.

27. It is, however, important to note that the fragments of English's French identity, so valuable to his success in business, cast suspicion on him and his wife during the Salem witch trials of 1692. English later became an Anglican and built Saint Peter's Church in Danvers, Massachusetts. Norton, *In the Devil's Snare,* 137, 140, 176; Bernard Bailyn, *The New England Merchants of the Seventeenth Century* (New York: Harper & Row, 1955), 144.

28. Secondary sources on Channel Islanders in early North America are surprisingly scarce. Notable exceptions are portions of Bailyn's and Norton's works, cited above.

29. *Records and Files of the Quarterly Court of Essex County* (Salem, MA: Essex Institute, 1911–21), 4:400.

30. *NEC* 1:204.

31. John Swarton to General Council, June 6, 1687, *DHSM* 6:264–65. Coleman states the grant was for fifty acres of land, though the petitioner requested only ten. *NEC* 1:204.

32. Whitmore, *Andros Tracts* 1:xxxiv, 53.

33. "Narrative of Hannah Swarton," 150.

34. The revocation of the Edict of Nantes coincided with James II's attempts to reassert Catholic control over the Channel Islands. A. C. Saunders, *Jersey in the Seventeenth Century* (St. Helier, Jersey: J. T. Bigwood, 1931), 169.

35. Kenneth Silverman, *The Life and Times of Cotton* Mather (New York: Harper & Row, 1984), 5.

36. Ralph Mollet, *A Chronology of Jersey* (St. Helier: Société Jersiaise, 1954), 25–29; Saunders, *Jersey in the Seventeenth Century,* 18.

37. Andros's own high Anglicanism is confirmed by the language of his will, which notes special days in terms of the pre-Reformation religious calendar. Bequests to family members were to be made based on an annual cycle of saints' and feast days. Whitmore, *Andros Tracts* 2:xlii.

38. The Casco Bay settlements include present-day Portland (Falmouth), North Yarmouth, Spurwink and Black Point (both part of Scarborough), and Purpooduck (South Portland). *NEC* 2:420.

39. Many thanks to Emerson Baker for this insight. Personal correspondence, July 23, 2004.

40. Separating captive families was a common first step in the acculturation process. For other examples see John Williams, *The Redeemed Captive Returning to Zion* (Northampton, MA: Hopkins, Bridgeman, 1853); Mary Rowlandson, "Sovereignty and Goodness of God," and John Gyles, "Memoirs of Odd Adventures, Strange Deliverances, etc.," both in Vaughan and Clark, *Puritans among the Indians.*

41. "Narrative of Hannah Swarton," 142.

42. Ibid., 149–51.

43. Ibid., 153.

44. Little, *Abraham in Arms,* 127.

45. "Narrative of Hannah Swarton," 154.

46. Mary Swarton spent six days at the Hôtel-Dieu in Quebec in 1693. It is likely that her mother visited her there since Hannah, redeemed in 1695, "had not seen [Mary] in two years before [she] came away." Marcel Fournier, *De la Nouvelle-Angleterre à la Nouvelle-France: L'histoire des captifs anglo-américains au Canada entre 1675 et 1760* (Montreal: Société Généalogique Canadienne-Française, 1992), 212–13; "Narrative of Hannah Swarton," 157.

47. *NEC* 1:206–7; Fournier, *De la Nouvelle-Angleterre à la Nouvelle-France,* 212–13. The family eventually expanded to include fifteen members. Coleman and Baker found baptismal records for only eleven: Fournier, working fifty years later, identified two more Swarton-Lahey children. Other captive New Englanders served as godparents.

48. "Lettre de Vaudreuil au ministre," 14 avril 1714. National Archives of Canada (hereafter NAC), ser. C11A. Correspondance générale 34:333–35.

49. Other widowed captives did the same. One was Mary Reed, a native of Braintree, Massachusetts, taken from Salmon Falls, who resettled with her family in Braintree after her redemption. *NEC* 1:191; *GDMNH* 580.

50. For Wheelwright family civic leadership in early Maine, see *GDMNH* 743–45. Mary's cousin John Wheelwright was one of the founding congregants of the First Church of Wells in 1701. One of the first events at the church was the baptism of his young children, including the future captive and nun Esther Wheelwright. *Records of the First Church of Wells, Maine from October 29, 1701, to October 21, 1810* (New York, 1918).

51. He was the son of Anne Marbury Hutchinson's sister, Esther. *GDMNH* 367.

52. Clark, *Eastern Frontier,* 47.

53. Ibid., 51.

54. Rishworth's ability to survive adversity was envied by many of his fellow settlers, making him enormously unpopular in his community. Charles Edwin Banks, *A History of York, Maine,* vol. 1 (Boston, 1931), 216.

55. Banks, *History of York,* 1:110–14.

56. Bourne, *History of Wells and Kennebunk,* 109–14.

57. Foster notes that this area of York was reserved for farmers of more modest means. He refers to James Plaisted as a "hardscrabble farmer," though he, like Mary, was tied to more prestigious family members like his brother, Portsmouth merchant Ichabod Plaisted. *Captor's Narrative,* 66; *GDMNH* 559.

58. Baker and Kences, "Maine, Indian Land Speculation, and the Essex County Witchcraft Outbreak of 1692," 167; Norton, *In the Devil's Snare,* 15, 21.

59. Quoted in Banks, *History of York,* 1:291.

60. Ibid., 1:294–95. This number is subject to some debate: Banks reports that forty-eight York settlers were killed, but Coleman puts the number closer to one hundred. Banks seems to have based his account on that of Cotton Mather in *Magnalia Christi Americana* (bk. 7), 77.

61. Donations for the redemption of captives came in from other Maine communities, and as far away as Dorchester and Plymouth. Banks, *History of York,* 1:296–98.

62. Foster, *Captor's Narrative,* 66.

63. These were Theodore Atkinson and his wife, Francis Tucker, and Elizabeth Alcock, a wealthy widow. *NEC* 1:226, 227, 229.

64. After Mary left the Gauchet household, her ex-mistress became an inmate of the Hôtel-Dieu of Montreal, where one of her daughters had preceded her. *DCB* 1:508; *NEC* 1:236.

65. *NEC* 1:79.

66. *YD* 4:77.

67. Mary neglected to renew the license in 1711 and was prosecuted for the oversight. *YD* 10:187.

68. *NEC* 1:238–40.

69. The growing number of so-called outlivers was a natural by-product of New England's geographic expansion in the latter half of the seventeenth century and caused concern throughout orthodox circles. Hambrick-Stowe, *Practice of Piety,* 244.

70. The contemporary problems geographical dispersion created for metropole New Englanders are articulated in two Mather publications, *Decennium Luctuosum,* and *Good Fetch'd out of Evil.*

71. When Susannah Johnson, a captive from New Hampshire, gave birth to her child while in Wabanakia, her Indian master reportedly exclaimed with joy, "Two moneys for me! Two moneys for me!" Colin Calloway, ed., *North Country Captives: Selected Narratives of Indian Captivity from Vermont and New Hampshire* (Hanover, NH: University Press of New England, 1992), 54.

72. When a priest could not be present, missionaries left lay neophytes, called *dogiques,* to administer sacraments, including baptisms. *JR* 27:65.

73. Daniel Scalberg notes that, as late as 1683, there were only twenty-five priests in New France covering a 620-mile area. Scalberg, "Religious Life in New France under the Laval and Saint-Vallier Bishoprics" (Ph.D. diss., University of Oregon, 1990), 39–40.

74. Using Emma Lewis Coleman's research, Vaughan and Richter determined that New England captives who became acculturated French Catholics outnumbered those who became transculturated Native Americans by a factor of more than four to one. Vaughan and Richter, "Crossing the Cultural Divide," 60–62.

75. See examples in Mather, *Decennium Luctuosum,* 63, 64, 71; Joseph Dudley to the Board of Trade, Dec. 2, 1712, *DHSM* 9:335; John March to Joseph Dudley, Nov. 10, 1703, *DHSM* 9:164.

76. *NEC* 1:232.

77. Drake, *Border Wars of New England,* 76. If mission priests encouraged these offenses, they did so in absentia: there is no record of active Je-

suit participation in any of the raids on the southern Maine settlements during King William's and Queen Anne's wars. See *JR* 67, passim.

78. Mather, *Decennium Luctuosum*, 77.

79. Ibid., 71.

80. Charles Hambrick-Stowe describes Samuel Sewall's profound concern for the soul of his own sickly child, whom he feared might die before baptism. The sacrament was quickly performed by his colleague, Samuel Willard, because "it seemed important to bring the child officially into the covenant as quickly as possible." So-called outlivers rarely had the opportunity to enclose the family sacramentally as quickly as their contemporaries in more established communities did. *Practice of Piety*, 9, 11.

81. Demos, *Unredeemed Captive*, 29.

82. The child was Hannah Parsons of Wells. Hannah, the niece of Esther Wheelwright, survived, matured in Canada, and married Claude-Antoine Berman, a military officer from an aristocratic family. By 1759 a widow, Hannah moved to France in the wake of the fall of Quebec and sold her home, ironically, to James Murray, the first British governor of Canada. Mather, *Good Fetch'd Out of Evil*, 35; *NEC* 1:410.

83. Jill Lepore discusses violence perpetrated by both Native Americans and New Englanders in *The Name of War*, passim. Increase Mather, Cotton's father, was the author of one of the major accounts of King Philip's War, *A Brief History of the Warr with the Indians in New-England* (1676).

84. Linda Colley explores these tropes in *Captives: The Story of Britain's Pursuit of Empire and How Its Soldiers and Civilians Were Held Captive by the Dream of Global Supremacy, 1600–1850* (New York: Pantheon, 2002), 151–52.

85. "Narrative of Hannah Swarton," 144.

86. Ibid.

87. Ibid., 150.

88. Jacques Valois, "Joseph Denys," *DCB* 2:174.

89. Sleeper-Smith, *Indian Women and French Men*, 102.

90. Chaplin, *Subject Matter*, 58.

91. "Relation of 1643–44," *JR* 26:15.

92. Modern archaeologists have found Jesuit rings throughout Maine. One of the most unusual finds, by Emerson Baker in 2003, was in the remains of English trader Humphrey Chadbourne's home. Shirley Jacques, "Treasure Uncovered," *Portsmouth Herald*, Aug. 14, 2003.

93. The Native American fondness for *piquage* rubbed off on the French, some of whom had tattoos themselves. As reported by Henri de Tonti, one French officer festooned his body with images of "the Virgin and the baby Jesus, a large cross . . . with the miraculous words which appeared to Constantine." Clearly inspired by the Indians, these images might have been their handiwork as well. Sayre, *Les Sauvages Américains*, 169–71.

94. Chaplin, *Subject Matter*, 64.

95. Sebastien Rale to his nephew, Oct. 12, 1723, *JR* 67:181.

96. Nash, "Abiding Frontier," 225.

97. Joseph Aubery, S.J., to Joseph Jovency, S.J., Oct. 10, 1710, *JR* 66:177.

98. Alice Nash, "Abiding Frontier," 227, 229.

99. For the Jesuits' use of peer pressure to enforce certain behaviors within the missions, see Bilodeau, "Policing the Wabanaki Missions in the Seventeenth Century," in Roeber, *Ethnographies and Exchanges,* 97–114.

100. "Journal of what occurred in the Abnaquis Mission from the feast of Christmas, 1683 until October 6, 1684," *JR* 63:35.

101. Claude Chauchetière to his brother, Aug. 7, 1694, *JR* 64:125.

102. *JR* 63:27.

103. Jacques Bigot to unidentified Jesuit, Oct. 26, 1699, *JR* 65:89.

104. John Gyles, "Memoirs of Odd Adventures, Strange Connections, etc.," in Vaughan and Clark, *Puritans among the Indians,* 129.

105. Moogk, *La Nouvelle France,* 8.

106. Williams, *Redeemed Captive,* 186–87.

107. Ibid., 185.

108. "Journal of what occurred in the Abnaquis Mission from the feast of Christmas, 1683 until October 6, 1684," *JR* 63:27.

109. Ibid., 63:29.

110. Sebastien Rale to his nephew, Oct. 15, 1722, *JR* 67:87.

111. "Narrative of Hannah Swarton," 153. Like other captives, Hannah was ransomed into the household of a high-level New French administrator. By and large, her material environment was "a great and comfortable change as to my outward man in my freedom from my former hardships and hardhearted oppressors." Hannah, however, never loses her sense of being in enemy hands, and proceeds to contrast this comfort with the "danger to my inward man" presented by her close proximity to evangelistic priests. John Williams of Deerfield was received in the home of Governor Vaudreuil himself, whom he described as "in all respects relating to my outward man, courteous and charitable to admiration." Williams, *Redeemed Captive,* 34.

Even Mather admits "the French . . . Treated [the captives] with a Civility ever to be acknowledged, until care was taken to fetch 'em home," and even conceded that mission priests could be "very civil" to their New England human booty. Mather, *Magnalia Christi Americana*, 69, and *Good Fetch'd Out of Evil*, 32.

112. Little, *Abraham in Arms*, 136.

113. Jacques Bigot to unidentified Jesuit, Oct. 26, 1699. *JR* 65:91.

114. As early as the 1640s, the Jesuits were at work translating key Catholic texts into native languages. One key effort was Jean de Brébeuf's Huron translation of the vernacular *Doctrine Christienne*, by Jacques Ledesme, S.J. Though this text was originally in French (and Latin), both languages would have been unfamiliar to English women, men, and children. Axtell, *Invasion Within*, 106.

115. *NEC* 1:359–60.

116. "Narrative of Hannah Swarton," 150.

117. The importance of public and group worship is discussed in Hambrick-Stowe, *Practice of Piety*, chap. 4, passim.

118. Williams, *Redeemed Captive*, 18. Williams's experience influenced Cotton Mather, who wrote in *Good Fetch'd Out of Evil* that the captives found the means to meet despite the moratorium—with, of course, the assistance of divine grace. Mather, *Good Fetch'd Out of Evil*, 13.

119. [John Stoddard], "Stoddard's Journal," *NEHGR* 5:33.

120. Vaughan and Richter assert this belief in their article "Crossing the Cultural Divide." The authors also were among the first to suggest that the ideological lines that separated Protestant and Catholic, New Englander from *canadien*, were perhaps less rigidly defined, especially when other factors such as distance, religious commitment and exposure, and age, to name a few, came into play. "Crossing the Cultural Divide," 87.

121. *NEC* 1:185, 194, 237.

122. *NEC* 1:184–87, 245, 410–12; 2:3–8; Fournier, *De la Nouvelle-Angleterre à la Nouvelle-France*, 180, 209, 216.

123. Aaron Littlefield, whose story is discussed in length in chap. 6 of this study, had his clothes hidden by the curé whom he served. New England negotiators got wind of this underhanded strategy and complained bitterly of the tactic to French officials. Williams and Stoddard to Vaudreuil, Feb. 2, 1713, *NEGHR* 5:28–29.

124. Grace Higiman was taken from Pemaquid along with her husband and children. The entire family might have returned intact, though the two Higiman children disappear from the historical record. The fact that Grace

does not mention them in her testimony suggests that they were not killed in the raid or in captivity. "Statement of Grace Higiman," *NEGHR* 18:161.

125. *NEC* 2:144.

126. *NEC* 2:19, 404; Fournier, *De la Nouvelle-Angleterre à la Nouvelle-France*, 166.

127. These were William Hutchins (Salmon Falls), and Joseph Stover and Charles Trafton (both of York), all of whom are discussed in detail in chap. 5. *NEC* 1:244–47, 391–93.

128. *GDMNH* 248, 504–5.

129. Ibid., 284.

130. Austen, "Captured . . . Never Came Back," 30.

131. Ibid., 31.

132. For church celebrations and their effects on the conduct of the congregants, see Moogk, *La Nouvelle France*, 255–60.

133. John Norton, *The Redeemed Captive* (Boston, 1748), 26.

134. Austen, "Captured . . . Never Came Back," 33–34.

135. For a contemporary account of the importance and celebration of the Feast of the Nativity of the Blessed Virgin Mary in New France, see *JR* 66:83.

136. *NEC* 1:13–15.

137. Moogk, *La Nouvelle France*, 238.

138. Austen, "Captured . . . Never Came Back," 28–38.

139. Mary Storer St. Germaine to Ebenezer Storer, July 17, 1727. Mary Storer Letters. MHS, Boston.

140. *NEC* 1:414.

141. Ibid., 1:161–62.

142. Ibid., 2:8.

143. Ibid., 1:321.

144. Charlene Black, "St. Anne Imagery and Maternal Archetypes in Spain and Mexico," in Greer and Bilinkoff, *Colonial Saints*, 4.

145. Hall, *Worlds of Wonder, Days of Judgment*, 10, 26.

146. "Clement" had been the choice for no fewer than four popes between 1592 and 1700. Foster, *Captor's Narrative*, 138.

147. *NEC* 1:231; *GDMNH* 441–42.

148. Mathew Cary to Massachusetts General Council, Nov. 1695. MSA, Boston, 38a:1–3.

149. Josiah Littlefield to an unidentified male Wheelwright relation (probably Captain John), in Maine, 1708. Quoted in Bourne, *History of Wells and Kennebunk*, 268.

150. Demos, *Unredeemed Captive*, 109; *NEC* 1:230–31.

151. Fournier, *De la Nouvelle-Angleterre à la Nouvelle-France*, 144.

152. Yves Zoltvany, "François Hazeur," *DCB* 2:275–76.

153. Illiteracy was common in New France, even among the well placed in colonial society. Greer, *People of New France*, 67; Magnuson, *Education in New France*, 103–4.

154. *NEC* 1:231, 408; Moogk, *La Nouvelle France*, 142; Fournier, *De la Nouvelle-Angleterre à la Nouvelle-France*, 128, 162.

155. Fournier, *De la Nouvelle-Angleterre à la Nouvelle-France*, 127, 144; René Jetté, *Dictionnaire généalogique des familles du Québec des origines à 1730* (Montreal: Presses de l'Université de Montréal, 1983), 398.

156. Austen, "Captured . . . Never Came Back," 35.

157. For a thorough description of the inheritance patterns and priorities of the nobility in New France, see Haefeli and Sweeney, *Captors and Captives*, 232–37.

158. These captives were Hannah Swarton, Margaret Gould Stilson, her daughter Mary Stilson, and a child from Dover, New Hampshire, Sarah Gerrish. The Champignys failed to convert the older women but made willing converts of the others. Mary Stilson remained in Canada, accepted baptism, and became in that sacrament and in marriage Marie-Madeleine Cardinet. The Champignys gave Sarah Gerrish over to the care of the nuns of the Hôtel-Dieu, with whom the child bonded. When she was told of her redemption and return to her New England family, she wept and refused to go. She was later found to have hidden a crucifix in her armpit when she left Canada. *NEC* 1:145, 175–78.

159. William H. Foster demonstrates how one particular settler used captive labor to improve her family's situation within Canadian society. William H. Foster III, "Agathe St. Père and Her Captive New England Weavers," *French Colonial History* 1 (2002): 129–41.

160. *NEC* 1:238.

161. Jean-Jacques LeFebvre, "Jean Baptist Migeon de Branssat," *DCB* 1:508; Foster, *Captor's Narrative*, 67.

162. Foster, *Captor's Narrative*, 68.

163. *GDMNH* 560.

164. There are no records of the spouses of captives petitioning the General Court of Massachusetts to declare a captive husband or wife dead—even in the absence of compelling proof that the partner in question survived the ordeal. Furthermore, no spouse appears to have attempted to obtain a divorce from a missing spouse on the grounds of desertion, though

on at least on one occasion a New Hampshire captive seems to have used her captivity as a convenient means to effect a "self-divorce," another practice to break apart undesirable marriages informally which was widely discouraged in New England. The reasons for this are obvious: captive wives and husbands had not voluntarily left their families, and their inability to return was more often a product of failure to negotiate effectively or meet demands of ransom than ambivalence on any captive's part to return to his or her family. The topic of self-marriage is explored in much more detail in the next chapter of this study. Morgan, *The Puritan Family*, 35; Nancy F. Cott, "Divorce and the Changing Status of Women in Eighteenth-Century Massachusetts," *William and Mary Quarterly* 3rd ser., 33:4 (1976): 588.

165. *NEC* 1:238–39.

166. It is also possible that she was indeed ill, especially since she was prosecuted for no further infractions of this nature. *NEC* 1:238–39; Foster, *Captor's Narrative*, 68.

167. Samuel Moody, "Doleful State of the Damned" (sermon; n.d.). Quoted in Banks, *History of York*, 32–33.

168. Norton, *The Redeemed Captive*, 9.

Chapter 3. *"Pits of Hell" and "*Ménages des anges*"

1. John Demos used the term "unredeemed captive" in his book of the same title. The term plays with the title of a famous captivity narrative, the Reverend John Williams's *The Redeemed Captive Returning to Zion*. The study itself tells the story of Williams's daughter, Eunice, who refused to be redeemed to New England, preferring instead to become a fully transculturated Native American. Nevertheless, Eunice and her Indian family maintained ties with her New England siblings. Demos, *The Unredeemed Captive*, passim.

2. For early American marriage practices and expectations, see David Hackett Fischer, *Albion's Seed: Four British Folkways in America* (New York: Oxford University Press, 1989), 78; Helena M. Wall, *Fierce Communion: Family and Community in Early America* (Cambridge: Harvard University Press, 1990), 49–53.

3. Wall, *Fierce Communion*, 51.

4. Quoted in Morgan, *Puritan Family*, 55. Morgan speculates that this undated sermon, contained in the collection "Boston Sermons," was delivered around 1673 or 1674.

5. On the dangers to the social order and punishments for self-marriage, see Demos, *Little Commonwealth,* 118–20; Allan Kulikoff, *From British Peasants to Colonial American Farmers* (Chapel Hill: University of North Carolina Press, 2000), 239; and Barry Levy, *Quakers and the American Family: British Settlement in the Delaware* (New York: Oxford University Press, 1988), 91–93.

6. Wall, *Fierce Communion,* 52; for an attempt by an elite Puritan family to have a daughter's unsuitable marriage legally dissolved, see also Michael K. Ward, "Rebecca Rowson: Portrait of a Daughter of the Puritan Elite in the Massachusetts Bay Colony," *New England Journal of History* 56:1 (1999): 22–35.

7. Cotton Mather, *Family Religion, Excited and Assisted* (Boston, 1714), 1.

8. Plane, *Colonial Intimacies,* 83.

9. I am thankful to Ann M. Little for encouraging this alternative reading of the historical evidence. Personal correspondence via University of Notre Dame Press, Nov. 30, 2008.

10. The "sacramental system" described by Cornelius Jaenen usually was attached to additional requirements, which included the consent of the two parties and their parents and guardians, counseling by the parish priest, investigation into consanguinity and affinity, and the publications of banns over three successive Sundays before the marriage itself was performed. As will be seen in the case of Rachel Storer, a number of these requirements were dispensed with. Jaenen, *Role of the Church in New France,* 135–37.

11. Captives would have received the sacraments of baptism, penance, the Eucharist, and confirmation prior to marriage. In all likelihood, the conferral of some of these sacraments was rolled into one pre-marriage ceremony.

12. Philip Greven, *The Protestant Temperament: Patterns of Child-Rearing, Religious Experience, and the Self in Early America* (Chicago: University of Chicago Press, 1977), 186.

13. Ira Berlin, *Many Thousands Gone: The First Two Centuries of Slavery in North America* (Cambridge: Harvard University Press, 1998), 1.

14. Attacks on Wells and its environs by Wabanaki or Wabanaki-French forces occurred on four separate occasions between 1691 and 1712 (June 1691, Jan. 1691/2, Aug. 1703, April 1712, and Sept. 1712). Drake, *Border Wars of New England,* 71, 76, 155, 286, 288. Following the destruction of Casco in 1690, Charles Frost reported that "nothing now remains Eastward of Wells," and warned that the town "will desert if not forthwith reinforced."

Charles Frost et al. to General Council of Massachusetts, May 22, 1690, Massachusetts Archives 36:77, MSA, Boston.

15. Malcolm Storer, *Annals of the Storer Family* (New York, 1924), 30. Storer, a descendant of the Storers of Maine, gave the family papers used to compile this narrative genealogy of his family to the Massachusetts Historical Society.

16. Samuel Penhallow, *The History of the Wars of New-England with the Eastern Indians* (New York: Kraus Reprint Co., 1969), 18. Penhallow's work is one of the few contemporary treatments of Queen Anne's War and a major source of details on the depredations that conflict wrought throughout northern New England.

17. Gallay, *Colonial Wars of North America*, 613.

18. Ibid., 613–14.

19. Ibid., 614.

20. Drake, *Border Wars of New England*, 207.

21. Ibid., 208.

22. Ibid., 198–99.

23. Gallay, *Colonial Wars of North America*, 615.

24. Ibid., 617.

25. May 5, 1725, Registre des congés, 1721–26, MG8–C8, 2:526–31, NAC.

26. The year before he accompanied his kinswomen, Dagueil had been entrusted to carry letters between Governor Vaudreuil and New York governor John Schuyler related to French intervention in Dummer's War. Schuyler to Vaudreuil, Nov. 21, 1724, *DHSM* 10:233–34.

27. Mary was the third of Joseph and Hannah Storer's daughters. *GDMNH* 304, 665. Children of both sexes, sometimes as young as four, were charged with the responsibility of minding younger siblings. See Laurel Thatcher Ulrich, *Good Wives: Image and Reality in the Lives of Women in Northern New England, 1650–1750* (New York: Knopf, 1982), 29, and *A Midwife's Tale: The Life of Martha Ballard Based on Her Diary, 1785–1812* (New York: Knopf, 1990), 243.

28. Mary's command of English made an impression on a New England visitor to Montreal, the Reverend John Norton. In 1746 Mary and her brother-in-law Dagueil paid a call on the minister to ask if he knew Seth Storer (he did not). *NEC* 1:419.

29. As described by Ann M. Little, the eighteen letters of the Storer family correspondence consist of nine from Mary to Ebenezer, one from Mary to Seth, one from Mary to her mother, Hannah Hill Storer, five from

Mary's husband, Jean Gaulthier *dit* St. Germaine to Ebenezer, one each from Ebenezer to Mary and her husband. Little, *Abraham in Arms*, 159.

30. Drake, *Border Wars of New England*, 71–72, 76–80.

31. For the structure, proportions, and flexible uses of Maine's frontier garrison houses, see Edward Bourne, "Garrison Houses of York County," *Coll MeHS* ser. 1, 7:114.

32. *GDMNH* 664–65.

33. Clark, *Eastern Frontier*, 67–68.

34. Penhallow, *History of the Wars of New-England*, 18.

35. Austen, "Captured . . . Never Came Back," 37.

36. *NEC* 1:414. None of the Storer women spent more than two and a half years among the Wabanakis, and possibly much less. Mary was redeemed some time before her baptism on February 25, 1704 (new style). For example, Mary Storer's Native American captivity lasted for at most six months, which meant that her marriageable years were spent almost exclusively in New France. This is not surprising, given that, as Evan Haefeli has demonstrated, conditions between the French and their Native American allies were shifting during Queen Anne's War to favor French captivity over Native adoption. Consistent with this new policy, payments of money or gifts were made to Native American captors to induce them to relinquish their prizes quickly. See Haefeli, "Ransoming New England Captives in New France," 118. This was the ideal, though not always the case. Esther Wheelwright of Wells spent six years among the Wabanakis of Norridgewock; many captives of Deerfield, Massachusetts, spent years, and in a few cases, the remainder of their lives among the various Native American groups who had established villages in the St. Lawrence Valley. See also Haefeli and Sweeney, *Captors and Captives*, chap. 8, passim.

37. Pierre Boucher ransomed at least three Maine captives: Mary Storer, Martha Grant of Salmon Falls, and Sarah Randall Cole of Saco. Sarah and Martha were both older when taken and were used as house servants until they were redeemed. Martha was baptized and actively engaged in the Catholic Church until she was returned; Sarah's religious activities in New France are unknown, though her two daughters did convert, and one married in New France. *NEC* 1:184–87; 2:13–15.

38. *NEC* 1:414.

39. There were also several powerful merchants in nearby Montreal who had the Gaulthier name. Ironically, several of them had been Huguenots before abjuring their faith as the price for settling in New France. Though

Jean Gaulthier *dit* St. Germaine has not been linked to these families through any of the standard family sources, it is possible that Mary was not the first birth Protestant of his intimate acquaintance. Jetté, *Dictionnaire généalogique,* 475; *NEC* 1:415–16.

40. Quoted in *NEC* 1:415. Theodore Atkinson, a Portsmouth merchant, was taken captive in the Candlemas raid on York and redeemed several days later at Sagadahoc. Though lacking in specific details about Mary's life, Atkinson's observation is nonetheless valuable: as one of the wealthiest merchants in Portsmouth, New Hampshire, he was a capable judge of what "living very grandly" entailed. Clark, *Eastern Frontier,* 260.

41. Ebenezer Storer followed the path of other promising young men out of Maine and neighboring New Hampshire. His contemporaries in these ventures included Wheelwright cousins, as well as members of the Plaisted and Shapleigh families. *GDMNH* 560, 624, 744.

42. John Langdon Sibley and Clifford K. Shipton, *Sibley's Harvard Graduates* (Cambridge: Harvard University Press, 1933–), 4:412–13; *GDMNH* 665.

43. The Copley portraits of Ebenezer Storer, his wife, Mary Edwards, and their children, Ebenezer II and Mary Green Edwards, hang in the American Wing of the Metropolitan Museum of Art. Ebenezer Sr.'s religious preferences are alluded to in the style of his clothes, which, though clearly well made of costly fabrics, were relatively plain in contrast to those of many of his peers, who were also painted by Copley. He and his son are also wigless, an indication, at least in Sr.'s case, that he sided with religious conservatives who saw in periwigs and other finery the demise of religious devotion and appropriate comportment during the first half of the seventeenth century. Carrie Rebora and Paul Straiti, *John Singleton Copley in America* (New York: Harry N. Abrams, 1996), 154, 243; *GDMNH* 665.

44. Sibley and Shipton, *Sibley's Harvard Graduates,* 12:208.

45. Ibid.; *GDMNH* 665.

46. Sibley and Shipton, *Sibley's Harvard Graduates,* 6:412–13; *GDMNH* 665.

47. Peter Moogk, *Building a House in New France: An Account of the Perplexities of Client and Craftsmen in Early Canada* (Markham, Ont.: Fitz - henry and Whiteside, 1977), 51–52.

48. Mary gave birth to nine children, five of whom lived to adulthood. She served as godmother for a number of her cousin Priscilla's children. *NEC* 1:414–15, 423.

49. Jean Gaulthier ("JG") to Ebenezer Storer ("ES"), March 20, 1748, Mary Storer Letters, MHS, Boston.

50. This route was most certainly familiar to Priscilla Storer's husband, Jean-Baptiste Dagueil, who had traveled it numerous times as an emissary and negotiator between New France and its English neighbors, a role he continued to play through Dummer's War. Ironically, it was Dagueil who carried peace overtures to New York from the French government during the latter conflict. John Schuyler reported to William Dummer that he had had "some descours with the said Daguiell Concerning ye warrs between New England and ye Indians." Schuyler to Dummer, Nov. 21, 1724, *DHSM* 10:234.

51. Mary Storer St. Germaine ("MS") to Seth Storer ("SS"), June 28, 1725, Mary Storer Letters, MHS, Boston.

52. Sibley and Shipton, *Sibley's Harvard Graduates,* 6:413.

53. Axtell, *Invasion Within,* 288.

54. Little, *Abraham in Arms,* 161.

55. MS to ES, July 13, 1725, Mary Storer Letters, MHS, Boston.

56. MS to SS, June 28, 1725; MS to ES, June 26, 1725, ibid.

57. MS to ES, July 17, 1727, ibid. Placing children out to work in the households of other families, particularly in those of extended kin, was a common practice in early New England. In *The Puritan Family,* Edmund Morgan posits that Puritan parents "did not trust themselves with their own children, that they were afraid of spoiling them by too great affection." Laurel Thatcher Ulrich concurs in *A Midwife's Tale,* and discusses the gendered aspects of this system. Morgan, *The Puritan Family,* 75–78; Ulrich, *A Midwife's Tale,* 81. Ann M. Little examines the components of gendered power as demonstrated within the Storer family story itself, concluding, "Stories like that of Mary Storer St. Germaine show the effects that choices like hers had on the workings of patriarchal power within New England families. . . . The Storer family was typical of other New England families . . . who . . . went to great lengths to recover their daughters and save them from the twin evils of French government and Catholicism, or punish them for their rejection of New England government and Protestantism. . . . New England families actively courted the return of male ex-captives by offering them cash and jobs, whereas female captives were offered little if any incentive to return." Little, *Abraham in Arms,* 164.

58. MS to ES, June 29, 1725, Mary Storer Letters, MHS, Boston.

59. MS to ES, July 17, 1727, ibid.

60. Sargent, *Maine Wills,* 306; Little, *Abraham in Arms,* 163.

61. Malcolm Storer described his ancestor as "the wealthiest man in Wells." His estate was valued at £1,481. Storer, *Annals of the Storer Family,* 36; *GDMNH* 665.

62. MS to ES, April 19, 1733, Mary Storer Letters, MHS, Boston.

63. MS to Hannah Hill Storer, April 1733, ibid.

64. ES to MS, May 24, 1733, ibid.

65. Little, *Abraham in Arms,* 164.

66. After the inheritance controversy, the correspondence between siblings apparently decreased in both volume and frequency. One letter in particular, in which Mary tells that she lost one of her sons "about a year ago," confirms a lengthy gaps between missives.

67. JG to ES, March 20, 1748, Mary Storer Letters, MHS, Boston.

68. Ibid.

69. Morgan, *Puritan Family,* 18.

70. Greven, *Protestant Temperament,* 21; Hall, *Worlds of Wonder,* 241.

71. Greven, *Protestant Temperament,* 257.

72. As in New England, religious and civil authorities in New France were clear in their assertion, as well as in their laws, that fathers were undisputed heads of family units, and children were bound by God, law, and tradition to acquiesce to the authority of both parents. See chap. 6 of John Demos, *A Little Commonwealth: Family Life in Plymouth Colony* (New York: Oxford University Press, 1970), and chap. 3 of Morgan, *Puritan Family.*

73. Church authorities and observers of French Canada noted with chagrin the absence of strong parental authority in New France. Speaking of *canadien* children, Charlevoix noted, "There is one thing with respect to which [family relations] they are not easily to be excused, and that is the little natural affection most of them shew to their parents, who for their part display a tenderness for them, which is not extremely well-managed. The Indians fall into the same defect." Pierre F.-X. de Charlevoix, *Journal of a Voyage to North-America* (London: J. Doddsley, 1761), 1:267.

74. Haefeli and Sweeney, *Captors and Captives,* 157–58.

75. In his drive to counteract the effects that the priestly authority of Père Meriel was having over his son Samuel, John Williams wrote to the boy, "Was Mr. Meriel a God, a Christ? Could he bear to hear such words and not reject them, replying 'Don't commit your soul into my hands, but see that you commit your soul into the hands of God through Jesus Christ, and do whatever God commands you in his holy word. As for me, I am a

creature, and cannot save your soul." Williams, *Redeemed Captive,* 67. As Erik R. Seeman has written, celibacy "seemed to threaten the New England model of social order, whereby religious and behavioral norms were supposed to be inculcated voluntarily within the family." Erik R. Seeman, "It is Better to Marry Than to Burn: Anglo-American Attitudes toward Celibacy, 1600–1800," *Journal of Family History* 24 (1999): 398.

76. James Axtell describes sources that note the abusive turns these relationships could take. Captive youngsters were flattered and cajoled, but persistent resistance could also result in beatings and other acts of physical abuse and humiliation meted out by laypeople, clergy, and religious. Axtell, *Invasion Within,* 295.

77. Morgan, *Puritan Family,* 67.

78. David Hall asserts that, though Protestantism dismantled much of the old Catholic world of ritual, it reemerged within Protestant communities, in particular in the celebration of sacraments that predated the Reformation. *Worlds of Wonder,* 19. Charles Hambrick-Stowe discusses the pan-Christian applications of sacrament in *Practice of Piety,* 123.

79. Greer, *People of New France,* 22.

80. *NEC* 1:243, 2:148.

81. Ibid., 2:147.

82. Clark, *Eastern Frontier,* 114.

83. Bourne, *History of Wells and Kennebunk,* 646–50.

84. Charles Clark observes that in 1726 virtually all Falmouth's sixty completed houses were unpainted. The town also experienced severe food shortages in 1732, 1737, 1741, 1748, and 1753. *Eastern Frontier,* 150, 159.

85. Louise Dechêne, *Habitants and Merchants in Seventeenth Century Montreal,* trans. Liana Vardi (Montreal: McGill-Queens University Press, 1992), 220–21.

86. Charlevoix, *Journal of a Voyage to North-America,* 1:113–14.

87. *MCPR* 4:68.

88. Bourne, *History of Wells and Kennebunk,* 54.

89. Axtell, *Invasion Within,* 314.

90. In *Frenchman into Peasants,* Leslie Choquette notes that many young men ended up in New France thanks to the efforts of military re - cruiters. Called *racoleurs,* these recruiters joined in the efforts to build the ranks of the French colonial military with civilian counterparts. Many were working against French Canada's unattractive reputation and, as stated above, provided enlisted men who rarely committed to life in the colony

after their military service was through. Choquette, *Frenchmen into Peasants: Modernity and Tradition in the Peopling of French Canada* (Cambridge: Harvard University Press, 1997), 123.

91. Ibid., 113.

92. Ibid., 19, 21.

93. Along with other members of his family, Jean-Baptiste Hertel was one of the architects of raids on Salmon Falls and Deerfield during Queen Anne's War. His older brother, Zacharie-François, led the French contingent of the Salmon Falls attack of 1690. Both portraits are in the collections of the McCord Museum of Art of McGill University in Montreal. Raymond Douville, "Jean-Baptiste Hertel de Rouville," *DCB* 2:54; "Fonds des Ordonnances des Intendants," 1:27–28, NAC.

94. Williams, *Redeemed Captive,* 87.

95. Ibid.

96. Notably, John Adams used the term, describing an incident where a "fine Gentleman" attempted to bribe three women into having sex with him as "debauching young girls." Quoted in Sharon Block, *Rape and Sexual Power in Early America* (Chapel Hill: University of North Carolina Press, 2006), 24. On other examples of the use of *debauch* and related issues, such as its implications for seduction stories that exclude clear-cut cases of physical coercion, see Block, 32, 213.

97. In *Rape and Sexual Power in Early America,* Block makes the distinction between coerced sex acts (those "not necessarily defined as rape in early America that nevertheless contained some degree of extorted or forced sexual relations") and rape, defined by the author for the purposes of her book as "forced heterosexual intercourse." Block, *Rape and Sexual Power,* 2.

98. Axtell, *Invasion Within,* 287.

99. The fact of French Canada's underdeveloped population also contributed to the drive to create unions "with a minimum of impediments and delay." Allan Greer, *Peasant, Lord, and Merchant: Rural Society in Three Quebec Parishes, 1740–1840* (Toronto: University of Toronto Press, 1985), 50–51.

100. Scalberg, "Religious Life in New France," 236.

101. *NEC* 1:423–24. Though the publication of banns in New France was used primarily as protection against consanguinity, it is important to note that the period of time it took to publish all three of the banns was also meant to discourage polygamy, and to create time for pastoral instruction on the responsibilities of the sacrament. Scalberg, "Religious Life in New France," 237–38.

102. Williams, *Redeemed Captive*, 83; Haefeli and Sweeney, *Captors and Captives*, 172.

103. James S. Pritchard, "Jacques Levasseur de Néré," *DCB* 2:432; *NEC* 1:423–24.

104. "Fonds des Ordonnances," 1:27–28, 40–41, NAC.

105. Scalberg, "Religious Life in New France," 240–41.

106. Ibid.

107. Jetté, *Dictionnaire généalogique*, 86. The problem of premarital pregnancies persisted in towns with transient populations, including those that had a significant military presence. For example, in his study of Sorel, a village on the outskirts of Montreal, Allan Greer demonstrates that premarital pregnancies peaked with Sorel's growing importance as a river community with ties to the interior fur trade. Its transient male population and garrisoned soldiers likely caused the spike. Greer, *Peasant, Lord, and Merchant*, 57–60. For *habitant* immorality as one of the greatest social problems to plague New France, see Jaenen, *The Role of the Church in New France*, 154–55.

108. Axtell, *Invasion Within*, 278.

109. Block, *Rape and Sexual Power*, 7.

110. The Cross of Saint-Louis was the highest recognition conferred for service to the French Crown; its recipients were officers whose "core values . . . were defined by honor and service to the king" and, by extension, the honor of the colony. Haefeli and Sweeney, *Captors and Captives*, 232, 237.

111. John Williams complained bitterly that French Catholic "adversaries did what they could to seduce our young ones to Popery." Williams, *Redeemed Captive*, 83.

112. This baby, Marie-Françoise, did not live long, nor did her brother, who was born two years later. Rachel perhaps had had other pregnancies, but if she did, the children did not live long enough to be presented for baptism, which in New France usually happened within a month of birth. Jetté, *Dictionnaire généalogique*, 86.

113. *NEC* 1:424; *GDMNH* 664.

114. For a comprehensive discussion of networks of female captives, see Barbara Austen, "Captured . . . Never Came Back," passim.

115. Jules Bazin, "Pierre Le Ber," *DCB* 2:377–78; Foster, *Captor's Narrative*, 24–25.

116. "Fonds des Ordonnances," 1:27–28. Card money was a rather informal form of currency devised by the military in Canada to meet its payroll before the arrival of a printing press in the colony. Playing cards were simply stamped with some official symbol and marked with the word *bon*.

A full card was worth four *livres;* half and quarter cards were worth forty and fifteen sous, respectively. *NEC* 1:408–9; Charlevoix, *Journal of a Voyage to North-America,* 1:147.

117. Though the Adamses had to leave their presumably sickly infant son behind in Quebec, the couple otherwise benefited enormously by James's willingness to do almost anything to escape New France, regardless of the potential penalty. Foster, *Captor's Narrative,* 137. For Catherine Adams, James's wife, marriage bound her to her spouse's fate, whose crimes in New France had the unlikely outcome of benefiting both of them. Vaudreuil could have sentenced James to death, but instead the governor used the situation to his advantage, offering to return them and their families in exchange for French prisoners in Boston. Vaudreuil à Dudley, Feb. 6, 1706. Quoted in *NEC* 1:400.

118. Jules Bazin, "Jean Berger," *DCB* 2:377.

119. Roger Magnuson asserts that the lack of a printing press was not due to a disregard for literacy in the colony, but because French printers and booksellers jealously guarded this important transatlantic trade. Jesuits and Sulpicians petitioned France for a press for the better part of a century, but the request was never granted. Magnuson, *Education in New France,* 107–8.

120. Bazin, "Berger," *DCB* 2:377.

121. Colonial Archives MG1-Série G3, F-644, NAC; Bazin, "Berger," *DCB* 2:378.

122. John Stoddard, "Stoddard's Journal," *NEHGR* 5 (Jan. 1851), 30.

123. The story of Christine's relationship with her mother and other captives is recounted in Alice Nash's essay "Two Stories of New England Captives: Grizel and Christine Otis of Dover, New Hampshire," passim.

124. Jean Berger transacted a series of leases for properties in Plaisance between Aug. 6, 1710, and May 18, 1713—in essence until the Treaty of Utrecht ceded the French fishing territories to Great Britain. "Dépôt des papiers publics des colonies; notariat," NAC 8:176.

125. Ibid.

126. For a description of housing and environment in French Plaisance, see Moogk, *Building a House in New France,* 72–73.

127. R. Cole Harris, *Historical Atlas of Canada,* vol. 1 (Toronto: University of Toronto Press, 1993), plate 25.

128. *GDMNH* 664; *NEC* 1:424–25.

129. MS to ES, July 17, 1727, Mary Storer Letters, MHS, Boston.

130. *NEC* 1:129, 2:92.

131. *NEC* 2:92.

132. For common pejoratives New England Protestants commonly used to describe Catholics, see Hanson, *Necessary Virtue*, 4, and Cogliano, *No King, No Popery*, 9, 15.

133. Mary Beth Norton, *Founding Mothers and Fathers: Gendered Power and the Forming of American Society* (New York: Knopf, 1996), 107, 128.

134. The Reverend John was a chaplain with Samuel Vetch's 1711 failed invasion of Quebec. His son Stephen, who had briefly accepted Catholicism while in captivity, was chaplain for a regiment during the first assault on the fortress of Louisbourg. Demos, *Unredeemed Captive*, 216.

Chapter 4. The Ways of Christian Industry

1. Sebastien Rale to his nephew, Oct. 15, 1722, *JR* 67:97.

2. The Governor's Speech, May 25, 1709, *DHSM* 9:296–97.

3. Samuel Shute "to the jesuit at Norigwalk," Feb. 21, 1718, *DHSM* 9:379–80.

4. Clark, *Eastern Frontier*, 111.

5. Ibid., 121.

6. Baker and Reid, "Amerindian Power in the Early Modern Northeast," 77–106.

7. Joseph Baxter, "Journal of the Reverend Joseph Baxter," *NEHGR* 21:52–53, 55, 57, 58.

8. The Medfield congregation kept the minister's salary at the same level for nearly two decades. Sibley and Shipton, *Sibley's Harvard Graduates*, 4:145.

9. These compensational assurances were only as attractive as the ability of the Massachusetts government and local militias to protect the region for settlement. Peter N. Carroll, *Puritanism and the Wilderness: The Intellectual Significance of the New England Frontier, 1629–1700* (New York: Columbia University Press, 1969), 119–20; Silverman, *Life and Times of Cotton Mather*, 50.

10. Samuel Shute to Philippe Rigaud de Vaudreuil, March 14, 1721, *Coll MeHS*, ser. 2, 1:379.

11. For an extensive treatment of the tradition of anti-Jesuit rhetoric in early modern English literature, see Garry Wills, *Witches and Jesuits: Shakespeare's "Macbeth"* (New York: Oxford University Press, 1995).

12. Cotton Mather, *A Letter to Ungospelized Plantations* (Boston, 1702), 10.

13. Hugh Adams, the frontier minister and doctor who treated Rale's various ailments, later became pastor of the congregation at Durham, New Hampshire. Calvert, *Black Robe on the Kennebec,* 172; Kidd, *Protestant Interest,* 108.

14. Hall, *Worlds of Wonder,* 240.

15. Quoted in David Murray, "Spreading the Word: Missionaries, Conversion and Circulation in the Northeast," in Griffiths and Cervantes, *Spiritual Encounters,* 45.

16. The concept of "heart religion" transcended boundaries of the major early modern Christian faiths. Teresa of Avila, for example, one of the great Catholic mystics of the sixteenth century, was, like many later Reformed Protestants, drawn to the concept through reading Augustine's *Confessions.* She wrote in her own spiritual memoir, *The Interior Castle,* that Augustine's story had coaxed her conversion from her so-called frivolous and dissipated life. Teresa declared, "When I reached his conversion, the voice which he heard in the garden, the Lord, I believe, made it ring in my ears, so keenly was my heart touched." Hambrick-Stowe, *Practice of Piety,* 27.

17. Hsia, *World of Catholic Renewal,* 32–33.

18. Most Jesuits spent at least several years refining their communication and teaching skills in the order's secondary schools and universities before applying them to the mission field. Axtell, *Invasion Within,* 75 n. 344.

19. Henry O. Thayer, "Ministry of the Kennebec, Period of the Indian Wars," *Coll MeHS* ser. 2, 9:266–67; Samuel Sewall, "A Memorial Related to the Kennebec Indians, 1717," *Coll MeHS* ser. 3, 1:365.

20. Cogliano, *No King, No Popery,* 9.

21. Axtell, *Invasion Within,* 275.

22. New France's church officials complained frequently that the *habitants* and, more frequently, the *coureurs de bois,* subverted the missionary work of both religious men and women. But the need to bring revenue into the colony meant that these efforts were often subverted by Canada's own government. Moore, *Indian and Jesuit,* 193; Axtell, *Invasion Within,* 64–67; Moogk, *La Nouvelle France,* 38–40.

23. As late as 1730, only one in four Canadian parishes had a resident curé, which hampered the clergymen's efforts to support moral reform. Magnuson, *Education in New France,* 96–97.

24. Jean-Baptiste de Saint-Vallier, *État présent de l'église et de la colonie française de la Nouvelle-France* (Paris: Robert Pepie, 1748; repr., Quebec: Côté & Cie, 1856), 6. Author's translation.

25. Quoted in James Phinney Baxter, *Pioneers of New France in New England* (Albany, NY: J. Munsell's Sons, 1894), 96.

26. The Massachusetts government hoped that a "civilizing program," as promoted by Protestant ministers, would greatly reduce the Wabanakis' need for land and succeed in luring them away from the Jesuits. As the rest of this chapter will discuss, the reverse almost happened, but with a few nuances that still permitted for the growth of English settlement. Axtell, *Invasion Within*, 249.

27. Sebastien Rale to Pierre Joseph de la Chasse, Aug. 23, 1712. Baxter, *Pioneers of New France in New England*, 256.

28. [Joseph Baxter], "Journal of the Rev. Joseph Baxter of Medfield, Missionary to the Eastern Indians, 1717," *NEGHR* 21 (Jan. 1867): 50.

29. For detailed maps of the dispersal of Wabanaki peoples in the seventeenth century, see Nash, "The Abiding Frontier," 56, 150.

30. Daniel K. Richter, *Facing East from Indian Country: A Native History of Early America* (Cambridge: Harvard University Press, 2001), 95.

31. This translation was one of the few produced for Protestant missionary work available in any Indian dialect. This choice of text shows the sheer volume of "catch-up" work that Protestant ministers would have needed to do before they could openly challenge the Jesuits' Christian hegemony. Axtell, *Invasion Within*, 251.

32. See Baker and Reid, "Amerindian Power in the Early Modern Northeast," passim; Axtell, *Invasion Within*, 253–54.

33. For detailed description and assessment of this complicated period in Wabanaki/Euro-American politics, see Morrison, *Embattled Northeast*.

34. New England critics, however, were careful to distinguish between unchristian people and unchristian acts. In what was perhaps an effort to legitimate the use of missionary techniques, William Dummer wrote to Philippe Rigaud de Vaudreuil that Jesuits, especially Rale, should strive to "[preach] Peace, Love, and Friendship Agreeable to the Doctrines of the Christian Religion." Lt. Govr. Dummer to Govr. Vaudreuil, Jan. 19, 1724, *Coll MeHS* ser. 2, 1:386.

35. General Court, Sept. 8, 1640, *MPCR* 1:74.

36. *GDMNH* 120.

37. William S. Southgate, "History of Scarborough from 1633 to 1783," *Coll MeHS* ser. 3, 1:154.

38. *DHSM* 4:169.

39. *DHSM* 4:151; James Finney Baxter, "The Abenakis and Their Ethnic Relations," *Coll MeHS* ser. 2, 3:202.

40. Bourne, *History of Wells and Kennebunk,* 66.

41. Quoted in John Reid, *Maine, Charles II and Massachusetts: Governmental Relationships in Early Northern New England* (Portland: Maine Historical Society, 1977), 53. Reid shows that Jordan was far from unique in his sentiments: many of Maine's Anglicans were incensed by Massachusetts's religious incursions in the province and sought to undermine them.

42. Quoted in Bourne, *History of Wells and Kennebunk,* 104.

43. Southgate, "History of Scarborough," *Coll MeHS* ser. 2, 3:22.

44. *GDMNH* 624; *Coll MeHS* ser. 1, 1:58, 171.

45. Robert Jordan's son, Dominicus, "the Indian Killer," successfully thwarted an assault on his garrison in King William's War, only to be killed himself in Queen Anne's. His wife and six children were taken captive. *GDMNH* 389.

46. This was Laurence Vanderbosk, likely a Walloon Huguenot. According to Mather, he fled Massachusetts and, when last heard from, was plying his trade in Cape May. Whitmore, *Andros Tracts,* 1:37.

47. *GDMNH* 94; George Folsom, *History of Saco and Biddeford* (Saco, ME: Alex G. Putnam, 1830), 168. An early biographer claimed Blackman "loved wealth as well as religion, and the praise of donors more than the praise of saints." Williamson, "Sketches of Early Maine Ministers," *Coll MeHS* ser. 2, 4:70.

48. Mary Beth Norton terms Blackman's initiative a "tragedy of errors." Having seized the Indians, Norton notes, "Maine's military and political leaders did not know what to do with them," and simply continued to detain them. Their retention led to more frontier raids by the Wabanakis. Norton, *In the Devil's Snare,* 95.

49. The captives were later released by Sir Edmund Andros, an act that reinforced New England suspicions that he was a crypto-papist and ally of the French. "Thomas Stevens's Deposition," Sept. 4, 1688, *DHSM* 6:421; Drake, *Border Wars of New England,* 11; Thomas Hutchinson, *The History of the Colony and Province of Massachusetts-Bay,* ed. Lawrence Shaw Mayo (Cambridge: Harvard University Press, 1936), 1:364–65.

50. Norton, *In the Devil's Snare,* 130.

51. Bourne, *History of Wells and Kennebunk,* 96.

52. Ibid., 99.

53. Joseph Emerson was the great-grandfather of Ralph Waldo Emerson. Well respected for his spiritual leadership, his departure to Massachusetts was felt keenly by his Maine flock. *GDMNH* 220.

54. Bourne, *History of Wells and Kennebunk,* 167.

55. Ibid., 170.

56. Martyn died of smallpox. *GDMNH* 464.

57. On "cursed" and "blessed" places and spaces, see Hall, *Worlds of Wonder,* 178; Gildrie, *The Profane, The Civil, and the Godly,* 173; Jon Butler, *Awash in a Sea of Faith: Christianizing the American People* (Cambridge: Harvard University Press, 1990), 39–41, 44–45, 54, 56–57, 63–65.

58. There is some confusion over the Dummer family's members and their fates during the wars of empire. Some sources describe Dummer's wife, Lydia, as a daughter of Edward Rishworth and sister of Mary Plaisted (discussed at length in chap. 2 of this book). Sybil Noyes et al. claim that Lydia Dummer was born into the Alcock family of York. She and her young son were taken captive after her husband was killed; both died on the trek to Quebec. Bourne, *History of Wells and Kennebunk,* 211; *GDMNH* 210–11.

59. Mather, *Magnalia Christi Americana,* 7:77.

60. Quoted in Banks, *History of York,* 1:292.

61. Louise Breen suggests Andros's success in bargaining with Maine's Indians and other groups led to the accusations of illicit dealings that relied on religious disloyalty. Among the frequently leveled charges were that Andros "loved" the Indians more than the English, and that his drinking with Native American women and providing the Indian allies with ammunition was something far more sinister than an attempt to woo them into an English alliance. Breen, *Transgressing the Bounds,* 217–18.

62. Increase Mather, "True Reformed Religion" (1690), in Whitmore, *Andros Tracts,* 2:218.

63. Swarton, "Narrative of Hannah Swarton," 150.

64. Increase Mather, "Further Queries upon the Present State of New England Affaires" (1690), in Whitmore, *Andros Tracts,* 1:202.

65. Bellomont to the Board of Trade, July 9, 1700, *DHSM* 10:69. The idea was still being considered as late as 1746. Governor Shirley to the Duke of Newcastle, Nov. 21, 1746, *DHSM* 11:347. In contrast to the sexual nature of the term *debauch* described in the previous chapter, the contents of Bellomont make it clear that the term had religious connotations.

66. Charles Clark notes that all were under thirty. The youngest, Samuel Moody, was only twenty-two when he came to the Maine frontier. Clark, *Eastern Frontier,* 82.

67. Joseph Dudley to the Board of Trade, March 1, 1708/9, *DHSM* 9:264.

68. Clark, *Eastern Frontier,* 83.

69. Noyes et al. describe Moody as "a frontier parson and fighting chaplain." *GDMNH* 487.

70. Clark, *Eastern Frontier*, 85.

71. *GDMNH* 487.

72. Samuel Moody started his career as a minister but, "prompted by duty some times as chaplain, or a lasting memory of the refugees he had seen as from childhood," decided to plow his efforts into military work. *GDMNH* 487.

73. Joseph Dudley to Samuel Moody, Nov. 12, 1712, *DHSM* 9:332–33.

74. Sebastien Rale to Samuel Moody, Nov. 18, 1712, *DHSM* 9:334.

75. Jacques Bigot to unidentified Jesuit, Oct. 26, 1699, *JR* 65:95, 97.

76. Ibid.

77. Vincent Bigot to George Turfrey, Sept. 9, 1700, MSA, Boston, 51:99–100.

78. William Stoughton to Vincent Bigot, April 10, 1701, *DHSM* 10:109–10.

79. Sebastien Rale to Pierre Joseph de la Chasse, Aug. 23, 1712. Quoted in Baxter, *Pioneers of New France in New England,* 256.

80. Jesuit mission work was laden with militaristic language: priests like Paul Le Jeune, the first superior of the Canada missions, and his colleagues spoke of themselves as "brave soldiers" who "built batteries" to "destroy the empires of Satan." Such usage was not new to the context of the Atlantic World; much of it was coined by Ignatius of Loyola himself and was applied to efforts to conquer Protestantism. Axtell, *Invasion Within,* 91.

81. Southgate, "History of Scarborough," *Coll MeHS* ser. 1, 3:116.

82. *DCB* 3:24.

83. Ibid., 2:544.

84. Ibid., 3:359.

85. Sibley and Shipton, *Sibley's Harvard Graduates,* 4:144.

86. Ibid., 4:148.

87. [Pejepscot proprietors] to Joseph Baxter, 1717, Doggett Family Papers, MeHS, Portland.

88. Ibid.

89. Ibid.

90. Ibid.

91. *DHSM* 23:94.

92. *DCB* 2:542.

93. Axtell, *Invasion Within,* 252–53.

94. Sewall was in Maine for the Arrowsic Conference, an attempt to create a lasting peace between the Wabanakis and the English. It was at this conference that Baxter was introduced as an alternative Christian leader. Ibid., 252.

95. Calvert, *Black Robe on the Kennebec*, 172–73.

96. Baxter, *Pioneers of New France*, 67; Calvert, *Black Robe on the Kennebec*, 172–73.

97. *DCB* 1:649.

98. [Baxter], "Journal of the Reverend Joseph Baxter," 53.

99. Ibid., 52.

100. C. Baker, *True Stories of the New England Captives*, 339.

101. Morrison, *Embattled Northeast*, 184.

102. Baxter, *Pioneers of New France*, 96.

103. Axtell, *Invasion Within*, 252–53.

104. [Baxter], "Journal of the Reverend Joseph Baxter," 54.

105. Ibid., 18.

106. Sibley and Shipton, *Sibley's Harvard Graduates*, 4:145.

107. Samuel Shute to Philippe Rigaud de Vaudreuil, 1722; reprinted in Baxter, *Pioneers of New France*, 127.

108. "Samuel Shute," *ANB* 19:909.

109. Francis Parkman, *Half-Century of Conflict* (New York: Library of America, 1983), 494; *New-England Courant*, Feb. 12, 1721/22; Fannie Hardy Eckstorm, "The Attack on Norridgewock, 1724," *New England Quarterly* 7 (Sept. 1934): 563.

110. Parkman, *Half-Century of Conflict*, 494–95; Kidd, *Protestant Interest*, 102.

111. Parkman, *Half-Century of Conflict*, 498.

112. *GDMNH* 311, 499.

113. Parkman, *Half-Century of Conflict*, 500; Kidd, *Protestant Interest*, 108; Axtell, *Invasion Within*, 253.

114. Francis Parkman offers detailed accounts of these conflicting stories in *Half-Century of Conflict*, 498–501.

115. Edward Bourne and Charles Banks, the nineteenth-century chroniclers of Wells and York respectively, assume that Jesuits incited the Wabanakis to attack English settlements, even against the latter's wishes. Such assertions seem to reinforce older views that Jesuits relied on coercive, if not supernatural, means to force their neophytes to do their bidding.

116. Quoted in *NEC* 2:134–35.

117. Memorial of a Conference at St. Georges River (1727), *DHSM* 23:214.

118. Ibid.

119. Ibid., 215.

120. Ibid., 216.

121. Quoted in *DCB* 3:24.

122. Letter from Indians to Gov. Burnet, Nov. 2, 1728, *DHSM* 23:232–33.

123. Among the more critical studies are Jennings, *The Invasion of America*, and Delâge, *Bitter Feast*.

124. For a detailed description of the literary history of friars, see Anne Barbeau Gardiner, "Judas-friars of the Popish Plot: The Catholic Perspective on Dryden's 'The Spanish Friar,'" *Clio* 32:2 (Winter 2003): 177. For a New England interpretation of the dangers of peripatetic preachers, see Cotton Mather, "A Letter, containing a Remarkable History of an Imposter." The author tells the story of one Samuel May, a high Anglican who attempts to make inroads while seemingly adapting himself to the New England Way. Mather describes May "not supposed for to be a *Minister*, but rather a *Mendicant*." Mather, *Magnalia Christi Americana*, 7:36.

125. Baxter, *Pioneers of New France*, 144.

126. Data compiled by the author using Thwaites, ed., *The Jesuit Relations and Allied Documents*.

Chapter 5. *Protestant Ornaments and Popish Relics*

1. Baker and Reid, "Amerindian Power in the Early Modern Northeast," 77.

2. Clark, *Eastern Frontier*, 262.

3. Mather, *Decennium Luctuosum*, 215. Quoted in Little, *Abraham in Arms*, 131.

4. John Gyles, "Memoirs of Odd Adventures, Strange Deliverances, &c," in Vaughan and Clark, *Puritans among the Indians*, 97.

5. Ibid., 99.

6. Gyles told a prospective Indian convert to Protestantism that "ye french have Compeld People so far as to burn em at ye Stake, to make them Pray as they Do, which is not according to Gods word, etc." Gyles might have drawn this conclusion because he had heard stories derived from, or possibly even had access to a copy of, Foxe's *Actes and Monuments*. This be-

lief in the cruel treatment of Protestants at the hands of Catholics, however, was reinforced by the mode of death of his brother, James, who had been burned at the stake at a Penobscot fort as punishment for attempting to run away. *DHSM* 10:384.

7. Garry Wills explores these themes in seventeenth-century English literature in *Witches and Jesuits: Shakespeare's Macbeth,* passim.

8. For the persistence of Catholic practice and supernatural components in Protestant worship, see Scribner, "The Reformation, Popular Magic, and the 'Disenchantment of the World,'" 475–94; Hall, *Worlds of Wonder,* 156–61.

9. Gyles's father was mortally wounded but had time enough with his sons to bestow a blessing on them and advise them on surviving their upcoming ordeal. He was then led away and executed. Gyles, "Memoirs of Odd Adventures," in Vaughan and Clark, *Puritans among the Indians,* 97, 99–100; *NEC* 1:169–70.

10. Gyles, "Memoirs of Odd Adventures," 97.

11. The priest was Louis-Pierre Thury, a Sulpician and close associate of the Baron de Saint-Castin. Thury was known for the particular enthusiasm with which he supported violent incursions against the English settlements. *DCB* 2:272.

12. The insidious practices of professed Catholics and the literary fables and tropes they inspired in early modern England are the subject of Frances E. Dolan, *Whores of Babylon: Catholicism, Gender, and Seventeenth-Century Print Culture* (Ithaca: Cornell University Press, 1999), passim; Wills, *Witches and Jesuits,* passim.

13. Quoted in Wills, *Witches and Jesuits,* 97.

14. Gyles wrote skeptically of a sacramental to protect crops from birds, the failure of which was blamed by the priest performing the ritual on the sins of the local people. Gyles, "Memoirs of Odd Adventures," 127–28. On the other hand, he met French Catholics, laypeople and clergy alike, who treated him with gentleness and courtesy. He became devoted to these captors, so much so that he gave up an opportunity to return to New England in order to protect their property from a party of English coastal raiders. For a comprehensive analysis of Gyles's "odd adventures," see chap. 4 of Foster, *Captor's Narrative,* passim. Gyles's adventures brought him into the company of virtually every Catholic borderland character that existed on early Maine's fringes. He lived with the priest (most likely Thury) who attempted to buy him, with Christian Maliseets, and lastly, with a French *habitant* couple, Marguerite Guyon and her husband, Louis Damours

de Chauffours, who purchased him shortly before Acadia was attacked by Protestant English and colonial forces in 1711. Foster, *Captor's Narrative*, 114–15, 123.

15. Clark, *Eastern Frontier*, 127.

16. "Letter of Capt. John Gyles to Lt. Gov. Dummer," April 25, 1727, *DHSM* 10:382–84.

17. Ibid., 10:384.

18. See Little, *Abraham in Arms*, 172.

19. In *The Practice of Piety*, Charles Hambrick-Stowe identifies the numerous texts that were considered for both Protestant and Catholic audiences. *Practice of Piety*, 35. Because of this broad, interfaith appeal, however, such "crossover" texts were sometimes the source of controversy in Puritan New England. Contemporary confirmation comes from Thomas Hutchinson, who wrote, "There had been a press for printing at Cambridge for near twenty years. The court appointed two persons in October 1662 licensers of the press, and prohibited the publishing of any books or papers which should not be supervised by them, and in 1668 the supervisors having allowed the printing 'Thomas à Kempis de imitatione Christi,' the court interposed, 'it being wrote by a popish minister, and containing some things less safe to be infused among the people, and therefore they commanded to the licensers a more full revisal, and ordered the press to stop in the meantime." Hutchinson, *History of the Colony and Province of Massachusetts-Bay*, 3:38.

20. Ibid., 1:257.

21. Hambrick-Stowe, *Practice of Piety*, 35.

22. John W. O'Malley, *The First Jesuits* (Cambridge: Harvard University Press, 1993), 259–60, 264–66.

23. The roots of Puritan disdain for holidays was based on the idea that all time belonged to God and was therefore impossible to differentiate from Catholic "ordinary time." It was not to be relegated to certain days or blocks of time, as it appeared to be according to the Catholic concept of the liturgical year. See James P. Walsh, "Holy Time and Sacred Space in Puritan New England," *American Quarterly* 23:1 (Spring 1980): 79.

24. These reforms were aimed at improving "the morals of the clergy and the laity," as noted by Richard Gildrie. "An important element of this reform was a more orderly Sunday observance, extended back ideally to Saturday evening, and suppression of wrestling, ale-drinking, dancing, and gambling in the churchyards on Sunday afternoons." Gildrie, *The Profane, the Civil, and the Godly*, 115.

25. *Catechism of the Council of Trent for Parish Priests, Issued by Order of Pope Pius V,* trans. Theodore Alois Buckley (London: G. Routledge, 1852), 248.

26. "George Town on Arrowsic Island, August 9 1717: A Conference of His Excellency the Governor, With the Sachems and Chief Men of the Eastern Indians," *Coll MeHS* ser. 1, 3:384.

27. Letter of Capt. John Gyles to Lt. Gov. Dummer, April 25, 1727, *DHSM* 10:383–84.

28. "Samuel Shute "to the jesuit at Norigwalk," Feb. 21, 1718, *DHSM* 9:376.

29. Hutchinson, *History of the Colony and Province of Massachusetts-Bay,* 2:241.

30. Jaenen, *Role of the Church in New France,* 143; Scalberg, "Religious Life in New France," 47.

31. *MCPR* 4:liv–lv.

32. Virginia DeJohn Anderson, *Creatures of Empire: How Domestic Animals Transformed Early America* (New York: Oxford University Press, 2004), 50.

33. See Hambrick-Stowe, *Practice of Piety,* 49; Walsh, "Holy Time and Sacred Space," 80–83.

34. Cheryl Wells, *Civil War Time: Temporality and Identity in America, 1861–1865* (Athens: University of Georgia Press, 2005), 1–3.

35. For seasonal devotional travels of a Pequawket woman, Molly Ocket, see Ulrich, *The Age of Homespun,* 258.

36. *YD* 2:Fol. 13.

37. Maine Protestant households continued to mark Christmas with ambivalence, if at all, until well into the nineteenth century. For a general description of Christmas in early New England, see Stephen Nissenbaum, *The Battle for Christmas* (New York: Knopf, 1996), 3, 27–28.

38. Joseph Dudley to the Board of Trade, Nov. 15, 1703, *DHSM* 9:153.

39. Walton saw in their absence the opportunity to cover the region with seven hundred men "from casco bay fort to Saint Croix." Shadrach Walton to Joseph Dudley, Nov. 20, 1703, *DHSM* 9:180.

40. "Journal of the Reverend Joseph Baxter," *NEHGR* 21:52.

41. These patterns continued well into the nineteenth, and even the twentieth, centuries. Laurel Thatcher Ulrich discusses these patterns as they affected her and her descendants in *Age of Homespun,* 258.

42. Philippe Rigaud de Vaudreuil to Sebastien Rale, Sept. 25, 1721, *DHSM* 23:109.

43. The reporter was John Gyles. John Gyles to the Government of Massachusetts-Bay, Nov. 15, 1741, Massachusetts Archives 31:334, MSA.

44. The Jesuits supported reverence for Marian power when they declared that "New France, with its King, acknowledged the Blessed Virgin as the Lady and Protectress of his Crown and all his Estates." William B. Hart, "The Cult of the Virgin Mary in Seventeenth Century New France," in Griffiths and Cervantes, *Spiritual Encounters,* 71.

45. For Puritans and their relationship with the Virgin Mary, in all its complexity, see Ursula Brumm, "The Virgin Mary among American Puritans: A Difficult Relation," *Amerikastudien* 47:4 (2002): 449–68, and Hart, "The Cult of Virgin Mary in Seventeenth Century New France," both passim. For the complicated English response to the Virgin Mary, and by extension, the implied power of women, see Dolan, *Whores of Babylon,* 111–12, 116–18.

46. These events were Sir William Phips's 1690 and Samuel Vetch's 1711 campaigns. Moogk, *La Nouvelle France,* 239.

47. Notes to audio recording *Victoires et Réjouissances à Québec (1690–1758),* L'Ensemble Nouvelle-France, Oratorio, ORCD-1450.

48. Moogk, *La Nouvelle France,* 71.

49. Quoted in Scalberg, "Religious Life in New France," 64. Kalm's narrative of his travels also includes on the most comprehensive descriptions of the public celebration of Marian festivals in Canada. The Feast of the Ascension of the Blessed Virgin Mary, which he observed in 1748, served double duty in celebrating Philippe Rigaud de Vaudreuil's own ascension to the governorship of Canada. Peter Kalm, *Travels into North America,* trans. John Reinhold Forster (Barre, MA: Imprint Society, 1972), 439.

50. Mather, *Decennium Luctuosum,* 127–28.

51. *JR* 67:85.

52. Charlevoix, *Journal of a Voyage to North-America,* 2:209. The owner of the original volume of the first English translation of this work wrote "damn'd stuff" next to this anecdote in the book's margin, which transferred to this facsimile version.

53. For the complete story of this New Hampshire captive, see Nash, "Two Stories of New England Captives." The public role for women in Marian devotional practices is described at length in Susan E. Dinan's "Spheres of Female Religious Expression in Early Modern France," in Susan E. Dinan and Debra Meyers, eds., *Women and Religion in Old and New Worlds* (New York: Routledge, 2001). It is also the subject of chap. 3 of Elizabeth Rapley, *The Dévotes: Women and Church in Seventeenth-Century France* (Montreal: McGill-Queens University Press, 1990).

54. Hannah Swarton, "Narrative of Hannah Swarton," 154.

55. *JR* 67:85.

56. An active promoter of Protestant interests in the area, Samuel was also related to several Canadian *dévotes*—one-time captive women who had become enthusiastic participants in the Canadian Catholic Church. Samuel's wife, Olive Plaisted, was the daughter of Mary and James Plaisted and half-sister of Mary (Soeur Marie-des-Ange) and Esther (Madame Lestage) Sayward. His niece, Mary Scammon, who was one of the few captives taken from Maine during Dummer's War, was a student in the Ursuline convent at Trois-Rivières until her illustrious marriage to Louis-Joseph Godefroi, Sieur de Tonnancoeur, in 1740. *NEC* 2:149. Also see chap. 3 of Foster, *Captor's Narrative.*

57. George Town on Arrowsic Island, Aug, 9, 1717, *Coll MeHS* ser. 1, 3:363–64.

58. Ibid., 368.

59. Samuel Shute "to the jesuit at Norigwalk," Feb. 21, 1718, *DHSM* 9:378.

60. Nicholas M. Beasley, "Wars of Religion in the Circum-Caribbean: English Iconoclasm in Spanish America, 1570–1702," in Margaret Cormack, ed., *Saints and Their Cults in the Atlantic World* (Columbia: University of South Carolina Press, 2007), 157.

61. Ibid., 157.

62. As told in Carol Berkin, *First Generations: Women in Colonial America* (New York: Hill & Wang, 1997), 3.

63. David Hall identifies a range of tropes in these wonder stories, some of which predate Christianity altogether. Others have pre-Reformation roots, and appear in early Christian works, including hagiographies. Hall, *Worlds of Wonder,* 74, 111.

64. The incident is recounted by Mary Beth Norton in *Devil's Snare,* 180.

65. One scholar notes that "while raging theological and ecclesiological conflicts divided Christians, religious experience in the practice of devotional life was remarkably similar." Hambrick-Stowe, *Practice of Piety,* 36.

66. Ibid., 28–29, 36.

67. Ibid., 29.

68. Hannah Swarton got her Bible and "other good books" from her fellow captives. John Williams received his from a French source, a "Monsieur de Beauville . . . who was a good friend to me . . . he lent me an English Bible, and when he went to France gave it to me." Swarton, "Narrative of Hannah Swarton," 155; Williams, *Redeemed Captive,* 44.

69. Given connections to the network of Continental Jesuit colleges that had English students, such Bibles were probably fairly simple for missionaries to request from European sources, and the Bible in English had been available from the late sixteenth century. Hsia, *The World of Catholic Renewal*, 82.

70. Shoemaker, *A Strange Likeness*, 24–25, 30.

71. One of the earliest examples of transculturated sacred space involves the Virgin of Guadaloupe, who allegedly appeared to an Indian at a site considered holy to Mexico's Aztec people. The story of this Virgin was widely disseminated throughout the Atlantic World; French Jesuits in the New World were likely aware of the site's transformation into one of the most revered in New World Christendom. See Kenneth Mills, "Diego de Ocaña's Hagiography of New and Renewed Devotion in Colonial Peru," in Greer and Bilinkoff, eds., *Colonial Saints*, 51–71.

72. Sebastien Rale to his nephew, Oct. 15, 1722, *JR* 67:87.

73. Beasley, "Wars of Religion in the Circum-Caribbean," 157.

74. Father Rallé's Address for the Indians, 1722, *Coll MeHS* ser. 2, 1:382.

75. Edward Muir, *Ritual in Early Modern Europe* (New York: Cambridge University Press, 1997), 186.

76. Hall, *Worlds of Wonder*, 117.

77. Governor Lincoln Papers, *Coll MeHS* ser. 2, 2:440–41; also described in Axtell, *Invasion Within*, 250.

78. *Boston News-Letter*, March 5–8, 1704/5.

79. Axtell, *Invasion Within*, 250.

80. Letter from the Indians to the Governor [of Massachusetts], 1720, *DHSM* 23:47.

81. Ibid., 23:89–92; Ekstorm, "The Attack on Norridgewock," 558.

82. Butler, *Awash in a Sea of Faith*, 13.

83. Thomas Coram to Lords Commissioners of Trade and Plantations, Jan. 28, 1729, *DHSM* 10:436–37.

84. This emulated the French habit of identifying one's neighborhood with the name of one's church—a pattern that persisted even when the churches themselves were no longer there, or were no longer Catholic. Choquette, *Frenchmen into Peasants*, 92.

85. Greer, *People of New France*, 36.

86. Considering the destroyed monastic institutions in the wake of the Henrician Reformation, Jon Butler observes that even destroyed build-

ings "could be made to proclaim Christianity," or celebrate the triumph of a specific Christian vision. Butler, *Awash in a Sea of Faith,* 13.

87. Baker and Reid, *New England Knight,* 90.

88. Though the chapel was a modest timber-framed and mud-walled structure, compared with the dressed stone walls that protected trade goods and food, its physical shape and bell tower called attention to its function as a church. For a comprehensive description of historical archaeology at Saint-Castin's fort, see Alaric Faulkner and Gretchen F. Faulkner, *The French at Pentagoët, 1635–1674* (Augusta: Maine Historic Preservation Commission, 1987); Baker and Reid, *New England Knight,* 90.

89. John Walter, "Popular Iconoclasm and the Politics of the Parish in Eastern England, 1640–1642," *Historical Journal* 47:2 (2004): 261.

90. Muir, *Ritual in Early Modern Europe,* 195.

91. Baker and Reid, *New England Knight,* 92.

92. Chaplin, *Subject Matter,* 58.

93. Quoted in Francis Bremer, "Endecott and the Red Cross: Puritan Iconoclasm in the New World," *Journal of American Studies* 24:1 (1990): 7.

94. Ibid., 6.

95. Ibid., 18.

96. Mary Caroline Crawford, *The Romance of Old New England Churches* (Boston: L. C. Page, 1903), 88–93.

97. Ibid., 93.

98. A detailed description of adaptive reuse of religious objects among the Hurons can be found in David Murray, "Spreading the Word in Northeast America," in Griffiths and Cervantes, *Spiritual Encounters,* 43–64.

99. Linda Breuer Gray recounts the origins of the Deerfield bell story and its applications to popular memory and history in "Narratives and Identities in the Saint Lawrence Valley," 157–62.

100. The bell has been on exhibit at the Maine State Museum since the middle of the nineteenth century. Collection of Norridgewock Artifacts, Maine State Museum, Augusta, ME.

Chapter 6. *"The Lord . . . Will Greatly Reward Me"*

1. Scribner, "The Reformation, Popular Magic, and the 'Disenchantment of the World,'" 483.

2. Butler, *Awash in a Sea of Faith,* 14.

3. Micheline D. Johnson, "Joseph Aubery," *DCB* 3:23–25.

4. Colin G. Calloway, ed., *Dawnland Encounters: Indians and Europeans in Northern New England* (Hanover, NH: University Press of New England, 1991), 4. A copy of this map is part of a permanent exhibit of the Maine State Museum, Augusta, Maine. In *Abraham in Arms*, Ann M. Little uses the example of a 1680 map of the same region, by an anonymous French source, to show the same visual distinctions made between representations of Catholic religious buildings (topped with crosses) and English ones (which are not, which the author sees as an indication of French disdain). Little, *Abraham in Arms*, 132.

5. *GDMNH* 438.

6. Ibid.

7. Laurel Thatcher Ulrich and, later, Barbara Austen have both demonstrated the connections among female New England captives in New France. Ulrich, *Good Wives*, 212–13; Austen, "Captured . . . Never Came Back," passim. However, to date no one has examined networks among both males and females according to region in New England, except Evan Haefeli and Kevin Sweeney, who limit their study, *Captors and Captives*, to the victims of the 1704 raid on Deerfield, Massachusetts.

8. Additional variations of the Littlefield surname can be found in New France, including "Lidfril," "Lightfil," "Litrefille," "Littlefiver," and "Litrephil." Gray, "Narratives," App. A-85.

9. *NEC* 1:403–10.

10. *GDMNH* 440.

11. The trade in captives between the French and Indian allies was so common and brisk that Governor Joseph Dudley accused his New France counterpart, Philippe Rigaud de Vaudreuil, of encouraging an "Algiers trade." See Haefeli, "Ransoming New England Captives in New France," 113.

12. *NEC* 1:404.

13. Vaughan and Richter note that only one in ten males taken from New England between 1675 and 1763 refused to return. "Crossing the Cultural Divide," 62. Ann Little notes that, though complications remained, males who converted to Catholicism were much more likely ultimately to receive their inheritance than were their female counterparts. *Abraham in Arms*, 155.

14. [John Stoddard], "Stoddard's Journal," 28–29. The hidden clothes had been supplied by Captain Thomas Baker, a member of the redeeming expedition and an ex-captive himself whose wife, also an ex-captive, would later testify that Aaron had willingly "turned papist."

15. *NEC* 1:404.

16. [John Stoddard], "Stoddard's Journal," 29.

17. The rule on naturalization was clearly not as absolute as it seems: Charles Trafton, Joseph Stover, William Hutchins, and Patience Hammons were all naturalized in 1710 and all returned to Maine after the Treaty of Utrecht. *NEC* 1:245, 247, 388–89, 392–93.

18. [John Stoddard], "Stoddard's Journal," 29.

19. *NEC* 1:405.

20. *NEC* 1:405, 409; see also Fournier, *De la Nouvelle-Angleterre à la Nouvelle-France,* 162.

21. *NEC* 1:405.

22. Ibid., 1:408. For the rules of *clausura* in theory and practice, see Susan Dinan, "Spheres of Female Religious Expression in Early Modern France," in Dinan and Meyers, *Women and Religions in Old and New Worlds,* 71–87.

23. *NEC* 1:408.

24. MS to ES, May 2, 1728.

25. Out of all female captives taken from New England between 1675 and 1763, 31.5 percent between the ages of two and six, and 53.7 percent of those between seven and fifteen, remained with their captors. For adult women (over fifteen), this number drops to 12 percent. Vaughan and Richter, "Crossing the Cultural Divide," 66.

26. Norton, *Redeemed Captive,* 23.

27. Little, *Abraham in Arms,* 154.

28. *NEC* 1:391–93. Ann Little notes the resemblance of this story to a celebrated early modern French case, described by Natalie Zemon Davis in her classic work *The Return of Martin Guerre* (Cambridge: Harvard University Press, 1983). Little, *Abraham in Arms,* 155–56.

29. *NEC* 1:408.

30. *GDMNH* 440.

31. Peter Moogk notes that Canada's *habitants* found potatoes unpalatable: turning to potatoes as sustenance was considered an act of desperation. Quoted in Moogk, *La Nouvelle France,* 229.

32. Norton, *Redeemed Captive,* 23–24.

33. *NEC* 1:406.

34. Ibid., 1:407.

35. The 1627 charter of the Hundred Associates stipulated that all settlers in the colony must be "natural-born, French and Catholic subjects." Protestants were denied the right to settle permanently in the colony or

acquire land. In 1676 the Sovereign Council of Quebec forbade Protestants to practice their religion together, and demanded that even temporary visitors "live like Catholics without scandal." Moogk, *La Nouvelle France,* 60; Bédard, "Les Protestants en Nouvelle-France," *Cahiers d'histoire* 31 (1978): 29–30.

36. *NEC* 1:408.

37. The "covenanted family" was a "web of mutual obligations" for which, as interpreted by John Cotton, "God hath made a covenant with parents and householders" which bound "wives and children, and servants, and kindred, and acquaintances, and all that are under our reach, either by way of subordination or coordination." Hence, a child who lived outside of that covenant was ineligible to partake in its protections and spiritual and worldly benefits—unless, of course, said child could be convinced to rejoin the covenant. See Fischer, *Albion's Seed,* 70.

38. For a general description of cloistered life in Old World and New (as compared with the freedoms of other types of post-Reformation women's religious communities), see Susan Dinan, "Spheres of Female Religious Expression," in Dinan and Meyers, *Women and Religion in Old and New Worlds,* 84. For specifics of French Canada, see Little, "Life of Mother Marie-Joseph de l'Enfant Jesus," and "Cloistered Bodies."

39. John Demos notes that the link between discipline and inheritance was indeed a component of many Plymouth colony wills. Demos, *A Little Commonwealth,* 103.

40. *NEC* 1:408.

41. "Dudley's list of unredeemed captives, 1710/11," Massachusetts Archives 71:765, MSA.

42. *MPCR* 4:144–45.

43. Ibid., 145.

44. Fournier, *De la Nouvelle-Angleterre à la Nouvelle-France,* 149. Trafton was at Esther Ingersoll's bedside with and appears to have been a spiritual protégé of Grizel Otis Robitaille, the Dover native, enthusiastic convert, and mother of Christine Baker. See also *NEC* 2:412.

45. *YD* 8:Fol. 85.

46. Sargent, *Maine Wills,* 571.

47. By 1714 Barsheba was living in Canada as Marie Wabert. Deborah Webber's will was probated on April 23, 1737. *NEC* 1:250; Sargent, *Maine Wills,* 545.

48. *GDMNH* 729.

49. Dominicus Jordan's will was probated on June 6, 1746. Sargent, *Maine Wills,* 640.

50. *NEC* 2:29.
51. *GDMNH* 191.
52. *GDMNH* 191; Sargent, *Maine Wills,* 434.
53. Sargent, *Maine Wills,* 525.
54. Ibid., 771.
55. Esther Wheelwright to Mary Snell Wheelwright, Nov. 26, 1747. Quoted in *NEC* 1:429–30.
56. *NEC* 1:430.
57. These items are still in use in the chapel of the Ursuline convent.
58. Barbara McLean Ward and Gerald W. R. Ward, "Sterling Memories: Family and Silver in Early New England," in *The Art of Family: Genealogical Artifacts in New England,* ed. D. Brenton Simons and Peter Benes (Boston: New England Historic Genealogical Society, 2002), 177.

Afterword

1. Edward Kavanaugh to William Allen, Jr., Nov. 14, 1832. Miscellaneous Manuscripts (422), MeHS.
2. Benedict Fenwick to William Allen, Dec. 13, 1832, MeHS.
3. Benedict Fenwick to William Allen, Dec. 8, 1832, MeHS.
4. *American Advocate* [Hallowell, ME], Sept. 9, 1833.
5. The evolution of anti-Catholic and anti-French rhetoric in eighteenth-century New England and the ameliorating effects of French support of the American Revolution are discussed at length in Cogliano, *No King, No Popery,* and in Hanson, *Necessary Virtue.*
6. Petition of William McClenachan, Aug. 20, 1740, *DHSM* 23:271.
7. "Order in Council to restrain Governor Belcher from Military Execution against Fredericksfort," Nov. 12, 1730, *DHSM* 11:66–67.
8. See Vaughan and Clark, "Crossing the Cultural Divide," 149 n. 2.
9. Axtell, *Invasion Within,* 150.
10. Thomas Kidd observes that "by 1727 the friends of the Protestant interest in New England had become thoroughly committed to a broad British Protestant identity, finding common cause with the Hanovarian monarchy and Whig Anglicanism." Kidd, *Protestant Interest,* 26.
11. J. G. Whittier, *The Poems of John Greenleaf Whittier* (New York: Heritage Press, 1945), 62–65.
12. For the historical underpinnings of Hawthorne's interest in Rale, see Hugh Dawson, "Père Sébastien Racle in History and Fiction: The

Background of Hawthorne's 'Bell' Sketches," *Essex Historical Institute Collections* 124:3 (1988): 204–12.

13. *GDMNH* 487.

14. Jenny Franchot, *Roads to Rome: The Antebellum Protestant Encounter with Catholicism* (Berkeley: University of California Press, 1994), 260.

15. For an old yet insightful assessment of the romanticization of Maine's colonial past, see Herbert A. Jones, *Maine Memories: Little-Known Stories about a Well-Known State* (Portland, ME: Harmon, 1940), 34–36; see also "Alexander Hamilton's Journal," June 14, 1722, in Baxter, *Pioneers of New France in New England,* 319–20.

16. Though they spelled their surnames differently, both men were descendants of the original Roger Dearing, who settled in Kittery in 1663. *GDMNH* 191.

17. Nathaniel Deering, *Carabassett: A Tragedy,* in Leola Bowling Chaplin, *The Life and Work of Nathaniel Deering (1791–1881) with the Text of Two of His Plays, "Carabassett" and "The Clairvoyants"* (Orono: University of Maine Press, 1934), 159.

18. *Carabassett,* act 3, scene 2. Ibid.

19. Nancy Lusignan Schultz, *Fire and Roses: The Burning of the Charlestown Convent, 1834* (New York: Free Press, 2000), 10.

20. Quoted in *Manufacturers' & Farmers' Journal* [Providence, RI], Aug. 18, 1836.

21. *Philadelphia Public Ledger,* Aug. 19, 1836.

22. William Allen to Benedict Fenwick, Sept. 27, 1836, MeHS.

Bibliography

Manuscript Sources

United States

Massachusetts State Archives, Boston
    Massachusetts Archives

Maine Historical Society, Portland
    Doggett Family Papers
    Miscellaneous Manuscripts

Maine State Museum
    Collections

Massachusetts Historical Society, Boston
    Fayerweather Family Papers
    Gerald Kelly Papers
    Francis Parkman Papers
    John Pike Journal
    Mary Storer Letters
    Cyprian Southack Letters
    Nathaniel Wheelwright Diary

Canada

Library and Archives Canada
  Série A23, Greffes de notaires de la Nouvelle-France et du Québec
  Série C11A, Correspondence générale, 1540–1784
  Série C8, Congés et permis enregistrés à Montréal

Newspapers

Boston News-Letter
Manufacturers' & Farmers' Journal
Philadelphia Public Ledger

Published Primary Sources

Baxter, James Phinney, ed. *Documentary History of the State of Maine.* 24 vols. Portland: Maine Historical Society, 1869–1916.

Baxter, Joseph. "Journal of the Reverend Joseph Baxter." *New England Historical and Genealogical Record* 21 (Jan. 1867): 45–59.

Calloway, Colin G., ed. *Dawnland Encounters: Indians and Europeans in Northern New England.* Hanover, NH: University Press of New England, 1991.

———. *North Country Captives: Selected Narratives of Indian Captivity from Vermont and New Hampshire.* Hanover, NH: University Press of New England, 1992.

Catechism of the Council of Trent for Parish Priests, Issued by Order of Pope Pius V. Trans. Theodore Alois Buckley. London: Routledge, 1852.

Charlevoix, Pierre F.-X. de. *Journal of a Voyage to North-America.* 2 vols. London: J. Doddsley, 1761.

Collection de manuscrits contenant lettres, mémoires, es autres documents historiques relatifs à la Nouvelle France. 4 vols. Quebec: Côté et Cie, 1884.

Hutchinson, Thomas. *The History of the Colony and Province of Massachusetts-Bay.* 3 vols. Edited by Lawrence Shaw Mayo. Cambridge: Harvard University Press, 1936.

Kalm, Peter. *Travels into North America.* Trans. John Reinhold Forster. Barre, MA: Imprint Society, 1972.

Lahontan, [Louis Armand de Lom d'Arce] Baron [de]. *New Voyages North-America.* 2 vols. Edited by Reuben Gold Thwaites. New York: Burt Franklin, 1970.

Libby, Charles Thornton, Robert E. Moody, and Neal W. Allen, Jr., eds. *Province and Court Records of Maine.* 6 vols. Portland: Maine Historical Society, 1928–75.

Maine Historical Society. *Collections of the Maine Historical Society.* Series 1 and 2. 19 vols. Portland: Maine Historical Society, 1831–99.

Mather, Cotton. *Decennium Luctuosum: An history of remarkable occurrences, in the long war, which New-England hath had with the Indian salvages, from the year, 1688.* Boston: B. Green and J. Allen, 1699.

———. *Family Religion, Excited and Assisted.* Boston, 1714.

———. *Frontiers Well-Defended.* Boston, 1702.

———. *Good Fetch'd Out of Evil.* Boston: Bartholomew Green, 1706.

———. *Magnalia Christi Americana.* London: Thomas Parkhurst, 1702. Reprint, New York: Arno Press, 1972.

———. *The Present State of New England Considered in a Discourse on the Necessities and Advantages of a Public Spirit in Every Man.* Boston: Samuel Green, 1690.

New England Historical and Genealogical Register. 101 vols. Boston: NEHGS, 1880–1947.

Norton, John. *The Redeemed Captive. Being a Narrative of the Taking and Carrying of the Reverend John Norton, When Fort-Massachusetts Surrendered to a Large Body of French and Indians, August 20th, 1746.* Boston, 1748.

Penhallow, Samuel. *The History of the Wars of New-England with the Eastern Indians.* Cincinnati: J. Harpel, 1859. Reprint, New York: Kraus Reprint Co., 1969.

Pike, John. "Journal of Reverend John Pike." Edited by Alonzo Quint. Cambridge: J. Wilson, 1876.

Records and Files of the Quarterly Court of Essex County. 8 vols. Salem, MA: Essex Institute, 1911–21.

Records of the First Church of Wells, Maine from October 29, 1701, to October 21, 1810. New York, 1918.

Rowlandson, Mary. "The Sovereignty and Goodness of God." In *Puritans Among the Indians: Accounts of Captivity and Redemption, 1676–1724.* Edited by Alden T. Vaughan and Edward W. Clark. Cambridge: Harvard University Press, 1981.

Saint-Vallier, Jean-Baptiste de. *État présent de l'église et de la colonie française de la Nouvelle-France.* Paris: Robert Pepie, 1748. Reprint, Quebec: Coté & Cie, 1856.

Sargent, William A., ed. *Maine Wills 1640–1760.* Portland: Brown Thurston, 1887.

———. *York Deeds.* 18 vols. Portland: John T. Hull, 1887–1910.

Sewall, Samuel. *The Diary of Samuel Sewall.* 2 vols. Edited by M. Halsey Thomas. New York: Farrar, Straus and Giroux, 1973.

Stoddard, John. "Stoddard's Journal." *NEHGR* 5 (Jan. 1851): 21–42.

Thwaites, Reuben Gold, ed. *The Jesuit Relations and Allied Documents: Travels and Explorations of the Jesuit Missionaries in New France, 1610–1791.* 73 vols. Cleveland: Burrows Brothers, 1896–1901.

Vaughan, Alden T., and Edward W. Clark, eds. *Puritans among the Indians: Accounts of Captivity and Redemption, 1676–1724.* Cambridge: Harvard University Press, 1981.

Whitmore, W. H., ed. *The Andros Tracts.* 3 vols. Boston: The Prince Society, 1868–74.

Williams, John. *The Redeemed Captive Returning to Zion.* Northampton: Hopkins, Bridgeman, 1853.

Winthrop, John. *The Journal of John Winthrop, 1630–1649.* Edited by Richard S. Dunn and Laetitia Yeandle. Cambridge: Harvard University Press, 1996.

Secondary Sources

Ahlstrom, Sydney E. *A Religious History of the American People.* New Haven: Yale University Press, 1972.

Anderson, Virginia DeJohn. *Creatures of Empire: How Domestic Animals Transformed Early America.* New York: Oxford University Press, 2004.

Austen, Barbara E. "Captured . . . Never Came Back: Social Networks among New England Female Captives in Canada, 1689–1763." In *New England/New France 1600–1850,* edited by Peter Benes. Annual Proceedings of the Dublin Seminar for New England Folklife. Vol. 14. Boston: Boston University, 1992.

Axtell, James. *The European and the Indian: Essays in the Ethnohistory of Colonial North America.* New York: Oxford University Press, 1981.

———. *The Invasion Within: The Contest of Cultures in Colonial North America.* New York: Oxford University Press, 1985.

Bailyn, Bernard. *The New England Merchants of the Seventeenth Century.* New York: Harper & Row, 1955.

Baker, Charlotte Alice. *True Stories of the New England Captives during the Old French and Indian Wars.* Portland, ME: Southworth Press, 1897. Reprint, Bowie, MD: Heritage Books, 1990.

Baker, Emerson W. *The Devil of Great Island: Witchcraft and Conflict in Early New England.* New York: Palgrave Macmillan, 2007.

————."Lithobolia: Frontier Prelude to Witchcraft in Salem." Paper presented at the American Historical Association Annual Meeting, Boston, Massachusetts, Jan. 2001.

————. *The New England Knight: Sir William Phips, 1651–1695.* Toronto: University of Toronto Press, 1998.

Baker, Emerson W., Edwin N. Church II, Richard S. D'Abate, Kristine L. Jones, Victor A. Konrad, and Harald E. L. Prins, eds. *American Beginnings: Exploration, Culture and Cartography in the Land of Norumbega.* Lincoln: University of Nebraska Press, 1994.

Baker, Emerson W., and James Kences. "Maine, Indian Land Speculation, and the Essex County Witchcraft Outbreak of 1692." *Maine History* 40:3 (Fall 2001): 159–89.

Baker, Emerson W., and John G. Reid. "Amerindian Power in the Early Modern Northeast: A Reappraisal." *William and Mary Quarterly* 61:1 (Jan. 2004): 77–106.

Banks, Charles Edwin. *A History of York, Maine.* Boston, 1931.

Barr, Juliana. *Peace Came in the Form of a Woman: Indians and Spaniards in the Texas Borderlands.* Chapel Hill: University of North Carolina Press, 2007.

Baxter, James Phinney. *The Pioneers of New France in New England.* Albany, NY: J. Munsell's Sons, 1894.

Beasley, Nicholas M. "Wars of Religion in the Circum-Caribbean: English Iconoclasm in Spanish America, 1570–1702." In *Saints and Their Cults in the Atlantic World,* edited by Margaret Cormack. Columbia: University of South Carolina Press, 2007.

Bédard, Marc-Antoine. "Les Protestants en Nouvelle-France." *Cahiers d'histoire* 31 (1978).

Belmessous, Seliha. "Assimilation and Racialism in Seventeenth- and Eighteenth-Century French Colonial Policy." *American Historical Review* 110:2 (2005): 322–49.

Bilodeau, Christopher. "Policing the Wabanaki Missions in the Seventeenth Century." In *Ethnographies and Exchanges: Native Americans, Moravians and Catholics in Early North America,* edited by A. G. Roeber. College Park: Pennsylvania State University Press, 2008.

Block, Sharon. *Rape and Sexual Power in Early America.* Chapel Hill: University of North Carolina Press, 2006.

Bonomi, Patricia U. *Under the Cope of Heaven: Religion, Society and Politics in Colonial America.* New York: Oxford University Press, 1986.

Bosher, J. F. *The Canada Merchants, 1713–1763.* Oxford: Clarendon, 1987.

Bourne, Edward E. *History of Wells and Kennebunk.* Portland: B. Thurston, 1875.

Brasseaux, Carl A. *The Founding of New Acadia: The Beginnings of Acadian Life in Louisiana, 1765–1803.* Baton Rouge: Louisiana State University Press, 1987.

Breen, Louise A. *Transgressing the Bounds: Subversive Enterprise Among the Puritan Elite, 1630–1692.* New York: Oxford University Press, 2001.

Bremer, Francis. "Endecott and the Red Cross: Puritan Iconoclasm in the New World." *Journal of American Studies* 24:1 (1990): 5–22.

Brumm, Ursula. "The Virgin Mary among American Puritans: A Difficult Relation." *Amerikastudien* 47:4 (2002): 449–68.

Burke, Peter. *Popular Culture in Early Modern Europe.* New York: Harper, 1978.

Burrage, Henry S. *The Beginnings of Colonial Maine, 1602–1658.* Portland: State of Maine, 1914.

Bushman, Richard. *From Puritan to Yankee: Character and the Social Order in Connecticut, 1690–1765.* Cambridge: Harvard University Press, 1967.

Butler, Jon. *Awash in a Sea of Faith: Christianizing the American People.* Cambridge: Harvard University Press, 1990.

———. "Historiographical Heresy: Catholicism as a Model for American Religious History." In *Belief in History: Innovative Approaches to European and American Religion,* edited by Thomas Kselman. Notre Dame, IN: University of Notre Dame Press, 1991.

Calloway, Colin G., ed. *After King Philip's War: Presence and Persistence in Indian New England.* Hanover, NH: University Press of New England, 1997.

———. *New Worlds for All: Indians, Europeans, and the Remaking of Early America.* Baltimore: Johns Hopkins University Press, 1998.

Calvert, Mary R. *Black Robe on the Kennebec.* Monmouth, ME: Monmouth Press, 1991.

Canup, John. *Out of the Wilderness: The Emergence of an American Identity in Colonial New England.* Middletown, CT: Wesleyan University Press, 1990.

Carroll, Lorrayne: *Rhetorical Drag: Impersonation, Captivity, and the Writing of History.* Kent: Ohio State Press, 2007.

Carroll, Peter N. *Puritanism and the Wilderness: The Intellectual Significance of the New England Frontier, 1629–1700.* New York: Columbia University Press, 1969.

Chaplin, Joyce. *Subject Matter: Technology, the Body, and the Anglo-American Frontier, 1500–1676.* Cambridge: Harvard University Press, 2001.

Chaplin, Leola Bowling. *The Life and Work of Nathaniel Deering (1791–1881) with the Text of Two of His Plays, "Carabasset" and "The Clairvoyants."* Orono: University of Maine Press, 1934.

Choquette, Leslie. *Frenchmen into Peasants: Modernity and Tradition in the Peopling of French Canada.* Cambridge: Harvard University Press, 1997.

Clark, Charles E. *The Eastern Frontier: The Settlement of Northern New England, 1610–1763.* New York: Knopf, 1970.

Clark, Emily, and Virginia Meacham Gould. "The Face of Afro-Catholicism in New Orleans, 1727–1852." *William and Mary Quarterly* 59:2 (April 2002): 409–48.

Cogliano, Francis D. *No King, No Popery: Anti-Catholicism in Revolutionary New England.* Westport, CT: Greenwood Press, 1995.

Coleman, Emma Lewis. *New England Captives Carried to Canada between 1677 and 1760 during the French and Indian Wars.* 2 vols. Portland, ME: Southworth Press, 1925. Reprint, Bowie, MD: Heritage Classics, 1989.

Colley, Linda. *Captives: The Story of Britain's Pursuit of Empire and How Its Soldiers and Civilians Were Held Captive by the Dream of Global Supremacy, 1600–1850.* New York: Pantheon, 2002.

Cott, Nancy F. "Divorce and the Changing Status of Women in Eighteenth-Century Massachusetts." *William and Mary Quarterly* 3rd ser., 33:4 (1976): 586–614.

Crawford, Mary Caroline. *The Romance of Old New England Churches.* Boston: L. C. Page, 1903.

Cronon, William, George Miles, and Jay Gitlin, eds. *Under an Open Sky: Rethinking America's Western Past.* New York: W. W. Norton, 1993.

Daniels, Christine, and Michael V. Kennedy, eds. *Negotiated Empires: Centers and Peripheries in the Americas, 1500–1820.* New York: Routledge, 2002.

Dawson, Hugh. "Père Sébastien Racle in History and Fiction: The Background of Hawthorne's 'Bell' Sketches." *Essex Historical Institute Collections* 124:3 (1988): 204–12.

Dechêne, Louise. *Habitants and Merchants in Seventeenth Century Montreal.* Trans. Liana Vardi. Montreal: McGill-Queens University Press, 1992.

Delâge, Denys. *Bitter Feast: Amerindians and Europeans in Northern North America, 1600–64.* Translated by Jane Brierley. Vancouver: University of British Columbia Press, 1993.

Demos, John. *A Little Commonwealth: Family Life in Plymouth Colony.* New York: Oxford University Press, 1970.

———. *The Unredeemed Captive: A Family Story from Early America.* New York: Knopf, 1994.

De Paoli, Neill. "Life on the Edge: Community and Trade on the Anglo-American Periphery, Pemaquid, Maine, 1610–1689." Ph.D. diss., University of New Hampshire, 2001.

Dictionary of Canadian Biography. 13 vols. Toronto: University of Toronto Press, 1966–.

Dinan, Susan E., and Debra Meyers, eds. *Women and Religion in Old and New Worlds.* New York: Routledge, 2001.

Dolan, Frances E. *Whores of Babylon: Catholicism, Gender, and Seventeenth-Century Print Culture.* Ithaca: Cornell University Press, 1999.

Drake, Samuel Adams. *The Border Wars of New England.* New York: Charles Scribner's Sons, 1897.

Dunn, Mary Maples. "Saints and Sinners: Congregational and Quaker Women in the Early Colonial Period." *American Quarterly* 30:5 (1978): 582–601.

Du Val, Kathleen. *The Native Ground: Indians and Colonists in the Heart of the Continent.* Philadelphia: University of Pennsylvania Press, 2006.

Eccles, William J. *The Canadian Frontier: 1534–1760.* Rev. ed. Albuquerque: University of New Mexico Press, 1983.

Eckstorm, Fannie Hardy. "The Attack on Norridgewock, 1724." *New England Quarterly* 7 (Sept. 1934): 541–78.

Evennett, H. Outram. *The Spirit of the Counter-Reformation.* Edited by John Bossy. Notre Dame, IN: University of Notre Dame Press, 1968.

Faulkner, Alaric, and Gretchen F. Faulkner. *The French at Pentagoët, 1635–1674: An Archaeological Portrait of the Acadian Frontier.* Augusta: Maine Preservation Commission, 1987.

Fischer, David Hackett. *Albion's Seed: Four British Folkways in America.* New York: Oxford University Press, 1989.

———. *Champlain's Dream: The European Founding of North America.* New York: Simon & Schuster, 2008.

Folsom, George. *History of Saco and Biddeford.* Saco, ME: Alex G. Putnam, 1830.

Foster, William H., III. "Agathe St. Père and Her Captive New England Weavers." *French Colonial History* 1 (2002): 129–41.

———. *The Captor's Narrative: Catholic Women and Their Puritan Men on the Early American Frontier.* Ithaca: Cornell University Press, 2003.

Fournier, Marcel. *De la Nouvelle-Angleterre à la Nouvelle-France: L'histoire des captifs anglo-américains au Canada entre 1675 et 1760.* Montreal: Société Généalogique Canadienne-Française, 1992.

———. *Les Européens au Canada des origins à 1765 (hors France).* Montreal: Les Éditions du Fleuve, 1989.

Franchot, Jenny. *Roads to Rome: The Antebellum Protestant Encounter with Catholicism.* Berkeley: University of California Press, 1994.

Gallay, Alan, ed. *The Colonial Wars of North America, 1512–1763.* New York: Garland, 1996.

Garrity, John A., and Mark C. Carnes, general eds. *American National Biography.* 24 vols. New York: Oxford University Press, 1999.

Gildrie, Richard P. *The Profane, the Civil, and the Godly: The Reformation of Manners in Orthodox New England, 1679–1749.* University Park: Pennsylvania State University Press, 1994.

Gould, Eliga. "Entangled Histories, Entangled Worlds: The English-Speaking Atlantic as a Spanish Periphery," *American Historical Review* 112:3 (2007): 764–86.

Gray, Linda Breuer. "Narratives and Identities in the Saint Lawrence Valley, 1667–1720." Ph.D. diss., McGill University, 1999.

Greer, Allan. *Mohawk Saint: Catherine Tekakwitha and the Jesuits.* New York: Oxford University Press, 2005.

———. *Peasant, Lord, and Merchant: Rural Society in Three Quebec Parishes, 1740–1840.* Toronto: University of Toronto Press, 1985.

———. *The People of New France.* Toronto: University of Toronto Press, 1999.

Greer, Allan, and Jodi Bilinkoff, eds. *Colonial Saints: Discovering the Holy in the Americas, 1500–1800.* New York: Routledge, 2003.

Greven, Philip. *The Protestant Temperament: Patterns of Child-Rearing, Religious Experience, and the Self in Early America.* Chicago: University of Chicago Press, 1977.

Griffiths, Nicholas, and Fernando Cervantes, eds. *Spiritual Encounters: Interactions between Christianity and Native Religions in Colonial America.* Lincoln: University of Nebraska Press, 1999.

Gura, Philip F. *A Glimpse of Sion's Glory: Puritan Radicalism in New England, 1620–1660.* Middletown, CT: Wesleyan University Press, 1984.

Hackel, Steven W. *Children of Coyote, Missionaries of Saint Francis: Indian-Spanish Relations in California, 1769–1850.* Chapel Hill: University of North Carolina Press, 2005.

Haefeli, Evan. "Ransoming New England Captives in New France." *French Colonial History* 1 (2002): 113–27.

Haefeli, Evan, and Kevin Sweeney. *Captors and Captives: The 1704 French and Indian Raid on Deerfield.* Amherst: University of Massachusetts Press, 2003.

Hall, David. *Worlds of Wonder, Days of Judgment: Popular Religious Belief in Early New England.* Cambridge: Harvard University Press, 1989.

Hambrick-Stowe, Charles E. *The Practice of Piety: Puritan Devotional Disciplines in Seventeenth-Century New England.* Chapel Hill: University of North Carolina Press, 1982.

Hanson, Charles P. *Necessary Virtue: The Pragmatic Origins of Religious Liberty in New England.* Charlottesville: University Press of Virginia, 1998.

Harris, R. Cole. *Historical Atlas of Canada.* Vol. 1, *From the Beginning to 1800.* Toronto: University of Toronto Press, 1993.

Heyrman, Christine L. *Commerce and Culture: The Maritime Communities of Colonial Massachusetts, 1690–1750.* New York: Norton, 1984.

Hill, Christopher. *The World Turned Upside Down: Radical Ideas during the English Revolution.* New York: Penguin, 1972.

Hinderaker, Eric, and Peter C. Mancall. *At the Edge of Empire: The Backcountry in British North America.* Baltimore: Johns Hopkins University Press, 2003.

Hsia, R. Po-chia. *The World of Catholic Renewal, 1540–1770.* New York: Cambridge University Press, 1998.

Jaenen, Cornelius J. *The Role of the Church in New France.* Toronto: McGraw-Hill Ryerson, 1976.

Jennings, Francis. *The Invasion of America: Indians, Colonialism, and the Cant of Conquest.* New York: W. W. Norton, 1976.

Jetté, René. *Dictionnaire généalogique des familles du Québec des origines à 1730.* Montreal: Presses de l'Université de Montréal, 1983.

Kidd, Thomas S. *The Protestant Interest: New England after Puritanism.* New Haven: Yale University Press, 2004.

Kolodny, Annette. *The Land before Her: Fantasy and Experience of the American Frontiers.* Chapel Hill: University of North Carolina Press, 1984.

Kulikoff, Allan. *From British Peasants to Colonial American Farmers.* Chapel Hill: University of North Carolina Press, 2000.

Lapomarda, Vincent A. *The Jesuit Heritage in New England.* Worcester, MA: College of the Holy Cross, 1977.

Lepore, Jill. *The Name of War: King Philip's War and the Origins of American Identity.* New York: Vintage, 1999.

Levy, Barry. *Quakers and the American Family: British Settlement in the Delaware.* New York: Oxford University Press, 1988.

Little, Ann M. *Abraham in Arms: War and Gender in Colonial New England.* Philadelphia: University of Pennsylvania Press, 2006.

———. "Cloistered Bodies: Convents in the Anglo-American Imagination in the British Conquest of Canada." *Eighteenth-Century Studies* 39:2 (2006): 187–200.

———. "The Life of Mother Marie-Joseph de l'Enfant Jesus, or, How a Little English Girl from Wells Became a Big French Politician." *Maine History* 40:4 (Winter 2001–2): 279–308.

Lucey, William Leo. *The Catholic Church in Maine.* Francestown, NH: Marshall Jones, 1957.

Magnuson, Roger. *Education in New France.* Montreal: McGill-Queen's University Press, 1992.

Marlowe, George Francis. *Churches of Old New England: Their Architecture and Their Architects, Their Pastors and Their People.* New York: Macmillan, 1947.

McDannell, Colleen. *Material Christianity: Religion and Popular Culture in America.* New Haven: Yale University Press, 1995.

Moogk, Peter. *Building a House in New France: An Account of the Perplexities of Client and Craftsmen in Early Canada.* Markham, ON: Fitzhenry and Whiteside, 1977.

———. *La Nouvelle France: The Making of French Canada—A Cultural History.* East Lansing: Michigan State University Press, 2000.

———. "Writing the Cultural History of Pre-1760 European Colonists." *French Colonial History* 4 (2003): 1–14.

Moore, James T. *Indian and Jesuit: A Seventeenth Century Encounter.* Chicago: Loyola University Press, 1982.

Morgan, Edmund S. *The Puritan Family: Religion and Domestic Relations in Seventeenth-Century New England.* New York: Harper & Row, 1966.

———. *Visible Saints: The History of a Puritan Idea.* Ithaca: Cornell University Press, 1963.

Morin, Marie. *Histoire véritable et simple: Les annales de l'Hôtel Dieu de Mon -tréal, 1659–1725.* Éditions critique par Ghislaine Legendre. Montreal: Les Presses de l'Université de Montréal, 1979.

Morris, Gerald E., ed. *The Maine Bicentennial Atlas: An Historical Survey.* Portland: Maine Historical Society, 1976.

Morrison, Kenneth M. *The Embattled Northeast: The Elusive Ideal of Alliance in Abenaki-Euroamerican Relations.* Berkeley: University of California Press, 1984.

———. "Sebastien Rale vs. New England: A Case Study of Frontier Conflict." M.A. thesis, University of Maine at Orono, 1970.

Muir, Edward. *Ritual in Early Modern Europe.* New York: Cambridge University Press, 1997.

Namais, June. *White Captives: Gender and Ethnicity on the American Frontier.* Chapel Hill: University of North Carolina Press, 1993.

Nash, Alice N. "The Abiding Frontier: Family, Gender, and Religion in Wabanaki History, 1600–1763." Ph.D. diss., Columbia University, 1997.

———. "Two Stories of New England Captives: Grizel and Christine Otis of Dover, New Hampshire." In *New England/New France, 1600–1850,* edited by Peter Benes. Annual Proceedings of the Dublin Seminar for New England Folklife. Vol 14. Boston: Boston University, 1992.

Nissenbaum, Stephen. *The Battle for Christmas.* New York: Knopf, 1996.

Norton, Mary Beth. *Founding Mothers and Fathers: Gendered Power and the Forming of American Society.* New York: Knopf, 1996.

———. "George Burroughs and the Girls from Casco: The Maine Roots of Salem Witchcraft." *Maine History* 40:4 (Winter 2001–2): 259–77.

———. *In the Devil's Snare: The Salem Witchcraft Crisis of 1692.* New York: Knopf, 2002.

Noyes, Sybil, et al. *Genealogical Dictionary of Maine and New Hampshire.* Portland, ME, 1928–35. Reprint, Baltimore: Genealogical Publishing Co., 1972.

O'Malley, John W. *The First Jesuits.* Cambridge: Harvard University Press, 1993.

Pacquet, Gilles, and Jean-Pierre Wallot. "Nouvelle-France/Québec/Canada: A World of Limited Identities." In *Colonial Identity in the Atlantic World, 1500–1800,* edited by Nicolas Canny and Anthony Pagden. Princeton: Princeton University Press, 1987.

Parkman, Francis. *France and England in North America.* Vol. 2, *Count Frontenac and New France Under Louis XIV.* New York: Library of America, 1983.

————. *France and England in North America.* Vol. 2, *A Half-Century of Conflict.* New York: Library of America, 1983.

————. *The Jesuits in North America in the Seventeenth Century.* Boston: Little, Brown, 1867. Reprint, Lincoln: University of Nebraska Press, 1997.

Plane, Ann Marie. *Colonial Intimacies: Indian Marriage in Colonial New England.* Ithaca: Cornell University Press, 2000.

Purvis, Thomas L. *Colonial America to 1763.* Almanacs of American Life. New York: Facts on File, 1999.

Rapley, Elizabeth. *The Dévotes: Women and Church in Seventeenth-Century France.* Montreal: McGill-Queens University Press, 1990.

Ray, Mary Augustine. *American Opinion of Roman Catholicism in the Eighteenth Century.* New York: Columbia University Press, 1936.

Rebora, Carrie, and Paul Straiti. *John Singleton Copley in America.* New York: Harry N. Abrams, 1996.

Reid, John G. *Acadia, Maine and New Scotland: Marginal Colonies in the Seventeenth Century.* Toronto: University of Toronto Press, 1981.

————. *Maine, Charles II and Massachusetts: Governmental Relationships in Early Northern New England.* Portland: Maine Historical Society, 1977.

Richter, Daniel. *Facing East from Indian Country: A Native History of Early America.* Cambridge: Harvard University Press, 2001.

————. *The Ordeal of the Longhouse: The Peoples of the Iroquois League in the Era of European Colonization.* Chapel Hill: University of North Carolina Press, 1992.

Roeber, A. G., ed. *Ethnographies and Exchanges: Native Americans, Moravians, and Catholics in Early North America.* College Park: Pennsylvania State University Press, 2008.

Saint-Pierre, Majolaine. *Saint-Castin: Baron français, chef Amérindien: 1652–1707.* Quebec: Les Éditions du Septentrion, 1999.

Salisbury, Neal. *Manitou and Providence: Indians, Europeans, and the Making of New England, 1500–1643.* New York: Oxford University Press, 1982.

Saunders, A. C. *Jersey in the Seventeenth Century.* St. Helier, Jersey: J. T. Bigwood, 1931.

Saunt, Claudio. "Go West: Mapping Early American Historiography." *William and Mary Quarterly* 65:4 (2008): 745–78.

Sayre, Gordon M. *Les Sauvages Américains: Representations of Native Americans in French and English Colonial Literature.* Chapel Hill: University of North Carolina Press, 1997.

Scalberg, Daniel Allen. "The French-Amerindian Religious Encounter in Seventeenth- and Early Eighteenth-Century New France." *French Colonial History* 1 (2002): 101–12.

———. "Religious Life in New France under the Laval and Saint-Vallier Bishoprics: 1659–1727." Ph.D. diss., University of Oregon, 1990.

Schultz, Nancy Lusignan. *Fire and Roses: The Burning of the Charlestown Convent, 1834.* New York: Free Press, 2000.

Scribner, Robert W. "'The Reformation, Popular Magic, and the 'Disenchantment of the World.'" *Journal of Interdisciplinary History* 23:3 (Winter 1993): 475–94.

Seed, Patricia. *Ceremonies of Possession in Europe's Conquest of the New World, 1492–1640.* London: Cambridge University Press, 1995.

Shoemaker, Nancy. *A Strange Likeness: Becoming Red and White in Eighteenth-Century North America.* New York: Oxford University Press, 2004.

Sibley, John Langdon, and Clifford K. Shipton. *Sibley's Harvard Graduates.* 16 vols. Cambridge: Harvard University Press, 1933–.

Silverman, Kenneth. *The Life and Times of Cotton Mather.* New York: Harper & Row, 1984.

Simons, D. Brenton, and Peter Benes. *The Art of Family: Genealogical Artifacts in New England.* Boston: New England Historic Genealogical Society, 2002.

Sleeper-Smith, Susan. *Indian Women and French Men: Rethinking Cultural Encounters in the Western Great Lakes Region.* Amherst: University of Massachusetts Press, 2001.

Smith, Mark M. "Remembering Mary, Shaping Revolt: Reconsidering the Stono Revolt." *Journal of Southern History* 67:3 (2001): 513–34.

Storer, Malcolm. *Annals of the Storer Family.* New York, 1924.

Stout, Harry S. *The New England Soul: Preaching and Religious Culture in Colonial New England.* New York: Oxford University Press, 1986.

Tanguay, Cyprien. *Dictionnaire généalogique des familles canadiennes.* Montreal: Eusébe Senécal & Fils, 1871.

Taylor, Alan. "Centers and Peripheries: Locating Maine's History." *Maine History* 39:1 (2000): 2–16.

———. *Liberty Men and Great Proprietors: The Revolutionary Settlement on the Maine Frontier, 1760–1820.* Chapel Hill: University of North Carolina Press, 1990.

Taylor, Aline. *The French Baron of Pentagouet: Baron St. Castin and the Struggle for Empire in Early New England.* Camden, ME: Picton Press, 1998.

Toulouse, Teresa A. *The Captive's Position: Female Narrative, Male Identity, and Royal Authority in Colonial New England.* Philadelphia: University of Pennsylvania Press, 2007.

Ulrich, Laurel Thatcher. *The Age of Homespun: Objects and Stories in the Creation of an American Myth.* New York: Knopf, 2001.

———. *Good Wives: Image and Reality in the Lives of Women in Northern New England, 1650–1750.* New York: Knopf, 1982.

Usner, Daniel. *Indians, Settlers and Slaves in a Frontier Exchange Economy: The Lower Mississippi before 1783.* Chapel Hill: University of North Carolina Press, 1992.

Vaughan, Alden T., and Daniel K. Richter. "Crossing the Cultural Divide: Indians and New Englanders, 1605–1763." *Proceedings of the American Antiquarian Society* 90:1 (1980): 23–99.

Vickers, Daniel. *Farmers and Fishermen: Two Centuries of Work in Essex County, Massachusetts, 1630–1850.* Chapel Hill: University of North Carolina Press, 1994.

Wall, Helena M. *Fierce Communion: Family and Community in Early America.* Cambridge: Harvard University Press, 1990.

Walsh, James P. "Holy Time and Sacred Space in Puritan New England." *American Quarterly* 23:1 (Spring 1980): 79–95.

Walter, John. "Popular Iconoclasm and the Politics of the Parish in Eastern England, 1640–1642." *The Historical Journal* 47:2 (2004): 261–90.

Wells, Cheryl. *Civil War Time: Temporality and Identity in America, 1861–1865.* Athens: University of Georgia Press, 2005.

White, Richard. *The Middle Ground: Indians, Empires, and the Republics in the Great Lakes Region, 1650–1815.* Cambridge: Cambridge University Press, 1991.

Willis, William. *The History of Portland.* 2 vols. Portland: Day, Fraser, 1831.

Wills, Garry. *Witches and Jesuits: Shakespeare's "Macbeth."* New York: Oxford University Press, 1995.

Index

Laura M. Chmielewski

is assistant professor of history at Purchase College,

State University of New York.

✦